What is Happening in Your Community?

What is Happening in Your Community?

Why Community Development Matters

Matthew J. Hanka

LEXINGTON BOOKS
Lanham • Boulder • New York • London

Published by Lexington Books
An imprint of The Rowman & Littlefield Publishing Group, Inc.
4501 Forbes Boulevard, Suite 200, Lanham, Maryland 20706
www.rowman.com

6 Tinworth Street, London SE11 5AL, United Kingdom

British Library Cataloguing in Publication Information Available

Library of Congress Cataloging-in-Publication Data

Library of Congress Control Number: 2021930855
ISBN: 9781498504911 (cloth)
ISBN: 9781498504928 (electronic)

Contents

Tables and Figures

TABLES

FIGURES

Acknowledgments

I would like to thank the following people for their support during the journey of my first published book. I will forever owe each of you a debt of gratitude.

I would like to thank my parents Marvin and Martha Hanka and my brother John-Michael Hanka, who have provided me enormous love and support throughout my life. Many thanks go to my wife, Annie, and my sons MJ and David for their support, love, caring, and understanding during this process.

Special thanks go to my friends Tom and Amy Quisenberry, Prasad Cherian, Dave Simcox, Nina Bambina, Andy Buck, Chailendu Pegues, the late Julian Bond, Katie Hecker Carney Bond, Liz and Rob Gutgsell, Philip and Amanda Hooper, Bill and Brenda Jeffers, Blair Jeffers-Farmer, Sarah Jeffers-Proebsting, Charmaine and Tom McDowell, John Gilderbloom, Stephanie Potter, Rob Henson, Amy Back, Liam Douglas, Silas Matchem, Chris Metz, Ruth Metzger, Zac Heronemus, Dave Goldblatt, Walt and Cecelia Garrison, Ali Miller, Brian and Barb Williams, Eric and Hillary Braysmith, Kathy Oeth, Erin Reynolds, Kathy Salomon, Kari Akin, Steve Williams, Ronda Priest, Steve Roosa, Todd Quire, Jason Emmerson, Silvia Rode, David Perlow, Terry Chambers, John Gage, Marcia Carmichael-Murphy, the late Lou Perry, Matt Evans, Ned Berghausen, John Glauber, Mario D'Sa, Charlie and Kristin Hudson, Kareem Usher, Nick Wildeman, Cara Stewart, Ashley McReynolds, Art Williams, Clark Exmeyer, Patrick Exmeyer, Jaci Wells, Jerry and Jen Reynolds, Kevin Valadares, Gerry Williger, Wes Durham, Shaun McKiernan, Matt McKiernan, Tami Jaramillo-Zuniga, Shanon O'Toole, Trisha Wright, Kristine Cordts, Traci and Steve Welp, Leigh Anne Howard, Mike Thissen, Peter Whiting, Nick LaRowe, and Bartell and Terri Berg for their continued support and friendship. Also special thanks to my friends in the Evansville Morning Rotary Club, Bruce Bryant, Brad Lisembee, Ken Horn, Chaze Patrick, Chris Kelly, Maryann Bryan, and Dave Meyers for their friendship and fellowship.

I would like to thank Senior Acquisition Editor for International/World Politics, Political Theory, Economics, and Security Studies for Lexington Books, Joseph Parry and his Assistant Editor Alison Keefner, and Assistant Production Editor Dominique McIndoe with Rowman and Littlefield Publishing for their patience, assistance, and support throughout the entire process.

Many thanks go to the book's contributors, including Dr. Trent Engbers, Dr. Mohammed Khayum, Ramona Harvey, Dr. Anne Statham, Dr. Helen Rosenberg, and Dr. John Gilderbloom for helping to make this book a success.

I would like to thank former University of Southern Indiana (USI) Master of Public Administration (MPA) student Misty Henry, former USI English student Lori Petty, and former Indiana University student Katherine Hitchcock who assisted me in the research and writing of parts of chapters 1, 2, and 9. I would like to thank again Katherine Hitchcock and Misty Henry, and thank former MPA student Ashley Hughes and MPA graduate Nick Wildeman for their assistance with disseminating the survey and going door-to-door collecting survey data, and to USI political science graduate Duncan Taylor for coding the survey data for the study featured in chapter 4. Also, special thanks to Joshua Calhoun, formerly with the City of Evansville Department of Metropolitan Development (DMD) for providing us the neighborhood maps for the study.

Thanks again to Dr. John Gilderbloom and the Center for Sustainable Urban Neighborhoods (SUN) at the University of Louisville where I served as senior fellow for four years and worked on grants evaluating the HOPE VI program for my doctoral dissertation in 2009 and for this book.

I would like to extend my appreciation to Mike Thissen for his assistance in my understanding of the Simplex facilitation method, and to Dr. Kathy Elpers for her assistance with the conclusion. Many thanks also go to Dr. Ramona Stone for her insight on the Liberty Green and Sheppard Square HOPE VI programs in Louisville, Kentucky.

I would like to thank Lynn Miller Pease from Leadership Everyone for her assistance in the VOICE visioning process; Jeremy Evans, Executive Director of the Dream Center for providing information on the Peacemakers program and the Jacobsville Kids Zone; and Bob Seymore from Engage Henderson, Rob Carroll from Audubon Kids Zone, and Lori Reed, former Executive Director of Habitat for Humanity of Evansville, for sharing their stories of the community development efforts in Glenwood, Jacobsville, and Henderson.

Thank you to my colleagues who worked through the Center for Applied Research (CAR) at USI on developing the framework of the Adaptive Collaborative Community Transformation (ACCT) model outlined in chapter 6, including Dr. Sue Ellspermann, the founding director of CAR, Elissa Bakke, former Assistant Director of CAR, and USI Associate Professor of Sociology Dr. Ronda Priest.

Also, thank you to my CAR and USI colleagues Elissa Bakke, Dr. Iris Philips, Dr. Mohammed Khayum, Dr. Ronda Priest, Dr. Marie Pease, and Dr. Katherine Draughon who worked on a study of the Habitat for Humanity Women Build program for Habitat for Humanity International that includes a study of the social capital implications of homeownership featured in chapter 3.

Thank you to Silas Matchem, Executive Director of the Evansville Promise Zone, Chris Metz, Executive Director of ECHO Housing Corporation (the convening organization of the Promise Zone), and Evansville Promise Zone consultant Dr. Dan Diehl of Diehl Consulting in Evansville for providing the housing data analysis that will be discussed in chapter 7.

Special thanks go to USI President Dr. Ronald Rochon, Provost Dr. Mohammed Khayum and College of Liberal Arts Dean Dr. James Beeby for awarding me the sabbatical to complete this book, and to the committees of the USI College of Liberal Arts Research Award (LARA) and College of Liberal Arts Faculty Development Award (CLAFDA) for awarding me course release time and financial support that assisted in the research of this book. Also, a special thanks goes to Marna Hostetler, Director of USI's Rice Library, for providing me an office to complete the writing during my sabbatical in the 2019–2020 academic year.

I would like to extend my thanks and appreciation to my colleagues in the Political Science, Public Administration, and Philosophy Department at USI, including my chair Dr. Oana Armeanu, and my colleagues Dr. MT Hallock Morris, Dr. Paul Raymond, Dr. Nick LaRowe, Dr. Trent Engbers, Dr. Mary Lyn Stoll, Dr. Chad Gonnerman, and Dr. Rocco Gennaro.

I also want to thank Kimberly Crum for her exceptional editing of the manuscript, and to Virginia Callan for her assistance in editing and formatting the manuscript.

Special thanks to Starbucks, River City Coffee in Evansville, Donut Bank Bakery in Evansville, Barnes and Noble in Evansville, the Evansville Vanderburgh Public Library, and the Nazareth Retreat Center in Nazareth, KY, for serving as quiet venues for me to write this book.

Foreword

I come to community development through a facilitation and creative problem-solving lens. An engineer by training, I have spent much of my career as a facilitator, trainer, researcher, and consultant in Simplex creative problem solving, a well-researched, applied problem-solving methodology, which balances creative and analytical thinking, helping teams reach consensus on problem finding, solution finding, and implementation. For twenty years, I consulted with more than 100 organizations ranging from small nonprofits to Microsoft in how these thinking skills could support better problem solving, strategic thinking, stronger outcomes, and engagement.

In 2006, I joined the University of Southern Indiana as the Director of the Center for Applied Research (CAR) with the opportunity to engage faculty, staff, and students to support southwest Indiana communities, businesses, and nonprofits. It was during this six-year endeavor that several of the projects discussed here emerged including the Glenwood, Jacobsville, and Engage Henderson community development initiatives. I was privileged to help shape the work of some very talented faculty and staff, including Dr. Matt Hanka and community leaders and conveners such as Lori Reed. I learned with them. We leveraged Simplex to provide the undergirding process that ensured the community was fully engaged, identified the challenges it could own and wanted to solve, developed comprehensive solutions it believed would solve these challenges, and was willing to "roll up their sleeves" to make those solutions happen. As their facilitator, I was entrusted to create an almost sacred space where stakeholders could share their hopes, disappointments, concerns, and ideas for the future in an atmosphere of respect, shared governance, consensus, creativity, and accountability. These experiences have forever impacted how I view community development best said by Margaret Mead, *"Never doubt that a small group of thoughtful, committed citizens can change the world; indeed, it's the only thing that ever has."*

In 2012, I left the University of Southern Indiana after being elected as a State Representative in the Indiana General Assembly and then served as Lieutenant Governor with then-Governor Mike Pence. We took office in 2013 where I oversaw six agencies including the "community building" agencies of Indiana Office of Community and Rural Development and the Indiana Housing and Community Development Authority (IHCDA). Within our agencies and the Lieutenant Governor's office, we used Simplex creative problem solving to develop innovative solutions and to better engage those we served.

Now as President of Ivy Tech Community College, the nation's largest singly accredited statewide community college system, we train in and use Simplex as our innovation and strategic thinking process while recognizing it also supports overall employee engagement. With nearly 20 campuses, over 40 locations, 150,000 students both on campuses and in high schools, and more than 7,500 faculty and staff across the state, Indiana counts on us to provide high-value, workforce aligned credentials for those who will enter the workforce and those that wish to transfer to pursue a bachelor's degree. At the core of everything we do are partnerships with employers, K–12 education, community leaders, and elected officials. These partnerships are built on trust, engagement, collaboration, and consensus. Goal 7 in our strategic plan is our community goal, that is, "putting more community in community college."

I commend Hanka for sharing these wonderful examples of community development to explore the theories, the challenges, and the opportunities we have in building and rebuilding communities that will be resilient, innovative, and empowered to become what only they can envision together.

—Sue Ellspermann, Ph.D.
President, Ivy Tech Community College

Preface

If you are tired of reading the endless stream of hundreds of articles and books by elite academics (mostly White) critical of modern community development practices as a conspiracy to rob and destroy the homes and communities of the poor, here is a brave "rethinking" that shows how communities can be regenerated with what former presidential candidate and former mayor of South Bend, Indiana, called "democratic capitalism."

Communities can be turned around from unlivable to livable, creating communities that are healthy, safe, sustainable, prosperous and equitable. It is a movement in which Dr. Matt Hanka has been involved and has documented himself. All communities can be regenerated with partnerships between community groups, government, and investors. Hanka worked as my top lieutenant in the Center for Sustainable Urban Neighborhoods (SUN) at the University of Louisville through several grants totaling $3.5 million that looked at the regeneration of neglected neighborhoods in Louisville, Newport, and Covington. He later left for a faculty position at the University of Southern Indiana in Evansville, Indiana, where he has become an important player in community development. In all these efforts of creating over 1,000 homes out of boarded up housing or building new houses on empty lots, nobody has been put out on the streets. Nevertheless, radicals will claim otherwise.

They forget to also note that community development efforts have created thousands of good paying jobs. For every million dollars of investment, 17 jobs are created, with 82 percent going to those with the highest rates of unemployment with only a high school education and 30 percent going to minorities. Community development equals community building, happiness, prosperity, health, and safety. As we say, what is worse than gentrification? No gentrification? Without investment, housing is abandoned. In Louisville's historic West End, 5,000 to 6,000 units have been abandoned due to lack of investment along with poor planning and tolerance of unbridled air, water, and soil pollution.

Hanka's book, *What is Happening in Your Community? Why Community Development Matters*, is a welcome and important contribution to community development. The breadth of the book is impressive, introducing readers to efforts that have been tried with both failures and successes. Hanka gives us an impressive tour of historic and current efforts to provide neighborhoods that are just, sustainable, and equitable. He shows a good understanding of and empathy to the dynamics of community development.

In an era of COVID-19, what makes community possible? We need to understand how community lifts our spirits. One of the most powerful arguments for renewing our neighborhoods comes from social critic Paul Goodman, who writes in his powerful book, *Growing Up Absurd*, "A man has only one life and if during it he has no great environment, no community, he has been irreparably robbed of a human right" (1960, p. 17). How do you make a great city? How do you make a great community? Goodman helps set our compass for why and how to create a community that inspires human happiness.

Communities exist as a meeting place and as a celebration of civilization, advancing humans to a higher place. Civilization would not be possible without cities. Think of the greatest thinkers, musicians, poets, writers, and inventors who needed a city to create and advance a better world. Before Christ, Plato believed that cities are based on justice and human virtues. Cities should be an incubator that maximizes potential, serves fellow citizens, and lives with universal truths and laws. Cities provide the space for people to meet, collaborate, negate, and create a synthesis of a higher knowledge. From a green urbanism perspective, cities are the solution to reversing climate change by reducing carbon emissions and by living in smaller, denser residences located closer to school and work.

It is difficult to ignore the effect of the Millennial generation on the vitality of cities. Millennials are in search of a more exciting and socially inclusive living environment. After being raised in the relatively boring and sterile suburbs, they are repelled by the sameness of national chains. They want the uniqueness of indie movies, food, art and music, and the excitement and feeling of "we-ness." They find the excitement of diverse communities with different cultural traditions in the city. Whether the attraction to cities is the connection to people or place, being green and less dependent on automobiles, being more walkable and accessible by bicycle, the health benefits of living in the city, or the proximity to cultural institutions, a new sorting is occurring in our cities and communities. People who live in cities are happier and healthier than those who live in suburbs.

Urban planners since Jane Jacobs believe that everyone has a right to a first-class neighborhood; nobody wants a second- or even a third-class neighborhood. Many of today's historic urban neighborhoods face challenges of urban pollution, brownfields, abandonment, crime, speedy traffic, and treeless streets. Still, there is tremendous opportunity for communities to reflect the dignity, pride, joy, and prosperity of its residents. Creating an authentic, livable neighborhood is a key to human happiness (Jacobs, 1961). Everyone has an equal right to a livable, safe, sustainable, accessible, and healthy neighborhood.

Hanka's book is the anecdote to the cynical rantings of any activist working to improve their neighborhoods. Yet as cities renew, rebuild, and repurpose themselves, Marxists claim that this back-to-the-city movement hurts low-income minorities by displacing them. This is nonsense. Hanka shows how rebuilding neighborhoods without displacement is doable. It is true that past attempts at urban renewal resulted in massive displacement of the poor, which was called "Negro removal" at the time, but the lessons were learned starting with the Clinton administration.

Why can't Black neighborhoods have the same kind of infrastructure and benefits as White neighborhoods, including clean air, parks, trees, calm streets, good housing, and homeownership? New investment is beneficial to homeowners. Their home values increase with more housing, shops, bicyclists, and pedestrians, and when there are more eyes on the streets, neighborhoods are safer. The key is not to stop gentrification, but to harness it to benefit the existing community. Black homeowners are delighted to see their homes increase in value.

Neighborhoods are better off in general with gentrification and the investment of new dollars. Downtown minority and poor neighborhoods are worse off without new investment, experiencing high rates of foreclosures, abandonment, and racial segregation. Moreover, Black neighborhoods want to see new developments in minority neighborhoods that include more than just halfway houses, homeless shelters, and drug rehab centers. Black leaders want cities and communities that build wealth.

We should reject the radical rhetoric that homeownership hurts Black communities. Ninety percent of all Blacks dream about owning a home yet only 38 percent are homeowners, while 78 percent of Whites are homeowners. Homeownership is the foundation to wealth building, equity, and an acceptable approach to reparations that rebuild Black neighborhoods that become prosperous. Homeowners are good stewards of the neighborhood who will advocate for calm streets and the enforcement of zoning and design regulations that reduce crime and significantly reduce the wealth gap between White and Black families.

Dr. Martin Luther King Jr. argued that you cannot get people to march and demonstrate unless you can get the poor to imagine a better life. Dr. King called for equality that included safe housing, health care, safety, and employment without the burden of discrimination. It is hard to argue that Dr. King did not go far enough, especially when you consider the long-term effects of civil rights legislation. Before civil rights legislation was passed in the 1960s, 30 percent of the U.S. population lived in inadequate housing without proper heat, water, and bathrooms; today, only 2 percent of Americans live in inadequate housing.

The civil rights movement has not only improved the lives of Blacks, but inspired other movements as well, making the lives of women, the elderly, the disabled, tenants, students, and the LGBTQ population better. However, we still have more work ahead and the key is addressing neighborhood decline. Hanka makes the argument that we need to pivot public administration programs 180 degrees to address the real problems in poor and minority communities. Academics should advocate for Black neighborhoods, where services, planning efforts, and investment lag severely behind affluent White neighborhoods. Blacks want to build wealth through housing as an anchor to greater equity.

Hanka's book is a much-needed contribution that gives us a model of best practices of community development, and a balanced and honest view of the ups and downs of community development. This book should be required reading in planning, public administration, political science, sociology, and Black studies. Most people want to invest in democratic capitalism, not undemocratic socialism. We have made great progress with community development thanks to Dr. Martin Luther King Jr., but we still have a lot of work to do.

—John I. Gilderbloom, Ph.D.

Introduction

Kentucky author, poet, farmer, environmentalist, and social critic Wendell Berry defined community "as the mental and spiritual condition of knowing that the place is shared and that the people who share the place define and limit the possibilities of each other's lives" that includes people's knowledge, concern, and trust in each other (1969, p. x). Everyone in a community shares something in common and plays an important role in the growth, development, and outcome of the community.

Before we understand community development, it is important to understand the nature of a community. A community is more than collections of people with common preferences, needs, or interests living together in a specific place, geographic area, or territory. In the 21st century, community takes on many different forms not spatially oriented, as with social media platforms, Facebook, Twitter, Pinterest, Instagram, Snapchat, YouTube, WhatsApp, TikTok, etc.

From the beginning of human settlements, human beings formed communities based on people interacting with each other for association, meeting basic needs, or protecting individual self-interest. People join and form communities because they feel safe, healthy, and are more satisfied than being alone. People also join and form communities because of a personal desire to be with like-minded people, learn new things from others, or grow as a person (Christian, 2007). Community enables us to make connections with other individuals and form "social networks and the norms of reciprocity and trustworthiness that arise from them," which Putnam defines as social capital (1993, 1995, 2000, p. 19). Social capital is valuable because of the benefits individuals and groups receive from contact and participation, which enhances participation in the civic sphere.

Communities are not static or stationary organisms. They are fluid and dynamic. As communities change, they grow and develop. From the ancient Greek *polis* to the early American settlers, communities evolved from fulfilling basic needs to becoming a microcosm of society. For philosopher John Dewey, community is an organic entity composed of aggregate needs and the combined interests of the individual, where everyone can improve oneself and achieve one's ends while improving the needs of the community (London, 2002).

How social groups improve themselves is important in understanding community development, defined as "a group of people in a locality initiating a social action process (i.e., planned intervention) to change their economic, social, cultural and/or environmental situation" (Christenson and Robinson, 1989, p. 14). Ferguson and Dickens (1999) define community development as "asset building that improves the quality of life among residents of low-to-moderate income communities" (p. 5). The development of a community is accomplished by all its members regardless of race, ethnicity, gender, age, socioeconomic status, political affiliation, religion, creed, or sexual orientation. Each member plays an active role in articulating their specific needs and desires for the community instead of merely being the beneficiaries of any development efforts (Abiona & Bello, 2013; Onyenemezu, 2014).

The role of community development has evolved over the last century, from its roots in Dewey's self-reliance ideology of the Progressive Era, to the New Deal policies of the 1930s that focused on federal government policies in addressing community problems through homeownership (i.e., the creation of the Federal Housing Administration [FHA] under the National Housing Act of 1934), job creation, and infrastructure building under the Works Progress Administration (WPA) and the Civilian Conservation Corps (CCC). Federal policies under urban renewal in the 1950s changed the way residents lived. Extensive slum clearance during urban renewal and the creation of the federal interstate highway system destroyed the inner-city neighborhoods that proliferated the growth and development of automobile-dependent suburbs.

Community development also addressed the structural and institutional causes of poverty through the creation of federal programs such as the Community Action Programs (CAP) and the Model Cities program under President Lyndon Johnson's Great Society of the 1960s, along with the creation of Community Development Corporations (CDCs) and Community Development Block Grants (CDBG) in the 1970s. The CDBG program gave state and local governments more latitude in spending federal funds to provide housing to low- and moderate-income residents and funds to revitalize neighborhoods and communities through blight elimination and economic development projects (Schwartz, 2015).

Communities were transformed by the Fair Housing Act of 1968, which focused on specific targets aimed at the expansion of building low-income housing, providing low-interest loans and rental subsidies for low and moderate-income households, and prohibiting discrimination in the sale or rent of a home on the basis of race (Schwartz, 2015; Massey & Denton, 1993). In 1977, the Community Reinvestment Act (CRA) outlawed the practice of redlining that targeted specific areas and neighborhoods based on racial and ethnic groupings.

The role of community development in the transformation of a community is critical to the survival of a community. This book examines the theoretical foundations and approaches to community development, such as self-help, technical assistance, asset-based community development (ABCD), and conflict models (Christenson and Robinson, 1989; Green & Haines, 2016). The self-help approach to community development is predicated on the notion that only the people can and should solve their community's problems (Bhattacharyya, 1995). The self-help model is influenced by a post-positivist approach from the social sciences which emphasizes that human behavior is best understood from the lens of the client who is the expert of his or her own life. In applying this perspective with a community lens, the client, or in this case the community, is the expert. The community developer serves as the guide during the development process, enabling the voices and narratives of the community to be heard and understood (Hutchison, 2019).

An effective community developer and a highly skilled well-trained convener will adopt a neutral position focused on process and capacity building (i.e., building leadership skills) more than specific results or bricks and mortar improvements. The community development convener's job is "to engage the people concerned in a process so that they themselves can identify what the problems are so that they 'own' the problems, which is the first necessary step for them to exert themselves for their solution" (Bhattacharyya, 1995, p. 63).

The technical assistance model of community development is rooted in the positivist model in social sciences, which uses scientific inquiry based on facts and data (Hutchison, 2019). This model is based on a community's lack of information and resources to solve its problems and is less concerned about capacity issues (Green & Haines, 2016). Sometimes, the community may lack knowledge to achieve their specific desires or the community lacks a leader with the knowledge to guide them (Onyenemezu, 2014). The challenge of this model is to bring in a consultant, facilitator, or expert with technical expertise, who does not work *for* but *with* the community.

The conflict model is rooted in communities having a lack of power. An organizer works within existing organizations in the neighborhood, chooses a problem, and organizes the community around that problem (Green &

Haines, 2016). Ferguson and Dickens (1999) identify five assets in community development, including physical capital, intellectual and human capital, political capital, financial capital, and social capital, which is the "stock of knowledge and other resources that enable members of a neighborhood or social network to help one another, especially in relation to education, economic opportunity, and social mobility" (p. 5).

A major goal of this book is to move the discussion beyond the implications of physical capital (e.g., bricks and mortar projects), human capital (e.g., workforce development, investments in education and training and additional benefits for workers), and cultural capital (e.g., skills, language, tastes, mannerisms, credentials) to discuss how social capital enhances a community's capacity to develop, revitalize, and transform itself through programs and initiatives designed and led by the community.

Current views on the impact of social capital acknowledge its contribution to sustainable economic development (Putnam, 1993, 1995; Coleman, 1990; Temkin & Rohe, 1998). Apart from being a determinant of economic growth and development, the bonds that result from social networks are critical to the survival of individuals and communities during times of economic difficulties (Whiteley, 2000). In a crisis, a person's family, friends, and associates are vital assets, enjoyed for their own sakes, because of closeness, or leveraged for material benefit (Woolcock & Narayan, 2000). When a group or community improves its social capital, change can happen, because people can leverage their networks to produce better results for themselves. For Woolcock (2000), "communities endowed with a rich stock of social networks and civic associations are in a stronger position to confront poverty and vulnerability, resolve disputes and take advantage of new opportunities" (p. 226; also cited in Woolcock, 2001, p. 67).

Despite the difficulty of measuring and operationalizing social capital, three dimensions are relevant in exploring the dynamics of homeownership, community development, and social capital. The first dimension is bonding social capital, which refers to the strength of family ties like a "sociological super glue" (Putnam & Feldstein, 2003, p. 2). The second dimension is bridging social capital, which refers to ties among friends and acquaintances like "a sociological WD-40" (Putnam & Feldstein, 2003, p. 2). The third dimension is linking social capital, which refers to formal ties linking individuals to voluntary organizations and associations (Putnam, 2000; Putnam & Feldstein, 2003; Woolcock, 2001; Sabatini, 2005).

High levels of linking social capital result in higher levels of civic involvement from individuals involved in these associations, such as neighborhood associations, block watch groups, bowling leagues, sewing circles, and political and religious organizations. This high participation collectively contributes to the overall health and quality of life of individuals and the entire community. More importantly, high social capital encourages active participatory democracy and governance, and positively contributes to the overall fabric of American society (Rohe, Van Zandt, & McCarthy, 2001). For Putnam (2000, p. 338), these are some of the external effects of social capital's contribution to the democratic polity. For Dewey, "democracy begins at home and its home is in the neighborly community" (Westbrook, 1991, p. 314). This neighborly community helps to inculcate strong democratic virtues and habits into the minds and hearts of citizens, such as civic-mindedness, cooperation, and public-spiritedness, which are some internal effects of social capital's contribution to democracy (Putnam, 1995, 2000, p. 338).

Social capital plays an important role in community development. In addition to providing the theoretical foundations of social capital and community development, this book will examine the practical applications of how housing policy interventions, service-learning programs, comprehensive community development, collective impact, and placemaking initiatives help improve the social capital of a community.

In the past decade, there has been a noticeable decline in the homeownership rate in the United States. During the same time, the number of persons who own their own homes because of nonprofit housing developers like Habitat for Humanity International has increased. Although bonding, bridging, and linking social capital are discussed conceptually, little empirical work has focused on these dimensions at a micro program level. Chapter 3 will examine social capital in context of the Habitat for Humanity homeownership program, where there are multiple opportunities for establishing and strengthening relationships. These relationships are formed from the time someone applies for a Habitat for Humanity home to paying off the mortgage for the home. Based on data from a survey instrument administered to a national sample of Habitat for Humanity homeowners who participated in the Women Build program, our analysis shows bonding and bridging social capital strengthened in the context of this program, while there was limited evidence that linking social capital was enhanced by homeownership.

Sean Safford's 2009 book, *Why the Garden Club Couldn't Save Youngstown*, introduces a revolutionary idea that much of a community's economic resilience is tied to its social capital. Recent research suggests social capital not only benefits those who develop it, but it can serve as a source of economic development in the communities in which it arises. Past quantitative research on the economic benefit of social capital has only examined the city or higher levels of aggregation.

Chapter 4 will present a study that measures social capital in three diverse socioeconomic neighborhoods to better understand how social capital can serve as a tool for economic development. An ordered probit regression model was developed to examine how individual and neighborhood levels of social capital benefit households within these communities. Moreover, this study addresses how differences in social capital across neighborhoods are explained by both individual and neighborhood characteristics.

Another practical application of community development is service learning. The National Youth Leadership Council defines service learning as "a philosophy, pedagogy, and model for community development that is used as an instructional strategy to meet learning goals and/or content standards" (NYLC, 2008). Service learning is also the mechanism to meet community needs combined with intentional learning goals, conscious reflection, and critical analysis (Jacoby, 2003). Putnam (2000) defines the norm of generalized reciprocity, which is the notion of doing something for someone without expecting anything in return, which Campbell (2000) argues can enhance social capital by involving young people and students in community service. Service learning as an investment in communities helps build social capital.

Chapter 5 will explore the connections between community development and service learning. We show that service learning is a valuable tool for those stakeholders engaging in community development, particularly with students and faculty at the University of Southern Indiana (USI), and community partners in Evansville, Indiana. Scholars including Mattessich (2009) argue that social capital is at the heart of community development, and if community development is about building capacity to effect change, then the social capital created from that change is critically important.

Putnam (1995, 2000) argues that social capital and civic engagement is declining because of generational change, pressure of time and money, residential mobility, the growth of demographic changes due to the growth of suburbanization and sprawl, and technological changes associated with electronic innovation (including the presence of television). The connections we make virtually, and the communities we form online, have taken on a different meaning over the past 20 years. Social media has also played a key role in how we define our interactions. Social media allows us to communicate with whomever we want, when we want, and as often as we want. As people have control over the context and content of social media communication, sometimes debates, dialogue, and discussions in online forums and chat rooms can be volatile, hostile, and hate-filled (Field, 2017).

Society seems to be losing valuable personal human connections that build community and social capital (e.g., neighborhood get-togethers, visiting friends at someone's home, or belonging to or participating in voluntary associations or organizations) because of the selective interactions we choose on the internet. The COVID-19 pandemic of 2020–2021 has forced individuals to practice social distancing, which resulted in the shutdown of everyday institutions (schools, college campuses, businesses, restaurants, government and office buildings) to prevent the spread of the virus.

This mandate of social distancing has established new social norms contributing to our rethinking of community. Social distancing has enhanced bonding and bridging social capital, such as looking out for one's family and friends from afar, checking in on them, and using social media to make connections previously made in person. However, the lack of physical and personal interaction in social settings, typically how we create and foster social networks, may affect how we socialize in our world for decades to come. How we understand, create, and maintain community may be forever altered by this pandemic.

This book represents 15 years of my work on community development and housing with the Center for Sustainable Urban Neighborhoods (SUN) at the University of Louisville and the Center for Applied Research (CAR) at the University of Southern Indiana. This book is unique because of the opportunity to tell the stories of how our model of comprehensive community development, known as the Adaptive Collaborative Community Transformation (ACCT) model, has transformed communities in the Evansville area. Chapter 6 will provide an overview of this model that employs the self-help model and the Simplex facilitation method that is the most effective in capturing what a community wants and needs to improve its quality of life.

Comprehensive community development involves an individual or organization that demonstrates an interest in community revitalization and a willing local leader or convener who can build a support group of volunteers with specific skills and capacities. The lead convener consults the users/consumers of the program, summarizes and integrates group efforts, builds leadership skills and group capacities, and graciously withdraws as the group becomes self-directed. These community leaders and conveners build the long-term sustainability and effectiveness of the efforts that will drive transformational change. Whatever the community development effort, Harwood (2015) says, "it is simply not possible to *impose* a strategy on a community; nor is it possible for a group to impose its own will. Rather, the trust is that it is necessary to work *with* the community" (pp. 5–6).

The lead convener is involved in conducting assessments, usually through surveys to engage neighborhood residents and train the teams of volunteers to engage with the neighborhood so they can understand and evaluate the needs of their community. Once the lead convener mobilizes and organizes volunteers, community leaders, and residents, a formalized steering committee is created to begin the community development process. The process involves a pre-consultation session, a community SWOT (strengths, weakness, opportunities, and threats) analysis, a community listening session, the development of a community vision and mission statement, a needs assessment of the community, and the establishment of priority teams to carry out the community's vision, mission, goals, objectives and strategies.

A major component of our community development model is using facilitation as a method to best capture what a community must do to improve and enhance quality of life. Dr. Sue Ellspermann, the founding director of CAR, former Lieutenant Governor of Indiana and President of Ivy Tech Community College, utilized the Simplex method during the Glenwood, Jacobsville, and Engage Henderson community development initiatives, which will be outlined in chapter 6.

Unlike traditional facilitation, community facilitation requires the utilization of skills, methods, and knowledge of large-scale vision development, the ability to work with larger teams, an understanding of the stakeholders who are invited to be a part of this process, being a trusted partner in the community, and the ability to reach consensus in a short period of time that results in action steps that will move the community forward (Ellspermann, 2008). The deliberate and intentional outcome of community facilitation and the effectiveness of the facilitator may determine if a community is ready for a revitalization effort. The Simplex method used by the Center for Applied Research and their trained facilitators to assist businesses and public and non-profit organizations throughout southwestern Indiana and the state of Indiana.

A major theme of community development that has evolved in the past decade, known as collective impact, "represents a fundamentally different, more disciplined, and higher performing approach to achieving large-scale social impact" (Hanleybrown, Kania, & Kramer, 2012, p. 2). For practitioners of collective impact, five conditions must be met: having a common agenda; a shared vision for change; shared measurements; mutually reinforcing activities; continuous communication; and backbone support (Kania & Kramer, 2011; Hanleybrown et al., 2012). Collective impact differs from the idea of isolated impact, which uses a single unitary independent approach, rather than developing networks to achieve a common agenda and goals.

Hanleybrown et al. (2012) also identify three preconditions for collective impact: an influential champion; adequate financial resources; and a sense of urgency for change. Together, these preconditions create the opportunity and motivation necessary to bring people who have never worked together into a collective impact initiative and hold them in place until the initiative's own momentum takes over.

CHAPTER OVERVIEWS

Chapter 1 examines the role of community in our society with specific examples, such as intentional communities like the Harmonists and the Shakers, an examination of various theoretical models of community development, the role of community building in community development, and a historical foundation of how community development evolved throughout the 20th and early 21st century.

Chapter 2 defines social capital and provides an overview on the literature of social capital, and some of its gaps and critiques, which includes Florida's creative class theory. Florida (2002, 2005, 2014) argues that the most effective development strategy in the post-industrial world is developing cities and localities that have a high creative class, which he defines as workers with occupations who "create meaningful new forms" (Florida, 2014, p. 38). These workers are divided into the super-creative core, who are scientists, engineers, professors, artists, entertainers and designers, and the creative professionals who work in knowledge-intensive industries such as technology, financial services, business, law, and health care (Florida, 2002, 2014).

To attract this creative class, cities and neighborhoods must provide certain cultural and social amenities, such as arts, professional sports arenas, museums, theaters, shops, and restaurants. These amenities will attract a diverse group of people and a highly educated, highly skilled workforce that will drive growth and economic development (Florida, 2002, 2005, 2014).

Florida is a critic of Putnam, who argues creative workers, as the drivers of economic development, are stifled by "strong ties" (Granovetter, 1973) that increase bonding social capital but decrease bridging social capital. Putnam believes high levels of bonding social capital create an environment that stifles creativity but promote trust and reciprocity with family and co-workers. Florida contends that "weak ties" (Granovetter, 1973) are more important because they require less investment, and it is easier to mobilize resources, ideas, information, jobs, products, and enterprises more rapidly. These weak ties also help to preserve the freedom and quasi-anonymity of creative people (Florida, 2002, 2014).

Although various measures outlined in the literature are used as predictors of high levels of social capital, little has been documented about homeownership as a predictor of social capital. Chapter 3 will examine how social capital is measured on the macro-level, through a study conducted by researchers from USI who developed and administered a survey to a representative sample of participants in Habitat for Humanity International's Women Build program. This analysis shows that bonding and bridging social capital were strengthened within the context of this program. Linking social capital was not strengthened, since only three out of 10 residents surveyed said they were involved in a community group or organization (Draughon, Hanka, Khayum, Opartny, Phillips, & Priest, 2012).

Chapter 4 will include a comparative study of three local neighborhoods in Evansville, Indiana, diverse with respect to affluence, socioeconomic status, and city investment: the Dexter neighborhood in the inner city; Glenwood in the southeast side of Evansville; and the Mount Auburn neighborhood in the city's westside to analyze the level of social capital in each of these neighborhoods.

Like the origins of community development rooted in the ideology of John Dewey and the Progressives, service learning is an important tool to examine social capital's effects on community development, which is examined in chapter 5 by Statham and Rosenberg. Chapter 6 showcases the uniqueness of our community development process, known as the Adaptive Community Collaborative Transformation (ACCT) model. Volunteers and facilitators are trained in the art and science of community facilitation, which can be used to determine what residents want and need to improve and enhance the quality of life of their neighborhood and community. This chapter will examine how this model was utilized in the Glenwood and Jacobsville neighborhoods in Evansville and the Engage Henderson project in Henderson, Kentucky, across the Ohio River from Evansville.

Chapter 7 will describe the theory of collective impact and will look at two case studies that utilize the collective impact model. The first case study is: a visioning process called VOICE initiated by Leadership Everyone (formerly Leadership Evansville) a nonprofit organization that specializes in transformational leadership development aimed towards bettering the Evansville community (Leadership Everyone [LE], 2021). The other collective impact case study features the Promise Zone, a program created in 2013 by President Barack Obama, which targets the most economically underserved and under-resourced areas in the nation. This case study showcases the Evansville Promise Zone, one of the 22 zones in the nation that received the designation in 2016.

Chapter 8 focuses on the HOPE VI (Housing Opportunities for People Everywhere) federal housing program, created in 1992 by the George H. W. Bush administration as a response to the National Commission on Severely Distressed Housing. The Commission showed that six percent of the nation's housing stock (86,000 out of 1.3 million units) was uninhabitable (U.S. Department of Housing and Urban Development [HUD], 1992; HUD, 1999, 2000; Popkin & Cunningham, 2000; Goetz, 2003; Popkin, Katz, Cunningham, Brown, Gustafson, & Turner, 2004; Brazley & Gilderbloom, 2007; Gilderbloom, 2008; Hanka, 2009; Hanlon, 2010; Schwartz, 2015; Clark &

Negrey, 2017). HOPE VI focuses on remaking community building, helping residents achieve self-sufficiency through improving education, job training, and homeownership through a case management program known as Community and Supportive Services (CSS) (HUD, 1992, 1999, 2000; Popkin et al., 2000; Popkin, 2002; GAO, 2002; Popkin, Katz, et al., 2004; Gilderbloom & Hanka, 2006; Brazley & Gilderbloom, 2007; Gilderbloom, 2008; Hanka, 2009; Schwartz, 2015). HOPE VI has reduced the isolation of public housing through scattered site development and leveraged public investments in community and neighborhood revitalization projects (HUD, 2000; Popkin, Katz, et al., 2004; U.S. Government Accountability Office [GAO], 2002).

HOPE VI improved the physical shape of housing and the configuration of community using New urbanist design principles. New urbanist neighborhoods utilize traditional urban form and historic patterns of development, using a mixture of housing types, and building designs. New Urbanist HOPE VI neighborhoods are walkable, sustainable, and pedestrian friendly. These neighborhoods calm traffic via narrower streets and wider sidewalks. Chapter 8 will examine the relationship between New Urbanism, HOPE VI, and social capital, and provide an overview and evaluation of the HOPE VI projects in Newport and Covington, Kentucky, located in the northern part of the state. This chapter will also provide an overview of three HOPE VI projects (Park DuValle, Clarksdale/Liberty Green, and Sheppard Square) in Louisville, Kentucky, the state's largest city, and examine the social capital implications of the HOPE VI program in these neighborhoods under study.

Today, people less often move to cities and communities where the jobs are. They move to the city and community of their choosing and then find the job because of the place. The place where we live tells a story. The values, characteristics, and identity of a place, including its history, geography, industry, institutions, culture, and landmarks, enhance a resident's attachment to place and community. Chapter 9 examines the various types of placemaking: standard, incremental, creative, and tactical. In this chapter, I show how local and regional examples of placemaking have impacted and transformed neighborhoods and communities.

The conclusion will provide a summation of the book's themes and questions. Are neighborhoods strengthened by community development programs, and is social capital enhanced by these programs? What are some of the lessons learned from the community development and collective impact models used in our case studies? What can we do to create, develop, enhance, and maintain the social capital in neighborhoods and communities while coping with 21st century challenges, like the COVID-19 pandemic of 2020–2021? How do we make the work going on in our communities, the social capital that's created out of these communities, and the efforts to make place matter in our daily lives?

Chapter One

What is Community and Community Development?

The concept of community is something that is not easily defined. It is something that can be touched, felt, experienced, lived, and seen. Community is a big part of the human experience and condition, but it can have many meanings, depending on the person and the context, so what community means in one context or culture might mean something different in another context or culture (Christensen & Levinson, 2003).

Each community is unique, not simply a collection of individuals or dwellings. There is a culture behind a community. Some have smaller communities within themselves. The boundaries, rules, and expectations of a community may not always be clear; some have simple or complex structures. The reasons for entering, belonging, and participating in a community depend on desired benefits. Within a community that builds social capital, one can feel safe and secure, feel a sense of belonging, make connections, and receive support.

There is a lack of consensus on a definition of community. Etzioni's (1996) definition of community has two characteristics:

> First, a web of affect-laden relationships among a group of individuals, relationships that often crisscross and reinforce one another (rather than merely one-to-one or chainlike individual relationships), and second, a measure of commitment to a set of shared values, norms, and meanings and a shared history and identity—in short, to a particular culture. (p. 127)

Community can consist of a unified body of individuals, interacting with one another in a common space, location, or place, whether it be physical, spatial, or virtual that invokes a commonality in which everyone shares particular interests, identities, and experiences (Edwards & Imrie, 2015). Community can also be a unit of social actors who share similar sociodemographic characteristics and concerns about a problem or issue that might transcend locality or place (Checkoway, 2013).

For philosopher John Dewey, community is developed and achieved by allowing everyone the opportunity to achieve self-realization, which is the freedom and opportunity to improve oneself as a social being (Westbrook, 1991). This allows a person to grow and evolve and to realize one's potential, which ultimately improves the community as a whole.

Community can also be a deeply felt experience entrenched in human needs (Fowler, 1991), providing "a clear sense of cultural purpose, membership, status, and continuity" (Nisbet, 1953, p. 64). At its core, community is a sense of belonging, an understanding of our connections to those who help weave its fabric, a fabric that occurs in many small unnoticeable steps based on the accountability, gifts, and generosity of its citizens (Block, 2008).

Community takes on many different forms, such as voluntary associations, places of worship, public spaces (plazas and playgrounds) and peer groups that may not require a physical space or location. A focus of this book is on community pertaining to space and place, where place itself, bound by geography, can enhance social capital. We argue that a few assets within a community, such as neighborhood associations, community development corporations (CDCs), and community-based organizations (CBOs), help people feel strong ties to place.

In discussing his quest for community, Nisbet (1953) states there are major moral and psychological forces that impact an individual's life from the family, the local community, and the church. Nisbet (1953) says that community

> is the area of association from which the individual commonly gains his concept of the outer world and his sense of position in it. His concrete feelings of status and role, of protection and freedom, his differentiation between good and bad, between order and disorder and guilt and innocence, arise and are shaped largely by his relations within this realm of primary association. What was once called instinct or the social nature of man is but the product of this sphere of interpersonal relationships. (p. 44)

Unfortunately, Nisbet (1953) argues that relationships with family, community, and church do not play a role in shaping an individual's place in the larger political and economic decisions of society, resulting in "profound dislocations in the primary associative areas of society" for the individual (p. 41).

Community, for Nisbet (1953), has two requirements that can influence its members: function and authority. The function of a community is the extended family, neighborhood, and one's social class that adds meaning to an individual's life, while the authority "must be closely united to objectives and functions which command the response and talents of [its] members" (p. xxvii). Community can also rely on moral suasion and coercion by "threatening their members with the stick of sanction if they astray, offering them the carrot of certainty and stability if they don't" (Pearson, 1995, p. 47; also cited in Christensen & Levinson, 2003, p. 226).

Although community refers to a village or town, post-industrial society has expanded community to include larger urban areas and even a global community (Fowler, 1991), especially with the formation of international institutions that make up a global community and global society. Etzioni (1996) argues that we have moved from community to society (*gemeinschaft* vs. *gesellschaft*), or a community of communities (the society at-large). Community is also participatory, republican (smaller), and existential, and "a realm where we find our origin and definition, the roots of our lives, the roots of communities in which we live or from which we may escape in order to live" (Fowler, 1991, p. 40).

The ancient Greek philosopher Aristotle believed that man by nature is a political animal *(zoon politikon)* and that man's nature of achieving the highest good (i.e., happiness) can be fulfilled in the *polis* (Greek for city state), the highest ideal of community (Aristotle, 2010). Aristotle says the *polis* is a partnership between a citizen and the state. Citizenship is about being ethical, moral, and attaining the highest good. It is a citizen's responsibility to make the community better, instead of just being a citizen that enjoys certain rights and liberties (Dagger, 1981).

Citizenship helps foster community and breeds civility and proper discourse. Citizenship is a public vocation that requires citizens to be fully active in the public affairs of the community. Citizenship requires citizens to exercise their own power instead of deferring or delegating it, act in the best interest of the community, hold ourselves accountable to the well-being of the larger society, and hold ourselves to the same standards as our elected representatives (Dagger, 1981; Block, 2008). As citizens, it is our responsibility to make one's neighborhood, community, city, or little corner of the world a better place.

Community grows out of the possibility of citizenship and the role and contribution citizens make every day (Block, 2008). The creation of a newly conceived community can allow residents to be more centered within the community and provide a vested stake and interest in shaping its character, which will increase and improve civic memory (Dagger, 1981).

For Aristotle, a lower level of community, such as family, is important since the family educates and socializes its members. Many times, extended family lives in close physical proximity, as is the case in Appalachia. Familism is a "family structure wherein family leaders emphasize the importance of subordinated interests to benefit the family over the individual, possess a strong sense of loyalty and family identification, and encourage a general reliance on others in the family" (Moreland, Raup-Krieger, Hecht, & Miller-Day, 2013, p. 670). Close family relationships result in close ties, often referred to as "strong ties" (Granovetter, 1973; also discussed in chapter 3). The Appalachian people, for example, value shared history and their ties with each other.

INTENTIONAL COMMUNITIES

Community can evolve organically, but also intentionally. Many of these communities serve as moral agents, where the community acts "as a building block of the moral infrastructure" that reinforces an individual's character (Etzioni, 1996, p. 187). Some of these intentional communities have communitarianism aspects and often have a religious orientation, including the Shakers, Quakers, and the Harmonists, along with other religious groups such as the Catholic Worker and Focolare, which we will further discuss in this chapter.

An intentional community is defined as "a group of people who have chosen to work together in pursuit of a common ideal or vision" (Christian, 2007, p. 115; as cited in Christensen & Levinson, 2003, p. 670). Intentional communities are purposeful, voluntary, and specific, as they establish group goals and solve social or cultural problems (Brown, 2002). Brown further explains:

> Intentional communities represent a kind of "voting with the feet"—a call to action that is personal and communal, bringing together the needs of the individual with those of other individuals, reestablishing the bonds that connect human beings but in a particular fashion, The members of these communities often see themselves at odds with or needing to withdraw from the larger society; however, that withdrawal occurs within the context of the larger society. (Brown, 2002, pp. 5–6)

Intentional communities vary in size, scope, function, and orientation, but more importantly, move "beyond the bounds of mainstream society by adopting a consciously devised and usually well-thought out social and cultural alternative," often characterized as a "we-consciousness that is separate from and in many ways better than the society from which they have emerged" (Metcalf & Christian, 2003, p. 670).

The Shakers

The Shakers emerged during the first and second periods of communitarianism and are considered one of the first utopian communities (Berry, 1992;

Brown, 2002). The Shakers originated in Manchester, England, often considered the epicenter of the Industrial Revolution in the mid-1700s, led by their founder Mother Ann Lee (Jennings, 2016). The earliest Shakers believed society was plagued with disease, war, and poverty, and must be remade to allow humanity to live together and develop a proper relationship with God (Brewer, 1997). Lee had experienced personal hardship earlier in her life, having been imprisoned for heresy and losing all four of her children. She professed that Christ appeared to her in a series of visions, to show human misery and sin, and felt Christ's presence in her blood and in her. Lee called herself Mother Ann as an Elder Sister to Christ, as Elder Brother in the faith (Holloway, 1966; Brewer, 1997).

Known as the "Shaking Quakers" under Mother Lee's leadership, the Shakers functioned as a sanctuary. They believed in divine revelation, strict celibacy, confession of sin, equality of sexes, and rejection of the doctrine of the Trinity (Father, Son, and Holy Spirit). They believed in the second coming of Christ and communal living and promoted the economic well-being of the society (Holloway, 1966; Berry, 1992). The original Shaker community of believers consisted of nine members in 1774 who lived on 200 acres in Niskayuna near Albany, New York, that eventually grew to 4,000 members by 1850 (Brewer, 1997). There were as many as 18 different Shaker communities stretching from Kentucky, Massachusetts, New Hampshire, New York, and Maine in the early days, where as many as 20,000 Shakers lived during the 200-year history of the Shakers (Brewer, 1997). Mother Lee died in 1784 and was succeeded by James Whitaker, who died in 1787 and was succeeded by Joseph Meacham. These three are considered the first elders and founders of Shakerism; they gave "intellectual and institutional coherence" to the Shaker movement (Jennings, 2016). In 1788, Meacham elevated Mother Ann Lee's most capable assistant Mother Lucy Wright as a co-elder and the eventual successor after his death in 1796.

Under Mother Lucy Wright's 25-year leadership, 57 different Shaker communities formed, with the largest located in New Lebanon, Ohio, with 375 members. The communities in Union Village, Ohio, Pleasant Hill, and South Union Village in Kentucky ranged between 200 and 300 members. The smallest communities were around 50 members in Watervliet, Ohio, Groveland, New York, and Shirley, Massachusetts (Brewer, 1997). At the time of Wright's death, half of the 4,000 active Shakers lived in four villages in Ohio (including White Water), the two in Kentucky mentioned, and West Union Village in Indiana (Jennings, 2016).

Much of the recruitment of converts to Shakerism occurred during revivals in the early 19th century. Each Shaker society was divided into two or more families with respect to property. Each community or village owned at least 1,000 acres to grow crops, and some turned the land into forest and sold the wood, which served as a principal source of income (Hinds, 1961). Each Shaker home and its furnishings were kept simple and plain. The Shakers produced their own furniture and necessities such as brooms, tubs, mops, sieves, mats, and washing machines (Holloway, 1966). The Shakers thought of their entire village as a church. The Shakers' "tidy, highly planned villages" and the simple and plain homes were considered earthly reflections of how everything looked in heaven (Jennings, 2016, p. 57).

The Shakers were the first utopian community movement that believed in Christ's second coming. Shakers did not socialize, which they believed took away from diligent work, and did not produce offspring, which contributed to the membership's decline. Membership dwindled after 1850 to as low as 94 members (Holloway, 1966). The last year of active Shakerism was considered 1922, due to an elder embezzling money and the accumulation of $14,000 in debt at Pleasant Hill in Harrodsburg, Kentucky (Neal, 1977).

According to Holloway (1966), the Shakers' restrictions on personal freedom and liberty and severe abstinence were balanced by highly skilled craftmanship, insistence of equality between men and women, and equality between race, religion, and ethnicity. As a community, the Shakers showed an ordered, successful, stable, prosperous society that was not monastic or secluded but "provided a solid and enduring foundation for others to build upon" (Holloway, 1966, p. 79).

The Harmonists and New Harmony

The Harmonists are a notable example of community often associated with the third period of communitarianism, or the so-called Utopian socialist period from 1824 to 1848 (Brown, 2002). Known initially as the Rappites, the Harmonist Society was established in Wurttemberg, Germany, in the 1780s by Father George Rapp, who was considered a "benevolent autocrat" (Holloway, 1966, p. 95) and who possessed innate intelligence and leadership skills. He also enforced minimal discipline and rules and regulations and possessed strong craftmanship and entrepreneurial skills (Rode, 2019). The Harmonists were stimulated by a creative spirit of unity, self-determination, pietism, the belief in a communal utopia, community goods, loyalty, subordination to whole, and a belief that the reorganization of society would lead to the salvation of the world (Pitzer, 1997).

In George Rapp's *Thoughts on the Destiny of Man*, he defines community:

> where those who occupy its peaceful dwellings are so closely united by endearing ties of friendship, confidence, and love, that one heart beats in all, and their common industry provides for us all. Here, the members kindly assist each

other, in difficulty and danger, and share with each other, the enjoyments, and the misfortunes in life; one lives in the breast of another and forgets himself, all their undertakings are influenced by a social spirit, glowing with noble energy, and generous feeling, and pressing forwards to the haven of their mutual prosperity. (quoted in Arndt, 1997, p. 71)

In 1805 when they first came to America, the Harmonists built a new settlement in Pennsylvania north of Pittsburgh called Harmony after Father Rapp met with President Thomas Jefferson to obtain land for his community (Rode, 2018). Harmony had 800 members, and 500 charter members joined Rapp to live a communal life as an economic necessity, fleeing the old world to be redeemed by the second coming of Christ (Pitzer, 1997; Jones & Pitzer, 2012). Rapp's Harmonist Society operated in three spheres: overarching millennial spiritualism joined with inner communal socialism and outer venture capitalism (Rode, 2019). The inner communal socialism was self-contained and separate from worldly society, in an orderly, harmonious fashion, through a rigid routine of work and prayer (Brown, 2002). Much of Rapp's power came from millennial spiritualism, based on the belief that the Messiah will return, that His return is imminent, and the events in the world were pointing in a utopian direction (Jones & Pitzer, 2012).

Many of the Harmonists did not have contact with outsiders, partly because Rapp prohibited them from learning or speaking English and refused admission to non-Germans (Jennings, 2016; Rode, 2019). The venture capitalist side of the Harmonists, through the expansion of agrarian methods, created lucrative markets in grains, corn, wool, whiskey, flour, and fur hats, which they shipped downriver to New Orleans (Jennings, 2016; Rode, 2019). This resulted in a high standard of living, including advanced health standards through good medical care and a clean water supply (Rode, 2019). The education of the Harmonists was led by Christopher Mueller from the original Harmony, Pennsylvania, settlement in 1805 (Arndt, 1997).

In 1814, the Harmonists sold the first community to Mennonite Abraham Ziegler for $100,000, moved west, and settled on land in Southwest Indiana on the Wabash River north of the Ohio River. They called this new community New Harmony. New Harmony became wealthy from the fruits of their labors. In 1817–1818, a new wave of immigrants from Wurttemberg, Germany, arrived in New Harmony.

In the 1820s, New Harmony was sold to Robert Owen, the Scottish industrialist and philanthropist, and the Harmonists developed a third community, Economy, once again in Pennsylvania (Pitzer, 1997; Rode, 2018). Owen had been successful in his industrial reforms in improving living and working conditions in New Lanark in his native Scotland, including restrictions of child labor in his factories. Owen used his factories as his own social laboratory where he was responsible for the moral, intellectual, educational, and physical health and well-being of his employees (Jennings, 2016).

Owen believed that the progress of man through control of the environment and the society, based on the political philosophy of Jean-Jacques Rousseau, can either create or destroy the happiness of man (Royle, 2003; Jennings, 2016). In 1816, Owen created New Lanark as a model village to promote welfare and education reforms, through the creation of the Institute for the Formation of Character. Owen believed that the New Lanark model, based on superior character and education, work, discipline, proper health care, and good housing, would ultimately overcome poverty and social disadvantage and thrive as a self-sustaining community (Edwards & Imrie, 2015). Owen hoped his model could be replicated abroad, resulting in his purchase of New Harmony from George Rapp in 1825 for $150,000, which included 20,000 acres of farmland, an orchard, a brewery, a vineyard, and approximately 200 buildings (Jennings, 2016).

Owen wanted to live out the socialist utopian community in New Harmony with residents of superior character and abundance, which can only be done if "individualism and selfishness of the nuclear family were replaced by life in the community" (Pitzer, 2004; Royle, 2003, p. 1051). Upon his arrival in New Harmony at the old Rappite church that became the Hall of New Harmony, Owen stated: "I (am) come to this country to introduce an entire new system of society; to change it from an ignorant, selfish system to an enlightened social system which shall gradually unite all interests into one and remove all causes for contest between individuals" (Holloway, 1966, p. 104).

After Owen signed the deed of New Harmony, he embarked on a trip in the eastern United States, including tours of Philadelphia and Pittsburgh, to extol the virtues of the new utopian society, and left his son William Owen and a small group of advisers in charge (Jennings, 2016). His most prominent visit was to Washington, DC, to convert the United States to utopian socialism (Jennings, 2016). He was received by outgoing President James Monroe, President-elect John Quincy Adams, and outgoing Speaker of the House of Representatives Henry Clay (soon to be Secretary of State). At the time of Adams's inauguration, Owen addressed a joint session of Congress to explain the reason why the United States was the perfect place for a new socialist system, as a model to create "communities of cooperation" (Jennings, 2016, p. 109). Owen believed that America's youth protected it from being poisoned by the "inertia and moral rot inflicting old Europe" (Jennings, 2016, p. 109).

While Robert Owen returned from the east in April 1825, 800 men and women of different classes, vocations, nationalities, and creeds, including freethinkers and atheists, had descended on New Harmony (Holloway, 1966). Owen partnered with fellow Scottish businessman William Maclure, considered the father of American geology, the founder of the Working-men's Institute, and a founder of the "Boatload of Knowledge" Society. This society, comprised of scientists and educators, boarded a boat in Pittsburgh called the *Philanthropist* for a voyage down the Ohio River to New Harmony (Pitzer, 1997; Jennings, 2016). Owen and Maclure created public schools in New Harmony—the first public schools in America. Education focused on learning by doing and Owen viewed "education as central to socialization" (Pitzer, 1997, p. 93).

When Robert Owen went back to Scotland in June 1825, New Harmony floundered through five different constitutions in six months. It struggled to interpret Owen's vision in his absence and was unable to shape and guide the community. Finally, they settled on a constitution to establish The Preliminary Society of New Harmony in May 1825 (Holloway, 1966). This new constitution placed Robert Owen in charge of the society for three probationary years, and each member was assured of equal privileges and advantages. The following February, another constitution was passed called the Conditions of the Community of Equality, which focused on community of property and equality between men and women in rights, freedom of speech, and action (Holloway, 1966; Jennings, 2016).

Owen believed community building, through benevolence to the poor and social responsibility of the workers, would shape and guide New Harmony. However, the lack of housing for every Harmonist, Owen's paternalistic rigidity, his unwillingness to loosen strict rules that prohibited residents from sharing property, and his prolonged absence ultimately doomed New Harmony. The Owenite New Harmony experiment failed (seven reorganizations and five constitutions in two years) (Pitzer, 1997) because he could not bring together and integrate the castes and divisions of people (lower classes and middle and upper classes) effectively. He failed to implement the community of property model, and there were fallings out between Maclure and Owen based on disputes on how to run the schools, as well as disagreements over slavery and financial partnerships (Jones & Pitzer, 2012).

Owen never effectively took on the hands-on role as the manager of New Harmony, leaving it to his son William and other advisers; consequently, he failed in fulfilling an important community building role of uniting all community members in "his inspired purpose" (Jones & Pitzer, 2012, p. 74). He also failed to motivate the citizens and workers to develop an effective and prosperous economy (Jones & Pitzer, 2012).

While the Owenite New Harmony experiment ended in a failure, despite successes with gender equality and women's rights, Owen himself viewed the experiment as a springboard for future socialist Utopian communities (Pitzer, 1997; Jones & Pitzer, 2012). His descendants played major roles in both New

Harmony's development and our nation's history. For instance, Robert Owen's son, Robert Dale Owen, served as an Indiana state representative and a congressman, and founded the Smithsonian Institution in Washington, DC, which was to serve as an educational facility and a free museum to benefit the American people (Weinzapfel, Bigham, & Branigin, 2000; Jones & Pitzer, 2012).

The twice-failed utopias of the Harmonists and Robert Owen, in the early 1800s, left the town in disrepair, especially after the land Owen bought from the Harmonists was sold off, during the rest of the 19th century and until the town's centennial celebration in 1914. In the late 19th century, New Harmony had low taxes and no water or sewer, little fire protection and electric service. The town's population declined 10 percent before the town's centennial (Weinzapfel, Bigham, & Branigin, 2000).

The preservation of New Harmony, especially with the failed Harmonist and Owenite experiments, began in 1937 with the establishment of the New Harmony Memorial Commission, along with the construction of the original labyrinth in 1939 and placement on the National Register of Historic Places in 1966 (Nicholson & Sabatino, 2019). In 1942 and 1969, master plans for New Harmony, showing future development opportunities for the town, were conceived. By 1973, a second New Harmony Memorial Commission was created to recommend legislation, and the following year, Historic New Harmony (HNH) was created as a nonprofit organization designed to raise money for its long-term preservation and development (Gorby, 2019).

The town evolved and embraced new and innovative changes with the construction of two projects that embody the notion of community: The Roofless Church and Tillich Park. These projects were financed through the work of Jane Blaffer Owen and Kenneth Dale Owen, the son of Robert Dale Owen and grandson of Robert Owen. Jane Blaffer Owen's father Robert Lee Blaffer founded Humble Oil and Refining Company (later known as Exxon). Along with her and Kenneth's family's fortunes (he founded an oil company), the Owens slowly rebought the land that Robert Owen had purchased from the Harmonists (Nicholson & Sabatino, 2019).

The Roofless Church is an example of modernist architecture, art, and landscape that served as a place of interdenominational worship and a refuge for solitary contemplation in a roofless open-air setting, which also include a small-enclosed chapel under a billowed shape shingled roofed dome (McAtee, 2019; Nicholson & Sabatino, 2019). The architects conceived the Roofless Church as a space that would concentrate the spirit and would bring peace to persons entering through its doors (Nicholson & Sabatino, 2019).

Tillich Park was conceived in honor the prominent Protestant theologian and existentialist Paul Tillich, who visited New Harmony and served as a spiritual mentor to Jane Blaffer Owen. Tillich died in 1965 and his ashes were scattered in the park. Tillich Park was designed to incorporate a grotto designed by architect Frederick Kiesler, but budgetary constraints and creative differences led to nixing the grotto. A rescaled park, designed by Robert Zion, featured a simplistic design with small open spaces combined with an evergreen forest spread throughout the park. The park also included stones with engravings of Tillich's famous sayings, including one encapsulating both the utopian communitarian history and the human and spiritual experience of the town: "Man and nature belong together in their created glory—in their tragedy and in their salvation" (as cited in Sabatino, 2019, p. xxx; see also Historic New Harmony, 2020), along with a plaque at the entrance to the park with the title of the lecture Tillich gave in New Harmony before the park's dedication: "Estranged and Reunited: The New Being. Paul Tillich, Pentecost, June 2, 1963" (as cited in Nicholson & Crout, 2019, p. 192; see also Historic New Harmony, 2020).

Perhaps the most outside-the-box idea emerged in the 1970s, after the establishment of Historic New Harmony and through the leadership of its first president. Ralph Schwarz oversaw the construction of a space integrating the past with the present and the future. This space would show how New Harmony had changed over time and illustrate new development in New Harmony that "makes explicit the multidimensional relationships between history, landscape, and civic engagement" (Nicholson, 2019, p. 293). Schwarz and HNH hired architect Richard Meier to create a building that would be located in the northwest corner of town next to the Wabash River that would be called the Athenaeum (in Greek, "a place of learning")—a fitting name, considering the important role an atheneum played in early 19th century urban American life as a place of intellectual and cultural discourse.

According to Schwarz, "the Atheneum is an Icon, an inspired place of arrival, introduction, reflection, circulation to elevated planes and overviews, a gateway down the ramp into the historic community, where the contributions of two utopian societies can still be appreciated . . . The Atheneum is an end in itself. It delivers its own inspired utopian message" (Nicholson, 2019, p. 267). Construction on the Atheneum began in 1975 and was completed in 1979. Meier argued the building "has to be attached to some program in New Harmony for which this building becomes used as a center of studies for whatever that may be . . ." (Nicholson, 2019, p. 292). In 1985, the University of Southern Indiana, an independent public regional university in Evansville, Indiana, 30 miles east of New Harmony, entered into an agreement with the Indiana State Museum and Historic Sites to oversee and manage 25 properties and buildings in New Harmony dating back to the Harmonist period.

Today, New Harmony is a vibrant community of 900 residents located in Posey County, with its own town council. Even now, the community is forward thinking like its predecessors in forming intentional community through the Harmonist and Owenite utopian experiments. The town has been forward thinking in the rebirth, preservation, and transformation of New Harmony through the efforts of Jane Blaffer Owen. The town is forward thinking in being a laboratory and classroom for archaeology and historic preservation, and the town is forward thinking in becoming a regional high-tech center.

Catholic Worker Movement

An important intentional community focused on community development and social justice is the Catholic Worker Movement, founded by Dorothy Day and Peter Maurin in 1933; it is one of the most influential lay Catholic movements of the 20th century. The movement comes out of the social teachings of the Gospels and the Church, using a third way of thinking called personalism, which responds to the issues and dangers of communism and capitalism (Wright, 2018). Charles Fournier, a contemporary of Maurin's, emphasized absolute value and dignity of each person made in the image and likeness of God, and a recognition of human freedom as the way one responds to a call demanding the action of another person (Wright, 2018). This action "requires the context of a community that provides the material and spiritual conditions necessary for persons to answer this call" (Wright, 2018, p. 53).

This human freedom is, ultimately, a uniting with God and serving God, oneself, and one's fellow man. Being responsible for oneself and responsible to others can lead to salvation, for Maurin, and only in community can one serve the common good and the moral good (Wright, 2018). Another dimension, emphasized by Dorothy Day, was distributism, a critique of communism and capitalism that "favor[s] private ownership for as many as possible, not just for the few" (Wright, 2018, p. 59).

Maurin and Day emphasized serving the common good as the principal tenets of the Catholic Worker movement, as outlined in four major points:

1. To reach the man in the street with social teachings of the church.
2. To build a lay apostolate through roundtable discussion for the clarification of thought.
3. To found houses of hospitality for the practice of the corporal and spiritual works of mercy.
4. To found farming communes to alleviate unemployment and to serve as agronomic universities. (Wright, 2018, p. 62)

Day formed the eponymous newspaper to spread the message of the Catholic Worker, a newspaper still published every week for one cent.

Day's conversion to Catholicism and the lives and experiences of the saints and the Gospels laid the foundation and framework of the Catholic Worker Movement. This includes the work and spirituality derived from St. Benedict's teachings (*Ora et labora*), the voluntary poverty of St. Francis of Assisi, and the scriptures, particularly Matthew 25 ("I was hungry and you gave me food, thirsty, you gave me drink, a stranger, and you welcomed me, naked, and you clothed me . . .") in carrying out the corporal works of mercy (feed the hungry, give drink to the thirsty, shelter the homeless, clothe the naked, visit the sick, visit the imprisoned, bury the dead) and the spiritual works of mercy (instruct the ignorant, counsel the doubtful, admonish the sinner, comfort the sorrowful, bear wrongs patiently, forgive all injuries, pray for the living and the dead).

The Catholic Worker Movement achieves community through its commitment to social justice through its houses of hospitality, where 204 of these houses exist in cities and towns around the world. Each community member practices voluntary poverty that allows the corporal and spiritual works of mercy to be realized. Many of these intentional hospitality communities house as many as 25 people, with many shared rooms. Everyone living in a house of hospitality, whether they are guests or permanent members, must help in housework, based on their abilities, and must share in the house's common spiritual practices (Wright, 2018).

Focolare Movement

The Focolare Movement is a Catholic international organization whose name means "hearth" or "fireside" in Italian (Focolare Movement, 2021). The Focolare Movement's aim "is to contribute to building a more united world in which people value and respect diversity" inspired by Jesus' prayer to the Lord: "May they all be one" (Focolare Movement, 2021; Gold, 2003). The movement was founded in 1943 in Trent, Italy, by Chiara Lubich, who focused on the ideas of unity and brotherhood among all peoples. As of 2011, there are 140,000 core members in 182 nations, with approximately two million affiliates (Allen, 2011). The Focolare Movement has the strong endorsement of the Pope and the church hierarchy (the foundress Chiara Lubich enjoyed a weekly audience with His Holiness St. Pope John Paul II). The Focolare Movement's rules dictated that the president of the movement must always be a woman. The Focolare Movement's multidenominational focus allows members to belong to other churches and religions, fostering interreligious dialogue (Allen, 2011). Lubich received the Templeton Prize for Progress in Religion in 1977, the highest honor for her and the Focolare Movement's interreligious work.

Unity is at the heart of the Focolare's charism, based on the realization of the infinite love of God based on the New Testament teachings of doing God's will. The notion of Jesus in the midst when "two or more are gathered in His name" (Matthew 18:20) is an example of community. Lubich states that we can only become fully human when we let the light of God enter our lives fully, "a light that can penetrate and harmonize all of life's particular aspects" (Masters & Uelman, 2011, p. 43). This light penetrates every aspect of life for individuals who become members of a Focolare community.

Men and women who have made lifelong commitments to the Focolare Movement are called *focolarinos* and *focolarinas*; together, they are *focolarini*. These men and women take private vows (as opposed to religious vows) of poverty, chastity, and obedience, to live a life of unity and love, and to live in a community where material and spiritual goods are shared. Each *focolarini* household is designed to meet each person's necessities. The *focolarini* work in professions in the outside world and share their wages and salaries with the movement. Responsibilities for daily life, prayer, meals, cleaning, study, and other tasks are shared by each member of the household.

Focolarini can be married and have children, like other lay Catholic movements (Masters & Uelman, 2011). Many of the *focolarini* households maintain a spirit of family, community life, and personal commitment to the Focolare every day (Focolare Movement, 2021). Some live in larger communities known as a Mariapolis—a city of Mary—throughout Europe and around the world, including one in Hyde Park, New York, in the United States (a few hours north of New York City). Individuals in the movement younger than 30 who have not made a lifelong commitment or taken vows are identified in groups the movement calls Gen (or the new generation of the Focolare Movement) and are classified either Gen 1, 2, 3, or 4 depending on the individual's age (Focolare Movement, 2021).

An important element of the Focolare Movement stems from a concept known as the Economy of Communion (EoC). This concept was developed by Lubich in 1991, and draws upon individuals in every sector of society, such as entrepreneurs, workers, directors, citizens, scholars, and economists to commit to helping persons with material and spiritual need "in promoting a practice and an economic culture imprinted on communion, gratuity and reciprocity" (Focolare Movement, 2021). The economy of communion draws on Christian values and spirituality by living a life of poverty based on God's Providence and giving oneself to others' individual needs. This economy of communion is not only "a form of spiritual edification but also a means of emancipation for the poor" (Gold, 2003, p. 147) based on a communion of good where everything is based on each other's needs.

This economy of communion manifests itself in a community based on free market and business regulations and standards, where the profits or proceeds from a company or enterprise are divided into three parts: one part to the poor; one part to reinvest in the company; and one part for the formation of the people (Gold, 2003). Since its inception in 1991, 767 businesses around the world follow the Economy of Communion model. Many of them are small businesses in a wide variety of sectors. Most of them are in Europe (469) with 233 in Italy, 176 in Latin America, 48 in North America, 50 in Asia, 15 in Australia, and 9 in Africa (Gold, 2003).

COMMUNITY BUILDING

While we've been discussing different examples of communities, it's important to understand the role of community building as an effective tool in community development aimed to address poverty and other social issues. Community building is defined "as a variety of intentional efforts to organize and strengthen social connections or to build common values that promote collective goals or achieve desired outcomes, such as neighborhood improvement, health care for children and families, etc." (Christensen & Levinson, 1999, p. 246). Hess (1999) emphasizes community-building projects that seek to build new relationships, developing changes out of these relationships, while emphasizing existing assets rather than provision of services to address community deficiencies.

Community building provides neighborhood residents with a right to place, defined by the "social meaning of locales" (Lepofsky & Fraser, 2003, p. 128). Lepofsky and Fraser (2003) believe the distinction between space and place impacts resident involvement in their neighborhoods and communities and "limits the ability for residents to actualise change without professional community builders" (p. 132).

The National Community Building Network (NCBN) believes community building should replace feelings of dependency with "attitudes of self-reliance, self-confidence, and responsibility" (Kingsley, McNeely, & Gibson, 1997, p. 3). If done effectively, community building places great emphasis on participation by residents, emphasizing the "self-help" approach. Effective community building emphasizes developing a vision tailored to their specific needs and setting an agenda and action steps based on collective and individual assets (Kingsley, McNeely, & Gibson, 1997). Community building emphasizes building human capital and social capital, particularly internal social capital that focuses on values and relationships people have, and selects relationships to strengthen, renew, and rebuild community (Kingsley et al., 1997; Hess, 1999).

The NCBN focused on seven themes of community building: 1) a focus on specific improvement initiatives in a manner that reinforces values and builds social and human capital; 2) broad resident involvement; 3) comprehensive, strategic, and entrepreneurial; 4) asset-based; 5) tailors itself to neighborhood scale and conditions; 6) strengthens community institutions and enhances outside opportunities of residents, by collaboratively links to the broader society; 7) consciously changes institutional barriers and racism (Kingsley, McNeely, & Gibson, 1997).

Effective and successful community building relies on three categories: 1) the various characteristics of the community, which includes the community awareness of an issue, based on the community's motivation, the social and geographical attributes of the community and the residents, and their ability to reach consensus and cooperate; 2) the community building process itself (akin to maintaining one's individual health), including the components by which people attempt to build community such as widespread participation, good communication, linkages to organizations outside the community, the right training to gain community building skills, and the right mix of resources; and 3) the actual qualities and characteristics of the community building organizers themselves, such as leadership, commitment, experience, trust, being organized, flexibility, and adaptability (Mattessich & Monsey, 1997; as cited in Mattessich, 2016).

Community building is distinct from community organizing in its value to and interest in the public. The process relies on relationships, especially with local government officials, to carry out goals and objectives, whereas community organizing relies on tackling issues through direct public confrontation and action, demanding the government, rather than the community members solve the problems. Hess (1999) emphasizes a symbiotic relationship between community building and community organizing, wherein community builders can assist community organizers with the tools necessary to increase resident engagement in the community without relying on external agents, while community organizers can help community builders with the means to confront imbalances between the external costs and community members.

Walsh (1997) conducted case studies in Savannah, Georgia, South Bronx, and Baltimore, Maryland, that looked at community building through the lens of poverty. Community building analyzes poverty not only as a lack of jobs and income, but as a lack of networks and relationships to deal with an intricate web of connected problems such as poor schooling, bad health, family troubles, racism, crime, and unemployment (Walsh, 1997). As we will examine in chapter 9, one of the greatest community building initiatives in community development and revitalization is placemaking, which builds trust, helps communities increase resiliency, builds community capacity and social capital, and engages residents with their neighborhood's changes and people's perceptions of the neighborhood (Enterprise Community Partners, 2020).

Community building is a difficult task, especially difficult for populations whose social and physical mobility are hindered or curtailed, specifically our senior population. For instance, the three plagues that impact a senior citizen living in place in institutionalized senior care are loneliness, helplessness, and boredom (Thomas, 2006). In the early 1990s, a new approach, the Eden Alternative, transformed and improved the quality of life of one long-term nursing care facility in upstate New York into "a worldwide movement to reform the structure and practices of long-term care as a whole" (Thomas, 2006, p. 217) through love, respect, dignity, tenderness, and tolerance.

The Eden Alternative restructured long-term care through the creation of resident-centric housing with senior citizens aging in place. One initiative includes the creation of Green Homes communities, built in a grid with ten elders per dwelling. These dwellings are equipped with the latest technologies in patient care and are appropriately designed with accessible cabinets and appliances, private rooms and private baths, but also include common areas with plants and small gardens, animals, and children (Thomas, 2006; Tedeschi, 2018). Eden Alternative's model is sometimes referred to as MAGIC (Multi-Ability Multi-Generation Inclusive Community).

Dr. Bill Thomas, a Harvard-trained physician and geriatrician, is a renowned expert in aging in place and a revolutionary thinker in the future of senior care facilities. In October 2018, his team constructed a house on the University of Southern Indiana campus using a refabricated housing system called Minka (Japanese for "house of the people"). Minka homes are built to meet the needs of differently-abled persons, using universal design for greater accessibility and smart house technology (Tedeschi, 2018; Changing Aging, 2018). The MAGIC/Minka project serves as "a laboratory that will help students and faculty explore innovative approaches to protecting and extending the independence of older people (USI, 2018). This program also includes an undergraduate course on participatory design. The MAGIC/Minka model is taught at USI each semester.

The main strategies from Minka and MAGIC were inspired by the first-generation Eden Alternative. Thomas shares ten lessons, each offering a different approach to the conventional way of dealing with housing the elderly and building community.

I.   The three plagues of loneliness, helplessness, and boredom account for the bulk of suffering in a human community,

II.   Life is a truly human community revolving around close and continuing contact with children, plants, and animals. These ancient relationships provide young and old alike with a pathway to a life worth living.

III. Loving companionship is the antidote to loneliness. In a human community, we must provide easy access to human and animal companionship.
IV. To give care to another makes us stronger. To receive care gracefully
is a pleasure and an art. A healthy human community promotes both
activities in its daily life, seeking always to balance one with the other.
V. Trust in each other allows us the pleasure of answering the needs of the
moment. When we fill our lives with variety and spontaneity, we honor
the world and our place in it.
VI. Meaning is the food and water that nourishes the human spirit. It
strengthens us. The counterfeits of meaning tempt us with hollow
promises. In the end, they always leave us empty and alone.
VII. Medical treatment should be the servant of genuine human caring,
never its master.
VIII. In a human community, the wisdom of the elders grows in direct proportion to the honor and respect accorded to them.
IX. Human growth must never be separated from human life.
X. Wise leadership is the lifeblood of any struggle against the three
plagues. For it, there can be no substitute. (Thomas, 2006, pp. 199–200)

Minka homes, and the MAGIC model, have transformed our thinking of community building for the elderly and individuals with disabilities and aging in
place. This is an excellent model of community to be developed in the future.

WHAT IS LEADERSHIP?

Books and articles have been written *ad nauseum* about leadership. Even in the
vast literature, there is acknowledgment that we cannot agree on a definition of
leadership. No one has satisfactorily defined leadership, and there is no more
agreement on what leadership is not (e.g., seniority of position, management,
attributes, status, power, etc.) versus what leadership actually is. Packard says,
"Leadership appears to be the art of getting others to want to do something you
are convinced should be done" (quoted in Kolzow, 2009, p. 120).

Leading a community development project differs from leading a private
or nonprofit organization. Organizations have hierarchical structure; communities are more democratic and egalitarian, requiring consensus building.
Many communities lack indigenous leadership able to build capacity. Consequently, true leadership development is critical and necessary for the sustainability of a community (Green & Haines, 2016).

For a community leader, leadership does not seek to motivate followers by
providing rewards in exchange for performance, support, and effort (i.e., give
employees something the leader wants in exchange for getting something

they want). Community leadership is less transactional than transformational. A community building facilitator must transcend narrow self-interest in pursuit of higher goals for the benefit of the community and nation. A transformational leader creates an uplifting vision and uses symbols to focus efforts, evoke ideals, and challenge group members to view new perspectives.

The transformational leader is not a top-down leader who wants to be elevated. Rather, the convener is the "social architect" who uses knowledge and capacity to provide opportunities to engage in and take ownership of the community building process (Block, 2008). This convening leader "creates experiences for others—experiences that in themselves are examples of our desired future. The experiences we create need to be designed in such a way that relatedness, accountability, and commitment are every moment available, experienced, and demonstrated" (Block, 2008, p. 86). The role of convener for the community development model will be further explored in chapter 6.

WHAT IS COMMUNITY DEVELOPMENT?

Just like the term *community*, community development has been difficult to define (Bhattacharyya, 1995). In fact, numerous authors state how confoundingly ambiguous, challenging, complicated, and perplexing community development has been to define (Bhattacharyya, 1995, 2004; Honadle, 2007; Sanders, 1958; Onyenemezu, 2014). Bhattacharyya (2004) and Christenson and Robinson (1999) argue its definition is based partly on one's experience in the field, expanded and applied universally to rural and urban areas.

A broader, more holistic, national, and global definition by the United Nations for community development is "the process by which the efforts of the people themselves are united with those of governmental authorities to improve the economic, social, and cultural conditions of communities, to integrate these communities into the life of the nation, and to enable them to contribute fully to national progress" (as cited in Christenson & Robinson, 1999, pp. 13–14). Among the numerous definitions of community development, Checkoway (2013) offers a simple one: "a process in which people join together and develop programs at the community level" (p. 473). Perhaps the best definition of community development is from Christenson and Robinson (1989), who define it as "a group of people in a locality initiating a social action process (i.e., planned intervention) to change their economic, social, cultural, and/or environmental situation" (p. 14).

Onyenemezu (2014) defines community development as an amalgam of "community" and "development." Community is defined as "a social system where people live sharing common life, geographical location, common socio-economic, cultural and political characteristics, having a feeling of oneness and a sense of belonging which enable them to pursue one goal" (p. 210). Development is defined as an "improvement in the quality of [the] socio-economic, political, cultural, and environmental life of people [in a community] including their life expectancy" (Onyenemezu, 2014, p. 210).

In addition to development on the community level, Sanders (1958) identifies development that occurs on regional, or district, and national levels. At the community level, decisions can be unique and tailored to one community. At the regional or district level, decisions are applicable to the needs of multiple communities that may share many similarities but differ in specific needs. The emphasis is on providing services that the community cannot effectively offer or provide. At the national level, decisions are made for the greater good, putting communities in a beneficiary position rather than planning actively for specific needs.

Sanders (1958) also describes four types of practitioners in community development: local lay leaders, resident professionals, outside professional organizers, and multipurpose community development workers. Local lay leaders include those with varying degrees of expertise such as church leaders, local organization leaders, volunteers, and local politicians. They are closest to the community and have status within the community, so they are best to gather quick responses to the needs and changes from the community. Resident professionals are specifically trained for a task and often do not reside within the community they are hired to assist. Outside professional organizers are also skilled in specific tasks and are temporarily hired by a national agency to organize without understanding the welfare of the community in which they are working. Because they lack the knowledge and understanding of that community, they are unable to seek solutions for unique issues and ultimately remain tied to the agency that hired them. The multipurpose community development worker is usually sent into a community to assist with any local projects and "to train local leadership so as `to work oneself out of job' in that community" (Sanders, 1958, p. 10).

Agency is "the capacity of people to order their world, the capacity to create, reproduce, change and live according to their own meaning systems, to have the powers to define themselves as opposed to being defined by others" (Bhattacharyya, 2004, p. 12). Instead of the community having decisions made for them, in which the improvements may or may not actually be helpful, the goal is to enable community members to assert their needs and ideas for improvement. Bhattacharyya (2004) uses the term *human development* to define agency under the "creation and promotion of people's choices and capabilities" (p. 13). Furthermore, community development is about generating critical consciousness in the minds of the people in the community by first addressing problems that the people in the community own and define while understanding the "structure of causes" that brought about the problems, followed by taking action towards solving the problems (Freire, 1973; Bhattacharyya, 2004, p. 13).

HISTORY OF COMMUNITY DEVELOPMENT

The origins of community development are traced back to how American society first understood poverty in the late 19th and early 20th century. This period is known as the Progressive Era, although the term did not emerge until the middle of the 20th century (Phillips & Pittman, 2015). Social interventions aimed to address poverty, according to the Progressives, were comprehensive and focused on an array of problems (poor health and sanitation, overcrowding, poor education, access to employment) facing the impoverished—a reaction to the ills of capitalism rather than simply poverty and limited access to financial resources (Phillips & Pittman, 2015).

One early manifestation of comprehensive community development was through the settlement house movement led by reformer Jane Addams. The reformers' efforts to improve social ills extended into neighborhoods, where the settlement houses were located, first in New York and Chicago. The settlement house movement often viewed their efforts as "municipal housekeeping" (Von Hoffman, 2012). The urban reformers argued that

> poverty was not an isolated individual pathology, but an all-encompassing social condition characterized by social and cultural isolation, overcrowding, and chronic disease. These conditions led to delinquency, crime, vice, family disintegration, and other forms of social disorganization that characterized urban industrial slums. Fixing the environment—whether by cleaning up the tenements or improving neighborhood residential composition—was a way of breaking the vicious cycle of urban poverty and physical decay. It would also, not coincidentally, help to protect and preserve the social peace. (O'Connor, 1999, p. 84; as cited in Patterson, 1994, pp. 23–24)

A major evolution of dealing with social issues and poverty stemmed from our growing understanding of physical and spatial inequalities and disparities, which led to the evolution of the field of urban planning in the early 20th century. Urban planning is a technical field that requires advanced training and expertise in land use, development, spatial analysis, and urban development, which enabled the public to better understand the social implications of planning the built environment. Urban planning's early accomplishments included Daniel Burnham's first plan of Chicago, the creation of new planning schools, the first planning textbook, *Introduction to City Planning,* by Benjamin Marsh in 1909, and the formation of the American Institute of Planners (AIP), later known as the American Planning Association (APA). While attempts by outside experts aimed to rid the inner city of its ills, they were often counterproductive. Von Hoffman (2012) states that "if Progressive reformers left the useful legacy of trying to counter the many aspects of poverty, they also handed the less useful principle that outside experts would save society by imposing reforms on the people they were trying to help" (p. 12).

Another important chapter of the history of community development is the New Deal, a series of federal programs in the 1930s designed to address the needs and problems in cities and communities after the Great Depression, particularly in housing. The major goal of New Deal housing policy was to promote and encourage homeownership, which was achieved through the Home Loan Act of 1932 that created the Home Owners' Loan Corporation (HOLC) and the National Housing Act of 1934 that established the Federal Housing Administration (FHA). These laws allowed the federal government to insure mortgage loans that protected banks and lenders in case of default, while increasing funds available to lenders and borrowers for building and purchasing new homes (Schwartz, 2015).

However, the FHA imposed strict standards on who qualified for these insured mortgage loans, which led to the practice of redlining. Redlining targeted specific areas and neighborhoods based on racial and ethnic groupings and used color-coded maps to indicate where mortgages would be issued, based on four categories of neighborhood quality. The lowest category, Category 1 (A), was coded green and consisted of all-White, all-Protestant American business and professional men. Categories 2 and 3 (B&C) were racially and ethnically mixed and Jewish neighborhoods coded either green or blue. Black segregated neighborhoods were Category 4 (D) and coded in red. Private banks and lenders would not lend to groups that lived in redlined areas (Massey & Denton, 1993; Rohe & Watson, 2007; Hayden, 2003; Schwartz, 2015; Baradaran, 2017). Banks relied heavily on the HOLC's "procedures (and prejudices)" in putting together its own maps to make its own loan decisions, thus further institutionalizing redlining, discrimination in housing, and disinvestment in black neighborhoods (Massey and Denton, 1993, p. 52).

The Housing Act of 1937 created the United States Housing Authority (USHA) that provided loans and subsidies to municipal housing authorities, to eliminate slums and provide low-income public housing. The federal government provided the loans while local governments exempted the housing costs from personal and property taxes (Schwartz, 2015; Marcuse, 2001). This act was designed to develop housing for poor residents in urban areas by requiring cities to target specific areas and neighborhoods for different racial groups who were not eligible to receive loans. Ethnic minorities could only receive loans in certain areas, which resulted in an increase in residential racial segregation in the United States.

The Housing Act of 1949, which began the era of urban renewal, was a compromise between the liberal and conservative housing policy approaches and served as the federal government's framework for urban redevelopment over the next two decades (Kleinberg, 1995). This act increased federal funding for slum clearance and public housing. A city housing authority selected a renewal site, purchased the given site at fair market value, cleared the site, and sold the land to a private developer at a lower price than the private developers would have paid in the private market. The federal government subsidized two-thirds of the "write down" costs associated with purchasing and clearing the property, while the local authority paid one-third of the cost (Kleinberg, 1995; Schwartz, 2015; Marcuse, 2001).

Much of public housing created in the 1930s during the New Deal was built to address a housing shortage for middle-class and working-class White families, who either lost their jobs and their homes during the Great Depression or could not find housing because it was not available (Rothstein, 2017a). For this new public housing, only $1/3$ was for African Americans and was segregated from the White public housing projects (Rothstein, 2017a). The FDR administration, through the newly created Public Works Administration (PWA), instituted a "neighborhood composition rule" (Rothstein, 2017a, p. 21; Von Hoffman, 2012) that referred to the neighborhood's previous racial composition in building new public housing. White neighborhoods could only house White tenants, Black neighborhoods could only house Black tenants, and already integrated neighborhoods could house both White and Black tenants (Rothstein, 2017a).

Ultimately, the federal government violated this rule by enforcing segregation in integrated neighborhoods, making these areas for Whites only. Excluding Blacks and other minorities from these neighborhoods forced them to live in more crowded, less stable public housing developments (Rothstein, 2017a). When vacancies in these public housing developments opened, created by Whites who fled to the suburbs because of industry and jobs leaving the inner city, they were filled by the Black families who remained (Rothstein, 2017a). Since many Black households were too poor to pay the full cost of housing, the federal government began subsidizing the cost of the public housing (Rothstein, 2017a).

The Works Progress Administration (WPA) provided $111 billion in 1935 for public projects aimed at building highways, streets, utilities, bridges, and other major infrastructure; many communities benefited from such needed projects, which provided opportunities to learn labor skills and gain job experience and fair wages (Schwartz, 2015; Green & Haines, 2016). Also, the Social Security Act of 1935 created the social security program that we know today—a social insurance net aimed to eliminate elderly poverty where individuals pay into a program to offset any lost income in old age and unemployment, separate from the public assistance program that served women and children (O'Connor, 1999).

Because of the Housing Act of 1949, urban renewal broke up established central city neighborhoods for new development initiatives, resulting in extensive clearing programs of inadequate and substandard public housing (Rohe & Watson, 2007). In total, the federal government spent over $213 billion in urban renewal programs between 1953 and 1986 (Williamson, Imbroscio, & Alperovitz, 2003). The architectural nature of early public housing developments, both low-rise barracks-style housing and the destruction of the old housing stock, produced unsuitable neighborhoods and massive dislocation of residents. Newer public housing was constructed in the form of high-rise public housing buildings (Williamson et al., 2003) that isolated residents from the surrounding streetscape with no access to transportation and social services and lacked any outdoor exterior amenities and features (Schwartz, 2015). The creation of LeCorbusier-style high-rise concrete apartment units, instead of single-unit housing (e.g., Robert Taylor Homes and Cabrini Green in Chicago), and the lack of "defensible space" (Newman, 1973) caused public housing to become a magnet for crime, vandalism, and drugs, which helped contribute to creating and perpetuating the culture of poverty (Wilson, 1987).

Traditional public housing in the 1930s, before and after urban renewal, alienated residents from their homes, giving them little control over its uses, such as interior design, living space, and entertaining guests (Gilderbloom, Brazley, Alam, Ashan, & Ramsey, 2002). More importantly, the plain ordinary, prison-like quality of public housing created a sense of stigmatization for the poor and marginalized who were confined to live in these dwellings. This stigmatization continues to be prevalent in public housing in many small and large cities throughout the United. Wilson (1987) argues that the stigmatization and the traits of the culture of poverty "assume 'a life of their own' and continue to influence behavior even if opportunities for social mobility improve" (p. 137).

White families who left for the suburbs benefited from New Deal federal government programs, through the HOLC, FHA, Veterans Administration (VA) and the creation of the Federal National Mortgage Association, known as "Fannie Mae." This agency provides low interest mortgage loans for 20 years, insures mortgages that cover 80 percent of the purchase prices, and facilitates the sale of mortgages in the secondary market (Baradaran, 2017). FHA conducted its own appraisals and instituted a "whites only requirement" to ensure loans did not default, which ultimately made racial discrimination a part of the mortgage and lending process by denying loans exclusively to African American or even integrated neighborhoods (Freeman, 2012; Rothstein, 2017a).

The FHA also devised an underwriting manual in 1935, for real estate agents and appraisers, with specific instructions. An example: "if a neighborhood is to retain stability, it is necessary that properties shall continue to be occupied by the same social and racial classes. A change in social or racial occupancy generally leads to instability and a reduction in values" (Rothstein, 2017a, p. 65). In a May 2017 interview on National Public Radio (NPR), Rothstein says that "what the federal government did, the FHA, is guarantee bank loans for construction and development to [suburban developments like] Levittown on condition that no homes be sold to African Americans and that every home have a clause in its deed prohibiting resale to African Americans" (Rothstein, 2017b).

FHA and VA policies, which were bolstered by the passage of the GI Bill that provided VA guaranteed mortgages and college scholarships and loans for veterans, favored lending towards the construction of single-family homes in predominately White middle-class neighborhoods, compared to multifamily units in traditional inner-city, African American and non-White neighborhoods. According to Freeman (2012), FHA guaranteed mortgages for its first 26 years at $730 per person in Fairfax, Virginia, outside Washington, DC, while guaranteed mortgages were only $87 per person in DC itself. Levittown in Long Island, New York, guaranteed mortgages of $610 per person, but only $10 per person in the Bronx in New York City. The creation of the alphabet soup of federal agencies such as HOLC, FHA, VA, and Fannie Mae helped move credit and loans towards new White homeowners, that "coupled with postwar economic growth, created a robust, homeowning, capital creating and predominantly White middle class," and "made the Black ghetto a permanent feature of the twentieth century" (Baradaran, 2017, p. 103).

Another major contributor to the destruction of urban communities was the result of the Federal Highway Act of 1956, one of the largest public works programs in U.S. history. This legislation began the proliferation of people moving from downtown and into the suburbs and was another response to federal policies on the future development of central cities with respect to the Housing Act of 1949 (Walker, Kulash, & McHugh, 2000; Kleinberg, 1995). During this time, a person's life, including one's home, job, office, school, and recreation and entertainment activities, was relocated to the suburbs. The growth of the suburbs helped "smooth the route home from work" (Eversley, 2006) and was facilitated by the presence of one-way streets and "the speedy entrance and exodus of commuters" to the suburbs (Walker, Kulash, & McHugh, 2000).

38 Chapter One

The interstate federal highway system that moved people to the suburbs destroyed minority and working-class neighborhoods and communities that further segregated African Americans and poor Whites from access to jobs and services located in the suburbs (Kleinberg, 1995). They were trapped in substandard housing and lacked the transportation, money, resources, and opportunities to move to the suburbs, mainly encouraged by policies set by the FHA dating back to the 1930s.

The late 1960s and early 1970s were a favorable climate for liberal housing policy (Marcuse, 2001). In 1961, Jane Jacobs provided a strong critique of urban renewal in *The Death and Life of Great American Cities* by arguing that extensive slum clearance only added to the existing problems. She adds: "At best it merely shifts slums from here to there, adding its own tincture of extra hardship and disruption. At worst, it destroys neighborhoods where constructive and improving communities exist and where the situation calls for encouragement rather than destruction" (1961, p. 270). Jacobs identifies the problems of urban renewal as paternalistic and describes the notion of perpetual slums that show no sign of improving and often regress after a slight improvement (Jacobs, 1961). To overcome this urban renewal mentality, Jacobs argues that

we must regard slum dwellers as people capable of understanding and acting upon their own self-interests, which they certainly are. We need to discern, respect, and build upon the forces for regeneration that exist in slums themselves, and that demonstrably work in real cities This is far from trying to patronize people into a better life, and it is far from what is done today. (1961, p. 271)

The Civil Rights Act of 1964 was important for federal housing policy by removing racial deed restrictions and restrictive covenants, the legally enforceable provisions of deeds that prohibited owners from selling or leasing their properties to specific racial groups (Plotkin, 2001). The Supreme Court successfully overturned the constitutionality of race restrictive covenants 16 years earlier in the 1948 ruling of *Shelley v. Kraemer* (Schwartz, 2015). This Supreme Court ruling and the Civil Rights Act of 1964, however, did not end the use of restrictive covenants in open White neighborhoods like Levittown to other racial or ethnic minority groups, nor did it end the practice of redlining (Freeman, 2012). The Fair Housing Act of 1968 prohibited discrimination in housing and the real estate market by making it unlawful to refuse to rent or sell a home based on race and barred discrimination in real estate advertising (Schwartz, 2015; Massey & Denton, 1993). As Rothstein (2017a, 2017b) contends, much of this act protects future discrimination, but it did not or could not fix the 30-year legacy of government sanctioned residential racial segregation in both public housing and homeownership.

The new chapter in community development in the 1960s became known as the War on Poverty and the Great Society created by President Lyndon Johnson. This ambitious policy agenda created programs that moved from "the bricks and mortar focus of urban renewal to the 'human face' presented by the problems of urban economic decline" (O'Connor, 1999, pp. 100–101). The passage of the Economic Opportunity Act of 1964 created the Community Action Program (CAP), the Special Impact Program (SIP), and the Department of Housing and Urban Development (HUD), while the Demonstration Cities and Metropolitan Development Act in 1966 created the Model Cities program (O'Connor, 1999; Green & Haines, 2016; Schwartz, 2015). What separated these programs from the New Deal was the bottom-up approach through local community involvement and the participation from the people in the communities receiving support, compared to the top-down overly bureaucratic intervention from the federal government during the New Deal and urban renewal periods (Von Hoffman, 2012). Johnson's urban polices, overall, added much needed infrastructure to cities (Glickman & Wilson, 2008).

CAP was the War on Poverty's signature program and was designed, created, and implemented by the people, centered around the Chicago sociological school of community competence. The Chicago model enabled local leaders to plan and build their own efforts outside of city government control through "maximum feasible participation" from the residents (Von Hoffman; 2012; Green & Haines, 2016; O'Connor, 1999). The Model Cities program involved more local planning control to city officials, instead of CAP working around city and elected officials (Green & Haines, 2016). Model Cities called for an investment of local sites "for a comprehensive plan of rebuilding, economic revitalization, and service provision and expression," which according to labor leader Walter Reuther created "architecturally beautiful and socially meaningful communities in large urban centers and to stop erosion of life in urban centers among the lower- and middle-class population" (O'Connor, 1999, p. 104).

The third major War on Poverty program was the Special Impact Programs (SIP) created by New York senators Robert F. Kennedy and Jacob Javits, which used Brooklyn's Bedford-Stuyvesant neighborhood as its first model. SIP focused on specific geographic targets in neighborhoods with high concentrations of poverty, where development funds were provided in the form of block grants to community-based organizations (O'Connor, 1999). Unfortunately, the rocky start and the lack of an institutional home—it was shared with multiple offices and departments before landing in the Office of Economic Opportunity (OEO)—failed to produce the promised impact, especially in reducing the number of households in poverty or creating new jobs (O'Connor, 1999).

Green and Haines (2016) state that the Community Action Program (CAP) was one of the War on Poverty's most controversial programs because of its misunderstanding over local participation and control. It was often seen as working around and away from local officials, which may be one factor that contributed to the inner-city violence in the 1960s. However, it was the SIP and the Model Cities program that provided the first funding and model for the creation of community development corporations (CDCs) (Stoutland, 1999).

CDCs are nonprofit organizations that revitalize "a clearly defined geographic area—often an urban neighborhood scarred by decades of disinvestment and concentrated poverty or an isolated and underdeveloped rural area" (Williamson et al., 2003, p. 213). From its origins in the 1960s, and as the Model Cities and the CAP were phased out by the early 1970s, CDCs emerged as a catalyst for local economic and community development in distressed areas, giving residents a voice and greater local control development process in their communities (Williamson et al., 2003).

A CDC serves many important roles and wears many hats. CDCs construct new homes and rehab existing homes, assist with home financing, and provide employment counseling, job training, and placement, as well as emergency food assistance services to the homeless (Schwartz, 2015). A staff and board of directors of a CDC consists of residents, along with community leaders and representatives from various local institutions that work with the community (West, Kraeger, & Dahlstrom, 2016). While CDCs are engaged in the big picture in major economic development initiatives, they also are involved in many "community-building and social-capital-oriented activities" such as cleanup programs for the neighborhood, childcare programs, leadership development training programs, and community policing efforts (Williamson et al., 2003, p. 217).

Since the 1980s, much of the CDCs success has been in housing development (Stoutland, 1999) and other bricks and mortar development for neighborhoods, using CDBG and federal and state funding, HOME and Section 8 programs, and the Low-Income Housing Tax Credit (LIHTC) created in 1986 under the Tax Reform Act. The LIHTC is an indirect subsidy and the most dominant source of equity funds financing affordable housing (either at 4 percent or 9 percent equity), and can be claimed over 10 years (Rubin, 2000; Mallach, 2009). To qualify for the LIHTC, 40 percent of units are for renters that earn 60 percent area median income (AMI) (Schwartz, 2015). In fact, by 1990, CDCs accounted for 13 percent of all federally supported housing production (Walker, Simonson, Kingsley, Ferguson, & Boxall, 1994).

Another major function of a CDC is the creation of community development financial institutions (CDFI). These entities provide services to communities already underserved by traditional financial institutions, such as credit, loans, and investments through community development banks, credit unions, microcredit and microenterprise programs, and venture capital funds (Williamson et al., 2003; Baradaran, 2017). The creation of a fund for CDFIs in 1994, and the strengthening of the Community Reinvestment Act (CRA), proved to be successful in assisting economically challenged communities where traditional banks and institutions lacked the wherewithal to lend to low- and moderate-income households and Black and minority businesses (Williamson et al., 2003; Von Hoffman, 2012).

Several criticisms have been made about CDCs and their role in the community. Many activists and academic observers, according to Williamson et al. (2003), believe CDCs have become corporate-minded and less community-minded over time. They often operate autocratically as individual leaders' personal fiefdom, with less focus on democratic control and accountability. Another criticism of CDCs is their inability to initiate programs on a large scale and the inability to maintain a consistent, adequate, and sustainable funding stream and long-term viability strategy. CDCs only focus on housing, according to many critics of CDCs, and not enough on initiatives that address community problems, even though housing finance and development has been one of the more successful components of CDCs over the years.

A major contributor to community development occurred under the Housing and Community Development Act of 1974, which created the Community Development Block Grant (CDBG) program, ostensibly replacing the urban renewal and Model Cities programs (Schwartz, 2015). Block grant programs like CDBGs are modeled on the new federalism approach of President Richard Nixon, in which federal funds given to state and local governments gave governments discretion and authority over how the funds would be spent.

For the first 40 years of the CDBG program, $144 billion in grants were given to state and local governments covering a wide range of activities (HUD, 2014). CDBG funds can be used to remove blight, eliminate slums through clearance and property site acquisition, construct new housing and rehab old housing, build public facilities and infrastructure (i.e., street improvements), assist immediate needs of lower income individuals and families, and fund small businesses and other economic development initiatives (Schwartz, 2015; Green & Haines, 2016; HUD, 2016).

CDBGs also provide allowances to low-income households in the form of rental subsidies for residents to pay for the cost of a private rental unit or an apartment, known as the Section 8 program. These subsidies cover the difference between 30 percent of the tenant's area median income (AMI) and the adjusted fair market rent prices (Schwartz, 2015). For developers, Section 8 also allows residents to depreciate their allowances, thereby reducing federal income taxes (Schwartz, 2015). Section 8 rental subsidies were followed by the introduction of tenant-based vouchers in the 1980s. These vouchers allowed tenants to choose any kind of housing as long as it followed HUD program requirements, although the landlords were not required to participate in the program (Varady & Walker, 2003; Varady, Walker, & Wang, 2001).

Each community receiving CDBG funds must submit a comprehensive plan every five years on how they want to use their funds. This plan includes an outline of goals and strategies and an extensive public input process (Green & Haines, 2016). Evansville, Indiana's recent consolidated plan from 2015–2019 includes the city's plan to spend CDBG funds and Emergency Shelter Grant (ESG) funds, and includes strategies related to housing, individuals and families experiencing homelessness, the city's community and economic development strategies, along with articulating the planning, administration, management, and oversight of any federal, state, or local programs that receive these funds (DMD, 2018). For cities receiving CDBG funds, 15 percent can be allocated to local nonprofits and social service agencies providing public services to the community (HUD, 2016).

Like the CDBG program, the HOME Investment Program is a federal block grant program created in 1990 that provide grants ($1.5–2 billion per year as of 2009) to state, county, and local governments that met certain need and size criteria for a variety of affordable housing purposes, for low to moderate income households, such as new construction and rehabilitation, and assistance for low income individuals and families who wish to buy or rent, similar to Section 8 vouchers (Mallach, 2009). HOME funds also can be used as gap funding with LIHTC in affordable housing development.

The policies implemented under urban renewal shifted towards developing new communities in the late 1960s and 1970s. The Fair Housing Act of 1968 also focused on specific targets aimed at the expansion of building low-income housing, low-interest loans, and rental subsidies for low and moderate-income households (Marcuse, 2001; Schwartz, 2015). Much of the growth of public housing, from urban renewal through the 1980s, through direct government opposition to integration and deliberate *de jure* segregation, occurred as a result of opposition by neighborhood, community, and NIMBY (Not in My Back Yard) groups to keep public housing out of their neighborhoods (Wilson, 1987; Calhoun, 1994). This opposition came mostly from the government rather than the private sector. Redlining, exclusionary zoning, and the creation of massive public housing projects in low-income areas helped to intensify racial segregation. This environment contributed to high concentrated poverty, violent crime, lack of employment, racial and institutional discrimination, and social isolation, which are the "social and institutional mechanisms that enhance patterns of social dislocation" caused by racial subjugation, class transformation, and decline of the social organization of the inner city (Wilson, 1987, pp. 137).

The remedy to end redlining practices and disinvestment in low and moderate income and minority neighborhoods occurred through the passage of the Community Reinvestment Act of 1977, which require banks and financial institutions to finance low-income housing in specific geographic places, including high poverty, underserved neighborhoods (Briggs, 2005). The CRA outlawed the practice of discriminatory redlining, although it did not stop it altogether. It was designed to be color-blind to act as an incentive to encourage home mortgages loans, small business, and banking services to low-income and minority communities (Briggs, 2005; Rohe & Watson, 2007; Baradaran, 2017). In the first thirty years of the CRA, from 1977 to 2007, $4.59 trillion has been given for community reinvestment and development (Von Hoffman, 2012).

The Johnson administration in the late 1960s saw the introduction of government funded assistance for mortgage and rental assistance for low-income housing through the Government National Mortgage Association (GNMA, aka Ginnie Mae). Ginnie Mae spilt off from Fannie Mae after the Fair Housing Act privatized Fannie Mae in 1968 (Baradaran, 2017) to "bring global capital into the housing finance system—a system that runs through the core of our nation's economy—while minimizing risk to the taxpayer" (Ginnie Mae, 2020). Ginnie Mae's mortgage-based securities are the only ones that have the "full faith and credit" guarantee from the federal government (HUD, 2020a). Around this time, the Federal Home Loan Mortgage Corporation (FHLMC, aka Freddie Mac) was created to go into the secondary private mortgage market to sell these mortgage-based securities (MBS) to investors (Baradaran, 2017). Freddie Mac issued production certificates that grouped mortgages together and allowed investors to buy a slice of the mortgages grouped together and receive a share of the dividends on the entire group of mortgages (Baradaran, 2017).

Mortgage-based securities transformed the mortgage market because they separated the borrower from the lender. Based on a complex mathematical formula, both the bank and the borrower assumed less risk. Banks and lenders issued loans that the secondary market would buy, so the banks did not track the loans and did not track whether the borrowers were paying the loan back to the bank or to the lender (Baradaran, 2017). Over time, these practices may have contributed heavily to the financial housing crisis of 2008–2009.

President Jimmy Carter and his administration created a robust federal urban policy designed to address severe urban problems. Of the $8.3 billion appropriated to tackle Carter's urban policy initiatives, $7.2 billion was earmarked for jobs and investment in distressed inner cities (Kingsley & Fortuny, 2010). The passage of the Housing and Community Development Act of 1977 led to Carter's New Partnerships program and the creation of Urban

Development Action Grants (UDAGs), designed to stimulate economic activity and revitalization in America's most distressed urban areas (Webman, 1981). The law and the UDAG program lacked specifics on the kinds of private investment allowed. Grants were awarded only if private firms secured a commitment to stimulate economic activity in the area (Webman, 1981). Five hundred and twenty grants were awarded in the first two years of the program from 1978 to 1980 totaling $961.5 million each year, with the top quartile of all distressed cities receiving approximately 45 percent of the funding for all approved projects (Webman, 1981).

Federal urban policies of the 1960s and 1970s focused on alleviating poverty through the programs mentioned earlier. President Ronald Reagan paid little attention to urban economic growth and developed little to no federal urban policy during his administration, leaving it up to the states and cities to deal with urban problems. The Reagan administration sought to empower residents by focusing on social and private investment and asset building. While the Reagan administration introduced an economic recovery program, the UDAGs were discontinued and CDBG funds and other housing program funding decreased under Reagan's watch. In 1986, the Reagan administration proposed the Public Housing Homeownership Demonstration (PHHD) program, which experimented with the sale of public housing units to tenants to become homeowners (Schwartz, 2015).

In 1980, the Ford Foundation, along with support from major corporations, formed an intermediary organization to support CDCs known as the Local Initiatives Support Corporation (LISC) whose mission was "resident-led, community-based development organizations transform distressed communities and neighborhoods into healthy ones—good places to live, do business work and raise families" (LISC, 2020; as cited in Mallach, 2009, p. 187). LISC provides assistance in the form of loans, grants, and other technical assistance and expertise to CDCs and helped link them to the federal government and financial institutions (Kingsley et al., 1997; Von Hoffman, 2012).

Since the 1980s, LISC has invested $11.1 billion towards the development of 277,000 affordable housing, retail space, and schools and childcare facilities and recreational areas (Von Hoffman, 2012). In the 1980s, lending expanded in communities, to include loans for social assets such as childcare and youth programs through programs such as Enterprise Community Funds and Low-Income Investment funds. Community Development Financial Institutions (CDFI) discussed earlier were designed to provide loans through banks and credit unions to promote social progress.

President Bill Clinton made community development a major component of revitalizing cities through economic empowerment and job creation in distressed communities. The administration created the Empowerment

Zone (EZ) and Enterprise Communities (EC) program in 1993. These initiatives were modeled on comprehensive community-based strategic planning "aimed at the economic, physical, and social development of the neediest urban and rural areas in the United States" (Hebert et al., 2001). This program involves building partnerships and community capacity between cities and different levels of government.

The four major principles of the EZ/EC programs are 1) economic opportunity through the creation of new jobs; 2) sustainable community development; 3) community-based partnerships including all segments of the communities (i.e., residents, government officials, community groups and organizations, social service providers, and the private sector); 4) a strategic vision for change through a comprehensive revitalization map that describes what a community wants to become (Hebert et al., 2001). Communities that received the EZ designation have benefited from tax incentives, grants, and loans to leverage and attract private investment and create jobs and businesses opportunities in distressed communities (Hanka, Kumaran, & Gilderbloom, 2007; Green & Haines, 2012).

Since its inception in 1994, 72 urban areas received some form of EZ/EC designation. Of the 72 sites, six urban Empowerment Zones were created in Atlanta, Baltimore, Chicago, Detroit, New York, and Philadelphia/Camden. Poverty rates at the time were roughly four times higher in the Empowerment Zones and Enterprise Communities than in the surrounding metropolitan areas, with 40–50 percent poverty rates in the Atlanta and Philadelphia Empowerment Zones alone (Hanka et al., 2007). At least 45 percent of the working-age population was unemployed. The proportion of individuals neither working nor in school was 80 percent higher than in the surrounding metropolitan areas, while less than half of persons in these empowerment zones had a high school diploma (Hanka et al., 2007).

Each designated EZ and EC was eligible for tax-exempt bonds for certain private business activity, and special consideration was granted for requested waivers of federal regulations and preferential treatment in competing for numerous federal grant programs (Hanka et al., 2007). In addition, businesses in Empowerment Zones were eligible for a 20 percent employment tax credit for the first $15,000 in wages, on each employee who lived within each zone, if the business did a substantial portion of its business within each enterprise zone (Hanka et al., 2007).

Qualified Empowerment Zone businesses were also eligible to receive additional allowances ranging from $10,000 to $20,000 for expenses on depreciable property in the first year of acquisition. States and localities were eligible to issue tax-exempt facility bonds for certain business activities within empowerment Zones. EZs were granted preferential status in the competition for certain federal grant programs and special consideration for waivers of federal regulations (Hanka et al., 2007).

Approximately $110 million in Social Service Block Grant (SSBG) funds were given to the six empowerment zones, which leveraged $2.62 billion in local public and private investment and the creation of over 30,000 new jobs (Hanka et al., 2007). More than $2 billion in private investment was made, and much of the new investment ($1.7 billion) was targeted toward economic opportunity and investment activities, such as business-related job retention, expansion, relocation and creation, investment pools for capital access and innovative financing needs, job/occupational skills training, and entrepreneurial and business support services and assistance (Hanka et al., 2007).

Community development in housing also includes the HOPE VI program, starting with the George H. W. Bush administration and continuing into the Clinton and George W. Bush administrations, following the philosophy of homeownership, which we will discuss in greater detail in chapter 8. Clinton is also responsible for reforming welfare (welfare to work) and expanding the Earned Income Tax Credit (EITC) for working families.

The George W. Bush administration created an Office of Faith-Based and Community Initiatives (OFBCI), now called the Office of Faith-Based and Neighborhood Partnerships for Community Services. OFBCI harnessed the capacity of community-based development organizations (CBDOs), CDCs, and faith-based organizations to solve problems in housing and community development (Glickman & Wilson, 2008). More than $2.2 billion in competitive social service grants have been awarded to faith-based organizations, since its inception, through states in the form of formula grants (U.S. Government Accountability Office [GAO], 2006).

There are obvious and evident limitations of faith-based organizations (FBOs), such as potential violation of the First Amendment's establishment clause, prohibiting use of taxpayer funds for prayer, worship, religious, instruction, proselytization, or other activities that discriminate on the basis of religion (GAO, 2006). Faith-based organizations experienced obstacles and limitations in financial and organizational capacity, technical assistance, and training (GAO, 2006) to effectively carry out housing programs.

The next iteration of housing and community development after HOPE VI occurred through the Choice Neighborhoods program under the Obama administration. This program was similar to HOPE VI in the goal of replacing severely distressed public housing centered around three goals: 1) transform distressed public and assisted housing into energy efficient, mixed-income housing that is physically and financially viable over the long term; 2) support positive outcomes for families who live in the targeted developments and in the surrounding neighborhood, particularly outcomes related to resident health, safety, employment, and education; and 3) transform neighborhoods of poverty into viable, mixed-income neighborhoods with access to well-functioning services, effective schools and educational programs, public assets, public transportation, and improved access to jobs (HUD, 2020b; Pendall & Hendey, 2013).

Choice Neighborhoods applies a comprehensive planning approach to community development that requires communities receiving grants to develop a transformational plan that not only guides the implementation of a housing plan but develops strategies that improve the overall conditions of the residents targeted (i.e., in income, healthcare, education, and employment opportunities, and the overall conditions of the neighborhoods itself) (HUD, 2020b).

On August 31, 2011, five Choice Neighborhoods applications received awards totaling $122 million, which included the Quincy Corridor neighborhood in Dorchester, MA; Grove Parc Plaza in the Woodlawn Area in Chicago, the Iberville/Tremé neighborhoods in New Orleans; the Eastern Bayview in San Francisco; and the Yesler neighborhoods in Seattle (HUD, 2020b). The smallest budget is $4.7 million for the Quincy Corridor, about one-tenth the size of the largest, Iberville/Tremé at $44.9 million (Pendall & Hendey, 2013). Like HOPE VI, Choice Neighborhoods calls for "extensive use" of mixed financing to carry out the one-for-one replacement requirement in each of the program's five implementation plans (Pendall & Hendey, 2013).

The newest iteration of community development is the creation of Opportunity Zones (OZ) created as a part of Tax Cuts and Jobs Act of 2017, under the Donald Trump administration, to encourage and stimulate development in economically distressed communities where investors may be eligible to deduct taxes made on capital gains earnings (IRS, 2019). According to the Tax Policy Center, 12 percent of all Census tracts (8,762) are in Opportunity Zones in 18 states, and officially designated by the U.S. Department of the Treasury. The average median income in Opportunity Zones is $33,345, with the average poverty rate (32 percent) and the unemployment rate (13 percent) in the opportunity zones are far above the national average. Like its predecessors of the Enterprise Zones, Opportunity Zones can leverage federal dollars.

For the most part, a lot of successful economic growth in cities and communities in the 21st century has occurred not because of federal programs but through a successful global economy, as well as various cultural and economic development trends, such as the back to the city movement, attracting the creative class, a subject we will discuss throughout the book (Katz & Nowak, 2017; Florida, 2002, 2014).

MODELS OF COMMUNITY DEVELOPMENT

Ledwith (2011) describes community development as grounded in people's everyday lives, set within the narratives of people and their stories, and in the ways practitioners of community development put ideas into action. Ledwith (2011) also encourages practitioners to employ Paolo Freire's critical pedagogy to address society's issues as outlined in his famous *Pedagogy of the Oppressed* (Freire, 1970; Hustedde, 2015). Education is designed to create critical autonomous thinkers that understand how power and domination are demonstrated through our everyday experiences (Ledwith, 2011, p. 53). Freire (1973) suggests humans are active participants in the world, and that they work to create their own epochs, but "to help men (and nations) help themselves, to place them in consciously critical confrontation with their problems, to make them the agents of their own recuperation" (p. 16).

Asset-Based Community Development (ABCD) Model

Ennis and West (2010) propose that all citizens have strengths or assets that can be utilized to improve and enhance their lives. This strengths-based approach brings citizens together as a larger, linked network, where their capabilities can be greatly increased. To obtain the intended goal, Ennis and West (2010) describe two aspects of the strengths-based approach: internal looking, based on the ability to control our actions by "locating, articulating, and building upon strengths or assets," and external looking that challenges the current social context that have an adverse impact on people and communities (Ennis & West, 2010, p. 405).

The four principles of this asset-based community development (ABCD) model complement the felt needs, self-help, and participation models previously discussed, where change must come from community (felt needs), development must build upon existing capabilities (self-help), change should be relationship driven (participation), with a fourth principle focused on the community's assets. Assets consist of primary building blocks (either individual or organization assets), secondary building blocks located within communities that the community does not control, and potential building blocks located outside of the community where the community has no control (i.e., social welfare) (Ennis & West, 2010).

The ABCD model enables community members to recognize their individual strengths and join with other community members to enhance those strengths. Once joined, the community can move forward to develop new relationships and new skills with a sense of ownership in their felt needs, which inspires them to act (Ennis & West, 2010). Further, the community can search for potential bridging social capital with agencies that will be able to best provide them the assistance they need on their own terms. This potential could be bridging with nonprofit associations outside of the community or government agencies, who are "invited into dialogue by the community and invited to share in and support the community's vision for itself" (Ennis & West, 2010, p. 406; see also Mathie & Cunningham, 2003).

Ennis and West (2010) bring the ABCD model back down to the reality of structural limitations. For many communities, where development would be needed, there are issues regarding racism, sexism, and ageism, issues involving marginalized groups with fewer strengths such as the disabled, elderly, and the long-term unemployed, and issues regarding capitalism and globalization that communities have no control over. These issues inhibit the ability for all community members to take part in determining the felt needs of the community and make it difficult to instill empowerment with an outside force (structure) limiting the community's development.

Felt Needs and Self-help Models

Bhattacharyya (1995, 2004) describes community development in terms of three principles: self-help, felt needs, and participation. Felt needs are people's perceptions of their community's deficiencies and "the process of assessment, setting priorities, and designing programs based on people's definition of their community's problems" (Wade, 1989, pp. 116–117). The people in the community define felt needs that are relevant to their community and find solutions that directly respond to their specific needs as they see fit. It is important to complement felt needs with self-help, because it is too easy to define the felt needs then sell those needs to the people as the solution (Bhattacharyya, 2004).

Both self-help and felt needs lead to participation, when people are encouraged and emboldened to actively engage in the relevant improvements they seek, and to take pride and ownership in the community (Onyenemezu, 2014). This participation allows individuals and groups "left out" with fuller access to the skills, tools, knowledge, and benefits necessary to fulfill their needs and be self-sufficient (Wade, 1989, p. 118; as cited in Onyenemezu, 2014). With participation, the community developers must not begin a project in a community with "any preconceived notions either of the problem afflicting the people or of its solutions, but with an attempt to elicit the felt needs of the people" (Bhattacharyya, 1995, p. 64).

Abiona and Bello (2013) found that when the government provides services to the people, without allowing the opportunity for self-help or allowing the people to decide their felt needs, there is no longer a sustained effort on the part of the people to continue participating when the government pulls out.

Felt needs are often viewed as addressing dissatisfaction over a lack of needs and are "reflections of past and current inadequacies" (Wade, 1989, p. 119) that do not orient towards any real change in the future. Felt needs must move beyond addressing a problem in the past and present, by looking at new opportunities for community change in the future, which Wade (1989) calls "anticipatory needs" that "shifts from correcting what is wrong to creating what will be, from deficiencies and problem solving to capacity building and capability" (p. 119). Anticipatory needs always orient towards an "imagined" future through using futuring techniques led by the people in the community, a strategy that follows the logic and approach of the self-help model.

Self-help is based on the notion that the community members themselves identify their biggest problems and issues, so they can work to create effective solutions (Bhattacharyya, 1995). The community must be engaged and involved from the beginning of the process to assert their wants and needs on any planned improvement.

Self-help is a new iteration of felt needs because it requires a realization by the people to know how to deal with the problems moving forward. The self-help approach to community development involves a well-trained highly skilled convener or facilitator who adopts a neutral position and is focused on process and capacity building. All three principles, on their own, are worthless in overcoming the needs of a people and change the community unless all three work together.

Technical Assistance Model

In addition to the self-help model, Green and Haines (2016) discuss a model of technical assistance in community development. While some communities assess their community and identify the community's needs and problems, residents often look outside the community for the help. This creates a dependency for which the communities rely on resources and expertise, because the communities themselves believe that the issues and problems are too complex to solve by themselves (Green & Haines, 2016). The complexity of the problem for the technical assistance model is based on a lack of information. This approach requires the use of experts or consultants with specific technical expertise and is more concerned about the outcome of the efforts than in building the capacity of the residents (Green & Haines, 2016; Christenson & Robinson, 1989).

Community development is about engaging a community, and at times it is not always what you might think they need or want. For several years, I was a participant in the International Service-learning program (ISLP) at the University of Louisville (UofL) in Louisville, Kentucky. According to its mission, the ISLP program "provides experiential education in which students engage in activities that address human and community needs together with structured opportunities intentionally designed to promote student learning and development. This interdisciplinary program contributes to campus internationalization by infusing the classroom with various cultures to prepare students to be more receptive to global and comparative perspectives" (University of Louisville, 2019). Their footprint has extended into countries such as Belize, Croatia, Ghana, and the Philippines.

One of the most fundamental questions asked in an international service-learning project, or for any community development project is, what can we do to improve and enhance the quality of life of one's community? The ISLP at UofL worked with partners in Belize, Central America, in the mid-2000s. Effective community development strategies, as we explore in this book, do not assume what a community wants and needs. One of the villages we worked with was in Gales Point, Belize, a small village on the Gulf of Mexico, and much of the infrastructure had been demolished by Hurricane Hattie in 1961. Instead of needing or seeking clean water or another resource we thought the citizens needed, the community said they wanted to create a women's softball team. Period.

The University of Louisville's Sport Administration program went to work and helped develop the infrastructure, equipment, and training necessary to make this happen. Teams of faculty and students from the University of Louisville did not impose their values on the group and provided the appropriate assistance towards a common goal. The following year, the Gales Point women's softball team invited the team from UofL back to Gales Point for a friendly game of softball in the mid-afternoon sun and were soundly defeated by the women's team the university team helped to create. Everyone from the softball team, the village, and the UofL students and faculty were happy with the outcome.

Conflict Model

Conflict is a behavior threat by one party directed at the behavior territory (rights, interests, privileges) of another party (Robinson, 1989). This model of community development focuses on individuals and groups who lack power and resources and feel oppressed by the power structure in the role of facilitator, organizer, and advocate (third party). Power can be defined as the control of access to resources (land, labor, capital, money, knowledge, etc.), the ability to influence and control others to get the outcomes and results you want, and who controls the rules of the game and who keeps those rules in place. In the case of communities and community development, power is necessary to revitalize communities and build capacity (Hustedde, 2016).

Dahl (1961) outlines power as the ability of an individual or group (group A) to make another individual or group (B) do something that B otherwise would not do. Bachrach and Baratz (1970) discuss the two faces of power. The first face of power emphasizes the decision making by those in power. This is where A has power over B only when A affects B that is contrary to the interests of B, which is often done through A's superior bargaining power (see also Lukes, 1974). The second face of power involves non-decision-making, where A devotes energy to construct barriers against the participation of B, often referred to as the mobilization of bias (Bachrach & Baratz, 1970). Group A works to restrict the scope and access of B into decision making arenas, through institutional inaction, force, threat of sanctions, rules or procedures to keep B's issues off the political agenda, and establish new barriers or symbols that prevent B from taking any action against or make any demands upon A (Bachrach & Baratz, 1970).

Gaventa (1980) outlines the three dimensions of power that build upon Dahl (1961) and Bachrach and Baratz (1970). These dimensions identify the means and the power processes of the "social construction of meaning and patterns that serve to get B to act and believe in a manner in which B otherwise might not, to A's benefit and B's detriment" (pp. 15–16). Power enables A to psychologically influence and shape the consciousness of B's wants, shapes how B becomes aware of the inequalities that exist between A and B, and enables B to become aware of its own powerlessness, regardless of the strength and power of A. If you can control what people think and feel, you have a lot of power. Power and the exercise of power is not always concentrated in formal institutions of government and spheres of influences. Power is often more dispersed across various actors in the civic, private, and social sectors (Katz, 2017).

Conflict and power differences are integral parts of life, existing everywhere between social classes, ethnic groups, race, religion, gender, age, and countries. Communities often use conflict to upset and undermine the status quo (i.e., protests, boycotts, and resistance), even if conflicting or competing groups refuse to negotiate or change their position (Hustedde, 2016).

A major champion of the conflict model designed to upset the status quo is renowned community organizer Saul Alinsky (1971), who wrote the famous *Rules for Radicals*. A community organizer chooses a problem to address and organizes the community around the problem that is often seen as a winnable win. This model has a normative emphasis on justice and equality, and emphasizes tactics that are direct and confrontational but do not always use force or other coercive measures (Christenson & Robinson, 1999),

An advantage of the conflict approach is that while change can occur in a short period of time, certain tactics take much longer and are often more strategic. One organizational model that fits into the conflict approach is the Direct Action and Research Training (DART) organization that "bring(s) people together across racial, religious and socioeconomic lines to pursue justice in their communities" through obtaining victories on a number of issues such as affordable housing, health care, crime reduction, environment, public transportation, and education, in more than 150 communities (DART, 2020).

The DART approach relies on an intentional ground effort led by trained organizers, many of these organizations consisting of religious congregations (i.e., Citizens of Louisville Organized and United Together [CLOUT] in Louisville, Kentucky, and Congregations Acting for Justice and Empowerment [CAJE] in Evansville, Indiana) The DART method follows three stages: listening, research, and action. Listening involves a gathering of organizations or congregations in a community conversation to discuss community problems. It is through these conversations that areas of common concern will emerge. During this meeting, participants vote on the top priorities the organization will pursue during that coming year. The second stage, research, allows committees to research short- and long-term solutions to the problems, and to determine the key players in the community with the authority to implement these proposed solutions (DART, 2020). The research or knowledge side is important in linking knowledge to action as a way of changing society, according to the conflict theory framework.

The third stage, known as action, involves a large public meeting often called a Nehemiah Action Assembly (DART, 2020) based on the Book of Nehemiah from Hebrew Scriptures and the Old Testament that describes the power of organized people coming together to achieve justice (DART, 2020). This assembly brings together all member congregations to hear reports on the information and research from the past year, hear testimonies from individuals who are directly impacted by the issue or problem, followed by an invitation to individuals who have influence and would be in the position to either accept or reject the demands (the solution to the problem) set forth by the direct-action group (DART, 2020). Starting in 2004, CLOUT demanded for the Louisville Metro government to pass an ordinance to establish an affordable housing trust fund. Once CLOUT achieved that victory to establish the fund, the organization continued for several years to pressure the Louisville mayor and the Louisville Metro Council to provide funds for the affordable housing trust fund. It took a decade to get it properly funded, thanks to the persistence of CLOUT using the DART methods.

Critics of the DART methods feel the approach is too rigid and confrontational and fails to account for the context and constraints of the local political environment. Leaders are accused of using strong-arm tactics to guilt the necessary authorities to agree to their demands. It also ignores the "less controversial and more orderly parts of society and does not show understanding the role of symbols in building solidarity" (Hustedde, 2015, p. 31). Supporters believe that the direct-action approach under the conflict model of community development produces definitive outcomes and results that are specific, measurable, and relevant.

Chapter Two

What is Social Capital?

Although there is no consensus on a precise definition of social capital, there are some recurring themes in the literature. Broadly defined, social capital embodies the "connections among individuals—social networks and the norms of reciprocity and trustworthiness that arise from them" (Putnam, 2000, p. 19), while Woolcock (1998) defines social capital as "the information, trust, and norms of reciprocity inherent in one's social networks" (p. 153).

Bourdieu (1986) defines social capital as the result of the capacity (actual and potential resources) of an individual's position or membership in a group or network, particularly one's position in the political or economic power structure. Coleman (1988) defines social capital by its function within a social structure and suggests that changes in the relationships among people facilitate actions. These structures, whether it is an organization, family, or church, might be more suited to develop norms that reinforce trust and reciprocity than other structures and institutions. Loury (1977, p. 100) defines social capital as the development of relationships and networks that "promote or assist the acquisition of skills and traits valued in the marketplace."

Emery and Flora (2006, p. 62) define social capital as "the glue" that holds the community together that reinforces trust, reciprocity, and social norms across communities (as cited in Rogers & Jarema, 2015, p. 22). Earlier studies of cities from the mid-20th century defined social capital "as a community resource that built trust, facilitated cooperation, and solved collective-action problems block by block in cities" (Hoyman and Faricy, 2009, p. 316; see also Jacobs, 1961). Social capital and social networks are valuable because social networks affect the productivity of individuals and enhance relationships with others. Woolcock and Narayan (2000) define social capital as "the norms and networks that enable people to act collectively" (p. 226). Previous research indicates that communities with more dense relationships and connections tend to exhibit greater economic dynamism. Putnam (1993) further impresses that without social capital, regions would suffer in their ability to grow professionally and economically.

Social capital refers to interpersonal resources that individuals can access through networks and can explain through two forms of relationships: weak ties and strong ties (Granovetter, 1973; Bourdieu, 1986; Steffensmeier & Ulmer, 2006; Beaudoin, 2009). Strong ties exist among individuals connected within densely knit, homogenous networks such as those involving kin and close friends. Weak ties are defined by Granovetter (1973) as relationships and networks that extend beyond one's family or social group and exist among individuals connected within sparse, heterogeneous networks such as those involving acquaintances. Weak ties suggest relationships that exist to gain access to information (social media sites, large associations) or resources, without much interaction, and often existing in formal organizations and work settings (Granovetter, 1973).

Granovetter (1973) describes these weak ties as "bridges" and conversely states that "no strong tie is a bridge" (p. 1364), while Jacobs (1961) calls weak ties "hop-skip links" (p. 1375). These weak ties inhibit the ability for low-income or geographically immobile individuals to find better job opportunities since low bridging social capital prevents access to information from these networks (Loury, 1977; Hoyman & Faricy, 2009).

Measuring social capital poses a few challenges and problems (Bourdieu, 1986; Coleman, 1988). Social capital is less tangible than other types of capital, making it difficult to consistently measure. Multiple variables impact social capital and have been interpreted in a variety of ways, resulting in a lack of universal understanding of social capital (Paxton, 1999; Costa & Khan, 2003; Siegal, 2013). The social capital literature identifies three key indicators of social networks: civic engagement, participation, and trust (Bourdieu, 1986; Coleman, 1988; Putnam, 1995; Woolcock & Narayan, 2000; as cited in Majee & Hoyt, 2013, p. 112). Curley (2010) found statistically significant differences among indicators of social capital across racial/ethnic groups, language, marital status, and place attachment. Social relationships do not occur in a vacuum, and there are other factors that may detract from or enhance the ability of social capital to positively impact a community or individual (Siegel, 2011).

DIMENSIONS OF SOCIAL CAPITAL

Despite the difficulty of measuring and operationalizing social capital, three dimensions of social capital exist. The first is bonding social capital, which refers to the strength of family ties. The second is bridging social capital, which refers to ties among friends and acquaintances. The third is linking social capital, which refers to formal ties and relationships that link individuals to institutions and organizations (Putnam, 1995, 2000; Woolcock, 2001; Sabatini, 2005). At the most basic level, studies of social capital have distinguished between bridging and bonding social capital (Putnam, 2000). Bridging social capital includes outward looking networks that connect diverse groups of people, while bonding social capital refers to inclusive social networking within homogeneous groups (Siegel, 2011). Bonding social capital provides mutual access to resources to cope with daily life, while bridging social capital is essential for gaining access to information and diverse resources (Johnson, Honnold, & Threlfall, 2011).

Saegert, Thompson, and Warren (2001) argue there are four kinds of bridging social capital in low-income impoverished communities: 1) bridging ties across or between local institutions, such as churches, tenant associations, and local community development corporations (CDCs); 2) making connections between different low-income communities or neighborhoods that often need to cooperate with each other to pursue initiatives of mutual benefit; 3) forging connections between the poor and more affluent communities to form allies to combat poverty; and 4) connecting people and communities nationally as a way to generate power and change, despite the problem occurring at the local community level.

Linking social capital extends beyond the debate and distinctions between bonding and bridging social capital and is defined as the "norms of respect and networks of trusting relationships between people who are interacting across explicit, formal or institutionalized power or authority gradients in society" (Szreter & Woolcock, 2004, p. 655). Linking social capital exists between individuals in vertical relationships, based on relative power or authority that can be used to access resources, services, jobs, or power through funders, government, or a community organization (Hawkins & Maurer, 2010; Woolcock, 2001; Szreter & Woolcock, 2004; Claridge, 2018).

Emery (2013) created a typology of youth development activities and social capital based on low and high levels of bonding and bridging social capital. Ideal type 1 (low bonding/low bridging) is individual focused, where the participants are involved in self-directed activities or projects (e.g., solo music performance). Ideal type 2 (low bonding/high bridging) is mentor-focused and individual project focused. Ideal type 3 (high bonding/low bridging) focuses on participants working together as a group on an activity with shared interest (e.g., band camp). Ideal type 4 (high bonding/high bridging) emphasizes participants work working together and learning about community issues while connecting with organizations engaged in community development efforts.

Emery (2013) stresses the importance of having a balance of strong bonding social capital while allowing for new connections. She gives an example of youth bonding with each other, then bridging with other youth and melding into a larger bond. Subsequently, they bridge with adults for information and resources, who in turn may bond with the youth seeking their participatory capacity and begin to see them as equals. The larger bonded group can link with speakers and resource organizations helpful to the youth's cause. Furthermore, "the building of social capital engenders the development of collective norms of reciprocity that reinforce the need for community engagement among youth and adults alike" (Emery, 2013, p. 58).

Kinsey (2013) found similarly that 4-H clubs, while attending to the human capital of individuals, increase the number of connections and instill strong bonding and bridging connections and social capital using the Targeting Life Skills model (Hendricks, 1998). 4-H has four categories (head, heart, hands, and health) and eight sub-categories (thinking, managing, relating, caring, giving, working, living, and being). For instance, giving includes such skills as community service, volunteering, responsible citizenship, and contributions to group effort. Working includes teamwork and self-motivation. Caring includes nurturing relationships, concern for others, and sharing. Relating includes accepting differences, social skills, cooperation, and communication (Hendricks, 1998). While the 4-H model is geared to developing educational and skill development programs, these sub-categories also lead to building social capital by forging new bridges and strengthening bonds.

Kinsey (2013) and Enfield (2008) also argue that 4-H programs enhance social capital. Enfield (2008) says "Through ties and connections at the family, neighborhood, school, and community levels, young people gain access to a multitude of opportunities, experiences, and forms of support, including those in the areas of education, jobs and careers, emotional growth, and life skill development, all of which help with a successful transition to adulthood" (pp. 9–10).

Kinsey (2013) also identifies four main crucial elements of the 4-H experience: belonging, mastery, independence, and generosity. Mastery and independence are related to human capital while belonging and generosity are related to social capital. Right after an individual's physiological and safety needs are met in the hierarchy of needs (Maslow, 1943), the need for love and belonging in the hierarchy of prepotency encompasses the ideas of trust, cooperation, and social connectedness that helps build bonding and bridging social capital.

Baker and Johannes (2013) asked youth programs to map their social connections. They found a rippling effect showing that the connections they build as a young person will advance their ability to connect and strengthen those connections later in adulthood, as well as benefiting the community in which they live. Emery (2013) took Baker and Johannes's (2013) ripple mapping data a step further and concluded that "an interaction between bonding and bridging social capital can lead to a spiraling up of social capital with the capacity to have an impact on the entire community" (p. 51; see also Woolcock, 1998). Emery (2013) found that the youth identified a critical planning period where the creation of norms around trust and reciprocity was established. This development of bonding social capital between peers led to the development of bridging social capital to adults and other community members who could assist with information and resources regarding youth issues.

SOCIAL NETWORKS

To add to the bonding, bridging, and linking social capital of community members, groups, and outside agencies, Hill (2002; cited in Ennis & West, 2010) shares four key features of social networks: 1) network structure, which includes network size, connectedness, concentration or dispersion, accessibility, degree of clustering, and heterogeneity or homogeneity of the actors; 2) network process, including network content, frequency and intimacy of contact, durability and intensity of ties, and reciprocity; 3) function, which is the purpose the network serves for the community; and 4) the composition of the network, including the culture of the community, where one would find support in closer personal networks or in broader social obligations.

Gilchrist (2004) explains the importance of social networking in community development:

> Networks that connect individuals and different sections of the local community are an invaluable resource, functioning as communication systems and organisations mechanisms. The development of "community" is about strengthening and extending networks of relationships between individuals, between organisations and, just as importantly, between different sectors and agencies. Working to establish and maintain these networks is fundamental to effective community development work. (p. 25; cited in Ennis & West, 2009, pp. 409–410)

Woolcock and Narayan (2000) developed four views of social capital. The first view, the communitarian view, is composed of community groups and voluntary organizations that argue social capital is inherently good, more is better, and its presence always has a positive effect on a community's welfare. A downside to this extra social capital can have a negative effect on development, for what Rubio (1997) and Woolcock and Narayan (2000) call "perverse social capital" (p. 229; see also Rubio, 1997). High solidarity that comes with bonding social capital can lead to economic prosperity, as in the case of Kenya. According to an assessment by Narayan and Nyamwaya (1996), 200,000 community groups were active in central Kenya, but many were not connected to outside groups which did little to change or improve their impoverished situations.

The second view, the networks view, consists of entrepreneurs, business, and information groups. The network of business owners or entrepreneurs relies initially on family and friends and their close social bonds, but ultimately would break from these bonds to form relationships and networks where the "bridging social capital is more abundant and economic opportunities more promising" (Woolcock & Narayan, 2000, p. 233). The third view, the institutional view, formed by Knack and Keffer (1997) views the presence of social capital based on the strength of the political, legal, financial, and economic institutions that protect civil and political liberties, rule of law, transparency, and accountability.

The fourth view, the synergy view, combines Woolcock's (1998) typology of capacity, autonomy, and embeddedness previously discussed with bridging social capital and governance. The levels of bridging social capital are dependent on the capital of the state and its relationship to society and are based on the interaction between social networks and the formal institutions and its economic well-being. These levels (positive to negative) may determine whether the state is mired in conflict, violence, and anarchy, or whether it is a stable state based on cooperation, trust, and the efficiency and effectiveness of the institutions (Woolcock & Narayan, 2000).

Putnam (2000) has argued that social capital, through informal groups, formal organizations, and internalized trust has been declining (Schwadel & Stout, 2012). Putnam (1995, 2000) highlighted factors relating to the decline of social capital, such as changes in the traditional family structure, suburban sprawl, increased cultural diversity, advancement of technology, and generational differences.

Schwadel and Stout (2012) studied age, period, and cohort effects on social capital, and found that informal association with neighbors (bonding social capital) declined across periods while informal associations with friends outside of the neighborhood (bridging social capital) increased across birth cohorts. Formal associations were stable across generations except for slightly higher formal associations for the early 1920s and the early 1930s birth cohorts. The results show that the number of types of voluntary organization memberships varies moderately by birth cohort and by period. These changes do not suggest declines in social capital but suggest that changes in social capital are more complex than previously thought.

Trust declined considerably across both periods and cohorts, where the oldest cohorts are less trusting than the cohorts are in the 1920s through the 1940s. Future research should look at this effect, and how it impacts the quality and value of social capital, even as people continue to volunteer and be active in their communities. Most proponents of the decline in social capital believe that the change happens across birth cohorts rather than simply across time periods.

According to Mannheim (1952), "Individuals who belong to the same generation, who share the same year of birth, are endowed, to that extent, with a common location in the historical dimension of the social process" (p. 290; as cited in Donovan and Hoover, 2014, p. 137). The across-cohort increase in socializing with friends outside of the neighborhood, however, can create opportunities and resources for people and communities and ultimately produce a different kind of social capital, one better fit for our more globalized society (Schwadel & Stout, 2012; Quan-Haase & Wellman, 2004).

Decreases in traditional forms of social capital are offset by increases in other, newer forms, such as internet groups and virtual associations (see Costa & Kahn, 2001; Ladd, 1999). Empirical evidence is limited, because it focuses on a single aspect of social capital (informal association, formal association, or trust) and uses techniques that do not disentangle period and cohort effects, but it does suggest social capital declines in the latter category.

CIVIC ENGAGEMENT AND PARTICIPATION

High levels of social capital tend to result in higher levels of civic engagement from individuals who are involved in community and voluntary associations (such as neighborhood associations, block watch groups, church-based groups, work-based groups, bowling leagues or other sports teams, sewing circles, etc.), participation in political and religious organizations, and activities. This high participation collectively tends to contribute to the overall health and quality of life of individuals and the entire community, and more importantly, encourages active participatory democracy and governance, and positively contributes to the overall fabric of American society (Rohe, Van Zandt, & McCarthy, 2001; Putnam, 2000).

Communities with high levels of social capital have more efficient political structures and more responsive political elites. Members of these communities show greater levels of civic engagement and participation in politics (Putnam, 2000). Westlund and Adam (2010) point out that associational activity membership and economic factors, especially on the regional and local levels, may be stronger and have more impact on the national level than family, school, work, media, and public policies.

Contemporary research generally confirms the Putnam (1993, 1995, 2000) thesis that social networks and neighborly attitudes help support democratic participation. For example, a sense of community and empowerment, especially in a high poverty community, leads to a discussion of community issues that impact people's daily lives (Bolland & McCallum, 2002). Lelieveldt's (2004) three measures of social capital are neighborliness, sense of duty, and trust, and there are different mechanisms that connect them to participating in either informal governance (e.g., checking in one our neighbor's homes and the neighborhood children), taking action on neighborhood problems (e.g., cleanliness, noise, crime watchdog), and participating in a neighborhood improvement program.

For neighborliness and social networks, Lelieveldt (2004) argues it's about having enough information. For trust, it is about reciprocity, and for sense of duty, it's about having feelings of obligation. Neighborliness and sense of duty have led to increased participation in programs by residents aimed towards improving their neighborhood (Lelieveldt, 2004; see also Hays & Kogl, 2007). However, not all forms of social capital have a direct link with participation. Trust, for instance, has an ambiguous effect (positive in participation in neighborhood improvement organization, absent in informal governance and negative in tackling problems) (Lelieveldt, 2004). Citizens seem more motivated to participate at a neighborhood level than at a higher level.

In low trust societies, legal contracts and enforcements are more effective due to the inability of social capital to perform the tasks. Problems of resource allocation are easier to solve in higher trust societies due to actors being able to collectively solve problems (Ostrom, 1990; Ostrom, Gardner, & Walker, 1994; Whiteley, 2000). With the appropriate social capital available, the actors can negotiate more effectively and reduce further transaction costs better than outside agencies. Without the need for additional resources from outside agencies, overseeing a job or providing goods or other services, economic growth can flourish.

According to Putnam (2000), the "long civic generation," those who came of age before and during the World War II period (those born before 1930), showed high social capital levels. The baby boomers (born between 1946 and 1964), who grew up during the Vietnam War and Civil Rights Movements, showed lower levels of social capital. Generation X (born between 1965 and 1980) should have even lower levels because of the perception of economic risk and vulnerability (as cited in Schwadel & Stout, 2012; Kiesa et al., 2007).

The Millennial generation (born in the 1980s and later) has shown high levels of civic engagement, suggesting an increase in social capital (Kiesa et al., 2007). This may be a result of the more intense political environment created by the events of the early 21st century. Proponents of period-based changes in social capital point to historical events and eras such as the Vietnam War and 9/11 and their effects on social capital levels as evidence (Schwadel & Stout, 2012). However, this theory seems inadequate because the aspects of social capital, such as trust, vary across cohorts (Dalton, 2005).

Scholars believe that there is a definite tie between social capital and citizen engagement and participation in the community. Portney and Berry (1997) showed that neighborhood associations are the most effective at creating grassroots political participation, especially in African American neighborhoods, more than participation in citywide issue groups, crime watch groups, social service groups, and other self-help organizations (see also Hays & Kogl, 2007). This likely stems from the fact that shared everyday circumstances in a place can motivate members of a neighborhood to participate. This suggests great complexity in the relationship between social capital and organized political activity; neighborhood and political associations are distinct from the closer relationships between the people of the neighborhoods. Portney and Berry (1997) state that "neighborhoods are where the bonds of community are built. They are the wellsprings of social capital. People's sense of community, their sense of belonging to a neighborhood, their caring about the people who live there, and their belief that people who live there care about them are critical attitudes that can nurture or discourage participation" (p. 633).

Hays and Kogl (2007) emphasize the importance of neighborhood as a place where this connectedness occurs, which they define as "a unit of political representation and action, especially for lower-income residents and for minority populations that are not adequately represented through other mechanisms" (pp. 181–182). They looked at the relationships between neighborhood-based social networks and attitudes, as well as participation in neighborhood associations in Waterloo, Iowa, a small Midwestern college town. Hays and Kogl (2007) argue that class-based political organization is relatively weak compared to place-based political organizations.

An individual's interactions with others may build social capital, for example, but depending on the larger economic and political power structures around him, that individual's actions may or may not make resources for his or her community. In other words, residents of low-income neighborhoods may not be able to channel their support networks into political or economic representation. While Putnam (1993, 1995, 2000) believes that all networks create social capital, critics argue that forms of mobilization of his version of social capital only give citizens symbolic rather than real political or economic power (Cohen, 2001; Halpern, 2005; Miraftab, 2004).

TRUST

Działek (2014) focuses on social capital as a norm of trust, consisting of either personal trust (confidence in and reciprocity with people one knows personally) or generalized trust (trust in all people, including strangers). Quality social connections are a major component of resource attainment, including financial resources (Bourdieu, 1986; Coleman, 1988; Lorenzen, 2007; Działek, 2014). Quality social connections provide high quality information and resource exchanges, which leads to improvement and goal attainment (Portes, 1998). The denseness of network relations is important but useless if the information lacks substance due to inadequate trust, which is why trust and the density of connections are equally important (Działek, 2014). If social capital is the glue holding communities together, then trust is the lubricant that makes organizations run more efficiently (Fukuyama, 1999).

Some communities in great need of development may not have highly educated and trained individuals; this problem can be remedied with the appropriate assistance. The ABCD model discussed in the last chapter seeks out the hidden strengths currently in the community. From there, those with the education or training in each area can teach others who are lacking in these strengths or assets. In more dire situations, an advocate may be brought in to offer basic education and training in the felt needs the community has chosen to tackle. During these educational and training events, community members come together to bridge their current individual resources and inevitably build stronger bonds and bonding social capital (Baker & Johannes, 2013; Emery, 2013).

Putnam (2000) discusses the role of voluntary associations in influencing the economy (see also Portes, 1998; Woolcock, 1998; Działek, 2014). Many groups are homogenous (family, race, occupation, political affiliation, residential location) and often develop strong bonds as a result. Voluntary associations can break the homogeneity that hinders creativity and entrepreneurship by forming strong links where access to new resources becomes available to individuals in different groups. For development to proceed in poor and low-income communities, the initial benefits of intensive intra-community integration must give way over time to extensive extra-community linkages as discussed in Woolcock's (1998) social capital typology. Too much or too little of either social capital dimension at any given moment will undermine economic advancement (Woolcock, 1998).

Działek (2014) shows that "while membership in associations and trust in public institutions had a positive influence on the economic development of the countries in the region, the level of trust to others did not exert any significant influence" (p. 181). Działek's (2014) own study of economic growth in Polish regions found that social capital did not show any significant direct influence on economic growth, but social capital better explains the differences in economic resources and human capital.

These findings differ from Działek's (2014) comparison to Raiser, Haerpfer, Nowotny, and Wallace's (2002) study on post-communist countries, which stresses social capital's importance. Działek (2014) offers a question about the difference in findings: "Is it because the resources of social capital are too limited to exert any significant impact?" (p. 188). He explains that Poland's density of connection, even at its highest, is still lower than Western European nations where there have been significant demonstrations of social capital influence on economic performance. Additionally, Działek (2014) wonders if Poland is suffering "from a negative usage of networks and the positive and negative impact of social capital level each other out" (p. 188). Further, Działek (2014) notes that the degree of economic modernization may play a role in the opportunity for social capital to make an impact.

Westlund and Adam (2010) analyzed the two most common measures of social capital: trust in others, and the number of associations and the number of memberships in these associations. While the focus on economic measurements is low, trust is used as a proxy for social capital and theoretically increases economic capacity by reducing transaction costs and speeds up information and resource transfer coinciding with the reciprocity principle (see also de Tocqueville; 1966: Whiteley, 2000). As the state collects resources and redistributes them, so do voluntary organizations that create mutual obligations (Westlund & Adam, 2010). Westlund and Adam (2010) conclude that on a national level, trust shows a positive relationship and associations are negative, while on the regional level, associations and trust still have a positive effect.

How is social capital created in the first place if it has never existed at all? Whiteley (2000) states, "If little or no social capital exists in a society to begin with, it is very difficult to create it, since anyone who tries to cooperate in such a society will simply be exploited" (p. 448). To remedy this, strangers must be willing to take the risk and trust others without the expectation of reciprocity; they must rely on generalized reciprocity or "pay it forward" ideals (de Tocqueville, 1966; Putnam, 1993, 1995, 2000; Whiteley, 2000).

Some researchers explain practicing and maintaining generalized reciprocity by putting their trust in voluntary activity (de Tocqueville, 1966; Putnam, 1993, 1995, 2000; Whiteley, 2000), for "trust is more likely to emerge in response to experiences and institutions outside the small associations than as a result of membership" (Whiteley, 2000, p. 449; as cited in Levi, 1996, p. 48). Whiteley (2000) argues that there is "no evidence of a relationship between voluntary activity and economic performance in a cross-national sample of

countries, although they do identify a relationship between economic performance and trust" (p. 449; as cited in Knack & Keefer, 1997). Arrow (1972,
p. 357) says, "Virtually every commercial transaction has within itself an
element of trust, certainly any transaction conducted over a period. It can be
plausibly argued that much of the economic backwardness in the world can
be explained by the lack of mutual confidence" (as cited in Hoyman & Faricy, 2009, pp. 317–318). There is a level of interpersonal trust required in all
transactions of goods or services delivered to a recipient.

Florida, Cushing, and Gates (2002, p. 20) speak to the restricting nature
of social capital theory stating that "relationships can get so strong that the
community becomes complacent and insulated from outside information and
challenges." Hoyman and Faricy (2009) confirm that bonding (between homogenous social groups) social capital had a negative effect on job growth,
but "social networks have been shown to be an important factor in the development of human capital" (p. 330, see also Coleman, 1988). Emery (2013)
also finds that excessive focus on bonding between in-group members will
inhibit expansion and acceptance of new members.

Long-term relationships, such as family, church groups, and small associations, have strong senses of reciprocity (Hoyman & Faricy, 2009). Hoyman
and Faricy (2009) also point out that attitudinal differences in trust account
for varying economic performances of countries. Putnam (1993, 1995, 2000)
and Coleman (1988) identify that trust encourages better government services
and encourages societies to put less effort into putting resources in protecting
themselves. Emery (2013) agrees that strong ties are required to move forward with development, as each participant believes they can trust the others
will know the expected norms from the group and pull their own weight in the
process. Putnam's (1995) idea of reciprocity allows for individuals of high
trust to be assured that they will eventually receive what they give.

The social network theory fills in ABCD model's shortfalls of focusing too
much on the assets of community members without paying much attention
to bringing those assets together. Ennis and West (2010) explain that social
networks may tie members by trust, economic exchange, or friendship among
other relationships and these networks can be small (e.g., family groups) or
large (e.g., city community and welfare referral networks). Putnam (1993)
writes that "the density of formal and informal institutions directly dimin-
ishes the costs of collective action for an area and therefore creates a regional
comparative advantage" (as cited in Hoyman & Faricy, 2009, p. 318). Furthermore, a more developed, civic community can result in higher growth
rates and government efficiency and belonging to associations increases community members' "habits of cooperation, solidarity, and public-spiritedness"

(Putnam et al., 1993, pp. 89–90; Putnam, 1995, 2000, as cited in Hoyman & Faricy, 2009, p. 318).

CRITIQUES OF SOCIAL CAPITAL

Urban growth has led to the rise of an elite economic base with a highly educated, highly skilled workforce in finance, media, and information technology that aim towards leisure pursuits related to their work (Clark, Lloyd, Wong, & Jain, 2002). Large cities like Chicago, New York, and Los Angeles, and medium to small cities such as Oklahoma City, Evansville, Omaha, Lubbock, Burlington, and Augusta, Georgia, are guided by the principles of the growth machine (Logan & Molotch, 1987). The growth machine consists of a coalition of elected officials, business elites, the local media, utilities, real estate developers, and auxiliary players such as organized labor, small retailers, museums, civic organizations, universities, and other professionals who play an important role in developing the right political and economic conditions for the growth of the city's business climate and the success of major economic development initiatives in a community or city (Logan & Molotch, 1987).

Florida (2002, 2005, 2014) argues the most effective development strategy in the post-industrial world is developing cities and localities that invest in human capital, such as workforce development, investments in education, and training that yield marketable skills, and emphasizes individual responsibilities and employment opportunities (Green & Haines, 2016). This particularly includes cities that have a high creative class. This class consists of highly skilled, highly educated workers such as scientists, engineers, professors, artists, and writers known as the super-creative core, along with creative professionals in law, business, health care, and financial services (Florida, 2002, 2014), compared to the working class (manual laborers) and the service class (bartenders, waitresses, maids, food service workers, etc.).

Florida (2002, 2005, 2014) argues that having high levels of talent, technology, and tolerance (the "three Ts") will attract this creative class. Talent, for Florida (2002, 2005, 2014), is based in "the ability to generate new knowledge or to convert existing knowledge into economically successful applications" (Krätke, 2010, p. 835). A person's education, background, skills, training, occupation, employment, and position in the labor market is often referred to as human capital (Green & Haines, 2016). Technology is the key to economic growth for Florida (2002, 2005, 2014) in attracting creative workers who will design new innovations in business, industry, and manufacturing that, according to economist Joseph Schumpeter, will "enable capitalism to constantly revolutionize itself" (Florida, 2014, p. 229).

Tolerance can exist in both negative and positive terms. "Negative tolerance is the capacity to 'put up with' another's difference from self because the different other is simply not perceived and/or because the self and other do not intersect" (Lofland, 2000, pp. 146–147; as cited in Gilderbloom, Hanka & Lasley, 2009, p. 481) that may exist in separate but shared spaces. Positive tolerance is "the capacity to put up with an other's fully recognized differences from self . . . with a mild appreciation for, or enjoyment of, those differences" (Lofland, 2000, p. 147; as cited in Gilderbloom et al., 2009, p. 481) through multicultural and diversity programs.

More importantly, cities with a high creative class and high levels of talent, technology, and tolerance also have a high level of amenities. In order to entice economic development and urban growth and attract this creative class, cities must develop these amenities, which are non-produced public goods and non-market transactions that do not have an explicit price and are restricted to a specific territory that distinguishes it from other territories (Clark et al., 2002; Green, 2001).

Cities develop policies that enhance the neighborhoods by providing civic amenities, such as parks, restaurants, shops, museums, convention centers, and sports stadia as engines for growth and economic development (Clark et al., 2002). Many of these projects for economic development, especially sports stadia, are used as political tools to demonstrate progress and success in economic development, because cities must pursue interests to improve their economic base and competitive position in the overall economy.

Cities pursue these economic development projects because they are bound by their structure and left with little choice but to be competitive and aggressively pursue these developmental policies to establish their competitive advantage among other cities (Peterson, 1981). Cities are vulnerable to the relocation threats of businesses and firms and must provide all the basic amenities to maintain a quality of life and ensure jobs that attract new residents who will remain in the city. Professional sports stadia and franchises become a part of the whole amenities strategy for cities that pursue economic development policies (Euchner, 1993). The business community persuades the local community that such developmental strategies and amenities are positive and achieve the goals for everyone, when in reality these goals only achieve the interest of the business elite's growth machine, often at the expense of minority, inner city, poor neighborhoods that rely on redistributive policies (Peterson, 1981). These amenities, especially sports stadia, attract the "visitor class" and use the city's fiscal resources to accommodate this class, and other business elites, rather than using public resources to address the immediate needs of the multitude of citizens, especially those in these economically disadvantaged areas (Eisinger, 2000).

Certain cultural and social amenities, such as arts, professional sports franchises, shops, and restaurants, will attract a highly diverse group of people, such as minorities, gays, and bohemians, and a highly educated, highly skilled workforce in information technology, performing arts, and music that will bring a critical mass of people into a city or neighborhood to promote growth (Florida, 2002, 2005, 2014; Clark et al., 2002).

Florida (2002, 2005, 2014) developed several indices to measure the creative class. The Innovation Index is the number of innovations patented per capita. The Gay Index measures the representation of gay people within a region relative to the rest of the United States. The High Tech Index measures a metropolitan area's high-tech industrial output in relation to the U.S., the percentage of total economic output of a region from high-tech industries, compared to the U.S., and the presence of a creative class—the percentage of the population that consist of the super-creative core and creative professionals. Final composite measures combine all four of these indices (Florida, 2002, 2005, 2014).

Other indices Florida (2002, 2005, 2014) uses to measure the creative class are the Bohemian Index, which is the number of artistically creative people (artists, designers, musicians, composers, painters, sculptors, etc.) divided by the total population. The Talent Index measures the human capital in the region based on the percentage of the population with a bachelor's degree or higher. The Melting Pot Index measures the relative percentage of foreign-born people in a region. The Tech-Pole Index is a composite measure of the percentage of national high-tech output multiplied by the high-tech real output location quotient for each metropolitan statistical area (MSA). The Coolness Index is the percentage of population ages 22–29, combined with a measurement of nightlife (number of bars and nightclubs per capita), and a culture measurement based on the number of art galleries and museums per capita. A composite Diversity Index combines the Gay, Bohemian, and Melting Pot Indices (Florida, 2002, 2005, 2014).

Florida's analysis also shows that structural factors determine whether cities will become creative, such as the size of the city and whether the city is a state capital (Florida, 2005). According to Florida's (2005) analysis, six of the top 12 cities, in terms of their creativity indexes, are capital cities— Austin, TX, Boston, MA, Seattle, WA (Olympia is the capital of Washington but is located in the Seattle MSA), Minneapolis/St. Paul, MN, and Washington, DC. Only two of the bottom 10 in Florida's (2005) rankings are state capitals (Providence, RI, and Richmond, VA). These capital cities and the top 15 cities in the creativity index possess a high-quality lifestyle full of amenities, such as bars, restaurants, and nightlife, putting these cities into the category of "cool" (Florida, 2005).

Peck (2005) lays out Florida's argument of the "three Ts" to attract the creative class, saying that "growth derives from creativity and therefore it is creatives that make growth; growth can only occur if the creatives come, and the creatives will only come if they get what they want; what the creatives want is tolerance and openness, and if they find it, they will come; and if they come, growth will follow" (p. 757). The old models proposed cities should compete for businesses and firms, and people will move where firms locate. Florida's model suggests creative workers will move anywhere. These workers' values, such as individuality, meritocracy, diversity, openness, responding to challenge and responsibility, flexibility, peer recognition, location, community, and money motivate their decisions (Florida, 2002, 2005, 2014). The creative class for Florida:

> Created a lifestyle mentality, where Pittsburgh and Detroit were still trapped in that Protestant-ethic/bohemian-ethic split, where people were saying, "You can't have fun!" or "What do you mean play in a rock band? Cut your hair and go to work, son. That's what's important." Well, Austin was saying, "No, no, no, you're a creative. You want to play in a rock band at night and do semiconductor work in the day? C'mon! And if you want to come in at 10 the next morning and you're a little hung over or you're smoking dope, that's cool." (Dreher, 2002, p. 6; also cited in Peck, 2005, p. 756)

While Florida's concepts make sense in theory, Krätke (2010) reports empirical research shows otherwise. Some have criticized Florida for misunderstanding the causes of economic growth. Peck (2005) questioned the causal logic of Florida by arguing that his conclusions are suggestive and correlative. Individuals may possess some talent, but they may not have the ability to grow within the structure in which they operate. Markusen (2006) identifies creative class members, who are not necessarily in creative occupations, arguing "occupations that exhibit distinctive spatial and political proclivities are bunched together, purely on the basis of educational attainment, and with little demonstrable relationship to creativity" (p. 1,921).

A community in need of development is likely to be extremely low on Florida's creativity indices. To develop a community, outside creatives need to be brought in before community development can take place (Montgomery, 2005; Peck, 2005). Florida offers no application for communities in great need of development and neglects, in his studies, any issues of urban inequality and poverty. One prominent critic of Florida's "three Ts" is Glaeser (2004), who argues it's not just the "three Ts," but rather the "three Ss" of "skills, sun, and sprawl" that drive relocation and economic development.

Glaeser argues, "most creative people are what most well-off people like — big suburban lots with easy commutes and automobiles and safe streets and good schools and low taxes" (2005, p. 654).

Hoyman and Faricy (2009) looked at creative class, human capital, and social capital theories across 276 American metropolitan statistical areas (MSAs) and found that the creative class and the "three Ts" were negatively correlated with economic growth, but human capital and social capital had varying levels of correlation with wages and job growth. Human capital was the best at predicting growth, while social capital did not predict job growth. Human capital suggests that higher concentrations of highly educated and highly trained individuals will increase growth. Also, human capital correlates with urban growth both in the service and knowledge economies. Individuals seek connections with others in similar positions and look for social capital within their human capital circumstances.

While Putman argues and provides his reasons for the decline of social capital, Florida (2002, 2005, 2014) suggests that creative workers tend to work longer hours, have more stress and pressures with work, and do not prioritize a work life balance. According to Putnam in the foreword to the Robinson and Godbey (1997) book *Time for Life* discussing America's "time famine," he says:

> the most worrisome social trend in America over the last several decades has been the widening gap in wealth and income between the social classes. Robinson and Godbey report a less noticed counterpart trend: less well-educated Americans appear to be enjoying more free time, whereas their college-educated counterparts, for the most part, are not. Paradoxically, as the authors put it, the "working class" is spending fewer hours at work, while the erstwhile "leisure class" has less leisure. (as cited in Florida, 2014, p. 126)

In terms of finding work where the jobs are located, weak ties—the bridging social capital that Putnam values—matter more than strong ties and have replaced the stronger ties that once structured society both in quality and quantity (Florida, 2002, 2014). Florida (2002) says

> instead of communities defined by close associations and deep commitment to family, friends, and organizations, we seek places where we can make friends and acquaintances easily and live quasi-anonymous lives. The decline in the strength of our ties to people and institutions is a product of the increasing number of ties we have. (p. 7)

The creative class values moving around from city to city, where the jobs and the amenities are what allows them to define and create their own identities.

CAN YOU HAVE TOO MUCH SOCIAL CAPITAL?

Putnam (2000) and other theorists say that we need more social capital because it is good for us; however, Field (2017) argues social capital has a "dark side" with negative effects, especially pertaining to inequality (p. 49). A major criticism of social capital is the assumption that a community with ample institutions, organizations, and people has a lot of social capital, but that is not always the case. Greely (1997) argues that the best measures of social capital in a community are activities that enhance the general welfare, such as volunteering (as cited in Johnson, 1999). Social capital is an important output performance in community development work among public and nonprofit organizations (Johnson, 1999).

Critics such as DeFilippis (2001) argue that Putnam (2000) misses the role of power in building social capital across networks and communities. Putnam sees a separation between economic capital and social capital, but DeFilippis (2001) says that social capital must reconnect with economic capital to have any impact at all, which he suggests can be done through mutual housing associations, community land trusts, CDFIs, and microenterprise lenders.

DeFilippis (2001) also disagrees with Putnam's assertion that social capital is something that an individual or community possesses. Communities and places are outcomes, not actors, and therefore cannot possess anything because a community or place is not "a function of the internal attributes of the people living and working there" (DeFilippis, 2001, p. 789). The outcomes, for DeFilippis (2001), "affect and constrain future possibilities . . . but also outcomes of a complex set of power-laden relationships—both internally, within the communities, and externally, between actors in the communities and the rest of the world" (p. 789).

Many discussions of social capital imply that poor neighborhoods have little social capital; however, there is little evidence that affluent neighborhoods have more social capital than poorer neighborhoods (Osterling, 2007). In fact, poorer neighborhoods have a lot of social capital, especially bonding social capital, but less bridging social capital necessary to promote economic activity that Putnam and others render "invisible networks unable to generate capital" (DeFilippis, 2001, p. 798). For instance, Cohen (2001) and Osterling (2007) argue that social capital may be used to acquire basic needs and connect resources, such as food, shelter, and housing, whereas affluent communities may use social capital to mobilize towards neighborhood preferences and outcomes.

Chapter Three

The Social Capital Implications of Habitat for Humanity Homeownership

Matthew J. Hanka, Mohammed Khayum,
and Ramona Harvey

Social capital focuses on the relationships and social networks that exist among people and the benefits that derive from them. A high level of social capital results from higher involvement and participation in the community through voluntary associations, such as bowling leagues, block watch groups, and civic and political organizations. Previous research indicates that communities with more dense relationships and connections tend to exhibit greater economic dynamism. This chapter examines connections within and between social networks that arise because of the Habitat for Humanity International builds and homeownership. In particular, the focus is on the impact of homeownership on the information, knowledge, and resource flows and the relationships formed after Habitat homeownership.

In a number of ways, homeownership serves to build social capital, but homeownership also benefits from existing social capital as well. Increases in social capital refer to increases in resources available for individuals and groups arising from their networks of relationships. Networks of relationships are valuable for individuals since they can play a critical role in accessing and transferring resources, including information and knowledge. Depending on the extent of an individual's network of social relationships, there also are important behavioral, perceptual, and attitudinal consequences (Knoke & Kuklinski, 1982).

This chapter empirically examines the dynamic between homeownership and social capital based on homes built by Habitat for Humanity International over a five-year period in their Women Build program. Responses from a sample of households, whose homes were built in partnership with Habitat for Humanity, provide insights about the relative changes in social network relationships and access to resources before and after heads of households became homeowners. This chapter examines the literature on social capital and its relationship with community development and homeownership, followed by an overview of Habitat for Humanity International, a section on our research question and methods, an explanation of the measures and variables utilized in this study, followed by the data analysis and conclusion.

As noted in the previous chapter, measuring social capital poses a few challenges. Social capital is less tangible than other types of capital, making it difficult to consistently measure. Multiple variables impact social capital and have been interpreted in different ways, resulting in a lack of universal understanding of what constitutes social capital (Paxton, 1999; Costa & Khan, 2003; Siegal, 2013). Curley (2010) found statistically significant differences among indicators of social capital across racial/ethnic groups, language, marital status, and place attachment. In contrast, Painter and Paxton (2014) found in another study that homeownership, age, the number of children in a household, and length of residence were associated with increased social capital formation through active memberships and community involvement. Conflicting findings occur in part because social relationships do not occur in a vacuum, and other factors may either detract from or enhance the ability of social capital to positively impact a community or individual (Siegel, 2011).

In particular, a high level of social capital represents resources that can be converted to other types of capital needed for survival and success (Whitley, 2013). Financial, social, and cultural capital tend to be linked (Steffensmeier & Ulmer, 2006; Beaudoin, 2009). Groups possessing one or two forms of capital can leverage one form of capital to strengthen another form of capital. Putnam (1995, 2000) highlighted factors relating to the decline of social capital, such as changes in the traditional family structure, suburban sprawl, increased cultural diversity, advancement of technology, and generational differences.

Bonding, bridging, and linking social capital are three dimensions of social capital that are relevant in exploring the dynamics of homeownership and social capital. Some groups of individuals are better able to access and utilize different types of social capital than other groups (Beaudoin, 2011). Many factors, including socioeconomic status and cultural backgrounds, influence one's ability to access and maintain social capital. Conventional culture is considered in terms of race and ethnicity, but there are increasing numbers of non-conventional, non-ethnic based groups with unique subcultures that impact how social capital is developed (Sharp, 2005). Cultural values impact the formation of social networks and trust levels, but more research needs to be done to clarify the interrelationship between cultural and social capital (Steffensmeier & Ulmer, 2006). Johnson et al. (2011) discuss how different ethnic groups and women may tend to have networks with more of one type of social capital over the other.

In the United States, evidence suggests that social capital has been declining. However, trends in social capital are complex phenomena with several factors affecting the development, maintenance, and value of social capital. The current review of the literature suggests that what was previously seen as a decline in social capital could be a fundamental shift from a reliance on bonding social capital to an increased reliance on bridging social capital. This change impacts some subgroups more significantly than others, resulting in a significant decline in social capital for some populations, but not others.

Members of certain minority ethnic groups are more likely to form bonding social capital ties and less likely to have bridging social capital ties across ethnic and socioeconomic lines, and therefore, benefit less from social capital (Beauvoir, 2009; 2011). Membership in a racial or ethnic minority is inversely related to social capital (Weaver & Rivello, 2006). Individuals from different racial and ethnic groups have varying cultural or subcultural norms and values, which impact how social capital is gained, maintained, and utilized. Some evidence suggests racial and ethnic minorities tend to trust public institutions less, compared to non-Hispanic Whites (Donner & Rodriguez, 2008). Ethnic minorities tend to identify with similar minorities while "dis-identifying" with other ethnic groups and gain fewer benefits from social capital than non-minorities (Beaudoin, 2009). Language skills can negatively or positively impact social capital. For those with English as a second language (ESL), individuals often lack the social capital conferred by language (Donner & Rodriguez, 2008; Curley, 2010).

Changes in the traditional family structure and shifting gender roles have resulted in an increase of single parent homes and an increase in female heads of households, which is relevant to this chapter's study focusing on the impact of a homeownership program that houses female heads of household. There is a strong relationship between a woman's level of social capital and her status (Caiazza & Putnam, 2005). Women with greater social capital enjoy greater status.

There also has been a significant change in the social roles of women since the 1970s. More women are heads of households, gaining post-secondary education and entering the workplace (Sharp, 2005). Traditionally, women have high levels of bonding social capital, but as roles shift, bridging social capital has become even more important. The level of education, socioeconomic status, and minority group status influences access to social capital. This is especially the case when it comes to bridging social capital (Johnson et al., 2011).

Minority females are more likely to be female heads of households and single mothers and are more likely to be less educated and poorer than the general population, thus limiting their access to social capital (Donner &

Rodriguez, 2008). Low-income women, especially minority women, have large bonding social capital but very shallow bridging social capital (Johnson et al., 2011). Social capital is important for a woman's success (Caiazza & Putnam, 2005). High levels of social capital increase a woman's likelihood of marrying and gaining employment, particularly for low-income single mothers (Johnson et al., 2011). Bonding social capital involves reciprocity, and in the face of diminished economic conditions many low-income women are experiencing declines in their ability to maintain the bonding social capital they rely on (Johnson et al., 2011).

Since the 1990s, wealth has become more unevenly distributed than income, and there is increased inequality of opportunity or social mobility for lower income individuals (Neckerman & Torche, 2007). The decline in social capital associated with rising income inequality is associated with decreased trust and participation (Neckerman & Torche, 2007).

Socioeconomic disadvantages are related to lower levels of social capital. Upper and upper-middle income youth have seen an increase in social capital, while there has been a significant decline of social capital among lower income youth (Sander & Putnam, 2010). The strength of a person's referral network plays a crucial role when it comes to job seeking success. The lack of bridging social capital networks limits opportunities for socioeconomically disadvantaged urban individuals. Often socioeconomically disadvantaged individuals are less able to capitalize on the connections they have because potential referrers are more guarded, for fear of providing a recommendation that may damage their reputation (Johnson et al., 2011).

One way to improve the social capital of the poor is to relocate individuals to neighborhoods that are more socioeconomically mixed. However, neighborhood resources and feelings of attachment and safety are stronger predictors of social capital than the socioeconomic mix of the neighborhood (Curley, 2010). The existence of a trusted network of relationships within a community promotes social capital and is a part of the neighborhood context. However, one problem with neighborhood social capital research is teasing out the effects of neighborhood characteristics to test the effect of social capital beyond neighborhood characteristics on economic outcomes (Brisson & Usher, 2007).

Greater access to fiscal capital is associated with greater access to, and the ability to benefit from, social capital (Steffensmeier & Ulmer, 2006; Beaudoin, 2009). Lockhart (2005) found that both secular and faith-based poverty-to-work programs increased both bridging and bonding social capital for participants. Low-income individuals could transcend social barriers more effectively with the supports provided by both types of programs. High levels of social capital increase average income while reducing income differences (Robison, Seles, & Jin, 2011).

In the context of the Habitat for Humanity homeownership program, there are multiple opportunities for establishing and strengthening relationships. These include connections that arise from the time someone applies for a Habitat for Humanity home to the time the mortgage is paid. With enhanced networks of relationships, there is increased access to a network of intangible resources. Social capital has several internal effects, which are the qualities that citizens gain from participation in local and neighborhoods affairs, such as civic-mindedness, cooperation, and public-spiritedness (Putnam, 1995, 2000).

Habitat for Humanity's unique structure has the potential for creating and strengthening social capital for volunteers, program participants, and the community-at-large (Hays, 2002). The formation of social capital through this organization can be especially beneficial to socioeconomically disadvantaged or marginalized individuals trying to gain access to resources that go beyond housing. For instance, Robinson and Martin (2010) looked at the impact of information technology on bonding and bridging social capital. They found that internet use decreased bonding social capital as people were interacting less with family and other traditional groups. When comparing non-internet users to internet users, there was an increase in interactions. which would promote bridging social capital between groups.

Homeownership is one factor that impacts social capital and is particularly associated with bonding social capital (Brisson & Usher, 2007). Home-ownership creates stability and an increased connection to the communities where the homeowners live (Wang & Graddy, 2008). Regardless of where a person lives, higher lengths of residency are associated with higher levels of social capital (Wang & Graddy, 2008; Whitley, 2013; Hopkins & Williamson, 2012). Older neighborhoods tend to have higher levels of social capital than newer developments, as measured by political participation, because older neighborhoods have had more time to develop dense social networks (Hopkins & Williamson, 2012). This association helps to explain how urban sprawl's longer commute times may be contributing to the decline of social capital in the United States (Putnam, 2000). High commute times are significantly associated with a lack of socially oriented trips. This suggests individuals with longer commutes have less access to social capital because the commute time hinders social capital building activities (Besser, Marcus, & Frumkin, 2008). As people commute, their ties to their neighborhood are weakened.

One potential problem shared by both long-standing rural communities and older more established urban neighborhoods is that the inherent, dense, and pre-existing social networks can make it more challenging for a newcomer to integrate into the community and develop individual-based social capital. This would be especially true if the community is close-knit and homogeneous and the newcomer has a different cultural background than most in the community. This problem is likely to be more pronounced in rural communities than urban communities, due to lower numbers of potential connections and decreased ability to look outside of the immediate community for support (Whitley, 2013).

Rohe, Quercia, and Van Zandt (2007), Rohe, Van Zandt, and McCarthy (2001), Rohe and Stewart (1996), and Baum and Kingston (1984) analyze the impact of homeownership on participating in voluntary associations and local and political affairs. The evidence suggests that homeowners tend to maintain and protect-their economic investment and commit to protect, improve, and influence the overall conditions of their neighborhood and community. According to Varady, Walker, and Wang (2001) and Rohe and Stegman (1994), homeowners expressed greater residential satisfaction than those renting and living in apartments. These sentiments of satisfaction among residents come from the personal attitudes of the residents themselves, the characteristics of their own dwelling units, and the physical, geographic, and socioeconomic status of the area.

Homeowners who reside in their homes for a longer period of time develop a sense of pride in ownership and a greater social attachment to their community, and thus, become more involved in community groups and voluntary associations (Rohe, Quercia, & Van Zandt; Baum & Kingston, 1984; Rohe, Van Zandt, & McCarthy, 2001). While the literature addresses the reasons why social capital has declined, including the issue of trust, little has been done at the individual level to examine how civic and voluntary organizations are helping to contribute to social capital development within communities and neighborhoods.

The literature references the relationship between social capital and community development on a macro level institutional analysis. Temkin and Rohe (1998) define and operationalize social capital in terms of sociocultural milieu, which is the social fabric and structure of the community and the identities, interactions, and linkages that manifest themselves from the social structure. The institutional infrastructure that measures the quality of formal organizations in a neighborhood is based on the presence of neighborhood organizations and the ability of these organizations to act on behalf of residents (Temkin and Rohe, 1998). Except for Hays (2002), who studied nine cities and their Habitat for Humanity affiliates, not much research has examined how nonprofit and community development organizations enhance social capital. There are gaps in the operationalization of social capital at the macro level vis-à-vis a more disaggregated focus, such as the extent or the lack of empirical study on bonding, bridging, and linking social capital.

HABITAT FOR HUMANITY INTERNATIONAL

Habitat for Humanity International (HFHI) is a nonprofit Christian housing ministry founded in 1976 by Alabama businessman Millard Fuller, who believed that every person deserves a decent, safe, and affordable place to live (HFHI, 2020a). Since its founding, Habitat has become one of the most recognized nonprofit housing organizations in the United States dedicated to addressing issues of poverty and housing, working in over 3,000 communities around all 50 U.S. states and 70 countries to qualifying families (HFHI, 2020a, 2020b). Over one million homes impacting over 29 million people have been constructed worldwide through the Habitat for Humanity program (HFHI, 2020b). This number is relatively small given the overall housing need, but a very impressive accomplishment for an organization made up of volunteers (Hays, 2002).

HFHI (2007) acknowledges that homeownership is more than just shelter for families. When people become homeowners, "families can provide stability for their children; a family's sense of dignity and pride grow; health, physical safety, and security improve; and educational and job prospects increase" (HFHI, 2007).

As one of the nation's largest nonprofit housing developers, Habitat for Humanity International is a minor part of the overall housing sector, but its impact on low-income residential housing has been considerable (Smith, 2013). Habitat for Humanity offers opportunities to families who otherwise could not afford homeownership. In most cases, prospective Habitat homeowner families make a $500 down payment and contribute 300 to 500 hours of "sweat equity" on the construction of their home or someone else's home (HFHI, 2020c; Rohe & Watson, 2007).

Habitat for Humanity International (HFHI) initially refused to accept federal funding, but in 1986, that policy against receiving federal funds was revised so federal funds could be accepted to purchase land, and cover infrastructure and administrative costs (Smith, 2013). Restricting acceptance of federal and state money was purposeful as HFHI feared reliance on federal funding would compromise the Christian mission (Hays, 2002; Smith, 2013). However, HFHI has become increasingly reliant on federal funding since 1996 when it started receiving federal Self-Help Homeownership Opportunity Program Grants (Smith, 2013).

Habitat affiliates are "community-level Habitat for Humanity offices that service a specific area in partnership with and on behalf of Habitat for Humanity International" (HFHI, 2020d). Each affiliate coordinates all aspects of builds on a local level. In 1986, Habitat's U.S. affiliates began receiving funds in the form of Community Development Block Grant (CDBG) funds (Smith, 2013). All affiliates are encouraged to be self-supporting, but HFHI will solicit contributions on behalf of affiliates and distribute federal funds on a competitive basis.

In return, all affiliates are expected to tithe 10 percent of unrestricted cash contributions to support international operations (Smith, 2013). Currently, there are more than 1,400 affiliates in the United States and about 70 national organizations around the world coordinating Habitat efforts to address low-income housing needs (HFHI, 2020a, 2020d).

One potential benefit of Habitat for Humanity programs examined by Hays (2002), is the creation and strengthening of social capital for volunteers, program participants, and the community-at-large. According to Hays (2002), Habitat can "support the development of social capital by anchoring an individual's sense of obligation to others" (p. 250). The formation of social capital can be especially beneficial to socioeconomically disadvantaged or marginalized individuals trying to gain access to resources that go beyond housing. Hays (2002) looked at the following four goals, which, if achieved, would result in positive social capital for a community:

- Mobilizing resources that would not otherwise be mobilized to address community problems, including the redistribution of significant amounts of resources to address inequality and achieve outcomes a market system does not
- Raising awareness about community issues which would otherwise go unnoticed
- Creating linkages which would not normally exist between disparate social groups
- Empowering social groups that normally have little influence

Hays (2002) examined Habitat for Humanity affiliates in cities with a population of 100,000 or more to best understand how Habitat functions in complex urban environments. Hays (2002) found Habitat's ability to mobilize volunteers makes it an engine for social capital formation. Habitat for Humanity builds social capital because it promotes social interaction within and between socioeconomic groups by increasing cross-socioeconomic interaction (Hays, 2002). Habitat involvement also promotes awareness of community need and creates one-on-one linkages between the volunteers and the families served, which otherwise would not have existed. Hays (2002) found that Habitat involvement empowered the middle-income volunteers but did little to empower low-income communities to deal collectively with housing problems. Thus, middle-income volunteers benefited more from the social capital created through this objective (Hays, 2002).

RESEARCH QUESTION AND METHODS

Because Habitat for Humanity focuses on participation and sustainable community engagement in all its activities, programs like Habitat for Humanity allow for an exploration of social capital dimensions and outcomes. Because of the availability and existence of longitudinal data in Habitat's homeownership program, this study provides an opportunity to empirically investigate the three dimensions of social capital (bonding, bridging, and linking) highlighted in the literature. We explore how social capital may change in association with general Habitat for Humanity builds and subsequent Habitat homeownership.

Do housing programs like Habitat for Humanity build social capital and if so, what kinds of social capital (bonding, bridging, and linking)? A major goal of this study is to examine the role of linking social capital (that is, formal ties linking members to voluntary organizations and associations) through an analysis of the Habitat for Humanity Women Build program.

An interdisciplinary team of researchers in the fields of sociology, social work, political science and public administration, and economics at the University of Southern Indiana, using input from staff of Habitat for Humanity International and their underwriters from the Whirlpool Corporation, created a self-administered, self-reporting, mail-back survey. The survey consisted of open- and close-ended questions about Habitat homeowners' perceptions of their homeownership experiences. The Habitat homeowner survey was subject to the Institutional Review Board (IRB) for the Protection of Human Subjects of Research at the University of Southern Indiana to receive approval before distribution. This process ensures that all research involving human subjects meets regulations established by the United States Code of Federal Regulations.

Habitat for Humanity affiliates across the United States provided the names and addresses of 1,801 Habitat homeowners from the past five years. Surveys were mailed with an introduction letter and a self-return paid postage envelope. Four weeks later, reminder postcards were mailed to non-responders to remind them to complete the survey and notify them another survey would be mailed soon. One week later, a second survey was mailed to non-responders. Of the original 1,801 mailed surveys, there were 1,728 usable addresses.

Most unusable addresses were returned as undeliverable for different reasons, such as moved, no forwarding address, and addressee not at that address.

Three hundred and twenty-three usable surveys were returned, resulting in an 18.69 percent response rate. This low response rate raises issues about the reliability and validity of using the sample responses to make statements about the population of homeowners with Habitat homes built over a five-year period.

A recent report on the future of survey research highlights the significance of these issues (Krosnick, Presser, Fealings, & Ruggels, 2012). According to the report, there has been a consistent and significant decline in response rates to surveys over the past 25 years. However, the report by Krosnick et al. (2012) also finds that survey results have maintained a remarkable level of reliability despite declining response rates, due in part through efforts to minimize nonresponse bias through improvements in survey design.

Keeter, Miller, Kohut, Groves, and Presser (2000) and Keeter, Kennedy, Dimock, Best, and Craighill (2006) cite studies that compare surveys with low and high response rates and show there is little difference in the validity and accuracy of those surveys with lower response rates (cited in Tighe, 2012). This also applies to affordable housing and housing assistance studies. Tighe (2012) conducted a telephone survey of attitudes of affordable housing with a 15 percent overall response rate from a sample representative of the overall voting population and a population affected by affordable housing and points out that "measurements of attitudes regarding affordable housing, poverty, and race are not likely to be severely affected by a low response rate" (Tighe, 2012, p. 971).

An examination of the geographic distribution of the population of interest indicates that ten states account for more than 70 percent of homeowners with Habitat homes built in the last five years. A comparison of the geographic distribution of the survey respondents with the population of interest shows that the sample is representative of the population regarding geographic distribution. Notwithstanding the problems associated with response and nonresponse bias, the representativeness of the sample at the zip code level serves to increase our confidence in the reliability of the sample responses to make statements about the population of interest. Based on the response rate, a 5 percent margin of error provides us with a 95 percent probability that statements about the population based on the sample responses are reliable.

A comparison of the socio-demographic and economic characteristics of residents and survey respondents, for the zip codes associated with the respondents, highlights some distinct differences. In particular, the average age of the survey respondents tended to be greater than the average age of all residents in the corresponding zip codes. The respondents were proportionately more female than the proportion of female residents in the corresponding zip codes, and the average income was lower for the respondents than for all residents in the corresponding zip codes. As a result, inferences from this study are limited to the population of interest, namely, homeowners whose homes were built through the Habitat for Humanity Women Build program.

Measures and Variables

The items in this study are grouped around scaled factors in several areas: neighborhood perception, behavioral and attitudinal perception before and after Habitat homeownership, community involvement, and social capital. Several items on the questionnaire, which sought to identify the respondents' perception about their neighborhood, were framed as yes/no questions. These items were combined to create a composite indicator of neighborhood perception.

Another set of questions asked respondents to report on various elements of their family life both before and after moving into their Habitat home. Eight questions were selected from the Family Inventory of Resources and Management on financial security, personal achievements, and socio-psychological issues, resulting in two scales: family state before Habitat homeownership and family state after Habitat homeownership (Draughon et al., 2012).

Questions centered on the respondent's community involvement, perceptions of their Habitat experience, and social capital were measured using a Likert Scale ranging from strongly disagree to strongly agree. Other items provide demographic information, such as age (measured in number of years), gender (male or female), ethnicity, marital status, and size of family (range from zero to nine children). The sample data was used to estimate several logistic regression models and to perform mean difference t-tests and chi-square statistical tests related to before and after homeownership perceptions and gender differences.

Data Analysis

In our sample, 86 percent are female and 14 percent are male. The number of children in the home ranged from zero to nine, with one being the most frequently reported. Adults in the home range from one to seven, with the most frequent number being two adults in the home, and the median age is almost 42 years.

Respondents answered several yes/no questions about various aspects of their neighborhood, including safety, activity, and utility issues. Combining these individual questions into one summative "neighborhood perception" scale provides a general view of the respondents' attitudes/feelings about their neighborhood. The combined score results in a scale range of zero (lowest perception level) to a high score of 11 (the most positive perception). Reliability assessment of the scale used Cronbach's Alpha resulting in an overall reliability score of .77, indicating the 11 items combine to form a single neighborhood assessment score. While a more specific and detailed analysis is gained from the analysis of each item separately, the analysis of the scaled factors provides an overall generalization of the results.

Table 3.1. Frequencies on Neighborhood Items

Survey Statement	YES N (%)	NO N (%)
I like living in my neighborhood.	279 (88.9%)	35 (11.1%)
I know my neighbors.	227 (89.6%)	32 (19.4%)
I feel safe in my neighborhood.	261 (84.7%)	47 (15.3%)
My neighborhood is clean.	251 (82.0%)	55 (18.0%)
My children can walk to school easily.	133 (51.2%)	127 (48.8%)
My children can walk to school safely.	141 (56.0%)	111 (44.0%)
My children can play safely in our neighborhood.	220 (82.1%)	48 (17.9%)
There are children recreation activities available near my home.	201 (66.3%)	102 (33.7%)
There are adult recreation activities available near my home.	168 (66.3%)	137 (44.9%)
I have choices for transportation in my neighborhood.	214 (69.0%)	96 (31.0%)
I am a member of a community group.	94 (29.8%)	221 (70.2%)

Source: Draughon, Hanka, Khayum, Opartny, Phillips, & Priest, 2012.

This study provides insights about networks of relationships arising from participation in the Habitat for Humanity homeownership program and the attitudinal, perceptual, and behavioral aspects of these networks of relationships. The first portion of the survey contains self-reported "yes" or "no" responses about the homeowner's neighborhood. When asked whether the respondent knew his or her neighbors (Q2), 89.6 percent responded "yes." However, when responding to the statement: "I am a member of a community group" (Q11), 70.2 percent responded negatively. These responses from the sample of homeowners suggest that bridging social capital was more evident than linking social capital in the Habitat for Humanity network effects.

Individual items were analyzed to gain an understanding of the number and percentage of responders' perceptions. Table 3.1 shows the number and percentage of responses to the yes/no self-report items regarding participants' neighborhoods. Most participants like their neighborhood (88.9 percent), know their neighbors (89.6 percent), feel safe (84.7 percent), and feel that the neighborhood is clean (82 percent). A little more than half of respondents feel their children can walk to school easily (51.2 percent) and safely (56 percent). Only 29.8 percent of respondents indicated that they were a member of a community group.

Survey questions also illustrate perceptual aspects of network effects related to homeowner status. From the statement in Question 12, "I seem to take more pride in my neighborhood now that I have a Habitat home," 93 percent strongly agree or agree. Responding to Question 14, "Habitat for humanity has helped me improve my job opportunities," 53.6 percent strongly agree or agree. Of the responses from Question 16, "I feel like I have more support now than before Habitat homeownership," 75.6 percent strongly agree or agree. The statement (Q20), "I have a greater sense of teamwork and community since becoming a homeowner," 85.8 percent strongly agree or agree. These responses indicate a strong connection between a sizable segment of respondents and a support network that transcends the Habitat for Humanity build experience.

Table 3.2. Aspects of Linking Social Capital by Gender

	Strongly Agree/ Agree		Strongly Disagree/ Disagree		
	Male N (%)	Female N (%)	Male N (%)	Female N (%)	Sig
I seem to take more pride in my neighborhood now that I have a Habitat home.	41 (97.6%)	232 (92.4%)	1 (2.4%)	19 (7.6%)	.217
Habitat for Humanity has helped me improve my job opportunities.	29 (74.4%)	121 (50.8%)	10 (25.6%)	117 (49.2%)	.006**
I feel like I have more support now than before Habitat homeownership.	37 (88.1%)	182 (73.4%)	5 (11.9%)	66 (26.6%)	.040*
I have a greater sense of teamwork and community since becoming a homeowner.	39 (90.7%)	212 (85.5%)	4 (9.3%)	36 (14.5%)	.359

* Significant at the .05 level.
** Significant at the .01 level.
Source: Draughon, Hanka, Khayum, Opartny, Phillips, & Priest, 2012.

Table 3.2 highlights responses by gender. From the statement, "I seem to take more pride in the neighborhood now that I am a Habitat homeowner," 97.6 percent of the males strongly agree or agree while the comparable percentage for females was 92.4 percent. From the statement "Habitat for Humanity has helped me improve my job opportunities," 74.4 percent of males strongly agree or agree while 50.8 percent of females strongly agree or agree. In relation to the statement "I feel like I have more support now than before Habitat homeownership," 88.1 percent of males compared to 73.4 percent of females strongly agree or agree. In relation to the statement: "I have a greater sense of teamwork and community since becoming a homeowner," 90.7 percent of males strongly agree or agree while 85.5 percent of females strongly agree or agree. A chi-square test indicates that there is a relatively small probability that the gender differences in response to the latter two items were due to chance. Perceptual aspects of social capital related to economic and support networks appear to be stronger for males compared to females in the survey sample. Males responded more positively to these items:

1. Habitat for Humanity has helped me improve my job opportunities.
2. Adults in my home are furthering their education now that we have a new home.
3. I feel like I have more support now than before Habitat homeownership.
4. I feel better about myself since I became a Habitat Homeowner.
5. My family's overall health has improved since moving into our Habitat home.

The results in Table 3.3 reflect responses about behavior and perceptions before and after Habitat homeownership. Potential family support appears to be stronger based on responses to the statement, "If a close relative was having financial problems, we could afford to help them out." The ability to help a close relative fairly well or very well increased significantly from a combined 18.3 percent to a combined 39.6 percent.

Table 3.3. **Aspects of Bonding and Bridging Social Capital**

	Before Habitat Home Ownership Number (%) Self-Reported		Today Number (%) Self-Reported	
	Fairly Well N (%)	*Very Well* N (%)	*Fairly Well* N (%)	*Very Well* N (%)
If a close relative were having financial problems, we could afford to help them out.	34 (10.9%)	23 (7.4%)	86 (27.7%)	37 (11.9%)
I was involved in neighborhood activities.	47 (15.2%)	51 (16.5%)	66 (21.5%)	75 (24.4%)

Source: Draughon, Hanka, Khayum, Opartny, Phillips, & Priest, 2012.

Before becoming a Habitat homeowner, 44 percent of the respondents were not at all involved in neighborhood activities, and approximately 24 percent were slightly involved, while 32 percent were involved fairly well and very well. When asked whether they are involved in neighborhood activities *today*, those responding fairly well and very well increased by approximately 14 percentage points. The survey data show that owning a Habitat home today resulted in a statistically significant difference in homeowners taking greater ownership in their neighborhood and its activities. Further exploration of factors that increase the likelihood of an increase in involvement in neighborhood activities indicate membership in a community organization, respondents knowing their neighbors, and the extent to which respondents stated they could not have owned their own homes without help from Habitat for Humanity, are statistically significant influences on this form of network relationships based on the logistic regression analysis.

Table 3.4 provides average scores of respondents regarding behavioral, perceptual, and attitudinal statements before and after Habitat homeownership. For each of the items, a paired comparison dependent t-test was performed. The results indicate that the difference in average scores is not explainable by stable characteristics of individuals in the study. In other words, the before and after differences were not produced by changes in characteristics such as race and gender.

Table 3.4.   Score Comparison Before and After Habitat Homeownership

	Before Habitat Homeownership Average Score	After Habitat Homeownership Average Score
Sometimes we feel we did not have enough control over the direction our lives were taking.	1.65	2.15*
Our family was under a lot of emotional stress.	1.35	2.23*
Many times, we felt we had little influence over the things that happened to us.	1.64	2.11*
If a close relative were having financial problems, we could afford to help them out.	0.75	1.31*
We were worried about how we would cover a large unexpected bill ($100 or more).	1.21	1.92*
In our family we felt it was important to save for the future.	2.15	2.52*
When we made plans, we were almost certain we could make them work.	1.84	2.27*
The members of our family respected one another.	2.46	2.60*
I was involved in neighborhood activities.	1.04	1.38*

(continued)

Table 3.4. *(continued)*

	Before Habitat Homeownership Average Score	After Habitat Homeownership Average Score
The children in my home made educational achievements.	2.16	2.46*
The adults in my home made educational achievements.	1.63	1.78*
The adults in my home made work-related achievements.	2.02	2.16*
I had attained personal financial security.	1.08	1.69*
I was able to focus on energy efficiency or being "green."	1.17	2.06*

All Items - higher scores indicate improvement.
*Difference between average scores significant at the .01 level.
Source: Draughon, Hanka, Khayum, Opartny, Phillips, & Priest, 2012.

CONCLUSION

Making and keeping connections are the foundations of social capital. Building a Habitat for Humanity home and participating in a Habitat build enhances relationships. Moreover, living in a Habitat for Humanity home represents a momentous transformation in the lives of homeowners. Habitat for Humanity builds homes and, therefore, provides tremendous opportunities for changing social capital and making a difference in people's lives.

Although the findings indicate an increase in satisfaction among new Habitat homeowners, these findings also suggest that there has been limited impact on a sizable segment of individual homeowners forming greater and stronger bonds and ties with the community and neighborhood, particularly in community and neighborhood organizations. As a result, bonding and bridging social capital were enhanced, but linking social capital was not as evident among homeowners whose Habitat for Humanity home was built in the last five years. The results show significantly high percentages of pride and ownership, among residents, in being new Habitat homeowners but do not translate into higher levels of involvement in their community or neighborhood.

Our findings suggest there are opportunities for Habitat for Humanity International and its affiliates to enhance civic participation among the new Habitat homeowners, an important component of increasing bridging, bonding, and linking social capital. We recommend that Habitat for Humanity promote and empower greater engagement and involvement in the community by residents. Habitat and its affiliate organizations may also consider providing additional services, such as civic engagement and leadership training and development programs to neighborhood residents, rather than simply hand over the keys to the new homeowners after the home is finished and dedicated.

One limitation of the study is the relatively low response rate to the survey, which brings the implications of response bias and nonresponse bias problems to the forefront. A comparison of the geographic distribution of the survey respondents with the population of interest shows that the sample is representative of the population at the zip code level.

Despite having a low response rate, we believe the data used for the study provides a unique perspective that does not exist in other data sets and believe that this will provide a basis for future analysis. Further recommendations may include a multi-mode survey (online and mail) or simply an online format that includes a larger sample size of addresses of Habitat build participants, and an expansion of the analysis to incorporate other owner-occupied homeowners in exploring the relationship between homeownership and social capital.

Chapter Four

Social Capital and Economic Development

A Neighborhood Perspective

Matthew J. Hanka and Trent Engbers

There is a growing consensus that social capital has an economic payoff for both individuals (Erickson, 2001; Knack & Keefer, 1997; Kim & Aldrich, 2005) and communities (Engbers, Rubin, & Aubuchon, 2016; Kawachi, Kennedy, Lochner, & Prothrow-Stith, 1997; Oh, Lee, & Bush, 2014; Safford, 2009) that invest in it. In some instances, social capital may be the determining factor in whether a community recovers from economic decline (Safford, 2009).

Over the past thirty years, there has been an evolving body of literature on social capital and economic development that demonstrates how strong social networks foster entrepreneurial activity (Kim & Aldrich, 2005), improve job prospects (Erickson, 2001), and support the development of human capital (Croninger & Lee, 2001). There have also been significant developments in the understanding of the effects of social capital on the outcome that matters most for many people: household income. However, this body of literature on social capital's income enhancing effects has been constrained by concerns about aggregation and the use of methodology with limited ability to demonstrate causation.

This chapter looks at the relationship between economic resilience and social capital at the micro-level. This chapter builds upon past research by looking at individuals' stocks of social capital and its effects on household incomes. Individuals are studied in the context of their neighborhood to control for macro-economic effects and to see the relative impact of neighborhood versus extra-neighborhood social capital.

Chapters 2 and 3 examined various definitions of social capital and its different types. Bridging social capital refers to the concept through which individuals are linked to others that fall outside their primary social circle. These relationships need not be substantive and are judged by their quantity and not their quality. Their primary advantage is providing access to non-redundant information. In terms of their economic effect, bridging social capital provides access to customers, producers, and suppliers necessary for economic growth (Kim & Aldrich, 2005). For example, Safford's (2009) comparative case analysis of rust belt cities find that bridging social capital explains Allentown, Pennsylvania's recovery during an economic decline. In contrast with Youngstown, Ohio, where social capital was concentrated among the economic elite, Allentown's bridging social capital cut across ethnic, religious, and economic groups. These crosscutting ties were enough to rebuild the economy in Allentown.

Bonding social capital differs from bridging in that its quality is based on intensity. Bonding relationships are high in trust and usually found within homogenous communities or in relationships based in shared history or experience such as familial or long-term friendship and work relationships (Coleman, 1988; Collins, Neal, & Neal, 2014; Putnam, 2001). The literature on bonding social capital has also emphasized the importance of community-based groups (Schnurbein, 2014). Nonprofits and other collective identity or service groups provide a place where individuals generate trust and form strong social ties. In recent years, these types of groups have also come to serve an important role in fostering economic development (Borzaga & De-fourney 2001; Stadtler & Probst, 2012).

ECONOMIC DEVELOPMENT

Economic development refers to the intentional process of increasing the trajectory of a community's economic growth curve (EDA, 2014). A community's economic development has been linked to a wide range of characteristics that include the community's institutions, geography, economic conditions, and social characteristics (Rodrik, Subramanian, & Trebbi, 2004). Community characteristics, such as a sound rule of law, clear state authority, and a government with enough capacity to provide services and enforce contracts, are critical for economic development (Rodrik et al., 2004). The economic development benefits derived from certain communities are based on that community's inherent geographic characteristics. Consider how climate, access to natural and other resources, transportation costs, and proximity to knowledge centers shift a community's economic potential. Likewise, economic trajectories are determined by the degree of market integration with a community, its macroeconomic conditions, the occupational and industrial mix of a community, and access to capital (Rodrik, Subramanian, & Trebbi, 2004). Lastly, economic development is determined by social conditions.

Among these, human capital has received the most attention in the literature (Benhabib & Spiegel, 1994; Machlup, 2014). However, entrepreneurial and business culture (Harrison & Huttington, 2000) and social capital (Engbers, Rubin, & Aubuchon, 2016) also have been shown to be important.

The effects of economic development are numerous and affect both social and economic conditions. Among economic factors, economic development is tied to job creation, GDP growth, trade, and increases in personal and household income. This study focuses on one aspect of economic development, which is the fostering of household income growth.

DETERMINANTS OF PERSONAL INCOME GROWTH

Like the process of economic development, personal and household income outcomes are associated with a wide range of determinants. These include both individual and social outcomes. Human capital accumulated through schooling and level of work experience is the biggest predictor of increases in income (Heckman, Stixrud, & Urzua, 2006). However, other factors such as personal health (Deaton, 2003), participation in illegal activities (Heckman et al., 2006), conducive family situations (Ellwood & Jencks, 2004), and access to transportation are also significant determinants (Hayaloğlu, 2015).

These individual factors are moderated by the social and economic conditions in which the household resides. In their studies of U.S. counties, Rupasingha, Goetz, and Freshwater (2002) find that in addition to the economic characteristics of the individuals, household income is also affected by social characteristics such as higher levels of ethnic diversity, lower levels of income inequality, and higher levels of social capital; the latter is particularly important for this study.

Culture

Culture, understood as "shared social practices and the values and beliefs that legitimate them" (Coyle, 1993, p. 20), has been found to be an important foundation for social capital (Platteau, 2000; Fukuyama, 2001) and subsequent economic development. For example, early work by Weber (1905), expounded on by Landes (1998), attributes the culture derived from the Protestant belief-system, such as hard work, thriftiness, and "honesty in business" (Trigilia, 2001, p. 429), as particularly important determinants of economic growth and development in Northern Europe and the United States. These particular cultural traits, coupled with the Protestant ethic's application of universal human rights to all individuals (Maridal, 2013), lead to a much broader understanding of the social circle and facilitated the establishment of social networks that have been instrumental in influencing economic growth and development of an area (Trigilia, 2001).

A well-cited example that builds on Weber's (1905) thesis of how cultural attitudes and behavior shape economic conditions is found in Banfield's (1958) analysis of social and economic life in the small village of Chiaromonte in Southern Italy. Banfield observed that the villagers tended to maximize the interests of their immediate family, over the interests of the citizenry, to such an extent that it led to isolation, nepotism, and widespread corruption. Banfield (1958) coined this lack of bridging social capital "amoral familism" and concluded that it prevented the village from addressing limitations on economic development such as extreme poverty, illiteracy, and basic infrastructure (see also Woolcock, 1998).

Using data from the World Values Survey (WVS), Marini (2004), and Maridal (2013) further developed and quantified Weber (1905) and Banfield's (1958) work by showing that certain cultural characteristics, which stimulate achievement-motivation (see also McClelland, 1961) and develop social capital, are necessary for economic growth and development. Achievement motivation is particularly important in the production stage, while social capital is necessary in the exchange stage and serves to enlarge economic markets.

Social Capital and its Economic Effect

While some of the earliest influential work on social capital has had an economic focus (Putnam, Leonardi, & Nanetti, 1993), more recent studies have made strides in using econometric analysis to demonstrate quantifiable effects of social capital on economic outcomes (Engbers, Rubin, & Aubuchon, 2016; Oh et al., 2014).

From a theoretical standpoint, there are multiple reasons to suspect an effect of social capital on economic development. These have been clearly articulated by Woolcock (1998). Woolcock suggests social capital affects job and income creation in four ways, which fit within a two-by-two matrix along the dimensions of embeddedness/autonomy and micro/macro scales. Micro social capital includes integration and intracommunity ties (embeddedness) or the linkage between extra-community networks (autonomy). In contrast, macro social capital features the synergy of state-society relations (embeddedness) or the organizational integrity of institutional capacity (autonomy). Macro embeddedness helps fosters ties that help groups overcome parochial interests necessary for long-term development such as when procedural requirements like citizen commissions encourage good governance while mobilizing community actors around shared interests. Macro autonomy is concerned with the use of traditional hierarchy for increased performance. Formal organization reduces collective action problems and facilitates the achievement of more socially optimal outcomes. Thus, communities with effective administrative systems are better able to deliver public services and foster trust in government.

At the micro level, embeddedness leads to access to the necessary economic resources that individuals need for economic advancement. For instance, families, religious and ethnic groups, or other tight-knit communities provide access to capital necessary for economic activity. Lastly, micro autonomy encourages economic actors to reach out beyond their primary community's interests to build linkages with outside groups. This reduces the likelihood that economic resources are drained by the community of origin (Woolcock, 1998). Empirically, these conclusions are demonstrated in a wide range of contexts. The following sections will begin by examining individuals within a context to better understand how social capital affects economic development outcomes, followed by a section on international and regional effects.

Individuals and Context

There is increasing evidence of an empirical relationship between social capital and economic development (Engbers, Rubin, & Aubuchon, 2017; Helliwell & Putnam, 1995; Rupasingha et al., 2002; Oh et al., 2014; Woodhouse, 2006). However, the research presented above is limited in a few ways. First, the international and regional studies usually do not acknowledge that social capital exists in a context. Consequently, to get a fuller understanding of social capital's effects on household income, it is useful to study individuals within a meaningful context. Studies of nations or metropolitan areas may underrepresent effects if the effect size is masked by the unit of analysis. Studies such as the one presented here allow analysis of specific types of social capital relationships. Conversely, the qualitative studies presented above highlight the importance of context in the economic effects of social capital, but rarely use a methodology appropriate for demonstrating clear association. This study attempts to rectify these shortcomings by applying quantitative techniques at the neighborhood level to better understand the effects of social capital on household income.

International and Regional Studies

One of the earliest studies to establish a link between social capital and economic development comes from the work of Putnam et al. (1993). In their qualitative analysis of Italian regions, they argue that Northern Italy has surpassed the South because of its unique stock of social capital. Unlike the South, where there is an established history of criminal and governmental corruption, Northern Italy exhibits a high degree of grassroots accountability. A tradition of involvement in civil society organizations and healthy governance in the North led to economic and political systems that overcame a history of authoritarianism to lead to more rapid economic growth (Putnam et al., 1993).

The findings from Putnam et al. (1993) have since been supported by statistical analysis. One early econometric approach found that trust and civic cooperation was a major predictor of economic performance and that these social capital effects were particularly prominent in countries with effective government, legal, and political systems. Interestingly, the same study found no economic effect associated with membership in civic organizations (Knack & Keefer, 1997). These results are at odds with those found using a similar survey methodology (Dakhli & De Clercq, 2004). This study suggests positive effects of trust and associational membership, but not civic behavior on cross-national innovation. This is further supported by a study that examined international development between 1970 and 1992 in 34 countries and found that social capital as measured by levels of trust has a significant impact on endogenous growth (Whiteley, 2000).

In addition to Safford's regional U.S. comparative study of bridging social capital, as discussed earlier, a regional study of two Australian towns facing similar economic challenges finds important economic effects (Woodhouse, 2006). Using a mix of qualitative and quantitative techniques and considering a wide range of social capital measures, such as informal associations (generalized reciprocity and bonding social capital), bridging social capital, family and work social capital, community engagement, and thin trust, this study finds that the greatest impact on economic development comes from bonding social capital, which results in both higher employment rates and a larger proportion of high income households (Woodhouse, 2006).

The quantitative research is equally inconclusive about the type of social capital that affects economic development. One of the first large-scale quantitative studies of social capital and economic outcomes found that bonding social capital as measured by the number of civic institutions per 10,000 individuals was statistically and substantively related to growth in per capita income (Rupasingha et al., 2002). Conversely, a recent study of social capital in the 50 largest municipalities in America suggests that bonding social capital has no effect on per capita income at the metropolitan level. However, they do find that social capital has an effect second only to education in predicting job creation. This is most prominent for their measures of bridging social capital (Engbers, Rubin, & Aubuchon, 2017). This suggests that the loose networks associated with bridging social capital foster community-level economic development by reducing the costs of transactions and by increasing the multiplier effects associated with economic development (Engbers & Rubin, 2016).

The value of bridging social capital for municipal economic development is further supported by evidence that shows that the number of nonprofits, rather than the volume of volunteering, matters. In other words, volunteering intensively for one organization (a measure of bonding social capital) has no statistical effect on a community's per capita income or job creation. However, the presence of nonprofits as a gathering place for crosscutting interaction creates positive economic effects (Engbers, Rubin, & Aubuchon, 2017). Likewise, Oh et al. (2014) show that social capital, in the form of intra-local and inter-local economic development partnerships, results in more joint ventures and public/private partnerships and economic development.

Individual

Like social capital studies at other units of aggregation, the earliest work on individuals was qualitative in nature. This study found that being a member of a tight knit community, such as that found when one lives in an ethnic enclave, leads to access to economic and other entrepreneurial resources. Consequently, bonding social capital provides access to resources that might be unavailable through traditional financial systems (Light, Kwoun, & Zhong, 1990). Likewise, a qualitative study of job success found that individuals, with high levels of social networks, can find better jobs and are of more appreciable value to their employers (Erickson, 2001).

Current quantitative research focuses on the benefits of bridging social capital that accrue to individuals. Much of this research focuses on the benefits of social capital to entrepreneurial activity, including the fact that those with larger social networks are much more likely to engage in entrepreneurial activity (Kim & Aldrich, 2005) and the size of an entrepreneur's social network is influential in their financial success (Baron & Markman, 2003). These effects are both direct through the skills associated with social capital (e.g., emotional intelligence, effective communication ability), and indirect through the social network and the benefits it provides in terms of access to resources and customers.

METHODS

This study attempts to learn more about how neighborhood and individual characteristics influence economic development and social capital. Past research examines only social capital at the city level or higher, but little is known at the neighborhood level. Methodologically, this study replicates Safford's (2009) findings using an alternative methodology. Unlike Safford's (2009) study, which effectively utilizes case studies and social network analysis, the methodology of this paper uses survey analysis of three Evansville neighborhoods with different socioeconomic status and policy interventions, in order to better understand how social capital can serve as a tool for economic development and to explain why some communities lag in jobs and growth. This study examines the effect of social capital across neighborhoods in Evansville and shows how differences are explained by the characteristics of the neighborhood and individuals. This study shows the relationship of social capital in multiple forms (e.g., bonding social capital, trust, neighborhood involvement) across neighborhoods in its association with household income.

It is not the intent of the authors to suggest that this method is superior to past qualitative studies but rather to triangulate past qualitative studies with quantitative data, thus presenting an alternative methodological approach (one that mixes quantitative data with analysis of micro regions) that enriches our understanding of the relationship between social capital and economic development.

STUDY CONTEXT

Evansville, Indiana, is a city located on the banks of the Ohio River in the southern part of the state of Indiana. Evansville is the third largest city in Indiana—an industrialized city that has experienced population decline and job loss throughout the past 20 years. The 2010 Census population for Evansville is 117,429. Evansville's population is 80.9 percent White, 12.6 percent African American, 2.6 percent Hispanic, and 1 percent Asian, according to the 2010 U.S. Census (U.S. Census, 2016). In the same census, 87.2 percent of the population age 25 or older in Evansville has a high school diploma or higher, while 18.5 percent of the population 25 years or older has a bachelor's degree or higher.

A study of a mid-size city like Evansville provides a number of benefits. A lot of studies have been published on larger cities, but much can be learned from medium size and smaller cities (Gilderbloom, Hanka, & Ambrosius, 2012; Hanka, Ambrosius, Gilderbloom, & Wresinski, 2015) that share similar neighborhood dynamics and have faced similar economic challenges.

The City of Evansville sample consists of residents within the boundaries of the Dexter, Glenwood, and Mount Auburn neighborhoods. These neighborhoods were chosen because of their diversity in terms of affluence, city investment, and policy intervention. The boundaries of the cities can be found in Figures 4.1, 4.2, and 4.3. There are 177 households in the Dexter neighborhood, 276 households in the Glenwood neighborhood, and 51 households in the Mount Auburn neighborhood.

Figure 4.1. Mount Auburn neighborhood. *Source:* Josh Calhoun, Evansville DMD

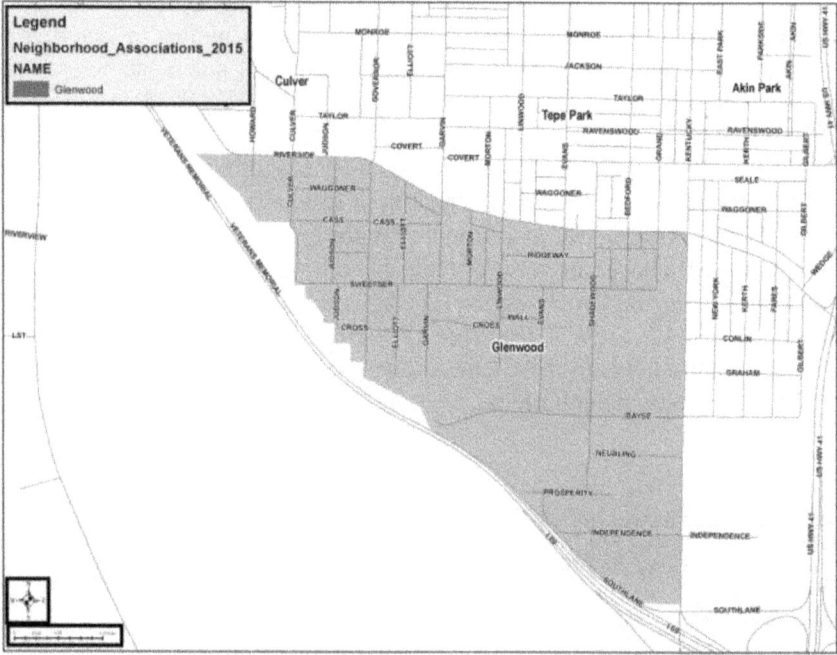

Figure 4.2. Glenwood neighborhood. *Source:* Josh Calhoun, Evansville DMD

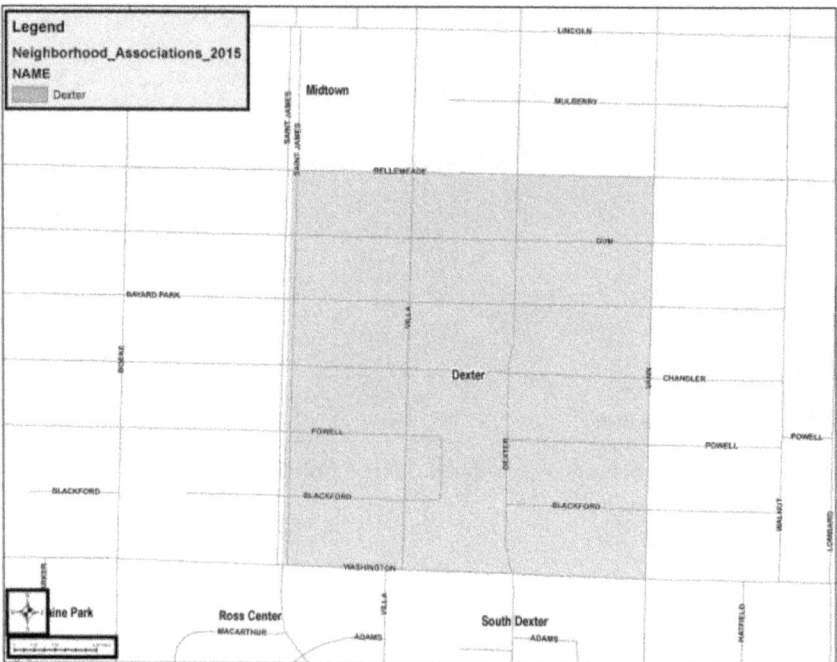

Figure 4.3. Dexter neighborhood. *Source:* Josh Calhoun, Evansville DMD

Data Collection

Safford's (2009) study of Allentown, PA, and Youngstown, OH, shows that some rust belt communities have fared better than others have. Using social network analysis, he finds that Youngstown failed to rebound from economic decline in the 1980s, because the social capital dynamics of the community limited access to resources and expertise necessary for recovery. Safford's study is relevant to this study in its understanding the economic effects of social capital at the neighborhood and individual level. For this study, data was collected through a 34-question survey instrument that looked at various social, economic, and demographic indicators. A combination of methods was utilized to increase the response rate. First, a trained graduate student employee from the Master of Public Administration (MPA) at the University of Southern Indiana, a high school intern interested in social research, and two faculty supervisors went door-to-door in the three neighborhoods (Dexter, Glenwood, and Mount Auburn) from Monday-Saturday in the spring and summer during various times of the day (in the morning between 10 a.m.–12 noon, early to mid-afternoon, and in the evening after 6:30 p.m.) and asked the head of household to complete the survey instrument. This step was designed to increase the number and quality of survey data, and it enabled the development of a definitive list of addresses for the second stage of the study.

During the second stage, residents who were unable to be contacted by door-to-door canvassing were sent a mail survey. As is best practice in survey research, to increase response rates, households were sent a postcard priming the respondent to compete the study. One week later, the survey was mailed with a self-addressed stamped envelope (Dillman, Smyth, & Christian, 2009).

The sample contained 504 usable addresses in the three neighborhoods (some houses were vacant). Completed surveys were received from 121 respondents from the three Evansville neighborhoods (57 in Dexter, 33 in Mount Auburn, and 31 in Glenwood). Thirty-seven percent of the completed surveys from Dexter, 36 percent of the completed surveys from Mount Auburn, and 24 percent of the completed surveys from Glenwood were completed going door-to-door. Sixty-three percent of the completed surveys from Dexter, 64 percent of the completed surveys from Mount Auburn, and 76 percent of the completed surveys from Glenwood were returned by mail.

Our survey response rate was 24 percent. Response rates differed by neighborhood with the most disadvantaged neighborhood, Glenwood, exhibiting an 11 percent response rate. The middle-income neighborhood, Mt Auburn, had a response rate of 65 percent, while the more affluent Dexter neighborhood had a response rate of 32 percent.

Variables

The unit of analysis is the individual, but the model includes neighborhood level variables to account for contextual effects on social capital. The study emphasizes the neighborhood level because past quantitative studies of the economic effects of social capital have been limited to higher levels of aggregated data. In addition to traditional individual-level control variables often used in neighborhood studies, such as homeownership, median income, hours worked, education level, and employment status, the study uses a variety of measurements common in the social capital literature that captures neighborhood level effects on social capital, such as frequency of socialization, a four question neighborhood involvement index, a four question neighborhood attachment index, and the number of neighbors known (Engbers, Thompson, & Slaper, 2017).

An additional advantage of this study is its control for macro-economic causes of income because all the participants are spatially concentrated within the same labor market. This study seeks to predict household income with bridging social capital variables, such as how many people do you know by first name, how many people do you know by face, number of different organizations respondent volunteered for in the past 12 months, and socialization (that reflect a wider range of connections) measured as an average of the following four items: had friends over to your home; been in the home of a friend of a different race or had them in your home; been in the home of someone of a different neighborhood; been in the home of someone you consider to be a community leader or had one in your home. Participation is another variable measured as an average of the seven kinds of participation from this survey: how many times the respondent worked on a community project; donated blood; attended any public meeting in which there was a discussion of local or school affairs; attended a political meeting or rally; attended any club or organizational meeting; gave $25 or more to charity; or volunteered.

Bonding social capital is measured as a ratio of hours volunteered per week divided by the number of organizations volunteer over the last 12 months. Generalized trust is measured using the standard General Social Survey measure of trust. Neighborhood attachment is measured as a mean based on a four-question index ranging from 0 (not answering the question at all) to 4 (answered positively on every attachment question). Neighborhood involvement is measured as a mean based on a four-question index ranging from 0 (not answering at all) to 3 (answered positively on every involvement question).

We include other social capital controls, such as the number of hours in a typical week one volunteers for an organization; population density measured in population per square mile within the neighborhood's boundaries, and a number of economic controls, such as average hours of week worked; college graduation rate measured in percent of the population with a college degree; median neighborhood income measured in thousands of dollars, and a dummy variable specifying male.

Method of Analysis

To better understand the effects of social capital on household income, a generalized logistic regression model using maximum likelihood estimation techniques was used to estimate the relationship between an ordinal dependent variable and a set of independent variables. For this logistic regression, the dependent variable is a four-point Likert measure of income: 1) less than \$25,000 per year; 2) \$25,000–\$50,000 per year; 3) \$50,001–\$75,000 per year, and 4) more than \$75,000 per year. While the model nests individuals within their neighborhood context, the limited number of neighborhoods leads one away for a hierarchical model. Rather, the model was run using robust standard errors clustered around each of the three neighborhoods. STATA was used to perform the regression using the following specification for the final analysis:[1]

$y_i{}^* = \beta1*$College grad $+ \beta2*$Frequency of socialization $+ \beta3*$ Different organizations volunteered in past 12 months $+ \beta4*$ Hours per work volunteered for organization $+ \beta5*$employment $+ \beta6*$Neighbors know by face $+ \beta7*$Currently enrolled in school $+ \beta8*$Neighborhood attachment $+ \beta9*$Trust $+ \beta10*$Male $+ \beta11*$Bonding social capital $+ \beta12*$Median neighborhood income $+\varepsilon_i$

Results

The results presented below highlight the important contextual differences in which social capital operates.

Descriptive Statistics

The neighborhood human and social capital descriptive statistics have been calculated in Table 4.1. Measures are drawn from either the 2010 Census or the survey instrument. This table includes variables not found in this model because of concerns about degrees of freedom. Dexter is the most affluent among the three neighborhoods, with a 2010 median household income of $46,521, compared to Evansville's 2010 median household income of $35,469 (U.S. Census, 2016). Only 2.4 percent of Dexter's population is below the poverty level of Evansville, compared to Glenwood. With a median household income at $30,161, 25 percent of Glenwood's population is below the poverty level. Mount Auburn's median income is $33,916, slightly lower than Evansville's median household income, but higher than Glenwood's, 14.8 percent of Mount Auburn residents live below the poverty level, which is higher than Dexter's, but lower than Glenwood's and Evansville's as a whole (20.5 percent) (U.S. Census, 2016).

Median housing value was the highest in the Dexter neighborhood at $137,064, while Glenwood's median housing value is $89,894, much lower than the median housing value for the City of Evansville ($107,876). Dexter's population of college graduates (39.6 percent) is twice as high as Mount Auburn's (18.3 percent), which is slightly higher than Glenwood (20.9 percent).

Table 4.1. Descriptive Statistics for Neighborhood Human and Social Capital

Variable	Dexter	Glenwood	Mount Auburn
College Grad Rate[s] (percent)	67.3	37.9	42.4
Socialization[s] (mean)	3.824	3.464	3.318
Hours Volunteered Per Week[s]	4.438	3.96	10.75
Neighborhood Attachment[s] (mean)	1.866	2.467	1.628
Median Income[c] ($US)	46,521	30,161	33,916
Population Density[c] (per square mile)	3785.71	1027.2	269.1
Homeownership[c] (percent)	96.4	74.1	93.9
Median Age[c] (years)	39.56	33.24	43.55
Percent Below Poverty Line[c]	2.4	25	14.8
Median Housing Value[c] ($US)	137,064	89,894	100,380
Percent Foreign Born[c]	1.8	4.1	0
Percent Non-white[c]	2.0	60	5
Neighborhood Involvement[s] (mean)	1.298	1.533	1.34
Participation[s] (mean)	2.68	2.326	2.438
Number of Memberships[s]	3.075	1.821	2.33

Note: s(survey), c (2010 Census data).
Source: Hanka & Engbers, 2017.

Table 4.2 below provides descriptive statistics for the interval variables, including socialization, hours volunteered per week, know respondent by face, neighborhood attachment, bonding social capital, and median income.

Table 4.2. Descriptive Statistics for Interval Variables

Variable	Mean	Stand. Dev.	Minimum	Maximum
Socialization	3.5911	1.57783	1	9
Hours Volunteered Per Week	5.48485	8.96144	0	60
Know by Face	19.5329	35.5206	0.1	300
Neighborhood Attachment	1.95592	0.7303	1	4.5
Bonding Social Capital	1.72698	2.70344	0	15
Median Income	38891.9	7358.52	30161	46521

Source: Hanka & Engbers, 2017.

Table 4.3 presents the results from the generalized logistic regression model predicting household income with the social capital variables but without any controls for human capital or neighborhood characteristics. Approximately 87 percent of the variation in household income is explained by the included variables in this model. All the predictors are significant for household income less than $25,000. Number of different organizations volunteered, trust and bonding social capital are negative, while socialization, hours volunteered per week, know person by face, and neighborhood attachment are positive. The magnitude of the coefficients for these variables is determinative, with bonding social capital, volunteering for different organizations, and trust having an odds ratio of near 0. The odds ratio for the other coefficients is so high that they have an overwhelming likelihood of falling into a higher income category. For household income between $25,000–$50,000, only socialization is significant at the .05 level and is in the negative direction. This translates into an odds ratio of 0.51 of falling into a higher income bracket. When predicting higher household income ($50,001–$75,000), socialization is negative and not significant. Number of different organizations volunteered is positive and significant at the .05 level, but trust is negative and significant at the .10 level. At this income category ($50,001–$75,000), there is a more moderate effect of the social capital variables with odds ratios ranging from .12 for trust to 1.69 for bonding social capital. However, these results should be considered with caution as the introduction of control variables influences these findings.

Table 4.3.   Generalized Logistic Regression Results for Household Income

Income Level	Variable	Unstandardized Coef.	Robust Standard Error	Z
<$25,000	Socialization	23.2784***	3.09847	7.51
	Different Organizations Volunteered	–885.91***	112.91	–7.85
	Hours Volunteered Per Week	1650.15***	210.129	7.85
	Know by Face	7.55943***	0.96654	7.82
	Neighborhood Attachment	177.887***	24.0353	7.4
	Trust	–364.49***	48.6205	–7.5
	Bonding Social Capital	–3332.6***	424.88	–7.84
	Constant	1388.75***	175.574	7.91
$25,000–$50,000	Socialization	–0.6737**	0.30436	–2.21
	Different Organizations Volunteered	2.39009	1.75003	1.37
	Hours Volunteered Per Week	–1.7933	1.56124	–1.15
	Know by Face	–0.128	0.10631	–1.2
	Neighborhood Attachment	–0.8958	1.34011	–0.67
	Trust	0.0125	1.9968	0.01
	Bonding Social Capital	5.32423	4.76976	1.12
	Constant	–0.2382	2.75112	–0.09
$50,001–75,000	Socialization	–0.3938	0.31594	–1.25
	Different Organizations Volunteered	0.46248**	0.21631	2.14
	Hours Volunteered Per Week	–0.1252***	0.04488	–2.79
	Know by Face	0.17075***	0.05057	3.38
	Neighborhood Attachment	–1.2053***	0.33189	–3.63
	Trust	–2.0904*	1.21606	–1.72
	Bonding Social Capital	0.52516***	0.16297	3.22
	Constant	0.44793	0.35771	1.25

*p<.1; **p<.05; ***p<.001
Pseudo R^2 = 0.8718
Source: Hanka & Engbers, 2017.

Our generalized logistic regression model in Table 4.4 includes the variables from Table 4.3, plus college attainment, employment status, school enrollment, a dummy variable specifying male, and median income of the respondent's neighborhood. The pseudo R^2 of this model is approximately 53 percent. For household income less than $25,000, number of individuals known by face is not significant, and college grad is significant at the .10 level.[2] All other variables are statistically significant, with odds ratios ranging from near zero for socialization, number of different organizations, employment status, neighborhood attachment and bonding social capital, to a largely determinative odds ratio for college graduation, hours volunteered, trust, male and enrollment in school. The odds ratio for neighborhood median income is 1.02.

Table 4.4. Generalized Logistic Regression Results for Household Income

Income Level	Variable	Unstandardized Coef.	Robust Standard Error	Z
<$25K	College Grad	33.45*	19.34	1.73
	Socialization	−37.04***	10.80	−3.43
	Different Organizations Volunteered	−22.84***	5.03	−4.54
	Hours Volunteered Per Week	32.30***	8.30	3.89
	Employment	−118.30***	35.06	−3.37
	Know by Face	0.07	0.08	0.92
	Enrolled in School	40.64**	20.16	2.02
	Neighborhood Attachment	−51.88***	17.17	−3.02
	Trust	269.05***	76.80	3.50
	Male	51.05***	13.27	3.85
	Bonding Social Capital	−61.38***	19.91	−3.08
	Median Income	0.02***	0.00	3.70
	Constant	−364.65***	126.01	−2.89
$25K–$50K	College Grad	−297.29***	13.41	−22.17
	Socialization	−59.78***	3.00	−19.94
	Different Organizations Volunteered	328.48***	16.94	19.39
	Hours Volunteered Per Week	−177.60***	9.44	−18.81
	Employment	−284.86***	13.63	−20.89
	Know by Face	−32.47***	1.53	−21.16
	Enrolled in School	−1327.22***	61.13	−21.71
	Neighborhood Attachment	301.55***	14.27	21.13
	Trust	−548.12***	25.10	−21.84
	Male	−191.12***	10.13	−18.87
	Bonding Social Capital	409.65***	22.92	17.87
	Median Income	−0.01***	0.00	−23.54
	Constant	3216.08***	142.79	22.52
$50K–75K	College Grad	0.07	0.38	0.18
	Socialization	0.71***	0.04	18.39
	Different Organizations Volunteered	2.18***	0.31	7.05
	Hours Volunteered Per Week	−0.78***	0.05	−15.64
	Employment	4.42***	0.11	38.97
	Know by Face	0.58***	0.13	4.36
	Enrolled in School	23.65***	2.70	8.76
	Neighborhood Attachment	−8.06***	1.29	−6.24
	Trust	0.14	0.22	0.64
	Male	7.04***	0.79	8.86
	Bonding Social Capital	5.38***	0.43	12.54
	Median Income	0.00***	0.00	6.69
	Constant	−89.77***	9.60	−9.36

*p<.1; ***p, <.001
Pseudo R^2= 0.5319
Source: Hanka & Engbers, 2017.

Consequently, men, students and college graduates are more likely to be in a higher income household than women, non-students, and non-college graduate respondents. Likewise, as one increases their hours volunteered and level of trust, their likelihood of being in the next higher income category increases dramatically.

For household income between $25,000–$50,000, all predictors are significant at the .001 level. The number of different organizations volunteered, neighborhood attachment and bonding social capital are positive predictors, while the other coefficients are negative. The odds ratios range from near zero for college graduation, socialization, number of hours volunteered, employment status, knowledge of neighbors by face, enrollment of school, trust and male to almost deterministic odds ratios for number of different organizations volunteered, level of trust and level of bonding social capital. Like the lower income category, being male and enrolled in school (though not a college graduate) increases the likelihood of being in a higher income category. Likewise, increasing levels of trust increases the likelihood of being in a higher income bracket. However, unlike those in the under $25,000 bracket, having a higher level of bonding social capital, and participating in a greater number of organizations, is associated with a dramatic increase in the likelihood of being in a higher income category.

For household income between $50,001–$75,000, being a college graduate and having a higher degree of trust are no longer significant. The odds ratio for neighborhood attachment and neighborhood income are near zero, but enrollment in school, being male, and having bonding social capital are quite high. The odds ratios for the other variables are much more moderate: socialization (2.03); number of different organizations volunteered (8.85); hours volunteered (.92); employment status (83.1); and knowledge of neighbor by face (1.79). This suggests men, those enrolled in school, and those with a high degree of bonding social capital are much more likely to be in a higher income category. For those individuals with incomes between $50,000 and $75,000, increasing socialization, the number of different organizations volunteered, the number of hours volunteered, and the number of neighbors known, have an increased likelihood of being in the highest income category. Additionally, those who are employed would also experience a greater likelihood of being in the next income category.

DISCUSSION AND LIMITATIONS

These results point to three contributions of this study: 1) a surprising finding about differences across income categories; 2) a nuanced understanding of the relative value of bridging and bonding social capital for economic development; and 3) the importance of neighborhood context in understanding the effect of social capital.

First, the generalized logistical model enables us to see that the impact of social capital is contingent upon the income category of interest. While being male or a student significantly increases the likelihood of being in a higher income for all economic strata, the social capital effects of the other variables of interest depend on the larger economic situation. For those individuals in the lowest income category (household incomes less than $25,000 a year), the range of social capital indicators is more limited than for higher income categories. Only level of trust and hours volunteered have a substantive effect. The average number of hours volunteered per week is statistically and substantively significant only for the lowest income category, suggesting either a bonding effect of social capital or a skill building effect of volunteering, where increased volunteering either signals marketable skills or workforce readiness.

These findings contrast to those in the $50,000–$75,000 income category, whose probability of being in a higher income category is influenced by a wider range of social capital indicators, including bonding social capital, socialization, the number of different organizations volunteered, and knowing neighbors by face. That said, the odds ratio for these are lower. This suggests that, while a wider range of social capital is influential for higher income individuals, the odds of increasing income categories associated with this social capital are more tempered. For those in the $25,000–$50,000 income category, a moderate number of social capital variables, including trust, bonding social capital, and the number of organizations are associated with a change in income status, and the change in likelihood is fairly dramatic. Consequently, studies of social capital and economic development that do not differentiate between income categories may mask or amplify the effect of social capital on income.

Second, until recent years, the preponderance of emphasis on developing social capital has been on building bonding social capital, as represented by the emphasis on involvement in voluntary organizations found in the work of Putnam and others. However, recently, scholars have tended to focus on the economic benefits of bridging social capital (Engbers, Rubin, & Aubuchon, 2017; Safford, 2009). This study finds a role for both bridging and bonding social capital. The direct measure of bonding social capital has a significant effect in increasing the odds of membership in higher income categories for the two middle-income strata investigated in this study. Likewise, trust, which is often classified as a form of bonding social capital, appears to be associated with increasing income for the two lowest income categories. The focus on trust supports one of the traditionally conceived causal mechanisms of social capital: the reduction of transaction costs. By building greater networks of trust, there is less need for formal, and often costly, transaction enforcement mechanisms. This increases the net economic benefit of any relationships.

For medium and high-income categories, the effect of bridging social capital, as measured by the number of different organizations volunteered and knowing neighbors' faces, appears to have a greater effect. Consequently, one should be hesitant to espouse blanket support for either bonding or bridging social capital but consider the moderating effect of economic and social network in judging the effect of social capital. This is in many ways consistent with both the weak and strong ties argument (Granovetter, 1973). Furthermore, unlike past research (Engbers, Rubin, & Aubuchon, 2017) that found bridging social capital's effect on job creation but not income, this study finds an effect on income; thus, stressing the importance of unit of analysis in social capital research. Aggregation at the MSA level may mask the effect on personal income that can be found when studies examine individual and neighborhood effects.

Third, the neighborhood level controls are statistically significant, suggesting that neighborhood effects are important in understanding income. This is most clearly visible as one compares the model with only social capital variables in Table 4.3 to the model with human capital and neighborhood controls in Table 4.4. Many of the variables that were not statistically significant in Table 4.3 become statistically significant in Table 4.4 showing that a failure to control for neighborhood related effects masks the potential impact of social capital. This important finding suggests that, while social capital can be used for economic gain regardless of the neighborhood context,[3] the effect needs to be understood within a cultural context. Thus, groups such as Habitat for Humanity International, which attempt to build social capital as a means of revitalization (which we saw in the last chapter), are not misdirected in their efforts but must take a more nuanced approach to thinking about social capital's effects.

The consistency with past research and high levels of statistical significance considering moderate sample sizes bolster the argument presented above, but some limitations remain. Perhaps the biggest concern includes issues stemming from the lower response rates.

First, the response rate differed among neighborhoods with low-income neighborhoods exhibiting lower response rates. This raises the risk of selection bias. This bias is undoubtedly a problem. The sample collected from this survey differs from census estimates in significant ways, including more education and whiter. Likewise, the low response rate may introduce other forms of bias, such as the likelihood that survey respondents differ from nonrespondents on unmeasured characteristics, such as being more extroverted or having other soft skills.

A second area of concern is perfect multicollinearity of control variables, which limits the number of neighborhood controls included. The model above included median income as a control of neighborhood level dynamics.[4] To better understand the effects of context, a wider range of neighborhood controls is needed. To do this would require increasing the number of neighborhoods examined, a strategy to be pursued by future scholars.

Third, the use of household income creates some limitation in interpretation of the data. Since the respondent may not be the primary income earner for the household, he or she may be unable to effectively judge household income. Alternatively, and perhaps more of a concern, the connection between social capital and the household income is more tenuous. The respondent may have a high degree of social capital, but this capital is unlinked to the household income.

Despite these conclusions, this study aids our understanding of social capital and economic development by showing that there are personal income benefits associated with social capital and that these benefits accrue to those with bridging and bonding social capital. However, this effect is depending on economic context and current economic status. Moreover, social capital effects appear to exist across neighborhoods, and that while neighborhood context is important for understanding income, the neighborhood effect does appear to nullify the effect of social capital.

NOTES

This chapter previously appeared as an article in the *Journal of Public and Nonprofit Affairs* [Hanka, Matthew J, and Trent Aaron Engbers. "Social Capital and Economic Development: A Neighborhood Perspective." *Journal of Public and Nonprofit Affairs* 3.3 (2017): 272–291] and was published and reproduced under the terms of Creative Commons Attribution License.

1. This model is somewhat truncated from the variables described above and represented in the descriptive statistics because of concerns about degrees of freedom in the model.

2. The percentage of college graduates and percentage employed are sensitive to model specification in terms of both their statistical significance and direction of impact even after neighborhood controls are included. Caution should be exercised in interpretation of these variables.

3. An early specification of the model included interaction terms for the neighborhoods and the social capital variables. These interactions were not statistically significant lending further credence to this claim.

4. The model was run with alternative neighborhood controls included such as racial composition, population density, and unemployment. These models were minimally different than the presented models in terms of coefficients on social capital variables.

Chapter Five

Service Learning and Community Development

Anne Statham and Helen Rosenberg

This chapter explores the connections between community development and service learning. We consider both the history and potential of service-learning projects done by university/college students, faculty, and staff to be a valuable tool for those engaging in community development.

SOCIAL CAPITAL AND NETWORKING

As implied in the definition offered by Checkoway (2013), networking is usually a main component of community development efforts. The networking involved is commonly aimed at enhancing access to resources that can be used for individual or group advancement. Most contemporary models stress social capital as a key mechanism for successful community development, while others have delineated more expansive forms of collaboration or collaborative partnerships (Ivery, 2010; DePaula, 2014; Sullivan et al., 2002; Moris & Frisman, 1987; Phipps & Shapson, 2009; Martinson et al., 2013; Harper et al., 2014; Tesdahl, 2015; Sales & Bush, 2000).

As discussed in chapter 2, social capital (Bourdieu, 1986) refers to actual or potential resources inherent in social networks, such as social support, social leverage, information, social control, and neighborhood/organization participation (Carpiano & Kimbro, 2016). Social capital is defined as the ability of people to organize, address, and alleviate current social problems in one's immediate community (Warren, Thompson, & Saegert, 2001). Taking this definition apart, we see that this is a quality of both groups and individuals, and at either level, is based in purposeful relationships (Warren, Thompson, & Saegert, 2001) with a goal of alleviating a community need and, subsequently, strengthening the community. In this context, community is defined by place rather than identity per sé (Checkoway, 2013). It presupposes that a community can solve its own problems and garner support from within or outside of its borders to do so. At the onset when confronted with inequalities and with an emphasis on organization and sharing resources, the goal is often to move toward equality of resource distribution.

In this chapter, we have applied Woolcock's (1998) model to assess the extent to which service-learning projects might promote community development. Woolcock's (1998) typology consists of two dimensions that describe expansion of social capital, one of embeddedness/autonomy, another micro/macro distinction. Micro level capital focuses on "necessary economic resources that individuals need for economic advancement," while the macro level capital focuses on bureaucratic efficiency and "features the synergy of state-society relations." At the micro level, Woolcock (1998) defines embeddedness as integration and intracommunity ties, which can be interpreted as a form of bonding social capital between individuals within groups of common identity.

For example, in studying how access to neighborhood resources served to mitigate the social strain on caregivers to promote their health and well-being, Carpiano and Kimbro (2012) found that people with higher levels of social support benefitted from neighborhood resources that relieved some of the strain of caring for children. "Consistent with Bourdieu's (1986) social capital theory, having high neighborhood attachment indicates a level of embeddedness in neighborhood networks that permits access to and use of network resources" (Carpiano & Kimbro, 2012, p. 244).

Woolcock (1998) defines autonomy as a linkage between extra-community networks, which can be interpreted as bridging social capital for individuals (see Coleman, 1988, and Putnam, 2000). Wiggins et al. (2013) describe how community mental health workers were trained to navigate the health care system in Honduras to access services for their community. In effect, they became social change agents, ultimately surpassing their roles as health promoters to participate in land reform and recuperation initiatives.

Macro embeddedness is a quality in which people with shared interests come to expand those interests to help their group or organization, often working toward sustainable development. Some notion of change that represents macro embeddedness is described in a case study (Martinson, Minkler, & Garcia, 2013) of senior volunteers who mobilized to combat ageism in California. Seniors' shared identity (embeddedness) was motivation to develop a statewide network to promote access to health care, transportation, and elder economic security. Macro autonomy is a means of achieving social outcomes by increasing efficiency *across* organizations to address public needs. "Communities with effective administrative systems are better able to deliver public services and foster trust in government" (Woolcock, 1998, p. 6), which involve bridging social capital or linkages between extra-community networks or among large bureaucratic systems on the macro level.

An example of this are the systems change activities (shared funds, partner collaboration within agencies across the community) of the Georgia Family Connection Partnership, a collaborative of local governments, education institutions, public health, social service, and community and faith-based agencies that used a multi-disciplinary approach to address community health, resulting in their ability to garner additional resources from state, federal, and private partners. This activity enhanced "the capacity of collaborative partners to work collectively toward resource development" (Harper et al., 2014, p. 355).

While chapter 4 focuses on economic development, this chapter expands to consider social and political development that can lead to empowering individuals and community organizations in achieving their goals in service-learning projects. Moreover, we ask if the efforts of service-learning practitioners advance social justice in their own and other communities.

The literature on community development is replete with examples of change efforts that operate on any one or a combination of the four levels described in the Woolcock (1998) typology. For example, a review of 269 articles on community practice interventions revealed macro practice interventions have both "psychosocial effects on participants . . . and physical, social, and economic changes in communities resulting from the interventions (e.g., improvements in affordable housing, infrastructure, employment, and education)" (Ohmer & Korr, 2006, p. 134). This meta-analysis underscores that macro social change can support both embeddedness and autonomy in developing social capital. In the process of social change, community organizations can move across cells, from micro embeddedness to macro autonomy.

In examining faith-based social movement organizations, Tesdahl (2015) highlights resource sharing among a cooperative system of leaders (micro autonomy), to organizational transitions maintaining unity and solidarity within member institutions (macro embeddedness), to increasing capacity in developing inter-organizational relations (macro autonomy). The Congregation-based Community Organizing model, developed by the Community Creating Opportunity in Kansas City, Missouri, engages professional community organizers to work across issues and promote cooperation among social movement organizations. They organize around each member organization's connection to an issue, enhancing each organization's capacity to mobilize labor resources and turnout around events for issues they care about.

Some of the efforts at creating change are quite ambitious, sometimes taking a global view of community organizing. Pillisuk, McAllister, and Rothman (1996) ask if social action based on local organizing can empower and restore communities in need by preventing post-industrial global technologies and economies from destroying the foundations and habitats of all living communities, examples of action flowing from built organizational capacity (macro embeddedness) or enhanced organizational collaboration (macro autonomy).

In the process of community development, leaders are created. Some are trained to be community health workers in Honduras (Wiggins et al., 2013), or become advocates of senior activists (Martinson, Minkler, & Garcia, 2013). Some also become grassroots community action organizers (Pillisuk, McAllister, & Rothman, 1996), while some students enter into caring professions in South Africa (Bozalek & Biersteker, 2010). A study of leadership levels in networked government in Canada found that middle-level managers were critical as change makers, compared to leaders at the front and center. Values-based and collaborative leadership seemed more important than transformational leadership in this New Public Management (NPM) era over the past 30 years. Supplementing this approach with action research can fill knowledge gaps and help these government workers access more resources in the form of leadership development (Wilkins, 2014), promoting the ability of government to solve problems, another example of autonomous macro-level social capital development.

Activities aimed at systems change predicted increased leveraging of dollar resources from state, federal, and private partners, but not from local groups or agencies in a project in Georgia that used a model of collaboration emphasizing autonomous decision-making of local stakeholders. A cross-lagged model showed that greater system change led to more leveraged dollars rather than vice-versa. The conclusion was that interagency-inter-organizational collaboratives are important for community health promotion and empowerment (Harper et al., 2014), evidence of macro-level autonomous social capital development.

Cooperation rather than competition seemed to result in more change and successful social activism in a study of Black and Latino groups in New York City, if not being "high jacked by entrepreneurial politicians who forego political principle and instead seek the best opportunity for personal advancement" (Sales & Bush, 2000, p. 19). Electoral strategies are often not enough, so groups without routine access to the power structure often need to include protest and civil disobedience strategies that disrupt the usual operation of the system (Sales & Bush, 2000).

SOCIAL JUSTICE AS A VALUED OUTCOME

Community development efforts are often aimed at low-income communities. People living in disadvantaged communities may lack the time, knowledge, and resources to advocate on their behalf to improve their collective lives, be it improving their neighborhoods or accessing goods and services taken for granted in wealthier communities. Barriers to collective action are the lack of a common identity or sense of community and the lack of a common goal that, if achieved, would relieve some burden experienced by the collective. In such communities, developing social capital through shared resources is one way of empowering and expanding the capacities of individuals and groups. Such communities rely on convergence from different organizations to share expertise to address and alleviate these problems.

This emphasis on expanding social justice is not necessarily the case for all community development projects, certainly not for projects related to gentrification. However, many of the authors cited here do see social justice as critical to the development efforts they are engaged in or chronicling. Checkoway (2013) refers to "the principles of equity and justice for all people, with an emphasis on those who are underrepresented or underserved" (p. 174). This often involves building the capacity of the organizations aiming to serve these communities (Barakat & Chard, 2002; Cramer et al., 2013; Gregory et al., 2012; Saunders & Marchik, 2007; Wiggins et al., 2013), the intended outcome of empowering a community or group that has been marginalized or cut off from resources (Barakat & Chard, 2002; Jones et al., 2009).

There were several ways the above projects attempted and advanced social justice. Senior activists gained recognition and support, combating ageism and invisibility in the program aimed at reducing ageism, and many seniors acquired emotional learning and networking benefits (Martinson, Minkler, & Garcia, 2013). The goal of the Community Capacitation Center in the Wiggins et al. (2013) study was to reduce health inequities, as the community health workers (trained as change agents) worked to improve constituents' skills and knowledge to promote health and well-being. Program participants subsequently reported improved health status and decreases in depression. Ohmer (2008) was also concerned with addressing the concentrations of health issues in distressed neighborhoods and pointed to a need for more effective evaluation processes at the macro level, looking at the economic, social, and physical changes that happen in communities experiencing interventions.

The main push of the environmental project described by Pillisuk, McAllister, and Rothman (1996) was to preserve the habitat and foundation of all communities, provide equal access to resources, and provide a voice in planning that promotes fairness, freedom and democracy. Tesdahl (2015) identified the various roles partners played at various times, the resources they shared, and the ways the organizations connected which had an impact on multiple ongoing issue campaigns at the neighborhood, regional, state and nation levels, all in an effort to address key issues around social justice. With a focus on healing racial and class divides, Sales and Bush (2000) consider the extent to which new social movements in urban areas result in cooperation, rather than competition between racial groups, as a mechanism for promoting equity, showing that cooperation between Black and Latino social action groups can lead to change toward greater social justice for both groups.

Action research can consolidate learning and fill knowledge gaps according to Wilkins (2014), who pointed to the need for reform of today's networked government to advance the common good in a time of government retrenchment. Wilkins (2014) argued there could be no public sector reform without capacity development; no transformation in today's networked government without collaborative leadership; no innovation without stewardship of strategic leaders. He asked if public managers have the right leadership values and competencies for the challenges they face.

A study by Bozalek and Biersteker (2010) involved the efforts of a team of students, but as with efforts around service learning discussed below, focused on developing awareness of racial and class differences. The workshop they participated in was designed to develop the capacity for respect, recognition, and understanding across racial and class boundaries, rather than producing actual change in a specific community. However, the results suggest that when students become better at examining the social, political, and cultural assumptions they hold about those of different races or classes, they become better change agents. Exploring power and privilege using "a pedagogical tool for anti-oppressive and reflective practice towards social justice" inclusivity is promoted, allowing people with different viewpoints to work together (Bozalek & Biersteker, 2010, p. 552).

In anticipating the potential for change, Harper et al. (2014) suggested the need to consider the impact of the relative strength of different systems' change activities in relation to the ability of coalitions to leverage resources. Addressing the need to teach social work students to conduct community level intervention research, Ohmer (2008) suggests building the evaluation capacity of community organizations to contribute to the evidence base of the project, while increasing collaboration among community-based organizations (CBOs) and university researchers, including students, through clear identification of activities and outcomes, using state of the art data management tools.

Connections between Models for Community Development and Service Learning

In much of the literature on community development and service learning, there is an underlying assumption that the best outcomes of these efforts are those going beyond treating symptoms or enlightening individuals about problems, to alleviating the problems. We see this in the emphasis on creating some change in community development circles and on addressing the underlying causes of observed problems in the field of service learning.

Both community development and service learning embrace an implied, if not explicit, focus on building social capital as a way of improving conditions in distressed communities. Community agencies and groups often seek out campuses as sources of innovative and strategic thinking or technological expertise to enhance their capacity to provide critical services to their clients or address specific constituent issues. In many cases, these agencies and groups mitigate homelessness, poverty, environmental injustice, and imprisonment, thereby serving the greater calling of promoting social justice.

As key stakeholders and collaborators with communities, resources from faculty and students cut across disciplines and have the potential to influence diverse sectors, such as health and the economy. In developing community capacity, both university and community combine resources using a bi-directional flow of information (Jones, Pomeroy, & Sampson, 2009) that identifies community needs and the direction that the university must take to address those needs. Both university and community partners are responsible for guiding the research/social action process leading to social change, resulting in the co-production of knowledge that, in conjunction with common needs, enables social change (Ivery, 2010; Phipps & Shapson, 2009).

Service learning affords students class time to work with communities, to help them solve one or more specific problems and potentially address larger social issues. Through their participation, students gain an understanding of community assets and needs and experience real-world problems that enhance in-class learning (Kapucu & Petrescu, 2006). Service learning is one way that advocacy strategies and resources, in the form of time and knowledge, are transferred to communities grappling with the need for social action. In the process of making change to benefit a disadvantaged group or address a community problem, students learn about community social problems and nascent ways to address them, while recipients of services can hone their skills for self-advocacy and community change. Students who serve by working with others can learn how to negotiate power differentials and develop teamwork to achieve a goal. Invariably, leaders emerge to achieve the goals of any project. In turn, those served reap benefits from servers, some developing their skills to change their own lives, but on a larger level, produce institutional change and sometimes, community change. As community members come to see community issues as collective problems and see themselves as drivers addressing and alleviating these problems, they will acquire the social capital needed to succeed. In this sense, we see a convergence of the goals of community development and many service learning projects.

Innovative programming for college students that contributes to community has strong positive effects over time. For example, engaging students with their communities affects student retention and successful completion of college, increased awareness of social problems in their own communities, and perceived personal efficacy to effect change (Reed, Rosenberg, Statham, & Rosing, 2015). Often, students who work with vulnerable populations in developing communities gain a new understanding of social conditions that contribute to marginalization and sometimes, students from these marginalized populations become civic agents for change when service learning involves social justice issues. Coterminous is students' realization that they are adding to the social capital of their communities as agents of the university (Jameson, Clayton, & Ash, 2013). However, not all of those involved in service learning realize this potential to contribute. Phipps and Shapson (2009) argue that universities still lack the capacity to inform public policy, since they largely work outside of the needs of community stakeholders.

One goal of service learning is to develop a shared sense of community sustained through continued communication, after a project has been completed. Even though many projects are only semester long, developing a sense of accomplishment within a community or organization can solidify relationships for future action toward problem solving. This sense of empowerment (Labonte, 1989) can be sparked by solving a problem common to both students and the underserved, but more importantly can develop skills for future endeavors. Two studies underscore the importance of communication in sustaining partnerships. Ivery (2010) found that having open communication among stakeholders when changes in agency leadership occurred allowed partners to readjust and recommit to a new or modified mission that further solidified the partnership. Gazley, Bennett, and Littlepage (2013) caution that only 46 percent of community partners reported they communicated with supervising faculty during projects, although representatives of 290 community agencies in Indiana ranked "clear and ongoing communication" as an essential factor in maintaining a good partnership.

Impacts on Students

Past research suggests significant impacts of service learning on students. Some studies point to general outcomes such as enhanced learning and professional skills development (Cunningham, 2001; Jackson & Sedehi, 1998).

But much research points to more specific impacts around commitment to social justice in various forms, with some students quite explicitly becoming more committed to social justice, advocacy, and civic responsibility (Mobley, 2007; Lewis, 2004). One study finds that students increased their capacity for critical thinking and questioning of conventional wisdom (Seider, Rabinowicz, & Gilmor, 2010), and another study showed that students realized enhanced possibilities for exercising responsibility and experiencing personal growth (Hondagneu-Sotelo & Raskoff, 1994).

Several studies reported that students who engaged in service learning became more likely to recognize social stereotypes and their functions, and to re-examine their beliefs compared to students who did not do service learning (Mobley, 2007; Lewis, 2004; Jarrott, 2001), and to develop a greater understanding of diverse groups of cultures within one's society (Mobley, 2007; Ryan, 2003; Cunningham, 2001). It also seems that students shift from individual to structural-level attributions of causes of poverty as they do service-learning projects (Seider et al., 2010; Jackson & Sedehi, 1998; Mobley, 2007; Lewis, 2004), moving from criticism of personal responsibility to a more sophisticated understanding of the structural roots of what they are seeing and experiencing (Cunningham, 2001; Jackson & Sedehi, 1998; Hondagneu-Sotelo & Raskoff, 1994; Polgar, 2008; Zander, 2006). Some students were inspired to become life-long change agents (Ruskay, 2012) and some changed their career goals to social change work as the result of their service learning experiences (Cunningham, 2001). Several studies suggested that students developed an increased sense of self-efficacy, becoming more convinced that they can make a difference in their communities (Mobley, 2007; Lewis, 2004).

Impact on Community

Past research also suggests the impacts of service-learning projects on the community. These projects can develop awareness of structural inequalities among community groups and may promote the potential for community change. Specific outcomes include: 1) developing awareness of the economic disparities for women and children, compared to men and adults, in ways that impact public policy (Seider et al., 2010); 2) developing mentors who become critically thinking citizens and stewards who address complex social justice issues and become a network for change (Ruskay, 2012); and 3) creating collaborative public photo displays to generate increased awareness of the underlying issues that create problems such as homelessness (Nichols & Winston, 2014).

These projects can help build collaborative relationships in the community with community partners (Ryan, 2003) by targeting high crime areas for intervention (Cunningham, 2001), by bridging the town/gown divide, generating trust (Blouin & Perry, 2009), and facilitating students to become organizational advocates who go beyond single class projects to develop internships and new career interests (Blouin & Perry, 2009).

These projects can also serve to empower the clients served. Home visits done by students in one project with high risk, poor, minority families fostered brief interventions that provided some relief from crises for individuals and families and offered information on community resources that generated trust within families in poverty (Jackson & Sedehi, 1998).

Service-learning projects can also help with capacity building. Specific examples include offering new ideas to improve organizational operations and helping staff to serve more clients and enhance the quality of the services offered, freeing up organizational resources (Blouin & Perry, 2009), and improving classrooms and availability of supplemental supplies at a child care center (Cunningham, 2001).

While the literature suggests service learning may have the potential to contribute to community development efforts, the literature on community development has yet to consider this possibility on a widespread basis. Few efforts at social change seem to include service-learning projects, but for those that do, the outcomes seemed to be beneficial for students in understanding the structural conditions that lead to inequality. Students are moved toward seeking social justice solutions for underserved populations and for the betterment of the larger community.

METHODS

This chapter uses Woolcock's (1998) typology to examine the extent to which community development is enhanced through service-learning projects. We consider two perspectives—those of faculty, and those of community partners who have participated in service-learning projects together. We ask if these projects, in achieving learning outcomes for students, also contribute to mutual solidarity (bonding social capital), expanded networks (bridging social capital), organizational and community enhancement, and/or the furthering of social justice—the four cells in Woolcock's (1998) typology. We use qualitative interview data, collected from 19 pairs of faculty and community partners to report the extent to which faculty, and their community partners, believed service-learning projects contributed to community development and social justice, and by implication, how useful service learning would be for community development efforts in general.

The research was conducted at two universities offering an array of service-learning classes in all disciplines. Each author accessed a list of courses with service-learning components from the administrative offices that coordinate such projects and began contacting faculty who supervised students, with the stipulation that faculty could provide the names of community partners who had worked with them on the projects. Faculty interviews occurred over the course of several years, but all partners were interviewed over a six-month period. For the most part, the authors interviewed faculty initially, asking them to choose one service-learning project they wanted to discuss, then interviewed community partners about their views on this same project. In a few cases, community partners were interviewed first in a larger study of partner perceptions, and then provided the names of the faculty they had worked with.

Of the 19 total pairs of faculty and community partners, eight partnerships were in social science courses, five with health and nursing courses, three with teacher education courses, two with engineering and business courses, and two with courses taught by a director of a student engagement office. All courses were listed as official service-learning courses in their respective institutions.

We wanted to learn if both faculty and community partners believed their projects helped build either individual or community capacity, if they felt their students understood the broader social justice implications of their work, and if the faculty and partner's views were consistent or divergent.

After a brief description of the project, we directly asked the following questions: "What were the benefits of the project? In what ways did the project help to strengthen your organization?" For the partners and faculty, we asked, "Did the project benefit the organization you worked with? If so, how?" We also asked, "Did the project strengthen the community in any way? In what ways did the project empower the people that you serve?" and, "Did the project promote social justice in any way?" We coded the results on our interviews using Woolcock's typology, examining the extent to which each service-learning project fell into one of the four cells. We further clarified faculty/community partner responses based on substantive themes within each cell.

RESULTS

Faculty and community partners agreed on their assessments of the impacts of the projects they collaborated on, but with subtle differences in emphasis. One of these differences involved the extent to which bonding occurred in the community or the university, in the latter case, within the service learning classes. Our partners were more likely to report change or bonding within their own groups or organizations, while the faculty focused on bonding within their classes and the changes in learning of their students. One challenge utilizing service-learning projects in community development is the primary focus of university faculty on the education of their students. As with many internship placements and community-based learning episodes, one possible issue, from the perspective of the community partner, is that the experience becomes much more valuable for the students than for the community organization. The education of college-level students is a worthwhile goal, and for many nonprofits, the preparation of future colleagues and staff members may provide a direct benefit in the future. However, these projects might not contribute directly to community development, the focus of our exploration here, and may drain the community organization of precious time and other resources in short supply.

The aim of service-learning projects is to create some change at the macro level. Community partners reported that students helped strengthen their organizations and their ability to serve more clients by taking over some staff duties and allowing staff to redirect their services. In many cases, students offered creative ways to enhance the functioning of the organization, offered ideas to staff on how to better provide services to clients, and consequently increased the capacity of the organization (macro embeddedness). Less often, service-learning projects connected agencies with other community resources (macro autonomy) and supported collaborations for their mutual benefit. In these cases, there was cooperation across organizations to achieve a larger, common goal or contribution to the greater good of the community, beyond strengthening the specific organization involved.

We explored the extent to which social capital was built in the form of micro embeddedness (bonding social capital) or micro autonomy (bridging social capital). Service-learning projects are, by definition, exchanges of resources between individuals in two networks, the community and the university, hence constituting micro autonomy. Most projects at the micro level involved students interacting with community members and training staff or clients. In return, the university students received valuable learning opportunities at their placements; students were reported to have benefitted immensely from exposure to these community networks, expanding their knowledge base and networks. Many of the clients served by the organizations also benefitted in a person-to-person exchange from their exposure to the university students doing the projects, especially the youth from the community.

Few projects measured bonding among students, members within an organization, or clients served by an agency (micro embeddedness or bonding social capital). Creating such bonding opportunities within the university classroom is not usually an explicit goal of service-learning projects; but, in some cases, both faculty and community partners indicated students and clients felt united toward achieving a common goal. Sometimes students were reported by the faculty member or the client to USI Service Learning that they are working with other students on the group projects, or faculty reported substantial time working on and/or discussing collaborative class projects in the classroom or within their own group in other settings.

In categorizing responses from faculty and community partners, we observed that most projects served to help organizations function better to achieve efficiency and sustainability (macro embeddedness) and/or connect people with others outside their immediate group (micro autonomy). At the other extreme, few organizations extended their efforts toward community development outside their boundaries for their mutual benefit. This type of macro autonomy requires complex negotiations and an understanding of larger goals toward community development—or the perception that a project has contributed to the common good in a community beyond benefitting the specific organization involved. This type of impact was reported by both service learning programs, but much less frequently than the result of strengthening specific organizations.

Micro Embeddedness: Accessing Necessary Resources within One's Group that Individuals Need for Advancement

Bonding Social Capital among University Students

There was little evidence that students gained competencies from their fellow students and teachers alone. Benefits to students included applying and increasing skills from classroom readings and developing creative problem-solving techniques. Some service learning involved the entire class, or a team in a class, working together in a way that promoted bonding. Often, when these skills developed in the classroom, they were honed in the community, hence an example of micro autonomy (students benefitting from exposure to a network outside of their own usual networks). Indeed, applying classroom learning to community experience is one main goal of service learning. What follows are examples of micro-embeddedness, for students and clients they served, resulting from service-learning projects.

In a communication class that developed an information campaign about alcohol and drug use for high school students, preparation for face-to-face interaction motivated service-learning students to expand upon current skills and become more creative. In-class learning became more "real," when students applied learning in their future interactions and when activities provided opportunities for capital building within the classroom setting. A communications professor said, ". . . The creative problem solving and marketing strategy process and what they know about the two converges into something real [by] having face to face contact with [high school] students." The faculty member further described how students, in their discussions with community partner, developed the target audience for their campaign. "Students and I shared the SWAT analysis and students posed questions and we had a conversation, and during that conversation she identified high school students . . . [as a] target audience. It was . . . an emergent . . . ongoing process. It takes time."

Another class worked on a computer system, matching donated musical instruments to students in need of them. This work also seemed to generate in-class bonding through the process set up by the faculty member: "It was a night class, and after the class we'd stay together and give some of the project designs. By the end of September, they had arrived at the design and started constructing the data base themselves. . . . As they started constructing . . . I would review the first parts of the project and they would take it back to the community partner, constantly getting feedback."

An engineering faculty member, who worked with a team of students designing pedestrian and bicycle trails, described a similar process: "Four or five civil engineering students worked on this project for their Senior Project in 2011. I was the faculty advisor. . . . Each student had a separate chunk of the project to complete. There was a retaining wall they had to deal with. It [was] . . . one of the largest projects I did with students. . . . They had a lot to get done. . . . They put together a good plan." In both cases, the students seem to have developed an enhanced sense of group process. A similar process was described by and connection with the faculty member.

A partner for a project on human trafficking described the process he observed within the class:

> The whole class presented . . . the professor divided 25 students into groups of 5 . . . and . . . they had to do a presentation to me and one of my other staff members on what [we] thought the best marketing plan was. . . . And then the professor asked us to rank them and . . . gave them a grade based on . . . that ranking. Instead of just picking the one that got #1, they decided as a class to pick the best ideas from each group and then . . . worked those ideas out.

A communications faculty described the work his class completed on an anti-bullying project:

Our class (Conflict, Mediation and Negotiation) looks at the systemic issues of bullying, why it occurs, and the communication that occurs (or does not occur) between and among kids, parents/guardians, teachers, and administrators. Students then create a one-hour training session that focuses on basic coping and conflict management skills. In essence, what these students learn is how to process a conflict episode, how to identify personality traits of the other person in that conflict, and how to work to resolve that conflict through strategic communication that is targeted toward specific personality types. We use short lectures, discussion, team building activities and experiential conflict resolution activities to illustrate these ideas.

Several faculty members also described spending considerable time in the classroom processing or reflecting on what was happening with the project. This special education class involved with Youth Build worked together, then spent considerable time discussing what had occurred:

The class met on Tuesdays and Thursdays each week, so on Tuesdays we went to YouthBuild and the students had either individual or small group literacy instruction time and then we all came together for a class lesson, which addressed a deficit area on the GED. The lesson was prepared and delivered by a team of two students. After our time together was done, I stayed behind and conducted a group discussion on what strategies the YouthBuild students felt were effectively used during the lesson and what areas they could make recommendations. On Thursday, the USI students would meet with me on campus and I would share the contents of the discussion as well as brainstorm as a class about positives, negatives, and ways to improve the lesson.

Some faculty talked about projects their students did together:

A small group of students was very interested in the topic of what is happening in Myanmar and the issue of human trafficking. They were very interested in what was happening abroad, but also in the U.S. The idea that it is happening on our own shores and in our backyards was alarming, raised a lot of awareness for them. They thought of it as something that happens in third world countries. They really wanted to be there in Myanmar, working with the victims and the rehabilitation they had going on. . . . But through that course, they learned how to build a campaign to address a broad issue, about the university's connection to global education, each benefitting, seeing they can address a global issue happening halfway around the world. . . . The students did not understand why people, governments, others were not doing something. They grappled with an understanding of the social injustice that they were seeing, why the Myanmar government, the United States government wasn't doing more. Some worked on government action, legislation here. A group did a project for a Change Maker Challenge competition and came in second place.

Even though students were divided into groups for many of these projects, the collaborations among themselves and with faculty seemed to support a developing a sense of unity as a group as they completed their final projects. Additional opportunities to bond occurred when students reconvened to revise projects in response to community partner feedback. The potential for competition was there in any one of these projects, yet the goal of creating a unified message to the community partner supported students' efforts to work together to create a common message.

Bonding Social Capital among Organizational Clients

Those who discussed client empowerment were mostly partners of social science faculty—from sociology, psychology, and social work. Often, they saw those they work with as having more confidence as the result of the projects—to pursue personal, educational, or career goals. A community partner at a Women's Shelter in Racine saw the project as helping clients achieve "a sense of community for the residents at the shelter. It builds comradery (sic) for the people at the shelter. . . . It allows for easier transition for the client to get to the next level. They use those skills to make choices."

This same project was developing and promoting a variety of skills that enabled clients to better handle complex problems, e.g., self-advocacy, empowerment, and critical thinking. The client said:

> It helps by understanding your own empowerment to make your own decisions. Many say I didn't have a choice, but there is always a choice. CR [conflict resolution] helps you determine your choices. Focuses on what is your responsibility, and the program fine tunes people's responsibilities and skills to make the right choices. This is the better way to deal with the conflict.

The faculty on this project saw the project as building bonding social capital among the residents:

> In the dialogues that take place in these workshops, residents have the opportunity to learn more about each other, and to initiate and strengthen supportive relationships. They listen to one another, offer advice, and share resources. The residents are empowered by feeling less isolated, and by forming mutually affirming and supportive relationships. They also develop a stronger sense of their own agency, including problem-solving and conflict resolution skills.

Skill building projects that required clients to work together to solve common problems promoted the most bonding. Similarly, students who had a unified goal seemed to develop bonds among themselves and with faculty. Working to help clients achieve personal goals, rather than working for a community partner per se, seemed to promote unity among students and clients as well.

Micro Autonomy: Accessing Necessary Resources Outside One's Group through Networking that Individuals Need for Advancement

Our interviewees reported more incidences of micro autonomy (bridging social capital) exchanged between university students and organizational staff and clients than intragroup exchanges. Exposing university students to new networks and resources, beyond those offered in the academy, is one essential goal of service learning, and they, in turn, offer their knowledge and innovative ideas to partner agencies and their clients. All faculty and community partners interviewed saw capital development involving micro autonomy.

Bridging Social Capital among University Students

Contributing to students' development was a major motivator for incorporating service learning into their classes; all but three faculty talked about this to some extent. Most of their comments pointed to the skills students learned that complemented the teaching and learning occurring in the classroom, as well as insights the students gained into future careers or work settings. A social work faculty member observed her students apply skills and competencies she had attempted to instill in the classroom, as they reflected on intake interviews done for a community-wide day connecting a wide range of resources to people who are homeless:

> Students had the opportunity to apply classroom learning, which advanced their overall learning. In their reflection papers students provided specific examples of their developing skills that are required by the Council on Social Work Education (CSWE), the accreditation body for academic social work programs. In addition to being able to better engage with individuals from diverse backgrounds, students were able to apply critical thinking and creatively problem solve, as situations arose in the interview setting and during the interviews.

Others also observed their students applying concepts from the material they were teaching:

> Students used the skills they learn in class and provided a service for members of our community. . . . Dental hygiene students provided non-surgical periodontal therapy to clients exhibiting moderate to severe chronic periodontitis. Services extended beyond those available during regular clinicals.

Only four of the community partners mentioned the goal of helping university students learn, but two of them talked about it quite extensively. When they mentioned this, they commented on broad benefits for the students participating in the project, rather than the honing of specific skills. One project at USI used engineering students to develop a plan for a trails system in the community sponsored by the Evansville Trails Coalition. The faculty member overseeing this project said:

> The college students who participated always tell me they get far more out of doing a real, hands-on thing than just some academic experience. That was especially true for this engineering student who worked on developing the trail. . . . It's a real thing . . . not just something they're studying in a book or some theoretical thing. . . . It exposes them to things they could do the rest of their life.

Faculty often saw the skills developed as direct preparation for future careers. This teacher education faculty said:

> The YouthBuild project was beneficial because it provided the USI students with a positive experience in dealing with secondary students in a non-traditional academic setting. It also gave them the opportunity to meet the needs of a diverse group of learners. . . . Many of the students they are teaching have a learning disability. They also get to experience planning and implementing various types of instruction.

Another said:

> It was very beneficial for the college students. . . . They got to do some hands-on teaching, got to design and implement lesson plans. It makes them more prepared to teach when they get into their own classrooms. . . . Teacher candidates learn how to manage small groups of students under guidance of a veteran teacher. They get a feel for the school setting and experience planning lessons. Early exposure to the classroom prior to student teaching is a valuable resource for our teacher candidates.

Community partners saw their roles with students as providing preparation for their future careers. This community partner helped students with resume writing and career development. Her faculty partner said this:

> X asks students, "What are you doing after this? What condition is your resume in? Look at your skills." Some of the students know they are going into OT. Some students are lost, and she helped them find a path—built their confidence. [She has] connections in the state, knows the jobs, career planning. She finds OT help and targets experiences and does lots of coaching and recommends where they should apply.

This same community partner realized that exposure to residents dually diag-nosed provided students with new awareness of whom they might work with in future careers.

> Part of their experience, they may find this is not work they want to do and not
> the population. . . . This is a really great opportunity for us to educate and . . .
> help to develop professionals who have a desire to work with people who are
> dual diagnosis. . . . We have some very unique people in a very specialized track
> who work with an agency focusing on those with dual diagnosis.

Many times, students benefitted from service learning in multiple areas. This communication professor said:

> My students had the opportunity to put theory into action, wrestling with com-plex and changing contingencies. They developed a stronger sense of their own
> agency and leadership skills. . . . Alumni report on how this experience has been
> helpful to them in their careers.

Other faculty commented on the increase in students' self-confidence in mak-ing a difference in their community. This faculty member felt her students had gained the confidence to work with a special population of women in an addiction recovery program: "Dental hygiene students completed oral assessments and provided education to residents of an addiction facility. . . . Students gained experience working with a population that they may feel uncomfortable around. They shared their knowledge and gained confidence." Another faculty member said: "We talk about client rights and they are trained in that . . . integration with the community. . . . We talk about why it's important if you cannot develop verbally, how do we ensure their rights . . . why it's [important] to be out in the community . . . without putting limits. We talk a lot about promoting independence."

Building Cultural Competency among University Students

Many service-learning projects focus on people who are homeless or low-income families and/or children, and thus directly address the issue of social justice, especially in developing students' level of awareness of inequality and its consequences in our society. Some faculty hoped this exposure to underserved populations, people of color, or people in poverty would give students a newfound understanding of people different from themselves, without the explicit goal of promoting social justice. Other faculty had a purposeful social justice mission for their projects, with the intention of of-fering some relief to people who were poor or disadvantaged. Thirteen faculty members across three of the discipline types represented here—social science (including communication), health professions, and teacher education—said these experiences served to break down stereotypes among their students. Broadening awareness for their students seemed to be a major reason for involvement in service-learning projects in the first place. More gratifying was the desire, on the part of some students, to continue to work with these populations after graduation.

At USI, students in the Master of Social Work (MSW) program interviewed people living in abandoned buildings and under bridges. A team from the ECHO Housing Corporation homeless shelter spent an entire class (three hours) educating social work students about issues homeless people face and strategies to readily engage, prior to students conducting any interviews.

The faculty member for this project noted that the students in the course learned a great deal about the causes of homelessness.

> Students shared that old stereotypes were dispelled, and they developed an awareness that anyone could become homeless. Many stated that some of the people they talked with had a college degree, and that others had worked all of their adult life until something outside their control had occurred—company downsized, closed, moved, or the individual suffered an injury or illness. The only real surprise students had was learning firsthand that a wide array of circumstances can lead to a person becoming homeless.

A partner working at another homeless shelter said, "Very interesting . . . the outcome from every semester . . . [university] students realized people in the shelter were so much like them."

Another project with an honors course, taught by a social science faculty, resulted in students learning a good deal about hunger in their community. "I think the students got a lot out of the experience. Many of them said they didn't realize that children in America and Evansville could be so hungry. The students learned that there was much worse poverty in their community than they imagined." One faculty member from a project on nutrition said, "The students were able to broaden their knowledge base about the homeless population here in the tristate area and to have a better understanding of HOW and WHY individuals become homeless or face food insecurities."

Stereotyping categories of people removes us from seeing them as human and just capable of adapting to life as we are. In the YouthBuild project, university students tutored other students who were working on their GEDs and developing skills so they could enter carpentry programs. This experience of service learning can dispel stereotypes about low-income youth for university students. The teacher education faculty member working with the YouthBuild Project said this:

I realized that the most significant part of the experience was that they realized their students [YouthBuild] have a beautifully complex and often difficult story which makes up who they are. The [university] students were able to see past the superficial relationship of students and teacher and see the YouthBuild participants as humans who are struggling to make a better life for themselves and their families through the pursuit of education.

Another project where students tutored and mentored students at a charter school in a low-income neighborhood provided teachers with needed time to work on lesson plans. The teacher education faculty member from this project said:

The main thing I expect my students to learn from their experiences is that not all their students come from the same background and family dynamics as the teacher candidates do. We try to have our teacher candidates in schools where they are encountering more diverse student populations including differing social economic backgrounds as well as culture. . . . I believe that the idea that not all children come to school ready to learn from loving and supportive parents is the biggest eye opener for the students. The realization that homework is not top priority for many parents and their children has caused them to stop and rethink some of their beliefs.

The teacher education faculty member also said: "The teacher candidates were surprised that there were so many children of poverty who were not only at, but above grade level and needing to be challenged. Somehow, they believed that all children of poverty were behind!"

Working in a low-income school had not been the original purpose of a recess supervision project done by the director of a student engagement office, but his partner in a school system was emphatic about the impact:

This idea that you . . . send people out into the world with a greater understanding of the community that they live in really helps . . . because I don't think people always really understand why schools are the way they are or all the different . . . children that we have in the schools and all the different challenges that they bring. And so, yes, to send out an educated workforce . . . some educated youth to be able to carry that message is . . . really helpful. . . . I love that point.

As with any service-learning project, while many students overcome stereotypes, some may have their prejudices reinforced. One faculty member said: "A lot of our students have never seen these students first-hand. The fear subsides after a few minutes of interacting and they find surprising similarities. I wouldn't go so far to say that stereotypes are broken, because several of them are reinforced as well."

A few faculty members worked with groups other than people who were homeless or low income. In another project, students worked with institutionalized people who were profoundly developmentally delayed.

> People aren't aware of these people with multiple problems, or if you are aware, you don't know how to interact with them. People don't know what to do. These students were glad they did this. They had this experience that this is a human being. I think that for some this is, "Wow, working with this population is an option!"

His partner concurred: "They . . . learn about people with dual diagnosis. . . . Look at people as not a part of a population . . . but how do you work with individual people. . . . Treat each person as an individual . . . enhance the community . . . not labeling . . ." This faculty member from the School of Nursing reported the following information:

> Prior to attending a health fair, almost all nursing students (83 percent) had "somewhat" or "little" awareness of the unique needs of the medically underserved Hispanic participants in their area. Because of this activity, over 90 percent of students reported they felt better prepared to provide health promotion screenings to the Hispanic population. In addition, 40.6 percent of students responded that while they had intended to practice in this area (i.e., with the underserved) before the program, this experience strengthened their commitment, and 15.6 percent of students who originally had not intended to practice in this area before the program said that as a result of this experience, they had changed their plans and would practice in this area.

The faculty member continued to report:

> Culturally, the students overcame some preconceived notions about this culture. For example, their idea of people in poverty who are from another culture was challenged: they assumed they would see fractured families with no cohesion or values, and they assumed that they didn't have jobs. What they learned is that this population is very family oriented, as they saw entire families coming to the health fair, and all the children were well mannered and dressed with care. The parents took pride in what their children were learning at school. They were not looking for a free handout—the fathers want and expect to provide for the family, and the children work hard to succeed at school to bring honor to the family. All these Hispanic participants had jobs and were working in the community, but they did not receive health care with the jobs they held.

Bridging Social Capital among Organizational Clients

Though not as numerous as for university students, our respondents discussed the bridging social capital that resulted from their interactions with youth in target community groups. Eleven faculty/community partner pairs talked about the importance of this interaction. Faculty remarks typically revolved around the strength of the relationships formed. Faculty pointed to students continuing to volunteer at the agencies where they did their projects. Another discussed a group of students who raised funds for playground equipment at a school after completing their recess assistance project. Some students returned after the semester when the equipment was delivered.

Some partners discussed the empowerment their youth clients had experienced, especially the social science faculty partners from sociology, psychology, and social work. Many believed student participants gained more confidence, as the result of the projects, to pursue professional and personal goals.

One partner emphasized the alternative role models provided for the youth she worked with in a low-income neighborhood. The university students helped them see college could be a possibility for them—and maybe a fun experience, too. University students can encourage them to go to school:

> Honors students mentor and work with kids and fill in whatever they need help with . . . do whatever needs to be done. The . . . students have been coming there for two years. Any time college students come . . . the kids don't often see these positive adult role models . . . young adults . . . trying to make something out of their lives and succeeding. So many kids have never made it out of this neighborhood. It opens their eyes. . . . The first thing they ask is where are you from and how did you get to do that. And they say, "Well, I was interested and just checked into it."

Another partner noted: "The other examples they see of success are in gangs or other such activities. This gives them an alternative view and it is fun too. They can see other options. [W]e have only eight staff members, and there is only so much we can do. My viewpoint is mine; they need to hear other views." Yet another partner noted: "By being there, people are already instilling self-worth in these kids, helping them see they need to stay in school— some were thinking, 'I don't need to finish eighth grade.' Now the older kids want to finish high school and go onto trade school, more schooling. Every student that comes there has something to do with that . . . has a good impact."

Students drew on their own educational experiences to augment the experiences of others, as noted by this education faculty member in commenting on her YouthBuild project:

The community benefitted from the YouthBuild project in the sense that the . . . [university] students had the opportunity to share their knowledge and skills with the YouthBuild organization . . . meet the individual needs of the Youth-Build students and create an engaging, successful education experience for them.

A social work faculty member pointed to help with character building, a goal of the programs she worked with, that the university students provided:

Character building is what this program really emphasizes, teaching the kids at a really young age . . . honesty, respect, integrity. This carries over into the school day. . . . We know if we teach these traits, they will carry over into adulthood. They are never too young to learn character-building skills There is too much going on in the schools; we don't have enough time to teach these skills. I wish I had more time to do this. We're constantly putting out fires just to provide some stability for the kids.

A communication faculty member discussed how the university students mentored the high school students about bullying:

These are students with behavioral problems, have failed several classes (and sometimes whole grade levels), have issues with attendance and sometimes have had issues with the law. They are placed in special classes to hopefully learn how to thrive in a public-school setting. If they do not, most likely, they will drop out. . . . I've learned that some of these students are in gangs or know people who are. Some work to help pay the rent for their family to stay in housing, and others have family members in jail due to drugs or violent offenses. It broke my heart to learn that several of the kids loved school only because they had somewhere to go besides home. . . . By targeting those who have been identified as "problem students," we may be able to . . . stop a future conflict from turning into a bullying episode.

Adult clients also gained resources through these projects. A nursing faculty member suggested that those her students were working with might have less anxiety about accessing health care, so they would be more empowered to seek care. "Exposure to nursing students may decrease anxiety for those who need to access health care services. Individuals were also made aware of resources in the community and how to cope with the challenges they face in their lives."

This community partner of another nursing faculty member stressed the ·impact of educational programming on women living in a homeless shelter:

Teaching about healthy foods and snacks to parents and children at the . . . [homeless] shelter (the presentations were separate and included actually preparing snacks). . . . Information on how to be a smart consumer of health care, including when to seek care and where and how to utilize cheaper medications (locations and lists for free and $4 prescriptions). . . . Any time college students come there . . . the kids don't often see these positive adult role models, even young adults, the college students, coming and trying to make something out of their lives and succeeding. The other examples they see of success are those in gangs.

Most often, we think of service learning as exposing students to real life situations that extend the applicability of what they learn in the classroom outside its walls. However, the exposure of students to clients and staff of community organizations changes all stakeholders in important ways. When we consider service learning using the definition of micro autonomy, i.e., knowledge and resource sharing that extends to groups outside one's primary groups, we expand narrow views of service learning to realize many unintended benefits. In many cases, these benefits are understood after projects are completed and faculty and community partners learn more about student experiences. Since many projects target people who are underserved, poor, or lacking knowledge to access resources, projects carry with them a social justice component, another consequence of service learning, often not realized nor intended by faculties and community partners.

The revelation that people in underserved populations are like many of the students who work with them shatters notions that all university students come from educated, affluent, stable families, and shatter stereotypical notions that students in poverty come from "broken homes" whose parents simply don't have the time or interest or cannot support their children academically. University students in this study often began to understand how circumstances, caused by multiple factors, lead to homelessness, poverty, and lack of educational advancement. Many of these circumstances are often beyond the control of those affected. Moreover, the experience of learning from others through interaction builds confidence in the capacity to advocate bettering conditions on for student and clients, thus building self-esteem and personal efficacy.

Evident from this review is the different emphasis placed by faculty and community partners on the benefits of service-learning projects. While faculty seem to focus on student learning and leadership skills, community partners focus on supporting and promoting self-advocacy skills in their clients. Yet, such different perspectives add to the experiences students reap from their service-learning projects—developing skills beyond the classroom, learning about various people and organizations in their community, and building leadership and a personal understanding of their future professional desires. In this endeavor, through experience and stories of client lives, students begin to understand the structural conditions creating circumstances faced by many people in poverty.

Macro Embeddedness: Strengthening Organizations toward Sustainability by Mobilizing Shared Interests

Another type of social capital frequently mentioned was at the macro level. In addition to substantial mentions of developing bridging social capital at the individual level, and some mention of building bonding social capital, our respondents frequently discussed the positive impact these projects had on the community organizations involved. This area drew the most comments from all respondents. In the Woolcock typology, this macro embeddedness goes beyond individual asset building to the development of entire organizations. In this case, the resources acquired promote organizational solidarity and, ultimately, sustainability.

These service-learning projects promoted macro embeddedness on a few levels. At the most basic, students performed administrative tasks that freed agency staff to serve more clients efficiently. However, this is a short-term fix as students leave projects and thus, leave agency staff to return to administrative tasks that students no longer perform. Highly valued, mostly by community partners, was the knowledge and creativity that students provided to help strengthen organizations for the long term. Through their creativity, students helped agencies improve their overall efficiency in ways that could be sustained after students left their placements.

For the most part, the faculty members seemed to have an accurate sense that their students' work benefitted the organizations they were worked with, and in more than half of the cases, this belief seemed to be deep and extensive. Partners agreed that these projects had functioned to strengthen their organizations. However, there were subtle differences in the specific ways faculty and partners saw the projects benefitting the organizations. At times, the faculty members focused more on the campus and/or the impact on their students, while partners focused more on the ways the university students could contribute to the work they were doing.

CREATIVITY AND INNOVATION

As expected, perspectives differed on the value of the project. One community partner felt the students contributed to the agency by developing assessments and treatment plans for profoundly disabled residents and interacted with them one on one. Additionally, "they would work with them on building social skills, might be as simple as sorting colors or objects. Students . . . bring different perspectives and stay on track in not getting stuck in a rut. Students come in with great ideas." The faculty member, on the other hand, made lengthy comments about what the students did, then at the end, stating it was not much help to the agency: "Students did training and made handouts for staff. . . . Not much contribution to agency . . . not the work that they were engaged in."

Another partner who worked with an international nonprofit organization noted that the university students were a source of ideas that helped agency staff see things in different and productive ways: "We try to let them come to our staff meetings and they have an equal voice like they are a full-time employee, and it is very interesting listening and hearing their ideas or . . . perspective. [M]ore than once where they have shaped the direction of the organization based on their input."

Direct Assistance in Accomplishing Goals

Projects helped organizations accomplish their goals. This was mentioned in general but was also noted more specifically when students brought additional resources to the agency, either in the form of their own expertise and experience, or by helping staff accomplish their tasks through training. This partner focused on the awareness built in the broader community through assistance with marketing of events.

> We do an annual fundraising event and a marketing class . . . took on how to best market that event. . . . So, what did we get out of it? We got more exposure, more tickets were sold. [T]he year before we had . . . 450 tri-staters come, and then last year when they did it, I don't know if it's necessarily because of them, but . . . we had 1,100 tickets that were sold, and 913 people showed up. . . . So, it was a big win for us. [T]hey used social media.

One faculty member, who also works as a school social worker, said that her project taught families how to access services for their children's education, furthering the goals of her school. In addition to promoting the mission of the agency, the project had a social justice component that enabled the school to take control of available community assets. She said: "This is a population that is often left out because there are so many barriers, transportation being one. The families can access the services without going to . . . [the] school, a long way away. . . . They are able to reach so many more kids and families who otherwise wouldn't be able to participate in such programs."

The faculty member's partner, who managed a local YMCA, an after-school program, and other youth development programs, said this:

I think number one, it supports the mission statement . . . that they will respond
to the needs of the community . . . immediately it provides a mode in which our
[K12] students can help us fulfill our mission. If we're not doing our mission,
then we're not existing as an organization. [I]t flows right in well. The secondary pieces were just creating better people in the world . . . as we create more
people who give back and take care of the world; that's really what it's all about.

Another faculty member discussed resources her class contributed in helping
the organization achieve its goals: "We were able to identify specific nutri-
ents that the [homeless shelter] patrons were lacking in and developed a list of
recommended food items that the [homeless shelter] could request to be donated to help fill in the nutritional gaps for their patrons." Her partner agreed,
and added a few other contributions the faculty member had not mentioned:

For the agency, we had . . . our massive food and kitchen operations—we're still
at 10,000 to 15,000 meals a month—it got some attention from professionals.
They gave us some good advice. . . . We also got a recipe book they developed,
which we have used. A longer-term issue has been more attention to nutrition
and food safety as far as our process, and the nutritional needs of that population.

According to this community partner, people who were homeless were getting more nutritious food and learning about food safety:

It provided more awareness about food safety and nutrition, since that is a big
part of the operation. . . . We want to provide food, but with dignity. A way of
conveying dignity to our guests is conveying that their nutrition is important.
It provided knowledge and awareness for workers throughout the organization.
They emphasized use of meat thermometers, different cutting boards for different foods, hairnets, and gloves, keeping knives separate, food storage and labeling. . . . We feel like we had a clarification of process. I think that it helped the
willing volunteer . . . the untrained person willing to help feels more confident
they are doing this right, following good practices.

Another faculty member discussed helping her partner's agency achieve its
goals about educating high school students about alcohol. Her partner also
focused on the importance of communicating about the issue, but on a different aspect of the collaboration:

Benefits to our agency are good quality videos that we can use. They reach a
population we don't necessarily reach, high schoolers and then colleges, and we
don't get into either . . . the peer-to-peer education, students with peers, talking
to classmates and high school students peer to peer. . . . We are working on a
town hall meeting for under-age drinking. Try to get people to understand the
process of drinking or overdrinking.

A Master of Information Systems (MIS) class provided an arts council with a technically efficient method for tracking the loan of musical instruments to K12 students by musicians. The faculty member discussed the benefits for the organization in some detail.

[The organization] gets instruments . . . they want to loan . . . out to students who are participating in music as part of high school. They had a data base system that wasn't . . . working well. [The students] went in and designed a database to keep track of instruments, who donated them and send out thank yous. [They created a] system of who they were loaned to and when are we getting it back . . . automated. Before, the project didn't know the status of an instrument. Now with a click of a button, they can show a report and see where instruments are. . . . Their processes became more efficient, an indirect benefit, appraisal for tax purposes.

Her partner agreed. "Easier than using the index cards. Helps us keep the records on how much impact."

A Health Education and Sports Management faculty member and partner discussed the contributions students made to a community garden project:

. . . winterizing gardens. Clean plots that people left. Put out wood chips around the paths for the winter so it's easier to work in the spring. They have easier clean up and in spring have plots ready. . . . [The community partner] helps because of manpower. Do the dirty work, moving heavy lifting and don't have a lot of people doing it. Makes it easy for them to have a sellable garden for people to work at.

Her partner agreed that the "dirty work" the university students were doing was valuable:

[We have] 120 plots and ask for $20 donations. That gets you compost, mulch, water for the season. Students cleaned up plots, weeded, checked if needed compost, added more compost. General maintenance of the . . . garden for the spring. They are all given plots that require a flower border. Some were cleaning out the flower border. That was the general aspect of what we were asking them to do. . . . They greatly benefitted [from the] work that we're doing repairing the garden for the 109 gardeners that were there. Pathways that needed weeding. Summer planting . . . we have a few volunteers but not many.

One step toward strengthening community is strengthening the capacity of individual organizations to accomplish their goals. Indeed, each agency contributes to social capital that will help sustain the larger community. There was no specific evidence that faculty or community partners shared this vision of their contribution to the whole community, though both faculty and community partners recognized how service learning supports the missions and work of their own organizations.

Service-learning projects sustained organizations to varying extents, based upon agency focus and need. Some agencies saw students as full partners in decision-making and benefitted from their creative ideas. Others limited students to specific tasks that, while supporting the mission of the agency, may not have taken full advantage of students' knowledge. For the most part, both community partners and faculty felt each project benefited agencies and students. Some projects had long-term benefits; these projects involved training clients to improve current skills that might transfer to life-long habits and/or providing technology to market, expand capacity, and improve organizational efficiency.

Macro Autonomy: Community Organizations Link with Outside Resources to Achieve Socially Optimal Outcomes So That Administrative Systems Are Better Able to Deliver Public Services and Promote Healthy Communities

There were relatively few references to perceived outcomes of these service learning projects, beyond enhancements to the specific organizations involved (macro embeddedness) or exposing individuals to new networks (bridging social capital or micro autonomy). This further impact, seen as macro autonomy in the Woolcock (1998) model, involves connecting agencies with other community resources, supporting collaborations for their mutual benefit, cooperation across organizations to achieve a larger, common goal, or simply contributing to the greater good of the community beyond strengthening the specific organization involved.

Connecting to Other Agencies for Bureaucratic Efficiency

The partner for the YouthBuild project gave the clearest example of bureaucratic efficiency, describing interconnections with other organizations and the willingness of the city government to provide funding when their grant funding lapsed.

> Our success rate was very high. . . . We had a 75 percent graduation rate. We were also getting help from USI's AmeriCorps Program at the time (in the Social Work program). . . . This is a Department of Labor Grant, although our agency (Evansville Housing Authority) is funded by HUD. This past year, no one in Indiana was funded for this program. The City was so impressed with what we have been doing, that they picked up the tab for this year. MPO had some funds to contribute. We are reapplying now. . . . The program is still going.

Work Force 1 is managing the educational program, through Vincennes University. They provide local instructors, who give participants individual attention.

He went on to discuss the impact the graduates of the program have had on the community:

> The graduates of the program have made a difference in our community. They have job skills that they didn't have before. Most of the young women went on to get a cosmetology certification. One young man became an electrician, and several have become carpenters. They have all stayed local. . . . Those that went on to get their GEDs are all better people, holding jobs. . . . We helped them move away from the unlawful activities they were engaged in before coming into the program. They now know how to get things the right way. . . . One person is a supervisor at Walmart, some working at Berry, Toyota, etc.; 70–80 percent are gainfully employed. They've learned what life is all about, how to raise a family properly. Very few have gotten into trouble with the law since leaving the program. Very few have gone back to "that way of life."

The education faculty working with him agreed that the success of the program participants had "a positive impact on the surrounding community."

Another example of inter-organization cooperation was the partner for the communications class working in a large youth-serving organization, who said she informed other organizations how to benefit from a connection with the university. This partner said, "With what our kids were able to take from it into the community, we would report on it at Site Council meetings for our neighborhood school, when we talked about activities we were doing, who we were bringing in and so forth. It helped other agencies see how they might connect with [the university]."

STRENGTHENING THE COMMUNITY, ALLEVIATING SOCIAL PROBLEMS

Other partners made the argument that a byproduct of their program's success was a stronger community. A staff member at a small after school program said this: "Kids are our future. The south side inner-city of Evansville is improving and the kids need to improve, to bring jobs back onto the neighborhood . . . for the whole city to improve. So many people will not come to our side of town because it is dangerous. The kids can't get out of it. It helps them grow. Helps the entire community."

The director of the program pointed to the impact for the individuals in the program, which translates into a more functional community:

One major goal . . . is to give the youth hope for the future, which they haven't had a lot of. We want them to believe they can do more than the gang activity, drug dealing, pimping, and prostituting that they see now as successful role models. . . . We have been successful in these efforts. In the current group of youth, we are working with, none of them have gotten pregnant, none have gotten in trouble with the law, over one-half of them have gainful employment this summer.

The belief that program success translates into a stronger community was echoed by the principal of the school where teacher education majors tutored and mentored. "In an indirect way, the better we can educate the children, the populace, the better off the community is. They are trying to help us better educate the children."

Our respondents also talked about the impact projects had had on a variety of community problems, ranging from bullying to homelessness to addiction. One social work faculty member saw the projects as raising the moral fiber of the community through the Positive Behavior Intervention Support process advocated by her partner who ran a large after school program.

Being a mentor provides a safe place for them to be after school. Keeps them off the streets during that time, 3 to 5 p.m.—when there is a high incidence of crime, when many kids are unsupervised . . . always looking for ways to provide on-site activities in their neighborhoods. . . . Character-building is what his program really emphasizes, teaching the kids at a really young age.

Another faculty described his students' efforts to address the issue of human trafficking:

They thought of it as something that happens in third world countries . . . through that course, they learned how to build a campaign to address a broad issue. . . . Our project helped the campus group build projects. . . . It had other implications. It led to the Scholars for Syria group, which sponsored refugees and did other activities . . . conversations. . . . The students didn't understand why people, governments, others were not doing something. They grappled with an understanding of the social injustice that they were seeing, why the Myanmar government, the United States government wasn't doing more. Some worked on government action, legislation here. A group did a project for a Change Maker Challenge competition and came in second place.

The communications faculty whose students worked on the bullying project believed they were addressing a critical community issue:

[It's] an attempt to provide a different message than what is out there. Generally speaking, the messages on bullying have been, "tell someone" if you're a victim and "you're going to get in trouble" if you're a bully. While these messages work superficially on the surface, they do not address the underlying issues of bullying in schools. By targeting those who have been identified as "problem students," we may be able to change the message to one of prevention rather than reaction and stop a future conflict from turning into a bullying episode. Some gained insights into their own problematic behavior.

His partner agreed it had made a difference: "Our kids took the scenarios, they role played, into their everyday lives. It gave them a different way to see how to react to situations other than with violence and conflict and hostility and negativity. We could see it impacted how they handled themselves outside on their own, with arguments, bullying situations, and so on."

PROMOTING A HEALTHY COMMUNITY

Several faculty and partners believed their projects had improved the health of the community. This nursing faculty commented on the impact of the health fairs her students had helped with in the Latino community:

> Over the past 5 years that I have been engaging with students in the health fairs, I have seen the participants beginning to change from being present-oriented and not really thinking about prevention and health promotion, to now taking initiative with their health care and getting appointments to be seen by providers. In the beginning, 80 percent of these Hispanic participants just went to the emergency room when things got bad—there was no thought for prevention or ongoing care, and now that is changing. They are now getting connected with health care providers. . . . We are making an impact in the community with this population and with our future healthcare providers through these health fairs.

Her partner agreed the project had had this impact:

> It gives the community members the opportunity for services they don't have otherwise. The whole family comes. [T]hey feel they can get all kinds of help right there. They have their medical exams on site at the monthly fairs, with a high amount of benefits. It really pays off, the preventive care and information. They were encouraged to change their eating patterns to prevent diabetes. The dieticians helped them know what to eat. [T]hey started doing this . . . to be more aware of their health, to understand the importance of prevention. This is a great service to provide, would be nice to do it again.

A nursing faculty said her students' projects with a neighborhood program resulted in "individuals . . . made aware of resources in the community and how to cope with the challenges they face in their lives." Her partner pointed to the impact on the community:

> They have had a big impact on the neighborhood that we serve. First, the knowledge they all get. They hear about issues with smoking, drugs, and alcohol, but to have the students come in with charts and pictures and see what it will do to you and your baby, that has a much bigger impact. We can see the mothers rethinking their behaviors and some come in say "I've quit smoking" or "I'm not drinking anymore." But it has had an even bigger impact on the youth who won't start these things in the first place. It's hard to evaluate that, not doing things, but we can see it is having an impact.

An engineering faculty member who helped his students with trails projects also believed they were contributing to the general health of the community:

> Assuming all communities are looking for improved health, it would help any community. Evansville doesn't have a good rating as far as we smoke too much and eat too much. Can burn up a few calories with the trails. Other Midwestern cities, Portland, have more bike paths. We don't have enough bike trails here.

The director of a large afterschool program took pains to be sure the youth he worked with understood the contributions they were making to the community at large:

> So, people don't just show up at a park and clean. . . . They understand if they're making a trail, the purpose is to provide an opportunity for people for decades to walk a trail and benefit physically, mentally, socially from that effort. It isn't just making a trail from here to there, that kids really understand why they're doing this and the impact they can have.

Two partners asserted that their projects had contributed to the aesthetics of the community. One argued that their project of matching musical instruments with interested students contributed to the general artistic atmosphere in the community:

> We all know that art and music seem to be disappearing more and more from the schools. . . . The program . . . fills a void. . . . It gives respect of the community. . . . Our purpose is to make sure that art reaches the people . . . young people, emerging artists, emerging art community. Everything that we do . . . is primarily meant to assist art and artists. . . . I think a community without art is a very sorrowful place because if you travel if you go anywhere in the world that is what draws people to a community. Racine has such an active arts community . . . creative. It's huge.

The partner for the community garden project believed it contributed to the general beauty of the community:

> I think it definitely helps the community as a whole. The garden is a showplace. Folks that come through . . . look at how the city in general is doing . . . [and] mention that they walk through the garden . . . everyone passes it sooner or later and people have a better feeling about the community in general. . . . Folks . . . see the garden looks so nice. . . . I wish my garden looked half as well. It helps with sense of community. They are proud of it. . . . The mayor has mentioned it in his address . . . sense of accomplishment. . . . The fact that we have gardens all over the city. . . . They now have a connection . . . feel better about the neighborhood. . . . It's a real sense of pride that the garden is there, that people go to the picnic table to talk and sit and enjoy . . . builds community. . . . Pick up the paper . . . story about the middle of nowhere you get a beautiful part of the city.

One social work faculty reported that her service-learning project had made a concrete contribution to the community by helping generate support for new supportive housing units. The faculty member said, "A report from the study was published on the Destination Home website, representing a major collaborative effort to end homelessness in Vanderburgh County. It was instrumental in the establishment of a new housing center for both homeless veterans and homeless families more generally, Lucas Place 1." Her partner concurred: "The information they came up with has been cited and used in other ways to support the need for housing resources in the community. . . . It did help make a case for supported housing. People in Indianapolis are still looking at it and citing that study."

Many of our participants believed their projects contributed to the community beyond strengthening the organizations involved. The impacts included increased levels of health, aesthetics, safety, and programs for the homeless. The seeds of community development are borne depending on the abilities of both individuals and organizations to develop a common identity, define who they are, develop common goals and, in the case of organizations, a common mission. Viewing the cells in Woolcock's (1998) typology that describe autonomy may contribute most to community development by reinforcing social capital between partnerships.

Social Justice Implications

Social justice efforts seek to right unequal distribution of resources within communities that bear an unfair burden of what Banerjee (2008) calls "bads." Examples of "bads" include communities of high poverty, which are defined as food deserts, lack of access to resources such as adequate transportation or health care, and lack of agents of power to confront institutionalized unfair distribution of services or resources. Merely giving to a community without addressing the underlying causes of inequality does not help that community develop the economic strength it needs to prosper.

When service learning has an explicit social justice focus, participants are more likely to tip the imbalance of unequal distribution of resources to create a more just system of access to goods and services. Most of the service-learning projects exemplified in this chapter had social justice components, in which participants contributed to underserved communities by offering clients new ways to access resources of which they were unaware. Nevertheless, six pairs of faculty-community partners did not mention or did not want to consider social justice as a contribution of their work with students in the community. When asked if the project promoted social justice, the community partner with the YouthBuild Project, a project for people in poverty wanting to earn GEDs and learn construction skills, stated, "Not sure about that. Don't know if it's made whole lot of difference. Not sure how to answer that, I don't want to give wrong information." An engineering faculty member was more specific in his response. "That's not really what we're shooting for, that type of thing, getting the students to incorporate design skills and write a report. Sometimes, the projects accomplish that, but doubt we did that on this one." Responding about the project that tutored students in an after-school program, the faculty member said: "Don't know how much it did that. If it did, it would be a broad definition of social justice. We didn't approach it that way. It wasn't so much about poverty, but about finding schools near the UE campus, so the students could get there, would be able to show up." In other instances, neither faculty nor community partners responded to the question.

When acknowledging a social justice contribution, some focused on the impact the project had on university students. A community partner from the Evansville, Indiana, school district says,

> The college student . . . is . . . someone who has gone through high school . . . gone on to college at USI or U of E, succeeded. They are doing well but they . . . frequently come from a background where they don't understand why a child goes to school without a coat on. "What do you mean they don't have a coat?" so once they've been exposed to the opportunities, to be around those families, they sort of get to see.

According to the community partner working with dental hygiene students on teaching clients about hygiene:

> I knew that the students would experience working with a culture that was not a typical culture in the dental office when I set up the WARM program, but

I had not pinpointed exactly what they would gain. Yes, they do learn about social justice, to a certain degree since many of the residents talked about not having access to dental services. They talked about the lack of money, Medicaid providers, transportation, and so on. Students always have a wide variety of comments pertaining to the event.

Most faculty and community partners emphasized the impact that service-learning had on recipients. The community partner who worked with nursing students reported that the project promoted social justice through client education. "Yes, to be more aware of their health, to understand the importance of prevention. This is a great service to provide."

A social work faculty member that worked with an after-school project said:

> Yes, some kids are not athletically or intellectually gifted, or in leadership positions because of their limitations, but in these programs that doesn't matter. They get an opportunity to shine and be important. They are judged by how they are. There are fair consequences to their actions by being rewarded for positive behaviors.

Overall impressions of responses to our question, "Did the project promote social justice?" suggest that social justice was not a primary goal for many of these faculty and community partners, thus it was not an explicit learning outcome for students. Although students were exposed to underserved populations in need, the projects did not specify promoting access to resources for people in poverty. Reflecting on a project on food and nutrition, a community partner says, "This might be a bit of a reach, but I would say something about it built more capacity in food service operations. We are feeding people three times a day, which is social justice. It improved our capacity to serve meals to homeless and hungry people."

Nevertheless, some faculty were purposeful in their choice of projects and acknowledged that social justice was a primary goal. A communications faculty who supervised students running an interactive workshop, related to decision-making and peer pressure, at the local Boys and Girls Club said the following:

> I wanted them to understand issues related to class, and perhaps social justice issues, but I wanted them to recognize how difference emerged and how they (might) respond as a result of the difference, real and perceived. I also wanted a level of sophistication in that understanding (beyond responses about how lucky and fortunate they are to not be raised like the kids . . .). In some instances that happened and in others not so much. Most were changed and in a positive way.

In response to the project on human trafficking in Myanmar, the faculty member noted the project's strong connection to social justice: "This project has a lot more connections to that. The students did not understand why people, governments, others were not doing something. They grappled with an understanding of the social injustice that they were seeing, why the Myanmar government, the United States government was not doing more."

There was great variability in faculty/community partners' acknowledgment of social justice as part of their projects' goals. Also, it appears that even if social justice was a goal, it was often not made explicit to students, so that students may have experienced some attitudinal changes, but may not have connected their experiences and changes to a goal of promoting social justice.

CONCLUSION

Connecting service learning to community development is a logical leap overlooked in much of the literature on community development partly because of the lack of theoretical underpinnings to understand this connection. Woolcock's (1998) typology offers a model for categorizing service learning so that we can gain a better understanding of how service learning contributes to developing social capital and enhancing community. The researchers can see more clearly where the connections are most likely to be and found more connections in the second (bridging social capital, micro autonomy) and third (macro embeddedness) cells of the model. There are exchanges on the individual levels that provide bridging social capital for both university students and the individuals they work with in the community. There are also many resources available that strengthen the organizations involved.

Organizations are strengthened when service-learning projects support organizational goals to reinforce the agency mission and use students as resources to help staff better serve clients (macro embeddedness), and communities are strengthened when organizations see themselves as part of a larger goal to deliver public services that create healthier communities (macro autonomy). On an individual level, students learn about their community and interact with people from populations they may have never encountered and youth in served agencies build bonds with university students (micro autonomy) and to a lesser extent, university students form bonds with other students in their classes (micro embeddedness).

While this typology helps us understand the connection between service learning, social capital development, and community development, and offers an estimate of the frequency to which projects fall into each category of the typology, we must acknowledge division of projects into discrete units is somewhat artificial. Often, projects fall into multiple cells within the typology or begin at one cell (micro autonomy) but expand their focus and accomplish larger goals (macro embeddedness). The advantage of using Woolcock's typology is to help understand the building blocks essential to community development and reach a better understanding of how process moves from simple to complex.

Our interviews with faculty and community partners reveal that community development is often not viewed as an explicit goal of projects. Faculty and community partners have differing goals for students and community agencies, although most believe their projects were beneficial to both. Additionally, with few exceptions, we found faculty did not recognize their projects' contributions to social justice until we asked the specific question in our interviews, although most projects had social justice impacts, serving people in vulnerable populations, people in poverty, and people of color. A few faculty members denied a social justice contribution or skirted the topic. Even though every project had political implications, many faculty members seemed to avoid politicizing service-learning work. These responses reinforce the conception of service learning as "doing for," a charitable enterprise, without recognizing that service learning has the potential to change communities for the better. Moreover, the refusal to acknowledge the goal of social change leaves students with an incomplete understanding of their potential as social change actors in their communities.

These types of projects may have varying levels of usefulness for those doing community development work, in that some faculty members may tend to skirt the crux of the issues. We advise those wishing to make use of service-learning projects in community development to explicitly explore the parameters and assumptions of projects and participants, to ensure they would have the potential to make a contribution. We recommend use of such projects in aspects of overall community development efforts where they stand to be most relevant—our results suggest in building bridging social capital and strengthening organizations.

The service learning programs involved in this study place heavy emphasis on working with nonprofit organizations in the surrounding community. This may be a large factor producing so many comments about strengthening organizations. Findings may differ for service-learning programs that work more with grassroots organizations or activist individuals, doing more participant action research.

Chapter Six

Adaptive Collaborative Community Transformation (ACCT) Model of Comprehensive Community Development

Community organizer Jim Caparo (2013) argues that successful community development must be comprehensive and all elements of a neighborhood or community (i.e., housing, health, safety, economic development, workforce deployment, education, and entrepreneurship) are important and strategic to each other. The needs and issues of a community are interrelated and cannot be dealt with independently (Janson, 2016). The work of many disciplines and program areas in community development must be simultaneous and connected because they add value to one another and yield results beyond what any one program can do by itself (Caparo, 2013).

Comprehensive community development is collaborative and relies on developing relationships and partnerships based on "exchanging information, altering activities, sharing resources, and enhancing the capacity of another for mutual benefit in order to achieve a common purpose" (Janson, 2016, p. 12; Himmelman, 2002, p. 3). This approach to community development can enhance bridging social capital and can stretch the capacity of an organization to have a larger impact and provide a greater range of services to the community, but it may require the organization to collaborate and coordinate across different sectors, fields, and levels of governments to appropriately address the structural issues and problems facing a community (Janson, 2016).

Comprehensive community development evolved through much of the 20th century through the New Deal, War on Poverty, and the Model Cities program, as discussed in chapter 1. The evolution of CDCs and the rise of the Local Initiatives Support Corporation (LISC), also discussed in chapter 1, transformed community development from a single-issue model to a model that addresses a broad range of social, economic, and physical needs of a neighborhood and community.

Erickson, Galloway, and Cytron (2012) use the term "community quarterback," to refer to the leader or convener of comprehensive community development who is responsible for developing a collective vision for the community, in addition to the day-to-day management of the organization's relationships, activities, and resources. Under the quarterback model, the leader or convener is more of a facilitator, compared to a traditional leader that is more hierarchical and controlling. A quarterback leader must be embedded in their respective communities, make decisions collectively towards a shared goal rather than control any outcomes, and make connections between people and organizations both inside and outside the organization (Onyx & Leonard, 2010; Janson, 2016). More importantly, the quarterback or convener must be a catalyst and build capacity to drive transformational change sustainable in the short and long terms, while also continuously collecting data and measuring and quantifying outcomes (Recker & Reed, 2013).

ADAPTIVE COLLABORATIVE COMMUNITY TRANSFORMATION (ACCT) MODEL

How a community transforms itself usually begins with a conversation the community has with itself over its future. The community will decide if it wants to have either a retributive conversation (whether it's a problem to be solved, a focus on fear or faults, or a focus on laws and oversight) or a restorative conversation (a possibility to be lived into, towards a focus on one's gifts and talents, a focus towards the betterment of the social fabric of the community, or to choose to hold the community accountable) (Block, 2008, p. 54).

A community development model that creates a new conversation focuses on what is possible and holds the community and individual residents accountable, which is at the heart of the Adaptive Collaborative Community Transformation (ACCT) model developed by researchers with the Center for Applied Research (CAR) at the University of Southern Indiana. The ACCT model uses the Simplex method, which is a facilitation method using creative problem solving that enables teams large and small to come up with creative solution to challenges facing their community (Basadur, 2003).

The ACCT model involves several major steps: the pre-initiative (which includes data gathering), the formalizing of the steering committee, community discussions (listening and visioning sessions), and community research, followed by engagement and action by the community. For the pre-initiative phase, an individual or organization demonstrates an interest in a community revitalization effort. Data is gathered through initial small group conversations to learn more about the community and to assess the community's assets. This phase should also include ethnographic training, which is the process by which researchers or participants immerse themselves into a group or culture over a long or extended period of time. After that time, researchers understand the community's identity and culture, know how the community lives, what the community says about themselves, what the community does, and what the community values (Schutt, 2015, p. 334; Armstrong, 2008, p. 55).

A pre-initiative is important to understand the starting point for a community from their perspective to gain buy-in and enthusiasm and build trust from the community. The local drivers and an initial informal support group should determine the necessary and sufficient components for a community development initiative. A willing and local convener in the community who can develop and communicate an initial vision, sell the initiative, and energize as many people as possible (approximately 50–100 people at first) must be identified. The convener must be a highly committed person who has a complex vision and knowledge of the community. The convener should know the conditions of the neighborhood, its culture, its social attributes, its attitude, and its readiness to determine if such an intervention for development and revitalization is appropriate.

When putting together such a team, several questions are important to consider: are the right people on the team? What is the mission of each team? What tools does the team need to be effective? In addition to the convener, it's important to intentionally select and recruit leadership that would serve on the steering committee, such as residents, community leaders, individuals who have diverse talents and viewpoints, high-capacity volunteers who have specific skills, and a project manager who can provide support both to the steering committee and the priority teams based on the goals that will be developed by the community during the process. Members of the steering committee will participate in the facilitated community discussion, led by a highly trained facilitator, to conceptualize a vision and to work on developing goals, objectives, strategies, and metrics that will set the future strategic direction of the community.

A community also needs seed money and support from public and private institutions and stakeholders from major institutions, as well as access to knowledge that doesn't exist in the community, such as subject matter experts (SMEs) or consultants, and other intellectual and organizational capital, who can engage in the process by presenting critical information (financial data, zoning data, metrics, etc.) relevant to the process (Ellspermann et al., 2010).

The formalized steering committee will engage in a community discussion in the form of a preconsult, a SWOT (strengths, weaknesses, opportunities, threats) analysis, and a community vision development and listening session that runs parallel with community research, such as surveys, focus groups, the creation of a community profile, and a widespread needs assessment.

A pre-consult is a meeting where the facilitator and consultant have an opportunity to meet their client (i.e., community or organization). This meeting allows participants to experience how the Simplex process works in real time (Thissen, 2020). The preconsult begins when a client has come to the realization that they want to do "something big that they have ever done before" (Ellspermann, Recker, & Kleindorfer, 2010). In the case with Habitat and the Glenwood Community Development Initiative (GCDI), Habitat for Humanity of Evansville Executive Director Lori Reed wanted to do more than build houses—she wanted to build communities and engage all stakeholders in the process, but she was not sure what it would look like (Ellspermann et al., 2010). The preconsult session began by involving several stakeholders to identify the lead convener and the steering committee members before the group listening and visioning session begins. At this session, the facilitator presents a list of questions that will set expectations for the facilitator, convener, and the community (Thissen, 2020).

ROLE OF THE FACILITATOR

Community visioning can be achieved through an appropriate level of facilitation, which is different from traditional facilitation in that it requires specific skills of working in large teams and knowledge of existing governance (Ellspermann, 2008). Traditional facilitation is primarily content based and focuses on providing expertise and solutions *for* the community (the technical assistance model of community development) rather than working *with* the community to empower its residents to solve their own problems (the self-help model of community development) (Ellspermann, 2008; Green & Haines, 2016).

For those working on visioning for small towns or in small to medium-sized communities, an effective facilitator requires "knowledge of large-scale vision development, an understanding of the stakeholders who should be invited to the table, an ease working with large teams (25 or bigger), a presence either in the community as a trusted partner, and the fortitude to help a large team reach consensus over a relatively short period of time closure and documented action forward" (Ellspermann, 2008, p. 3).

A highly skilled and competent facilitator also would be versed in appropriate strategic planning methodologies, such as SWOT analysis, developing mission and vision statements, and implementation planning. This person must demonstrate a proficiency in facilitating small and large groups and should be someone who can motivate and encourage positive change and can maintain trust and integrity with the convening organization (Ellspermann, 2008). The facilitator is not responsible for recommending solutions and should not appear to be the owner of the initiative. The facilitator should provide a process for the community to "organize the thinking" of the stakeholders that will lead to positive results (Ellspermann et al., 2010).

COMMUNITY SWOT ANALYSIS

Often known as the Harvard model, a SWOT analysis is an internal assessment used in strategic planning to gauge a community's capabilities relative to its mission, vision, capacity, and operating environment, by looking at the community's strengths, weaknesses, opportunities, and threats (Kearns, 2000; Helms & Nixon, 2010). Strengths are described by the things the community does well (e.g., assets, resources) (Renault, 2010). Weaknesses focus on how the community is underperforming or how poorly it is doing its work (i.e., limitations, restrictions, challenges) (Renault, 2010). Opportunities refer to the possibilities that may help the community achieve its goals. Threats focus on obstacles that pose potential harm or hinder the efforts of the community and the people the community serves (Renault, 2010; Bryson, 2011).

In a SWOT analysis, it is not enough to look at each of the categories or quadrants in a silo, but how they interact with each other. For instance, after a community identifies its strengths, it should find out how it can leverage its strengths to take advantage of opportunities as it plans for future actions, serving like a mini strengths-opportunities analysis (S-O analysis) (Renault, 2010). The community should identify weaknesses it can overcome in order to take advantage of opportunities (O-W Analysis), identify which weaknesses can be turned into strengths in the future (W-S analysis), and also how a community can minimize weaknesses and avoid threats (W-T analysis) (Renault, 2010).

When a community identifies threats, they should identify which threats prevent them from taking advantage of strengths (T-S analysis), but also identify which threats are needed in order to create future opportunities (T-O analysis) (Renault, 2010). For a SWOT analysis to be successful, three to five items should be listed for each category to prevent endless lists. Items must be clearly defined and be as specific as possible. The lists should rely on facts not opinions and be action-oriented.

COMMUNITY LISTENING SESSION

A community listening session gathers input from constituents or community members on a topic for the purpose of learning different points of view. A listening session can range in size from 10 to 200 people. If a listening session is greater than 50, the group can be broken into smaller breakout sessions. According to the Basadur (1999, 2003) Simplex model, a listening session is performed as a "vertical deferral of judgment," where the facilitator helps participants distinguish between unclear situations and well-defined problems, and between defining a problem and solving a problem, by avoiding passing bias or judgment on any comments (Sousa, Pellissier, & Monteiro, n.d.). It is important and critical to create an atmosphere of deferral for judgment to allow participants to comfortably share their ideas and thoughts (Ellspermann et al., 2010).

At the beginning of the listening sessions, the facilitator sets the tone for the day, identifying three to five open-ended questions. Before the facilitator invites group comments, participants must understand the Simplex ground rules to be used throughout the process. In Simplex, sometimes an icebreaker or a bonding activity helps put the group into a collaborative state of mind, focusing on the interests of the whole rather than one individual's or organization's interests. Simplex helps to create an environment where titles are removed, egos checked, and judgment deferred so participants can share anything (Thissen, 2020). The facilitator asks participants to avoid the use

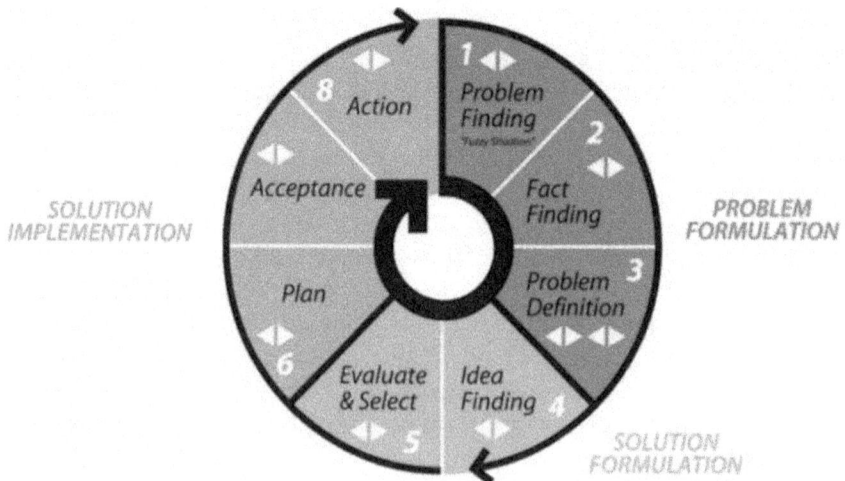

Figure 6.1. Eight-step wheel of the Simplex Process. *Source:* Basadur Simplex, 2003

of killer phrases, such as "Yes, that's a good idea, but . . ." or "We've never done it that way," or "It's not part of my job," or "It's against policy," or "It costs too much" (Basadur, 2003).

Three distinct phases and eight steps comprise the cyclic process of Simplex (Sousa, Pellissier, & Monteiro, n.d.; Basadur, 1999, 2003). The first three steps of the first phase are problem formulation, which includes problem finding, fact finding, and defining the problem without existing bias. Steps four and five involve solution formulation from idea finding and generation, to the evaluation and selection of the idea. Steps six, seven, and eight are known as solution implementation, which involves developing a plan, accepting the plan, and putting the plan into action (Basadur, 2003). Each step allows for divergence, which is the ability to imaginatively list as many facts, ideas, and solutions as possible without evaluation, judgment, or criticism (Basadur, 1999, 2003). Convergence allows the group to select the most important, insightful facts, ideas, or solutions, particularly using judgment, logic, and evaluation (Basadur, 1999, 2003).

According to Simplex facilitator and Indiana economic development official Mike Thissen (2020):

> A master facilitator practices the art of challenging difficult participants and establish the fact it is about collaboratively creating a plan an organization can implement. Also, the facilitator is not part of the implementation; they help put together the strategy but are not going to stay and be part of the organization. The actions are up to the participants.

The scribe is considered a vital position in a community listening or visioning session. This person writes down all responses from the questions throughout the session on flipchart sheets. The facilitator defers judgment by welcoming and encouraging everyone from the group to participate and provide input. After the questions have been answered and the comments have been recorded by the scribe, the facilitator may allow participants to place sticky dots on the comments they wish to emphasize.

After the group provides input, a SWOT analysis is conducted, enabling participants to identify each of the community's strengths, weaknesses, opportunities, and threats and their relationships across quadrants. Afterwards, the facilitator asks participants to converge on the most important strengths, weaknesses, opportunities, and threats; the group can complete this process through consensus or dots. Primarily, the community listening session will allow the steering committee to think about problems and possibilities as they begin to develop vision and mission statements.

COMMUNITY VISIONING AND MISSION DEVELOPMENT

A vision is a statement that transforms the community and provides a picture of what the community should look like and how it should act in fulfilling its mission (Bryson, 2011, p. 127). A vision is a declaration that also serves as a catalyst that can compel a community to move toward that dream (Maurer, 2000). A vision is an ideal, credible, unifying, attractive, and unique future picture of a community. A vision may be also community's "north star," the community's milestone or big hairy audacious goals (BHAGs), or a vivid image that describes the future state of the community (Ellspermann et al., 2010). A vision also facilitates goal setting and planning and sets priorities for the community by saying what they stand for and against (Maurer, 2000).

From a leadership community standpoint, visioning requires an inspirational and highly motivated leader who captures the energy and imagination, who captures the hopes, aspirations, ambitions, and values of everyone in the community to promote empowerment and change (Kearns, 2000). While a leader can be inspirational and highly motivating, relying too much on the leader during the community visioning can be detrimental because it relies too much on the leader's vision and traits may not easily be transferred or taught, and the leader might be blind to emerging threats in the environment (Kearns, 2000).

A vision statement is aspirational and not the goal or the end itself. Vision statements have no set length. Some visions are a few words, though some statements like John F. Kennedy's moon landing speech or Martin Luther King's *I Have a Dream* speech were much longer (Allison & Kaye, 2015). The vision statement should be inspirational and challenge the community to stretch its capacity to achieve its purpose and articulate how the community might look if it achieved its purpose (Allison & Kaye, 2015). The vision should be set on a timeline based on "how far one can see beyond the horizon" (Ellspermann et al., 2010). For the vision statement, the facilitator often engages participants in an exercise that asks them to look five to ten years in the future. Allison and Kaye (2015, p. 86) use an example of having participants imagine their organization is wildly successful and *The New York Times* wants to write about the organization. The exercise asks participants to think about the headline for the organization, what the article might say, and whom *NY Times* might quote.

Once the vision statement is developed and agreed upon, the facilitator will also help the group develop a mission statement for the community development initiative. The mission statement is a clarifying general statement of purpose that tells us why the community should be doing what it does (Bryson, 2011, p. 127).

Mission statements must be short, simple, and specific, and something that people can remember. They must also be realistic, motivating, compelling, and inspiring (Olsen, 2021). The statement must pass the disagreement test: If no one would disagree with the statement (e.g., "make the world better" or "act with integrity"), then the statement is too generic (Olsen, 2021).

Like the listening and SWOT analysis sessions, the facilitator will review the Simplex ground rules (and prohibit killer phrases), followed by a diverging and converging session that ask the following questions: What is our purpose? Whom do we serve? What makes us unique? After approximately 30 minutes of diverging on each of the three questions, the facilitator will ask participants to use dots to pick one or two items from the divergent list for each question, and the group will converge on items from each list that might be useful in the mission statement.

To finalize the mission statement, the facilitator breaks the group into teams of two to four people to craft a mission statement using the converged items. Each small team will present their mission statements, and the larger group will share what they like about each statement. Based on each small team's statement, the entire group will select the best one. The group can work together to craft the final wording and language of the mission statements and use portions from the small team's versions to develop a final mission statement. The scribe will assist the facilitator and the group on the language of the mission statement so that each participant understands the vision and mission statements they have created and developed.

STRATEGIC MAPPING

After developing the vision and mission statements, the facilitator will guide the community towards developing goals using the eight steps of the Simplex method. Using strategic mapping, the facilitator will ask the participants to identify "fuzzy situations" in the community as a starting point from which to work (Step 1). Through diverging, the group will identify as many fact-finding questions as possible (Step 2) and use the information from the SWOT analysis, before converging on the most intriguing facts or fuzzy situations that could assist the community in identifying the problem. In Step 3, based on the facts the group has considered, the group will map out a list on "How might we . . ." define the problem or problems, and through diverging and converging, will determine the best ways to the define the problem or problems. The "How might we . . ." question is considered the most important question in the Simplex process (Sousa et al., n.d.). After the group maps out each problem, the goals themselves emerge, are identified and agreed upon, either through consensus or using dots to capture the will of the group.

After the problems are defined and emerge as the goals after Step 3, the group will ask questions in Step 4 such as, "What is stopping us from solving the problem?" or "Why aren't we solving the problem?" which is now the proposed goal. Each goal at this point should be taken forward individually through the rest of the steps to flesh out the goal to develop objectives, strategies, and metrics. Diverging in Step 4 should generate ideas that might solve this problem or problems (goal) and converge by evaluating and selecting the best ideas for solving the problem or problems (goals) that ultimately become an objective and strategy for each goal. During converging in Step 4, the facilitator maps down each idea that may become an objective and strategy and the facilitator will ask the group participants to evaluate and select which goals, objectives, and strategies have enough support to move forward using dots.

Once the group forms a consensus on the major goals, objectives, and strategies, the facilitator will help the group, through diverging, to identify specific actions required to implement the plan, and through converging, will allow participants to select the most adequate actions in Step 6. Step 7 involves the necessary people in this process to ensure its feasibility, include those who did not participate in the earlier steps but who are indispensable to the project's success (Sousa et al., n.d.). Step 7 will also identify the owners of the new goals. Step 8 begins with each priority team starting with simple, specific, and realistic actions on their goal, objectives, and strategies.

COMMUNITY RESEARCH

According to Ledwith (2011), "research is integral to community development praxis; it is the way in which practice is kept relevant to the changing social and political context" (p. 34). A major part of the research under the ACCT model performed in parallel with the community discussions is the creation of a community profile. The community profile is critical to understanding the demographics and the makeup of the community, as well as the power on the individual, group, community, structure, and society (Ledwith, 2011). A community profile occurs in mutual partnership with the community in a systematic way that helps the community better understand the issues and challenges they are facing.

A community profile is defined as a summary of baseline conditions and trends that establish the demographic, social, and economic context of the community for assessing potential impacts and future decision making

(CUTR, 2000). The first component consists of an overview of basic demographic characteristics (age, race, ethnicity, educational attainment, disabilities), economic characteristics (employment, income, occupation types, overall makeup of labor force), and housing characteristics (age and type of housing, housing tenure, vacancy rates, types of occupancy, either renters or owners) (CUTR, 2000).

Much of the demographic, economic, and housing data can be obtained from federal sources (U.S. Census Bureau, Census Scope, American Fact Finder, USDA Economic Research Service data), along with state and local sources, chambers of commerce, school districts/boards of education, nonprofit organizations, and neighborhood associations (CUTR, 2000). For a community that is underserved and is seeking a community development initiative or intervention, understanding what poverty looks like is important (e.g., poverty rate, percentage of individuals and families receiving public assistance) (AmeriCorps VISTA Campus, 2021).

The second component of a community profile is identifying the issues and attitudes of the community. Much of this data will derive from the sources themselves through stakeholder interviews with community leaders who have lived in the community for a while and are knowledgeable about community affairs and issues, along with interviews of elected officials and representatives from other civic and nonprofit organizations (CUTR, 2000).

Oftentimes, for improving generalizability and validity, a survey may be administered to residents and stakeholders in the community. Another set of methods appropriate for this realm are holding community meetings, workshops, and forums, visiting the community, and observing it firsthand, or teaming up with a local historian or architect to do a walking or driving tour of the community or neighborhood. Secondary data can also be used, such as historical records, transcripts, newspaper articles, and comprehensive planning data (CUTR, 2000).

The third component of the community profile is an inventory of notable features of the community, such as community facilities and services (e.g., medical and health care, educational, religion, civic, recreation, historical, cultural and commercial), and an inventory of existing businesses, land use, transportation and cultural resources of the area, followed by a written summary of the profile's findings similar to an inventory map (CUTR, 2000). Like many aspects of a strategic plan, creating a community profile is iterative, and information not available at the beginning of the process may become available at any time during the process or at the end of the process.

COMMUNITY NEEDS ASSESSMENT

A needs assessment is a focused examination on the social conditions of a program intended to address the need of the program (Rossi, Lipsey, & Freeman, 2004). A needs assessment also refers to "measuring a discrepancy between what is and what should be" (Linfield & Posavac, 2018, p. 124). A needs assessment understands the nature and extent of the problem, identifies the users, collects information about a target population or community, decides what needs are being met and what resources exist, and determines needs not being addressed (Linfield & Posavac, 2018; Rossi, Lipsey, & Freeman, 2004).

Before we approach the needs assessment, it is important to understand what needs are. Bradshaw (1972) suggests several kinds of needs: a normative need, where a standard is established and certain people are not fulfilling the need they ought to have; a comparative need, based on one's position or a condition in a group compared or measured against one group; a felt need, which is the need received by those experiencing the problem; and an expressed need, which is articulated as a demand that needs to be put into action (as cited in Johnson, Meiller, Miller, & Summers, 1987, pp. 36–37).

Assessing these needs is a special case of citizen participation that involves collecting information about citizen preferences of programs and services and discovering the failures in the output or delivery of these programs (Summers, 1987). Needs assessment also takes a social indicators approach, where the needs are known by the community, and the evaluator measures how well the needs are being fulfilled, versus the self-report approach that assumes citizens need assistance in articulating their own felt needs (Summers, 1987).

Some common approaches of collecting new data for the needs assessment include focus groups and surveys, which can be general population surveys, target surveys, service provider surveys, key informant surveys, along with secondary data analysis such as the review of social indicators (e.g., income levels, occupation status, other demographics, social capital measures, neighborhood conditions, and community involvement) that reflect indices of needs, or a review of administrative and managerial records (Rotuman & Gant, 1987; Rossi et al., 2004; Linfield & Posavac, 2018). As one prepares to conduct a needs assessment, it is important to look at the most significant problems and concerns facing the community itself, such as an examination of the resources available in their community to address these issues, barriers to accessing these resources, and solutions that would help solve the problems and reduce or remove the barriers.

STRATEGIC PLANNING

A part of the community discussion and research that works in parallel should include an examination of the various trends and strategic issues facing the community or neighborhood. Trends are defined as a longitudinal statement of the general direction of change (gradual or long term) in the external environment that shapes the future of an organization, region, nation, or society (cited in Morrison, 1987; Simpson, McGinty, & Morrison, 1987; Morrison & Held, 1989; Lapin, 2004; Lapin, 2014).

Strategic issues are trends, developments, and dilemmas that affect an organization as a whole and its position in the environment (Thomas & McDaniel, 1990). Strategic issues may also include the challenges affecting an organization's mandates, its mission and values, its clients and users, the product or service level it provides, and the costs, finances, and management of the organization (Bryson, 2011). Dutton and Jackson (1987) say strategic issues can be described as threats and opportunities, that are also described in a SWOT analysis.

In developing a strategic plan, Lozier and Chittipeddi (1986) identify several stages in the planning process. The first is to scan the external environment to identify strategic issues and their impact on the organization and any probability of reoccurrence. Issues that are likely to require action can be handled as part of the organization's regular strategic planning cycle. However, current issues requiring immediate action might phrase the issue as a question and discuss the confluence of factors that make the issue strategic and discuss the consequences of not addressing these strategic issues.

Environmental Scanning

"Environmental scanning is a process that systematically surveys and interprets relevant data to identify external opportunities and threats. An organization gathers information about the external world . . . and itself. The company should then respond to the information gathered by changing its strategies and plans when the need arises" (Society of Human Resources Management, 2012). Environmental scanning is "a kind of radar to scan the world systematically and signal the new, unexpected, the major, and the minor" (Brown & Weiner, 1985, p. ix; see also Morrison & Held, 1989).

This process is a fundamental element of the strategic planning process that detects changes in the external environment. It defines potential threats or opportunities, and potential changes for the organization or a community caused by these changes and helps promote an orientation towards the future. Environmental scanning alerts the leadership of the organization to trends and emerging issues and predicts a future direction. A scan is a forecast that enables an organization to develop or change a strategic plan based upon external trends, events, developments, or ideas never encountered, to gain a competitive advantage. An appropriate scan may contradict previous assumptions or beliefs about what seems to be happening and has implications for the long-range program or management of the organization.

When looking at the trends in the external environment, the literature on environmental scanning focuses on trends. Grummon (2013) identifies five common categories for examining trends: demographics, economics, global education, politics, and technology. Some of these trends are either probable trends, which are those considered likely to occur based on supporting information demonstrating that the trend is developing, or plausible trends, which could occur and currently exist in the form of knowledge that may develop into a trend (Hanka, Valadares, & Bennett, 2015). Trends are also influenced by events: a non-repeatable occurrence at one point in time that is visible or dramatic and has a short-term effect on a system (Morrison & Held, 1989); an emerging issue, which is a controversy that may come from a trend or event that requires a response (Morrison & Held, 1989); or a wild card, which is the low probability of an event occurring (less than 1 in 10), with an extraordinarily high impact if the event actually occurs (Rockfellow, 1994).

University of Southern Indiana's Environmental Scanning and Strategic Planning Process

The University of Southern Indiana was founded in 1965 as a satellite campus of Indiana State University (ISU) in Terre Haute—two hours north of Evansville—and was created to respond to the need for public higher education in a region where it was sorely lacking. Prior to its founding, there was no public higher education institution in the region, mostly as a result of the "Indiana Plan," a gentleman's agreement among the heads of Indiana's four state universities, primarily led by Indiana University's longtime president Herman B Wells, that no new public university would be created in an area or region where a private college or university already existed (Heiman, 2011).

There was already a private college in Evansville, Evansville College, that was not accessible to many students and families unable to afford private school tuition, but Evansville College itself was struggling financially and at one point even sought Indiana University to take over (Heiman, 2011). Evansville was the largest city in Indiana without a public university and the president of Indiana State at the time ignored Indiana University's unwritten rule and sought to establish a satellite campus of ISU in Evansville. Finding a location for the new campus was based on the formation of a nonprofit organization—Southern Indiana Higher Education (SIHE)—which raised the money throughout the community to acquire the land (approximately 1,200 at the time; the campus is now 1,400 acres) on the western side of Vanderburgh County where Indiana State University–Evansville (ISUE) would be built.

The new campus was not ready until 1969 and ISUE used the former Centennial School in Evansville before it was completed. Since ISUE began in 1965, there was always a push, especially from the late Dr. David L. Rice, the first president of ISUE, to be an independent university, especially since there was a precedent for independence when Indiana State granted its Muncie campus in Eastern Indiana independence to form Ball State University. However as noted by Heiman (2011), the precedent fueled staunch opposition to another independent university in Indiana, and the state's two flagship universities, Indiana University and Purdue University, along with Indiana State's President Richard Landini, prevented ISUE from becoming independent.

In 1985, Indiana Governor Robert Orr, an Evansville native, signed the law establishing ISUE as an independent public state university, assuming the new name University of Southern Indiana (USI). The mandate of USI was clear: "to provide education to an underserved part of the state and serve as an engine for economic development" (Hanka, Valadares, et al., 2015, p. 4). USI's outreach and engagement efforts expanded regionally to meet the educational and workforce needs of the community and the region. For a university this young, USI has the makeup like a 21st century land grant, with a strong identity and a robust outreach and engagement operation that serves the Evansville community and the Tri-state region.

As of 2021, the University of Southern Indiana has 10,204 students enrolled in dual-credit, undergraduate, and graduate programs (USI, 2021a). USI has four colleges: the College of Liberal Arts; the Romain College of Business; the College of Nursing and Health Professions; and the Pott College of Science, Engineering, and Education, and 70 undergraduate majors, 13 master's programs, and two doctoral programs with a shift to more online course offerings (USI, 2021b).

In 2009, USI embarked on the process of developing its first formal strategic plan in its history, which was the first charge given by the Board of Trustees to the then-new president, Dr. Linda Bennett. The first strategic planning process involved feedback from discussion and focus groups consisting primarily of faculty and staff. Some external realities had an impact on the plan, such as the State of Indiana changing the funding criteria for higher education by moving from an enrollment-based funding formula to a performance-based approach using multiple formulae. This fundamental shift shaped a good part of USI's new strategic plan, as the institution relies heavily on state appropriations for much of its operating base. It was primarily a response to internal constituents and their agendas, for which six goals emerged in a new five-year strategic plan (2010–2015), along with a newly articulated vision statement, "shaping the future through learning and innovation" and a revised mission statement: "USI is an engaged learning community advancing education and knowledge, enhancing civic and cultural awareness, and fostering partnerships through comprehensive outreach programs. We prepare individuals to live wisely in a diverse and global community" (USI, 2020).

USI operationalized many aspects of its strategic plan between 2010 and 2013 while simultaneously attuned to the short-term political and environmental trends affecting its actions. In those three years, USI, much like many other state-based institutions, experienced reduced state funding support, demographic changes in the student body, and the entry into the market of new providers and programs (both online and for-profit). Nonetheless, the university forged ahead with its mission to be an engaged learning community. In 2008, The Carnegie Foundation recognized USI as an engaged university for "its efforts to integrate engagement into the curricula and expand its network of partnerships with regional businesses and public organizations" (Hanka, Valadares, et al., 2015, p. 2). This included the creation of many partnerships, including one with New Harmony in 1985 (discussed in chapter 1), through the formation of Historic New Harmony, which also partnered with the Indiana State Museum and Historic Sites.

In 2012, another partnership developed between USI and the United States Naval Surface Warfare Center (NSWC) in Crane, Indiana, one hour north of Evansville. NSWC-Crane personnel and business and engineering students and faculty from USI have collaborated on a number of projects, particularly the Technology Commercialization Academy (TCA), which develops commercial uses of technology, designed by Crane, for strategic military purposes (Hanka, Valadares, et al., 2015). This partnership with Crane assisted USI's efforts to begin the second iteration of the university's strategic plan.

Starting in 2013, Dr. Kevin Valadares and I helped the university and USI president Dr. Linda Bennett to perform an environmental scan for the next strategic plan to collect data on its distinctive competitive strengths in relation to the external trends that exist in our region, the state, the nation, and the world. The environmental scanning process grew out of the process Crane used. Dr. Bennett decided that USI should engage in that process for the USI community. We presented the results of our environmental scan to the annual conference of the Society for College and University Planning (SCUP) in Chicago in July 2015, and we published our results in a journal article later that year.

In 2015, the environmental scanning process helped inform the next strategic planning process and I served as a co-convener with Dr. Valadares. We convened a diverse steering committee of faculty, staff, alumni, students, parents, and community members. We organized workshops, meetings, and other planning exercises with multiple stakeholders and constituencies throughout the university, from executive-level administrators to low-level staff members. We sought input from all units and departments on our three strategic goals: 1) Excellence in Learning for the Entire USI community (i.e., expanding our connections into the region, state, country, and world, and enhance diversity in terms of teaching and learning that connect and engage); 2) Access and Opportunity by Design (i.e., increasing access to higher education, developing partnerships to promote opportunities for learning, and creating a diverse campus culture); and 3) Purposeful and Sustainable Growth (i.e., emphasizing community engagement, academic and outreach partnerships, growth in student enrollment and faculty, maintaining the quality of interdisciplinary learning and a sense of community). Each unit and department on campus examined one of the three goals and provided strategies and metrics on how their unit could achieve these three goals. These items were curated and archived in President Bennett's office. A number of these units of the university created effective strategic plans that aligned with the university's three overarching goals.

Once the strategic goals of the community have been developed, and the strategic direction of the community has been articulated, it is important for the community to identify person(s) who will own the goals as the strategic plan moves forward and is implemented. The following pages examine case studies of how we applied this model to comprehensive community development in two neighborhoods in Evansville, Indiana, and one neighborhood in Henderson, Kentucky.

GLENWOOD NEIGHBORHOOD

Glenwood is a neighborhood we examined in chapter 4. Located in the southeast side of Evansville, Indiana, Glenwood was a vibrant community. By the 1980s, families moved out of Glenwood and abandoned their homes, crime increased, the neighborhood school was declining, and there was a lack of business development in the area (Alvarez, 2012). However, Glenwood has benefited from government and policy interventions to transform and revitalize the neighborhood. Habitat for Humanity and its affiliates (including Evansville) build homes through volunteer labor based on a specific mission to produce affordable housing units for the communities that Habitat serves to provide a safe and decent place to live. In Evansville, the affiliate shifted its focus in the 2000s, under the leadership of Lori Reed, the

Executive Director, to play an important leadership role in community development, particularly in Glenwood.

According to Reed (2015), there were reservations initially from the Habitat Evansville affiliate, because the long-time supporters of the organization viewed community development as a distraction that deviated from Habitat's house building mission. A unique aspect of comprehensive community development is the long-term relationships that are developed, which often do not align with Habitat's approach of not staying too long in one neighborhood. Reed noted that the Habitat Evansville affiliate made strides to continue community development in Glenwood and realized that once the houses were built in two or three years, Habitat would move somewhere else, while the residents and homeowners would be committed to staying in their homes for 10, 15, 20 years, or the rest of their lives (Reed, 2015).

Reed went to other Habitat affiliates in the region and the nation to learn how affiliates built houses and communities so quickly, which over the past 45 years has earned Habitat for Humanity and its brand a lot of credibility. Interestingly, when Reed engaged in comprehensive community development in Glenwood, the Habitat for Humanity International movement itself was not into comprehensive community development, but by 2013, Habitat began to embrace comprehensive community development and collective impact. Ironically, the Evansville affiliate had curtailed its community development efforts at that time to focus solely on building houses, which as of the publishing of this book, has surpassed over 500 homes as an affiliate (Reed, 2015).

By 2007, informal meetings in the pre-initiative phase of the Glenwood Community Development Initiative (GCDI) were held, along with an initial assessment of Glenwood that measured the perceptions of the people, quality of housing, crime rates, employment, and educational rates. Eight to ten key volunteers from Glenwood, Habitat staff and volunteers from Habitat for Humanity and members of Crossroads Christian Church were trained through NeighborWorks America on the fundamentals and concepts of community development key in developing a common language among the key drivers and stakeholders. According to Reed (2015), community activities were held, including a community block party aimed at promoting awareness and support and recruiting volunteers to the effort in late summer 2008 for a neighborhood cleanup, three neighborhood festivals, and an increase in participation in the Glenwood Neighborhood Association, led by long-time resident Lucy Williams.

The first facilitated community discussion for the GCDI took place in November 2008 and was led by facilitator Dr. Sue Ellspermann, a Ph.D. in industrial engineering from the University of Louisville and a consultant on various projects in Indiana such as Evansville and Vanderburgh County's efforts to unify government, the State of Indiana's rural strategic plan, the town of Ferdinand, Indiana's 10-year vision, and the Glenwood, Jacobsville, and Henderson initiatives, highlighted later in this chapter.

The convener in the comprehensive community development efforts for Glenwood was Habitat for Humanity of Evansville, which provided backbone support along with the Glenwood Neighborhood Association (GNA) and helped advocate for mutually reinforcing activities among many stakeholders, including the school, Glenwood Leadership Academy, the PTA, students and teachers, Glenwood residents and businesses, the City of Evansville, and the Evansville Vanderburgh School Corporation (EVSC). The community needs assessment was conducted by a team of researchers with USI Center for Applied Research, and the community visioning session was conducted by Dr. Ellspermann several times in March, August, and November 2009, with a final session in early 2010 (Habitat for Humanity [HFH] of Evansville, 2011, p. iii).

From these community listening and visioning sessions, a vision statement emerged: "Glenwood is to be a model neighborhood valued for its improvements and spirit of community" (Fine, 2011, p. 3; see also HFH Evansville, 2011) based on improving the quality of life of neighborhood residents, as defined by six priority areas that became six goals: 1) housing/infrastructure will be improved and beautified to create a walkable, healthy, and safe community; 2) the school will be a center of the community where children and adults develop knowledge and skills necessary for successful lives; 3) the neighborhood's open space and structures will be clean and green; 4) the neighborhood will be a safe place for residents to live, play, and interact; 5) businesses will exist in the neighborhood to provide important goods/services and will serve as good community partners; 6) residents will have access to information and services related to health care, nutrition, and exercise (HFH Evansville, 2011).

Habitat convened the community development initiative by constructing 35 new homes between 2010 and 2012 for Glenwood residents, while the City of Evansville and Memorial Community Development Corporation (MCDC) also constructed homes in the neighborhood. Seventy-eight existing homes were given weather upgrades and 37 properties were torn down. The major successes included doubling the size of the newly renovated Glenwood Leadership Academy, which also received a $2 million U.S. Department of Education grant to enhance student quality and achievement and community engagement (Alvarez, 2012).

GNA also created a community garden that grew fresh produce and spawned the creation of a farmer's market. Crossroads Christian Church, the nondenominational megachurch in Evansville, raised money to support teachers, organized book drives, and organized lunches for teachers, parents, and students. Also, church volunteers mentored individual students, and one volunteer built a pergola at the community garden as part of an Eagle Scout project (Alvarez, 2012). Glenwood also received a full-service health clinic in the newly designed Glenwood Leadership Academy that was operated by the nursing program at the University of Southern Indiana's (USI) College of Nursing and Health Professions (CNHP), in partnership with St. Mary's Medical Center (now Ascension St. Vincent's) and Southwestern Indiana Mental Health Center (Alvarez, 2012).

Glenwood Analysis and Outcomes

Two surveys and a series of door-to-door qualitative interviews were conducted by student volunteers and USI researchers in the overall assessment of the Glenwood neighborhood (Phillips, Bennett, Opartny, Priest, & Khayum, 2008). The first survey to 356 eligible partner families received 107 resident responses (30 percent response rate). In terms of demographics, the median age was 44 years old, and most respondents were female. The median number of individuals residing in each home ranged from two to nine, with the median of three people, and the number of children per household ranged from 0–8, with two as the median number of children per household.

The survey results from the new Habitat for Humanity showed homeowners are substantially better off than before owning a Habitat home. Most partner families participating in this survey felt they are financially better off than they were five years ago, felt welcome in the neighborhood, and felt better about themselves since becoming a Habitat homeowner. The survey respondents also acknowledged they could not have owned their home without the help from Habitat for Humanity, and some residents became more involved in neighborhood activities. They reported an improvement in educational and academic achievement at the Glenwood Leadership Academy by doubling their Indiana Statewide Testing for Educational Progress (ISTEP) academic assessment scores, while homeownership in the Glenwood neighborhood increased by 18 percent. Also, Habitat homeowners reported a 35 percent decrease in food stamp usage, a 23 percent decrease in welfare assistance, and a 21 percent decrease in utility bill assistance after homeownership (Phillips et al., 2008).

In a second door-to-door survey, 127 homeowners responded out of a sample of 164 neighbors living near the Habitat development (77 percent response rate). The overwhelming majority of respondents were aware that Habitat homes were being built in the neighborhood but did not participate in the builds themselves. Of the respondents, 63 percent gave a high rating of the neighborhood. Seventy-seven percent were satisfied or very satisfied with the neighborhood as a place to live, around 64 percent felt they were a part of the neighborhood, and 70 percent felt they were somewhat or very much attached to the neighborhood. Eighty-five percent of all respondents had a positive identification about Habitat for Humanity of Evansville.

Seventy-eight percent of the respondents liked the Habitat home in their neighborhood, and 75 percent felt positive and took pride in their neighborhood regardless of income, education, gender, race, or number of Habitat homes, but only 26 percent of the respondents showed a high level of neighborhood involvement (such as involved in front door pride initiative, visited a neighbor's home, borrowed something from a neighbor, watched a neighbor's house, socialized with a neighbor, etc.). This suggested that bonding social capital was high, while bridging and linking social capital had decreased. The attachment and feelings the residents had for their neighborhood did not necessarily translate into involvement in the neighborhood.

A social work faculty member, and students trained in survey research methods, conducted 53 in-depth qualitative interviews to understand the individual experiences of Habitat homeowners as they moved through the process of becoming homeowners. The overwhelming majority of respondents believed that homeownership has increased their quality of life and their own individual sense of responsibility. They thought the Habitat staff was friendly and helpful, and the classes on budgeting and home maintenance and repair and sweat equity requirements were beneficial. Almost everyone encouraged their friends and relatives to become Habitat homeowners. Most of the residents interviewed (31) suggested the need for ongoing home maintenance and repair classes, as well as better education to the general public about Habitat's strict admission criteria and the path towards owning a Habitat home (Phillips et al., 2008).

One Glenwood resident stated that Habitat taught her a lot and increased her sense of responsibility as a Habitat homeowner:

> Once I assumed ownership, it (the house) was mine. I am totally responsible for not only making the mortgage payments, but also for the upkeep, inside and out, for my home. If something needs to be repaired, it is up to me to make sure that it is taken care of. When I used to rent, I didn't think about this as I would just call the landlord and take it for granted that it was up to him. Now, it's up to me to make sure everything keeps working right. (Phillips et al., 2008, p. 32)

Despite the successes and contributions of Habitat for Humanity of Evansville, as the convener of the Glenwood initiative, Lori Reed acknowledged that Habitat was limited in its role as convener because of its capacity and because of "its specific house building ministry and its limited geographical service area" (Recker & Reed, 2013, p. 4).

JACOBSVILLE NEIGHBORHOOD

The Jacobsville neighborhood is in the north central part of the city of Evansville, Indiana. According to the 2010 Census Data, the population of Jacobsville is 6,873 residents, and consists of 1.91 square miles (U.S. Census, 2016). The boundaries of the Jacobsville neighborhood are First Avenue to the west; Garvin Street from Illinois Street to Enlow Street, Enlow Street between Garvin and Governor Streets, and Governor Street from Enlow Street to Diamond Avenue to the east; the Lloyd Expressway and Division Street to the south and Diamond Avenue to the north. The Jacobsville neighborhood also includes the North Main Street Business District.

The Jacobsville neighborhood, established in 1863, was named after Hannah Jacobs and her farmhouse located at 609 W. Maryland Avenue (on the corner of Maryland Avenue and Oakley Street), which we refer to today as Old Jacobsville. The neighborhood was officially annexed as a part of the city of Evansville in 1868. As the city and neighborhood continued to grow, Jacobsville evolved as a blue-collar community, which included the Union Stockyards and Evansville Plate Works plant. Both are long closed (Historic Evansville, 2020). Over its history, Jacobsville has been a working-class neighborhood, that values its manufacturing past and the many jobs that were available to the residents. The closing of those companies has impacted quality of life and the environment of Jacobsville, including placement on the National Priorities List through the EPA Superfund program in 2004 (Wilson, 2020).

Currently, the neighborhood is home to several large employers, such as the regional utility company Vectren (a CenterPoint Energy Company), Berry Global, a plastics manufacturing business, Deaconess Midtown Hospital, and the Willard Library—Indiana's oldest public library building. The construction of the Lloyd Expressway 30 years ago also has physically isolated the neighborhood from downtown and the rest of the city.

In 2008, Dr. Ellspermann and her team engaged in a listening and visioning session in Jacobsville and conduced a SWOT analysis that resulted in a five-year vision to increase homeownership in the Jacobsville neighborhood, increase the number of quality rental properties, and reduce the number of boarded up homes. The major goals of the Jacobsville initiative were: 1) find ways to subsidize homeownership; 2) identify a few blocks in the neighbor-

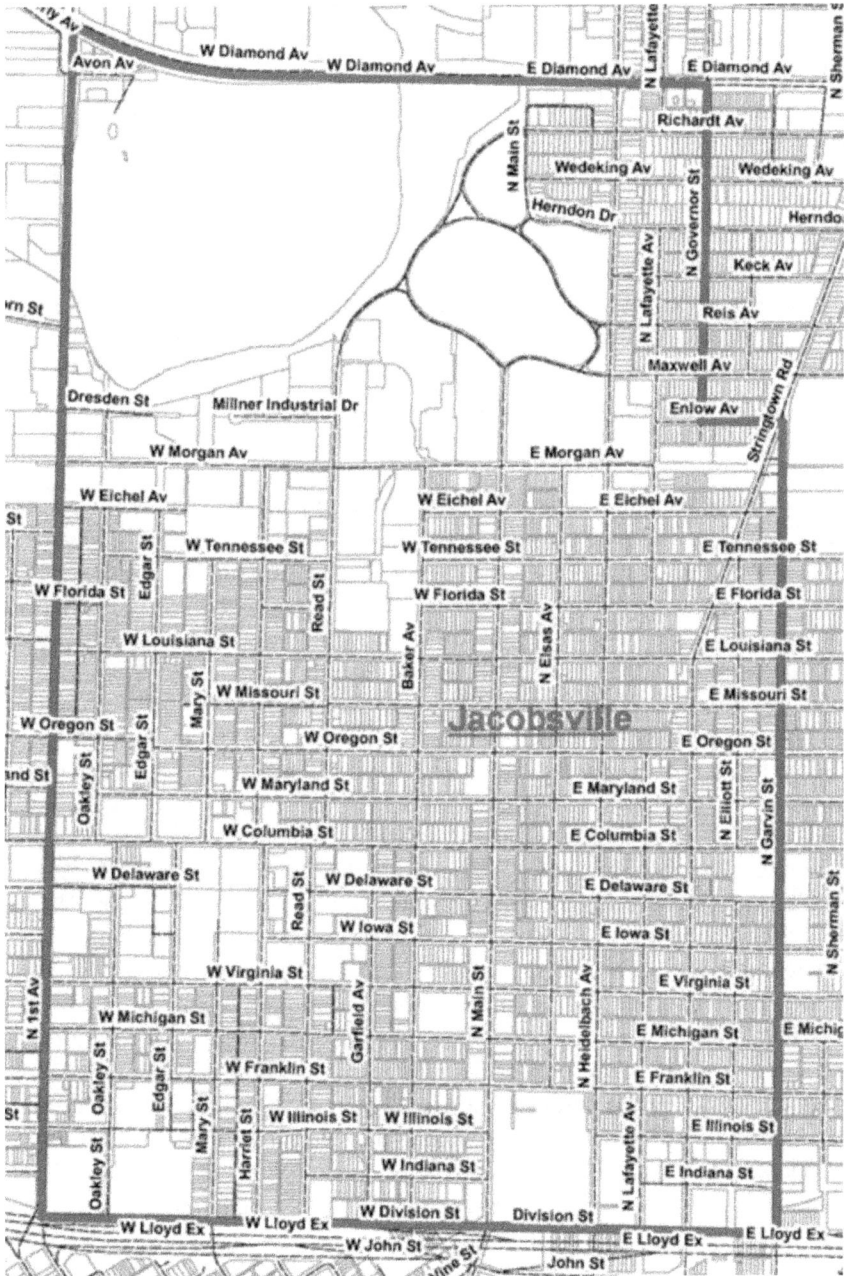

Figure 6.2. Map of Jacobsville, Evansville, Indiana. *Source:* United Neighborhoods of Evansville

hood to focus on revitalization; 3) attract more Jacobsville area employees to live and work here; 4) advocate for an ordinance ensuring rental property standards in the Jacobsville redevelopment area; and 5) reduce the number of boarded up homes in Jacobsville (JACC Strategic Plan, 2008).

Researchers at the University of Southern Indiana (Durham, Hanka, McKibban, Priest, & Raymond, 2012) conducted focus groups for employees who worked in Jacobsville, for residents and parents, and for small business owners. The major area of concern for all constituencies was the unsightly appearance of the Jacobsville neighborhood, due to its decay and decline. The employees cited safety as a major concern and wanted a greater and more visible police presence to reduce crime, especially drug crimes and thefts. While employees of Deaconess, Berry, and Vectren liked the central location of Jacobsville, many cited the lack of dining options and amenities in the neighborhood and expressed the need for greater interaction and engagement with the community (Durham, et al., 2012).

The residents and parents of Jacobsville were pleased with the Metropolitan Evansville Transit System (METS) bus service but wanted more walking and bike paths. They also expressed a lack of pride among residents, due mainly to the appearance and decay of the neighborhood, but they viewed this as a separate issue from crime. The residents also suggested including resources for children and spaces for recreation and community events, as well as improved communication and involvement by community leaders.

The small business owners cited the friendliness of the residents and believed the neighborhood should improve economic conditions by attracting new businesses, promote existing businesses, improve traffic flow, increase and improve affordable residential housing, create a more family friendly community, and improving the appeal of the area (Durham et al., 2012). While the business owners agreed with the residents and the employees that the appearance of the neighborhood should be improved, the business owners did not agree with the lack of safety, stating it was safer than what non-residents may have thought or believed (Durham et al., 2012).

The following year, Jacobsville Join In! (JJI) began, which allowed residents to work with formal and informal leadership to develop their vision and goals for the neighborhood and leverage resources. JJI was created through the involvement of stakeholders like One Life Church, Habitat for Humanity of Evansville, the Dream Center, Delaware Elementary School, and the Jacobsville Neighborhood Improvement Association (JNIA).

Jacobsville Redevelopment Area Plan

The 2013 Jacobsville Redevelopment Area Plan developed a series of visions, goals, and big ideas for the neighborhood. From the 2013 plan, a vision was created to "uplift the Jacobsville Neighborhood to a community of choice as a progressive location for business culture and a livable mixed-use neighborhood by creating an inviting, walkable and sustainable place to live, work and play" (JACC, 2013; DMD, 2018). There were ten goals, ranging from redeveloping brownfield areas, creating opportunities for greenspace, public spaces, and pedestrian connections through new parks, the implementation of a cohesive, neighborhood streetscape, preserving the character and historic cultural assets of the neighborhood for adaptive reuse, and collaborating with nonprofits and for-profit developers on affordable housing initiatives (JACC, 2013).

Eight ideas emerged out of the plan as a way of attracting young professionals to the Jacobsville neighborhood, with the potential for reinvestment in the neighborhood. These priority areas are: 1) expand the tax increment financing (TIF) district to provide opportunities for neighborhood revitalization; 2) improve the streetscape on key corridors in the neighborhood such as North Main Street, Franklin Street and Virginia Street; 3) strengthen neighborhoods, housing, and commercial areas; 4) develop a business or economic improvement district in Jacobsville (BID or EID) to target potential commercial activity in the North Main Street corridor; 5) develop better branding and wayfinding signage to promote the brand and identity of the neighborhood, including the establishment of gateway signs at major entry points into the neighborhood; 6) develop a land use strategy along the Lloyd Expressway that forms the southern border of Jacobsville; 7) develop sustainable development practices for the neighborhood in terms of site development, buildings, parks and recreation, utilities, arts and culture; and 8) revise zoning codes and design development strategies to align with the overall redevelopment vision of the neighborhood (JACC, 2013).

This master plan addresses the worn-out physical conditions of the neighborhood and the housing stock, which also fulfills the city's objective to "align the city's capital improvement projects with neighborhood planning efforts to leverage planned investment" (DMD, 2018, p. 34). The master plan also addresses the need for improvements on North Main Street, from the Lloyd Expressway to the south to Garvin Park to the north, including infrastructure replacements (new streets, sidewalks, crosswalks, bike lanes, traffic signals, traffic signage, new curbs, gutters, and drive aprons), along with improved street lighting (including decorative historic style streetlights), new street furnishings, and gateway welcome signage (DMD, 2018).

In 2018, the City of Evansville Department of Metropolitan Development (DMD) received, from HUD, a distinction as a Neighborhood Revitalization Strategy Area (NRSA) to create opportunities in four census tracts in the Jacobsville neighborhood that are economically distressed and that experience high vacancy rates, low homeownership rates, low home mortgage rates, high poverty rates, high home delinquency rates, and low median home sales prices, which will be incorporated into the city's upcoming consolidation plan submitted to HUD every five years (DMD, 2018).

The Dream Center, a local nonprofit organization located in Jacobsville, created a Kids Zone in the neighborhood, which mirrors the community development model of the Harlem Children's Zone (HCZ) created by educator Geoffrey Canada. Harlem Children's Zone began as a one-block model in the Harlem neighborhood in NYC in 1991 that grew to a 24-block area in the 2000s and is now a 97-block area. HCZ's goal is "to give our kids the individualized support they need to get to and through college and become productive, self-sustaining adults" (HCZ, 2020).

The Harlem Children's Zone (HCZ) developed a system or pipeline that provides continued support and reinforcement from a child's birth until college graduation, including various community services to support the child and the family along the way. The Harlem Children's Zone has served 12,000 children and 12,000 adults since its inception (Hanson, 2013; HCZ, 2020). Some of the programs include a baby college, a nine-week parenting class, and a path to the HCZ Promise Academies (I and II) that track students who gain admission to a charter school and those who do not. The Promise Academies include the "Three-Year Journey," the "Get Ready for Pre-K," and "Harlem Gems," along with the charter school that includes a grade school, middle school, and a high school (HCZ, 2020).

While in grade school, fifth graders are invited to an after-school program that helps the students' transition into middle school. While in middle school, students participate in a program titled "A Cut Above" aimed towards academic and leadership development, high school, and college preparation. When students enter high school in one of these two Promise Academies (Promise Academy II opened in 2013), they participate in either a college preparatory track or a career track that consists of the TRUCE (The Renaissance University for Community Education) program, the Employment and Technology Center, and the Learn to Earn program (HCZ, 2020). The college preparatory program, whose goal is "to increase college awareness, preparation, and attendance among high school students in Harlem" (HCZ, 2020) is an intentional year-round program. The College Success Office provides students information, assistance, and guidance towards the college admission process and prepares them for the academic rigor of college and university, while also providing support for these students once they enroll in college (HCZ, 2020).

In addition to preparing students academically for college, there are programs available for families, social services, health care services, and community building. The family and social service programs include Community Pride aimed to improve the empowerment and investment of Harlem. HCZ's Community Benefits Support Center provides residents free legal services and financial counseling, access to government resources, and tax preparation services for clients and their families. HCZ also sponsors four foster-care preventive programs, along with a mixture of community centers located in the neighborhood and inside a few public housing developments in Harlem. Jobson (2017) shows that the Promise Zone academies spend around $16,000 per student per year, while only $5,000 per child on average is spent on other HCZ programs.

While this comprehensive wraparound service approach to a child's education and academic readiness provides benefits and opportunities for participating individuals and families, some critics argue that Harlem Children's Zone is focused too much on education and not on the other social and emotional development needs that impact the progression and development of at-risk youth. Also, several studies criticize the metrics and empirics in determining school success, and question whether HCZ achieved the goals and outcomes that founder Geoffrey Canada claimed using a neighborhood approach rather than a school approach. Whitehurst and Croft (2010) compared HCZ test scores over a three-year period (2007–2009) with all charter schools in Manhattan and the Bronx. HCZ falls in the middle of the pack in terms of math (48th percentile) and english and language arts (37th percentile); thus, concluding "the HCZ Promise Academy is a middling New York City charter school" (Whitehurst & Croft, 2010, p. 6).

However, all the students in the Promise Academy's Class of 2012 passed the English exam for the New York State Regents diploma, and 90 percent or more of the students passed the Geometry, Algebra 2 and Trigonometry, and Integrated Algebra Regents exams (Hanson, 2013; as cited in Jobson, 2017). Dobbie and Fryer's (2009) study of HCZ shows improvements in english, language arts and math scores among elementary school students and improvement in math scores for middle school students, but the sample of students enrolled in the HCZ Promise Academies are not randomly selected. Students either self-selectively enroll in HCZ, are recruited in the neighborhood by HCZ, or are chosen by a lottery (Hanson, 2013). The apples and oranges comparison of "outcomes of HCZ children to the outcomes of other children in Harlem may be biased in one direction or another" (Dobbie & Fryer, 2009, p. 7). In fact, Dobbie and Fryer (2009) and Whitehurst and

Croft's (2010) studies are criticized for their snapshot analysis of HCZ (one test and one school) and because they did not perform a longitudinal analysis to measure student achievement over time (Hanson, 2013). Ultimately, President Obama used the model of the Harlem Children's Zone to create Promise Communities or Neighborhoods (Whitehurst & Croft, 2010; Jobson, 2017) that became the Promise Zone we will talk about in the next chapter.

The Jacobsville Kids Zone is using the model from the Harlem Children's Zone to create a 31-block service area in Jacobsville. The Dream Center adopted Delaware Elementary School as a laboratory to implement their model that focuses on the kids and not the program. This kid-centric approach focuses on three elements: 1) wrap-around care and services for each child by connecting and resourcing; 2) integrating into Delaware Elementary School through using full-time employees of Dream Center called Peacemakers (who work at Delaware half the time and the other half at Dream Center); and 3) creating academic interventions designed to improve reading and math scores (Evans, 2019).

According to Jeremy Evans, the Executive Director of the Dream Center, academic achievement and proficiency has improved in the first year under the Peacemakers program that targeted the population in the 12-block zone. Reading and math test scores increased 40 percent in the first year from 50 percent at or above grade level to 90 percent at or above grade level. In terms of child and student behavior, in-class disruptive and disobedient behaviors decreased 76 percent and decreased 92 percent among students paired with a peacemaker (Evans, 2019). Despite data limitations, due to the short period of time the program has been in operation, the initial results in the first year have shown a positive impact in these children's lives and their academic performance. Jacobsville Kids Zone has been innovative in its wraparound, holistic, kid-centric focus compared to Audubon Kids Zone located in the East End of Henderson, Kentucky (Seymore, 2020).

The Jacobsville community development initiative is a perfect example of comprehensive community development. The initiative focuses on a geographically defined targeted area of a city, has a strategic and a redevelopment plan in place, as well as access to important resources needed to improve the quality of life of the residents. Many constituencies, including residents and business owners, have been pleased with the progress being made in the neighborhood, especially with the collaboration and participation from multiple stakeholders in the community, but there is still work to do. One resident noted,

> When you look at trying to bring in [business], you got to have people in here to make any of this successful, people that actually live there where it's really

difficult to go in and replace one house on this block and a house on this block and, hey, we got an open lot to put one. You almost have to come in and start from scratch. . . . (Durham et al., 2012, p. 28)

The residents and the community have participated in the planning and implementation of the comprehensive community development efforts and have contributed to the economic, social, and human development of the neighborhood and the improvement of Jacobsville's quality of life.

ENGAGE HENDERSON

Engage Henderson is an organization sponsored by One Life Church, founded in 2010 in Henderson, Kentucky (south of Evansville across the Ohio River) and is focused on faith formation by serving the community. Founder Bob Seymore believes in the notion of community development, house-by-house and person by person, instead of program-by-program or citywide. Engage Henderson's mission is "to provide a process that creates partnerships with residents and community resources to improve the quality of life in targeted neighborhoods" (Hein, Hanka, & Gogel, 2013, p. 22).

Engage Henderson began from Seymore's work at the Evansville Christian Life Center to be a catalyst for neighborhood development in the East End of Henderson. Seymore saw the success of the Glenwood project and invited people from the neighborhood and community around the table over breakfast. Seymore often says: "Community development is bacon and eggs." This approach by Engage Henderson is tied to One Life's mission of serving people as Jesus would, and the church's desire to develop an outreach project without an ulterior motive. In an interview with Seymore (2015), he said:

We're going in to serve these people and that's very biblical to serve neighborhoods, serve people that struggle in poverty, but at the end of the day, what we have found is those relationships have created a lot of interest in who we are as a church, but again, we're not trying to trick you. If we give you benevolence and you come to church—if we give you something and you come, it's just we want to be givers and the response to that has been I want to see where these people come from.

The pre-initiative of the Engage Henderson process identified the convener who responds to the needs of the community to determine if the community is ready for development. The convener, "who acts much like a buzzing bee, cross-pollinating ideas from one part of the community to another," was identified as One Life Church (Hein, Hanka, & Gogel, 2013). The readiness criteria included an understanding of the community's defined boundaries, which is the East End of Henderson (east of N. Green Street and south of Second Street), an understanding of the community's current assets and the resident's perceptions of their community, along with a sense of "together-ness" that measured the strength of the community and the longevity of its residents (Hein, Hanka & Gogel, 2013).

During this pre-initiative phase, community stakeholders were identified to serve on the steering committee, which included the Evansville architectural firm VPS, Henderson City commissioners, local law enforcement officers, city planning officials, administrators and teachers of South Heights El-ementary located in the East End of Henderson, small business owners, and nonprofit organization leaders.

As in Glenwood, staff from the University of Southern Indiana Center for Applied Research (CAR) conducted the need assessment for the East End of Henderson and the Engage Henderson service area by conducting surveys and focus groups to assess the community strengths and community and residents' desires. Evansville architecture firms VPS and Bernard and Lochmuller also collected housing and infrastructure data that was used in the Sustainable Evansville Area Communities (SEAC) Millennial 2040 com-prehensive planning efforts.

Before any action or alignments occurred, the communities conducted visioning sessions led by Dr. Ellspermann using the Simplex community facilitation method. In these initial visioning meetings, Engage Henderson developed its vision statement: "Central to the Engage mission is the notion that residents themselves know best how to confront the challenges they face" (Hein, Hanka, & Gogel, 2013, p. 22).

Through an intentional design of the visioning process, community mem-bers voiced their priorities on what their community should look like, where 60 different priorities emerged at the first community meeting. At the next meeting, eight priorities were identified, followed by another meeting that paired the list down to six converged goals: 1) create a community event for the East End neighborhood; 2) create Wi-Fi accessibility to the community; 3) build on the strengths of South Heights School; 4) create an arts and res-taurant district; 5) provide a safe environment for kids from 2–10 p.m.; and 6) eliminate drugs from the East End neighborhood. During the final stage of action, the six priorities teams based on these goals were assembled that con-sisted of community members, subject matter experts, appropriate govern-ment officials, and individuals with a diverse array of talents and viewpoints.

According to Hein, Hanka, and Gogel (2013), Engage Henderson expe-rienced a disconnect, where many community members did not participate past the visioning part and did not participate in the priority teams, which was critical to the forward momentum and potential success of the Engage Henderson Initiative. CAR assisted in the project management and communication efforts through a project coordinator, communications intern, and a content expert. CAR also developed toolkits for each priority teams to implement their specific goals and strategies, best practices for managing teams, how to develop mission statements, how to identify measurable outcomes, and how to run a meeting effectively. Hein, Hanka, and Gogel (2013) noted that One Life and Engage Henderson relied on the CAR project management staff to provide the assistance to drive the engagement and reengagement process, instead of the organizations empowering the residents themselves.

The lack of involvement by residents in the priority teams forced Engage Henderson and One Life to combine the six goals into three overarching goals: 1) coordinate a mentoring programs; 2) recruit volunteers through the Community One website for infrastructure improvements; 3) expand the successful Blazer University program from South Heights Elementary to other locations in the East End of Henderson.

After the community engagement process, Engage Henderson aligned itself with South Heights, an elementary school in the city's East End, widely considered the poorest and the most at-risk, low expectations neighborhood in Henderson, which "had been dying on the vine for decades" (Carroll, 2020). Rob Carroll, the longtime principal of South Heights Elementary, used a model that heavily committed resources to a small group of 10 children at first. Carroll noted that the children served at South Heights are not just from "K–5, but K through life" (Carroll, 2020). Carroll and his team tracked this small group through high school, providing them with support and resources, almost like a "third parent" would, through nurturing, supporting, and mentoring. Recently, one of the young girls that worked with Carroll who attended South Heights 19 years ago graduated from Murray State University and recently graduated with a master's degree in education from the University of Louisville.

Approximately six to seven years later, as Engage Henderson went through its community development process, it aligned with Carroll's successful program at South Heights Elementary. Based on their introduction to Geoffrey Canada of the Harlem Children's Zone at the Global Leadership Summit, Seymore and Carroll decided to use the HCZ kid-centric model based on the success of the South Heights program that would eventually become known as Audubon Kids Zone.

Within the 10-block Audubon Kids Zone, the model focuses on five goals: kid-centric; zero through college; metrics matter; neighborhood support; and equipping for life (Audubon Kids Zone, 2020). There are 80–120 elementary age children and 200–270 school age in the Audubon Kids Zone, so there was no way they can serve everyone, according to Carroll (2020). They asked the question, "Do we serve a lot of kids with a few resources and support for each child, or do we serve a few kids and provide them as much support as we can?" (Carroll, 2020).

The smaller kid-centric approach has worked well in the first years of AKZ. According to Seymore (2020) and Carroll (2020), every AKZ student improved in their MAP Growth assessment scores (administered by the Northwest Evaluation Association [NEWA] to develop personalized learning pathways) in math, and 90 percent improved in reading. Eighty-one percent of the students are meeting or exceeding expected growth in math, and 65 percent are meeting or exceeding expectations in reading (Audubon Kids Zone, 2020). In math proficiency, 13 percent of AKZ students moved from below grade level to grade level or above in one year, and 23 percent of students moved from below grade level to grade level or above (Audubon Kids Zone, 2020).

Limited funding and resources have impacted the sustainability of the AKZ program, despite its success. One Life Church served as the convener of the Engage Henderson community development initiative and faced challenges engaging people in the community after the visioning sessions, as noted earlier, because it's a "small faith-based church with a primary evangelical mission," and does not have the capacity to be a full-fledged community development organization (Recker & Reed, 2012, p. 4).

Overall, the Adaptive Collaborative Community Transformation (ACCT) model has brought successful outcomes to the communities of Glenwood and Jacobsville neighborhoods in Evansville and the East End of Henderson. One of the unique features of the ACCT model is its adaptability and replicability, which helps communities build capacity. The model is driven by homegrown indigenous leaders, using a deliberate, intentional approach to determine community readiness for revitalization. If the community is ready to use an effective community developer and an effective and skilled facilitator through the Simplex method, the community can establish strategic, achievable, and measurable goals that will improve and enhance the quality of life of the community and its residents now and for future generations.

NOTE

Portions of this chapter are reprinted from Hanka, M. J., Valadares, K. J., & Bennett, L. L. M. (2015). Changing the landscape at the University of Southern Indiana through a locally developed, customized environmental scanning process. *Planning for Higher Education*, 43(2), 4–14., and are reprinted with permission.

Chapter Seven

What is Collective Impact?

Hanleybrown, Kania, and Kramer (2012) identify five conditions that must be met in order for any collective impact initiative to be successful. The first condition requires many groups to come together under one common agenda in order to further the vision and goals for change through agreed upon actions. The second condition is using shared measurements systems to collect data so that results are consistent across the board, efforts are aligned, and all partners are accountable. While participants and partners have different activities, they coordinate with a mutually reinforcing plan of action (the third condition) where each partner works towards the collective goal. Continuous and open communication is the fourth condition, where participants develop a culture of trust and collaboration through regular contact, transparency, and mutual vision. The final condition, backbone support, is created and managed through a separate organization equipped with the staff and skills responsible for coordinating the collective impact initiative, so the project remains focused on the goals (see also Kania & Kramer, 2011; Recker & Reed, 2013). The backbone support organization is responsible for "providing overall strategic direction, facilitating dialogue between partners, managing data collection and analysis, handling communications, coordinating community outreach and mobilizing funding" (Hanleybrown et al., 2012, p. 6).

   Collective impact, unlike community development, is not place or geography-based, but focuses on a subject area, such as education, substance abuse, health and wellness, or jobs. Collective impact focuses on how people across different disciplines and institutions come together to increase their impact by working together strategically. Collective impact is the synergy that results in different organizations working together to solve a complex problem.

Collective impact is different from collaboration. While collaboration means coming together to tackle a problem collaboratively that also fits their strategic ends and interests, collective impact moves an initiative forward using a "community wide strategic lens" aimed towards making systemic change based on understanding the costs of doing nothing, and creating solutions to the issues and problems that result in such systematic change (Hanleybrown et al., 2012)

The preconditions for a collective impact consist of an influential champion (which is the most critical point), adequate financial resources, and urgency for change. This influential champion's role is to "catalyze and support collective impact efforts, prevent overlap and duplication of efforts, and build capacity to utilize collective impact as a strategy to drive transformational change in the region" (Recker & Reed, 2013).

There are three phases in a collective impact initiative. Phase one consists of initiating action. It requires an understanding of key players, the baseline of the social problem, and the case for the change. Phase two consists of organizing for impact. It requires the players in the initiative to work together and create a supporting backbone infrastructure. Phase three is sustaining action and impact. This requires the pursuit of prioritized areas for action in a coordinated way through systematically collecting data. Phase three can take a decade or more to complete. The collective impact is a marathon not a sprint, noting that there is not shortcut in the long-term process of social change, and that progress takes time (Hanleybrown et al., 2012).

As we have discussed throughout the book about culture and its impact on building community, Harwood (2015) believes that culture, especially civic culture, is important for collective impact, which is defined as "a balanced political culture in which political activity, involvement, and rationality exist but are balanced by passivity, traditionality, and commitment to parochial values" (Almond & Verba, 1963, p. 30). This balance requires the active engagement and informed participation by citizens in politics and civic life as a part of one's civic duties. Such participation is necessary for the survival of a democratic state and critical for the survival of a community and the reestablishment of a "spirit of community" (Etzioni, 1993, 1996).

A civic culture within the context of a community shows

> how a community works—how trust and public will form, why and how
> people engage with one another, what creates the right enabling environment
> for change to take root and accelerate. It relates to the degree of readiness and
> appetite for change among leaders, groups, *and* everyday people. Civic culture
> helps to explain why some communities move forward and others remain stuck
> or treading water, and why some communities that make progress ultimately
> slide backward (Harwood, 2015, p. 6).

This chapter will highlight some important case studies of how the Stanford collective impact model applies to programs and initiatives in the Greater Evansville community.

EVANSVILLE VOICE VISIONING PROCESS

Leadership Everyone (now called Leadership Evansville) is a nonprofit organization founded in 1976 aimed towards training community leaders in the art of servant leadership, by engaging participants in an experiential learning process focused on individual learning and leading at their highest potential. Leadership Everyone (LE) provides community leadership programs several times a year for civic, public, and nonprofit leaders throughout Evansville, usually held in a retreat setting in New Harmony, Indiana (Leadership Everyone [LE], 2021). LE uses a servant leadership model where participants learn about their strengths, talents, and priorities. LE helps them use that self-knowledge through creating a personal timeline and a community timeline of the major events in the city's history that helps participants become better servant leaders and understand how they can make a difference in the community (Miller-Pease, 2015).

In 2012, the new mayor of Evansville, Lloyd Winnecke, was interested in initiating a public process aimed towards improving and transforming Evansville and wanted public input on how the city could achieve this vision. He sought the involvement of Leadership Everyone and Miller-Pease, who is a gregarious, enthusiastic trainer of leaders and the Executive Director of LE, to convene and facilitate this visioning process and serve as the backbone support organization for this collective impact initiative.

The new visioning process for LE in 2012 became known as VOICE, whose mission "brings together diverse servant leaders in our community in facilitator-led group discussions to draw out and capture everyone's ideas for the future. Together, we discuss our hopes and dreams for our community in a comfortable, open forum that is fun and inspiring, too. The sessions allow respectful conversations to take place, all voices to be heard, and every vision to be documented and shared. VOICE ensures that everyone in our community has the opportunity to take part in creating a desired future" (VOICE, 2013).

LE and the VOICE visioning process convened a series of 32 community listening sessions in 2012–2013 at libraries, schools, universities, churches, and community centers throughout the community (VOICE, 2015). One thousand seven hundred and twenty-one citizens participated in these sessions. Most of the visioning participants were white and female, and 1,100 of them were school-aged children enrolled from kindergarten through 12th grade. LE brought the VOICE process to various places throughout the community instead of going to LE. Every high school (public, private, parochial) in the city participated in these visioning sessions, occurring at various times of the day to accommodate different people's time and busy schedules.

At the beginning of each VOICE visioning session, whether it was a gathering of corporate leaders or a gathering of fifth-graders or high school students, Miller-Pease or a volunteer facilitator would read the book *The Flower Man* by Mark Ludy (2005). In the story, the flower man arrives in a town in the middle of the night and finds an abandoned house for sale. He buys the house, fixes it up, and plants a garden. Suddenly, the black and white images on the pages turn into color, including a girl he meets after he gives her a flower. As he does this, everything and everyone turns into color, transforming each person in the neighborhood. The people are now doing the work for themselves in their own homes and in their own neighborhood. Towards the end of the book, the flower man quietly leaves town, but the work continues.

The book has no words, but only images. You can go through the book multiple times and follow each character, including the flower man, and see the transformation unfold. *The Flower Man* shows a servant leader's heart and spirit by going into a struggling community. He did not point at others or blame others for what they were not doing. By fixing up his own house and sharing flowers with the neighborhood kids and residents, more people started to get involved and amazing things started to happen. The flower man is the catalyst for community development and collective impact. The flower man's attitude is powerful. He has an ability to share the work without controlling everything. He has the ability to let the people engage with their neighbors, build networks and social capital, and work towards change.

After participants in each session read *The Flower Man*, they were asked to do a community timeline and describe what is positive about Evansville right now. They were also asked to identify how Evansville should move forward and what Evansville should leave behind (see Figures 7.1 and 7.2). The larger the word, the higher the frequency of responses.

Reading *The Flower Man* and articulating positive statements, along with the carry forward and leave behind statements allowed everyone to prepare for further visioning. After this exercise, participants were broken into groups of three to four people and asked to draw their own vision of the future of Evansville on large flipchart paper. Each person shared their vision with their group and later to all participants in the VOICE session. After 32 visioning meetings and after everyone expressed their individual visions for Evansville's future, Leadership Everyone compiled all the visions and observes certain values that appeared consistently in these visions, such as being connected, diversity, engagement, sustainable, beautiful, inclusive, fun, hip, and innovative (VOICE, 2015).

Figure 7.1. Word Cloud of what VOICE participants would like to leave behind in Evansville's future. *Source:* Leadership Everyone

Figure 7.2. Word Cloud of what VOICE participants would like to carry forward into Evansville's future. *Source:* Leadership Everyone

From the compilation of these visions, three common themes emerged, and were presented by VOICE leaders at three big action meetings (BAMs). These themes—healthy greenspaces, city core, and experiences—were referred to as "flowerpots." The healthy greenspaces flowerpot, including one located on the westside of Evansville, focuses on the health and well-being of Evansville residents through outdoor activities designed to enhance quality of life, especially in the city's parks and trails system. The city core flowerpot focuses on the city's great neighborhoods and cultural hot spots in the city such as Franklin Street, Haynie's Corner, Downtown Evansville, Riverside Historic District, and the universities, and how the community can further support, connect, and promote these places in the city (VOICE, 2015).

The experiences flowerpot shows the multitude of existing opportunities people engage with in Evansville, as well as ideas for new and exciting events and activities to highlight, showcase, and celebrate in an organized and collective way (VOICE, 2015). This fits into the placemaking initiatives which we will discuss in chapter 9.

Results and Outcomes of the Flowerpot Meetings

As a result of the flowerpot meetings, some projects identified were already underway, but several new projects and events emerged. Several projects focused on creating a community garden. One is operated by a local nonprofit organization, Franklin Street Events Association, and is located on West Franklin Street in the westside of Evansville. Half of the beds in this garden belong to a different community nonprofit organization and the other half are available to any resident living on West Franklin Street (VOICE, 2015). Another garden project is the Culver Hoop House, a tunnel-shaped covered structure with raised garden beds that functions both in the warm growing seasons and in the cold winter months. Culver Hoop House also serves as an outdoor classroom to teach gardening, provide hands-on environmental education experiences, and increase young people's knowledge of fruits and vegetables and appreciation of healthy and nutritious eating habits (VOICE, 2013, 2015).

Another garden project is located at the city's main community center called the C. K. Newsome Family Learning Garden. This garden includes raised garden beds that feed the surrounding neighborhoods, using recycled material and featuring a whimsical design that provides an open and inviting space for the community. The family learning garden also includes a rainwater retention pond that irrigates the garden and prevents almost one-million gallons of storm water from flowing into the sewer and the Ohio River because of Evansville's combined sewer system (VOICE, 2013, 2015).

In the city core flowerpot, there was a desire to create cultural districts with the hope of increasing "the cultural value and understanding of Evansville who are out-of-town visitors, and that sell the quality of life to potential employers" (VOICE, 2020). Through signage, branding, and marketing strategies, and establishing venues to attract people, the project enabled five cultural districts in Evansville to emerge: West Franklin Street, Downtown Evansville, Haynie's Corner Arts District, North Main Street, and neighborhoods around the University of Evansville.

From the experiences of the flowerpot meetings, a series of regular and annual events emerged, such as the Franklin Street Bazaar and Parks Fest. During the summer months on Saturday mornings and early afternoons is the Franklin Street Bazaar, located on West Franklin Street on the grounds of the Western Branch Library. The bazaar offers locally grown and produced foods that follow safe harvesting and produce standards, supervised by Karen Blaize Conaway, the former Franklin Street Bazaar Market Master. The bazaar also offers a diverse array of food choices, and showcases local artists, live music, and children's activities (VOICE, 2020). The Franklin Street Bazaar space next to the Western branch library also includes events throughout the summer, such as outdoor concerts and movies that help create a unique sense of place along West Franklin Street.

Parks Fest is an annual festival held in September in collaboration with the Arts Council of Southwestern Indiana at Garvin Park next to Evansville's historic Bosse Field, the third oldest regularly-used baseball stadium in the United States. Parks Fest offers a wide range of activities, including live music from a wide variety of local and regional bands and performers, including country, bluegrass, and rock, along with family friendly activities for children such as bounce houses, hula hooping, face painting, along with a marketplace for local artists and merchants and a variety of local food venues (VOICE, 2015, 2020).

The common agenda and shared vision were realized by the city and Leadership Everyone. The shared measurement allows each flowerpot priority to measure the overall impact of the project, which evolved throughout 2014 and 2015. Leadership Everyone has expanded its scope to include other cities, towns, and counties in Evansville to make up the Regional VOICE initiative. Noting that data collection and measurements were limited in the VOICE visioning process, LE will use the experience of VOICE to carry forward to Regional VOICE with a survey questionnaire for participants and stakeholders.

The third criterion for successful collective impact, mutually reinforcing activities, has been beneficial through the partnership of many organizations in the creation of the city's cultural districts, and the creation of the Franklin Street Bazaar and Parks Fest. The continuous and open communication was developed through Leadership Everyone through the initial VOICE vision-ing sessions, the BAM meetings, and the follow-up flowerpot meetings. This developed and fostered a culture of trust and transparency through regular contact between LE and the public. LE represents everyone who participated in this process and as the backbone support organization, played a critical role in coordinating all the meetings, activities and projects and kept the drivers focused on the flowerpot goals and developing effective and successful outcomes.

LE and the VOICE visioning process embodies collective impact from the 3,200 participants in the initial VOICE vision session (1,700 in the 32 sessions and 1,500 people in the three [BAMs]). Also, 1,000 additional people participated in the 15 flowerpot meetings. As a result of this process, Leadership Everyone estimated approximately 30,000 have participated in the VOICE-inspired flowerpot projects, events, and activities, a few of which we have briefly highlighted (VOICE, 2015).

Much of the data collected from the participants in their personal visions have been used in other collective impact and regional economic development initiatives, which LE estimates have impacted over 250,000 people in the region (VOICE, 2015). This data has been included in such projects as the Regional Cities initiative from the Indiana Economic Development Corporation, the Millennial 2040 regional comprehensive plan, the Vanderburgh County Master Plan, the Downtown Evansville Master Plan, the Five-Year Consolidated Plan from the City of Evansville Department of Metropolitan Development (DMD) and HUD, and the Jacobsville Redevelopment Area Plan that we highlighted in the last chapter, as well as the application from the Promise Zone designation, which we will highlight below (VOICE, 2015).

PROMISE ZONE

An important model of collective impact is the Promise Zone (PZ) initiative. The Promise Zone was conceived by President Obama in his 2013 State of the Union Address and began the following year to create designations for high poverty communities in urban, rural, and tribal areas around the nation. The Promise Zone partners the federal government with local leaders to increase economic activity, improve educational opportunities, leverage private investment, reduce violent crime, enhance public health, and address other priorities identified by the community (HUD, 2020c).

Thirteen federal departments and agencies, ranging from Housing and Urban Development (HUD) to Agriculture, Commerce, Health and Human Services (HHS), and Education (among others) have partnered with 22 local communities throughout the United States using the principle of collective impact to improve the community and quality of life of its residents. A Promise Zone designation enables a community to earn preference points to apply for competitive federal grants, provides a federal liaison that helps the local Promise Zone connect with various federal programs and agencies that will benefit Promise Zone residents, and offers as many as five AmeriCorps VISTA members who work in the area to carry out the zone's mission and goals (HUD, 2020c).

Twenty-two communities were selected, including large cities such as Los Angeles, Philadelphia, Atlanta, and Minneapolis and Native American tribes such as the Choctaw Nation of Oklahoma and Pine Ridge Indian Reservation of the Oglala Sioux Tribe, South Dakota, as well as rural communities such as the Southern Kentucky Highlands and the Southern Carolina Low Country. Each had to demonstrate "a consensus vision for their community and its residents, the capacity to carry it out, and a shared commitment to specific, measurable results" (HUD, 2020c, Promise Zone Overview).

The designation requires each community to follow specific criteria outlined by HUD. This includes establishing a framework and layout of one or more census tract(s) or portions of census tract(s) across a contiguous geographical area. The geographic area must have a poverty rate of greater than 33 percent (with a priority placed between 34 and 49 percent), and a population greater than 10,000. In addition to the geographic and demographic requirements, the Promise Zone designee must identify the lead applicant (likely the convener) and the local leadership's demonstration of commitment to the effort, and how efforts are aligned with local needs and community assets, including school locations, areas of high crime, and areas where community development initiatives and other assets are present (Evansville Promise Zone, 2016).

Evansville was chosen on the third round of Promise Zone applications in June 2016; the designation is in effect for 10 years. The Evansville Promise Zone consists of the city's 10 highest poverty census tracts and neighborhoods covering the north central to the southeast sides of the city (see Figure 7.3). This Evansville Promise Zone is one of only two designations whose convening organization is not a city or municipality (the other being the Boner House in Indianapolis). The lead convening organization for the Evansville Promise Zone is ECHO Housing Corporation, and the lead partner is the City of Evansville Department of Metropolitan Development (DMD). Twenty-seven community agencies, otherwise known as implementation partners, have signed a memorandum of understanding (MOU) to support the mission and activities of the Promise Zone. These implementation partners range from nonprofit organizations, government agencies, social service agencies, businesses, banks, local universities, hospitals, health care provid-

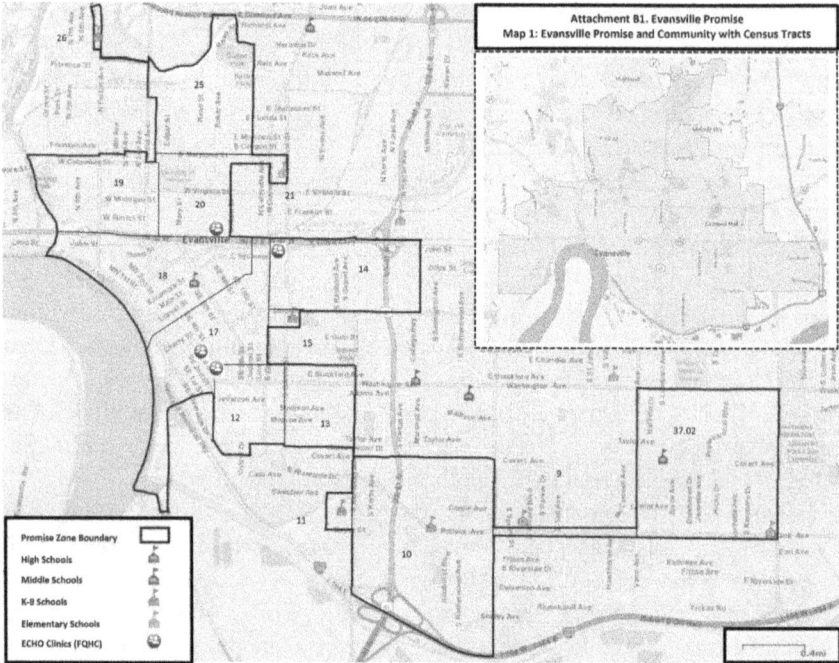

Figure 7.3.   Map of City of Evansville and Evansville Promise Zone boundaries. *Source:* **Evansville Promise Zone, 2019**

ers, churches, local foundations, and community development corporations (Diehl 2019a, 2019b).

The Promise Zone consists of a governance committee that ensures that it fulfills its legal, ethical, and financial responsibilities, assesses the progress towards the goals every month, troubleshoots conflict, reviews financials, and assists with any changes or modifications of assessment, consensus, approval, and revision of the goals. This committee consists of a representative from the lead partner ECHO Housing Corporation, the City of Evansville Department of Metropolitan Development (DMD), the evaluation partner team lead Diehl Consulting, a representative from the local school district (Evansville Vanderburgh School Corporation), a representative from United Neighborhoods of Evansville (an umbrella organization supporting the city's neighborhood associations), several residents that live in the Promise Zone, and representatives from each of the six workgroups in the areas of housing, crime, economic development, education, job development, and health, which align with the six goals of the Evansville Promise Zone.

The Evansville goals are as follows: 1) increase jobs opportunities through workforce development, family asset building and access to better transportation options; 2) increase economic activity and development through long-term growth and upgrading the standard of living for all citizens in the Promise Zone; 3) improve educational opportunities through a coordinated community school strategy that includes high quality early childhood experiences, community and school partnerships, systems that support learning, and connecting youth with resources to support postsecondary education; 4) reduce violent crime by working with neighborhood residents and stakeholders to generate and strengthen initiatives and community partnerships, community and proactive policing and focused activities, and reduce the number of physical locations in the PZ suitable for criminal activity; 5) promote the overall health and well-being of Promise Zone residents and their access to healthcare (mental, physical, and dental) and 6) increase access to quality affordable housing that elevate the quality of the neighborhoods in the Promise Zone (Promise Zone Application, 2016).

The workgroups consist of members from the PZ implementation partners and residents, who are responsible for monitoring the programs of the work groups' goals, collecting the necessary data to report to HUD and the governance committee, maintaining lines of communication with community partners to exchange information and resources, and addressing barriers and

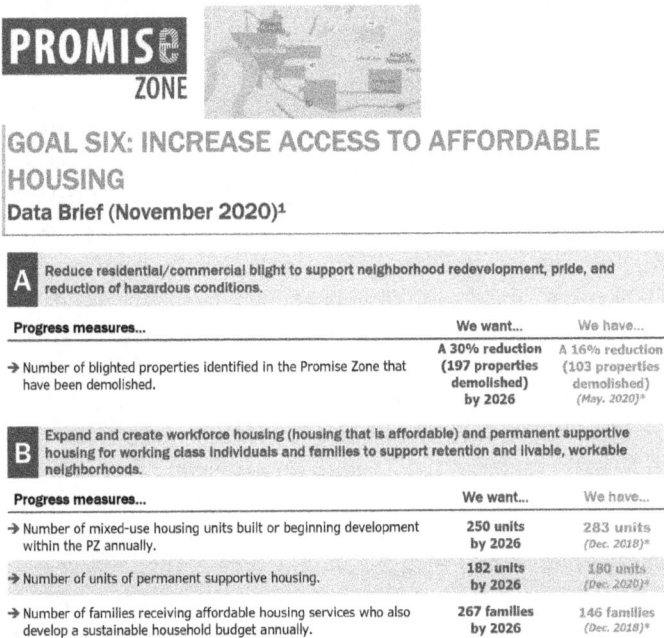

PROMISⓔ ZONE

GOAL SIX: INCREASE ACCESS TO AFFORDABLE HOUSING
Data Brief (November 2020)[1]

A Reduce residential/commercial blight to support neighborhood redevelopment, pride, and reduction of hazardous conditions.

Progress measures...	We want...	We have...
→ Number of blighted properties identified in the Promise Zone that have been demolished.	A 30% reduction (197 properties demolished) by 2026	A 16% reduction (103 properties demolished) *(May. 2020)*[a]

B Expand and create workforce housing (housing that is affordable) and permanent supportive housing for working class individuals and families to support retention and livable, workable neighborhoods.

Progress measures...	We want...	We have...
→ Number of mixed-use housing units built or beginning development within the PZ annually.	250 units by 2026	283 units *(Dec. 2018)*[a]
→ Number of units of permanent supportive housing.	182 units by 2026	180 units *(Dec. 2020)*[a]
→ Number of families receiving affordable housing services who also develop a sustainable household budget annually.	267 families by 2026	146 families *(Dec. 2018)*[a]

Figure 7.4. Evansville Promise Zone Goal #6: Increase Affordable Housing Data Brief (November 2020). *Source:* Diehl, 2020

challenges. Below is a data brief on the progress of the Promise Zone's Goal #6: Increase Access to Affordable Housing.

In its application for the Promise Zone designation, community leaders stated a goal of creating 250 new housing units within the Promise Zone. The Promise Zone has successfully reached its housing goals well in advance of the designation's 10-year timeline. This goal was met through the construction of Garfield Commons, a multi-unit development of ECHO Housing in spring 2018, a 45-unit complex in fall 2018 that transformed an old Catholic school, and a 27-unit project named Garvin Lofts that provided permanent supportive housing for the most chronically homeless and medically vulnerable homeless residents. In 2020, 144 units of market rate housing called the Post House, and 64 units in the original 1913 YMCA building, called Central Lofts, will be completed in Downtown Evansville, which is located within the Promise Zone.

Since 2016, the Evansville Promise Zone has received over $4 million in federal grants. Seven million dollars in local and state grants have been awarded, along with $2.86 million in capital investment in 2018, totaling $555.52 million in total leveraged economic development and capital improvements in the Promise Zone area (Diehl 2019a, 2019b).

The work of the Promise Zone is collective impact, which follows a common agenda and shared public goals that fit a common agenda. The Promise Zone has developed a theory of change and a logic model that guides the overall process. A theory of change defines how an intervention will create the desired change in which causal linkages among the various components of a program are articulated (Hill & Theis, 2010; see also Weiss, 1995). A theory of change consists of three main elements: the community problem or need; specific intervention; and intended outcome (Hill & Theis, 2010). The problem can be presented as a statement identifying the challenges and obstacles towards dealing with the problem. The intervention is presented as the mechanism for which the challenges, community problems, and needs will create the desired change and achieve the intended outcomes (Hill & Theis, 2010).

Theories of change are represented using a logic model, which illustrates "a visual depiction of the underlying program theory" (Hill & Theis, 2010, p. 357). A logic model also shows how a program will work under certain conditions to solve the identified problem or problems (Newcomer, Hatry, & Wholey, 2015). The logic model articulates a program's activities and its intended outcomes and results by depicting a causal chain of inputs (resources that are required to support the program), activities (the interventions or essential action steps to produce program outputs), and outputs (the products, goods, and services provided to the program's customers or participants). The end of this model includes the program's outcomes which are the expected changes or benefits to individuals, organizations, or other targets that result from the activity or output, either in the short-, medium-, or long-term (Hill & Theis, 2010; Newcomer et al., 2015). This is based on the notion that if we do x, then y will happen because of z.

The challenges and problems facing the Promise Zone communities are poverty, low educational attainment, low performing schools, blight, high crime, poor health, and poor, inadequate, and low-quality housing. If Evansville effectively leverages its community resources and assets through a comprehensive, coordinated, and collaborative effort in the six focus areas that help define the Promise Zone's goals, objectives, strategies, and metrics, this will improve the quality of life, prosperity, and vitality of the Promise Zone and all its neighborhoods. The common agenda, as outlined and articulated above, suggests that to have appropriate and effective buy-in, you ask all the stakeholders to commit to the common agenda by signing a memorandum of understanding (MOU) that describes what each person is committing to the project or initiative (e.g., process, data, etc.) (Kania & Kramer, 2011; Hanleybrown et al., 2012).

Shared Measurement

According to the shared measurement guidelines for effective collective impact, nearly 60 indicators have been selected based on the Promise Zone designation agreement. Data is available at different points during the year, including the monthly data collected, by Diehl Consulting in Evansville, from the different workgroups, along with the workgroups, tracked goals and data collection.

Through the assistance of Diehl Consulting, the Evansville Promise Zone conducted a community survey again in 2019 to a population size of 7,050 households randomly selected in the 10 census tracts of the Evansville Promise Zone. Three thousand three hundred twenty-four surveys were mailed to addresses that had already received the surveys during the first round, and 596 households completed the survey (Diehl, 2020). The survey instrument measured aspects of the Promise Zone that secondary data analysis cannot always capture.

Surveys conducted in 2017 and in 2019 measured the impact the Promise Zone has had on the community. Questions in the 2019 survey focused on perceptions of the neighborhood, community engagement, employment, resident engagement, neighborhood pride, opinions of neighborhood infrastructure, crime, safety, available services, access to healthcare and healthy food options, and perceptions of housing conditions. The survey results are generalizable to the entire Promise Zone and Diehl (2020) notes the different sample sizes between 2017 and 2019 with different margins of error between surveys. Only 387 individuals (+/– 5 percent) responded to the survey in 2019 compared to 596 in 2019, with a slightly lower margin of error (+/– 4 percent). Z-tests at the 95 percent confidence level were also conducted to note statistically significant differences between 2017 and 2019 (Diehl, 2020).

Demographic statistics of the Evansville Promise Zone are as follows: Around 54 percent of the survey respondents are female 60 percent are white; 55 percent have a high school diploma or less; 10 percent have a bachelor's degree; and 55 percent of the survey respondents are 45 years old or older. Survey participants reported living in their current neighborhood an average of 13 years (range of 1–91 years) and reported an average of 11 years living at their current address (range of 1–67 years). More than half of participants (53 percent) reported owning their home, while 47 percent reported renting (Diehl, 2020).

In terms of community engagement, the Evansville Promise Zone saw a major increase from 13 percent in 2017 to 26 percent in 2019, in terms of awareness about the PZ, and an increase from 12 percent in 2017 to 20 percent in 2019 in terms of understanding the PZ. Neighborhood pride had decreased, where 45 percent reported being proud to live in their neighborhood in 2019 compared to 54 percent in 2017. Little change occurred in terms of housing satisfaction and housing perception over the two years, despite meeting the goals and increasing the availability of affordable housing (39 percent of the respondents believed that run-down, blighted homes were a problem in the neighborhood in 2019 compared to 38 percent in 2017).

There are a lot of things that go into what makes a resident satisfied with his or her home or neighborhood. The Evansville Promise Zone is still working on identifying current resident needs or needs that are being met adequately, as illustrated by 56 percent of survey respondents' reported need for grocery stores, compared to 37 percent in 2017, while 20 percent identified needs in public transportation services in 2019, compared to 13 percent in 2017. And in 2019, more than half of the survey respondents identified childcare, youth programming, and shopping as needed services.

In terms of the third point of collective impact of mutually reinforcing activities, all implementation partners and their constituencies, the six workgroups and the governance committee, are engaged and working towards these goals. Continuous and open communication is key for the Promise Zone, through regular monthly newsletters. The most innovative communication tool devised by the Evansville Promise Zone was the creation of the digital app unveiled in December 2019, which allows everyone access to resources from the Promise Zone.

Evansville Promise Zone is a convener, an information gatherer and disseminator, and a resource for the public and the people who live in the Promise Zone. It maintains regular contact with citizens, partners, and stakeholders alike and operates with transparency and accountability. Diehl Consulting regularly monitors the Promise Zones to make sure each goal is met. ECHO Housing Corporation, the lead convening agency, continues to serve as the backbone of support, along with the City of Evansville and the Department of Metropolitan Development, the latter employing a liaison with the Promise Zone. This backbone support relies on resources to keep the activity going, and is responsible for building a culture of support.

OBSTACLES TO COLLECTIVE IMPACT

Collective impact, like any initiative, has its critics. Wolff (2016) argues that collective impact asks too much from the backbone support organization, resulting in a top-down organization instead of a collaborative and dispersed leadership structure. Sometimes, the backbone organization or its coalition has considerable resources and staff, and such organizations need to build leadership capacity rather than act as leadership.

Our two case studies belie these criticisms and represent effective backbone support organizations in their respective collective impact efforts. The effectiveness of the Evansville Promise Zone and Leadership Everyone comes from being composed of smaller organizations without top-down leadership. LE has a diverse board representing a broad range of stakeholders and the Promise Zone's implementation partners help support the work of the Promise Zone. With only one full-time staff member and the potential to hire several AmeriCorps VISTAs, with only three staff dedicated to Leadership Everyone, these organizations must build leadership coalitions and avoid being the sole leaders of the process.

In the VOICE visioning process, LE used a servant leadership model and a bottom-up strategy (lifting people up) to empower residents to take ownership of the VOICE projects, events, or activities to improve their community. The flowerpots comprising the three priorities of the VOICE visioning process have leaders and champions who have worked hard to reach their specific goals and objectives. Leadership Everyone provided backbone support, but the participants themselves led and directed these projects.

For the Promise Zone, the six workgroups are given latitude and discretion to carry out their work and achieve their particular goals, objectives, and strategies. The housing workgroup, which also serves as an umbrella organization of local housing organizations called HOUSE (Housing Organizations United Serving Evansville), developed a strategic plan last year where its goals aligned with the current goals of the overall Promise Zone. The leaders of each workgroup receive support from the director and the governance committee, but it is the workgroups themselves that provide the leadership for the zone and the communities impacted within the Promise Zone.

There are several obstacles to collective impact that can derail any long-lasting effects. One important obstacle to collective impact is the process of funding and support an organization receives, especially from grants. This process forces the funders to determine which organizations do the best job and produce the best results at solving a social problem (Kania & Kramer, 2011). At the same time, the nonprofits often highlight their own organizations' activities and achievements. This can pit nonprofit organizations against each other while they compete for the same dollars. This tension may result in an organization focusing only on their singular impact in the community, and how this singular model can be replicated to increase their impact individually and not collectively (Kania & Kramer, 2011; Hanleybrown et al., 2012). Any crosscutting issue, requiring more than one discipline or approach, cannot be negotiated effectively by an organization that is isolated rather than collaborative.

Another criticism of collective impact is that the involvement of competing organizations can make it difficult to develop partnerships with a common agenda. Competing organizations might be unwilling or unable to collaborate with one another, or unwilling to change, adapt, or behave differently in a collective impact process. As we have learned using the collective impact model, it is impossible to effectively solve a community problem through only one discipline or area of expertise, or by only one individual or organization. It takes all of us to come together to solve the problem and make lasting change.

Chapter Eight

HOPE VI, New Urbanism, and Social Capital

Matthew J. Hanka and John Gilderbloom

Homeownership is an important pathway towards building social capital. The best way to ensure livable and sustainable communities, and revitalize distressed communities, is through homeownership. A home symbolizes a family's social status and is seen as an alternative to renting or living in public housing (Hayden, 2002). Purchasing and owning a home not only improves one's credit and helps build equity but can boost a person's confidence and create a sense of self and self-identity (Gilderbloom & Mullins, 2005; Marcus, 2006).

The symbolic role of the home is an expression of the social identity that we communicate and display to our neighbors, community, and the world at-large (Marcus, 2006). Having a place to call home is critical in the personal development of an individual and an important vehicle for self-expression. For children, a home is a place for nurturance and socialization, and a base to explore their surrounding environment (Marcus, 2006). The context within one's home, furnishings, and personal effects are powerful statements about a person's identity. While a person's relationship with the physical environment around them changes over time, home is a place where a person feels a sense of control (Marcus, 2006).

Owning a home is a rite of passage, symbolizing a certain economic status, which increases an individual's satisfaction (Rohe, Van Zandt, & McCarthy, 2001). More importantly, owning a home is a crucial factor in increasing the economic and financial health, livability, and sustainability of a neighborhood, community, and city, causing property values to increase.

Owning a home has not always been an ideal of the "American Dream." Many Americans did not own homes before the early 20th century. Only 45 percent of the population owned their own home in the early 1920s, especially in urban areas. With the plight of tenements in major urban areas in the late 19th and early 20th centuries, there was a push by the federal government to reform living conditions in cities and encourage homeownership. Homeownership's most visible champion at the time was Secretary of Commerce Herbert Hoover, under Calvin Coolidge, who also served as president of the United States from 1929 to 1933 (Rohe & Watson, 2007).

Up until the 1920s, and before the Great Depression, the ability to afford and finance a home presented many obstacles. Mortgage loans required borrowers to put more money down on the purchase; the mortgage terms were short, and the monthly payments were high (Schwartz, 2015). The Great Depression forced many homeowners into foreclosure and default on their loans, where as many as half of all mortgages defaulted at the beginning of the loan terms (Schwartz, 2015). To remedy the foreclosure problem, Congress passed the Home Loan Bank Act of 1932, and the Home Owners' Loan Act of 1933, to allow banks to lend to borrowers with longer mortgage loan terms. This law also created the Home Owners' Loan Corporation to purchase and refinance mortgages that had gone into default (Schwartz, 2015).

Homeownership evolved with the growth of FHA and VA loans, as discussed in chapter 1. The growth of redlining as a result of discriminatory housing policy targeting specific areas and neighborhoods and based on racial and ethnic groupings and color coding determined that banks and lenders would not lend to groups living in redlined areas (Massey & Denton, 1993; Hayden, 2003; Rohe & Watson, 2007; Schwartz, 2015).

The growth of public housing during the New Deal was designed to address a housing shortage and help poor and middle-class Whites in central city neighborhoods. However, exclusionary zoning and racially discriminatory policies by the federal government prevented Blacks from owning homes in the newly suburban neighborhoods built for Whites, and the public housing that White families left for the suburbs became subsidized and substandard in their conditions. Also, the slum clearance programs under urban renewal created a massive dislocation of residents, many of whom were poor Black families who became concentrated in new public housing high rises, which isolated them from their surroundings with no access to transportation and social services (Schwartz, 2015).

The Fair Housing Act of 1968 focused on developing new communities during this time by expanding housing opportunities (rent and own) for low and moderate-income households in all neighborhoods, followed by a voucher program (i.e., Section 8) that allowed families to choose any kind of housing as long as it met requirements. In terms of penetrating the housing market through homeownership, Massey and Denton (1993) argued against the unfair spread of institutionalized racism and discrimination within the housing market and financial institutions. They argue that African Americans were guided into neighborhoods, less affluent and more racially mixed, a kind of *de facto* redlining, which was a violation of the law. Many financial institutions, such as banks and credit agencies, continued to violate the law. They viewed potential minority homeowners as a credit and financial risks and refused to grant loans and mortgages to communities with minority populations.

The Community Reinvestment Act (CRA) of 1977 required giving credit to banks and financial institutions to provide credit, mortgage loans, small business and banking services to finance housing in specific geographic places, including high poverty, low-income underserved minority neighborhoods, essentially outlawing redlining altogether (Briggs, 2005; Rohe & Watson, 2007). Despite the federal government's attempt to eliminate discrimination practices and policies, including redlining with the Fair Housing Act and the CRA, the damage to segregation in public housing and homeownership, had already been done (Rothstein 2017a, 2017b).

The National Commission on Severely Distressed Public Housing in 1989 estimated that six percent of the 1.3 million total housing units, approximately 86,000 total units, in the United States were severely distressed and uninhabitable (HUD, 1992, 2000; Popkin & Cunningham, 2000; Goetz, 2003; Popkin, Katz, et al., 2004; Brazley & Gilderbloom, 2007; Gilderbloom, 2008; Hanka, 2009; Hanlon, 2010; Schwartz, 2015; Clark & Negrey, 2017). The older model of public housing projects, where many poor minority populations were concentrated, was not safe for habitation (Wilson, 1987; Massey & Denton, 1993; Briggs, 2005; Lees, Slater, & Wyly, 2008).

Jack Kemp, the former New York Congressman and the Department of Housing and Urban Development (HUD) Secretary during the George H. W. Bush administration, passionately pushed for a federal program aimed toward homeownership for public housing residents by using a combination of public and private dollars, and the market, to encourage homeownership through the Housing Opportunities for People Everywhere (HOPE) program. HOPE came out of the Cranston-Gonzalez National Affordable Housing Act of 1990. Five previous iterations of HOPE focused on homeownership for public and Indian housing (I), multifamily units (II), single family homes to public housing residents (III), and homeownership and rental assistance and case management supportive services for elderly (IV and V) (HUD, 1992).

The last iteration, HOPE VI, was created in 1992 and initially called the Urban Revitalization Demonstration (URD) program to revitalize a small percentage of the most "severely distressed" public housing (Rohe & Watson, 2007; Clark & Negrey, 2017). HOPE VI aimed to eliminate inadequate public housing that were products of the urban renewal style of the 1940s and 1950s. By the 1980s and 1990s, cities replaced the old, run-down, inadequate and uninhabitable public housing (high-rise and low-rise barrack housing) with a mix of homes, apartments, and condominiums in mixed-income communities, providing self-sufficiency services to the residents through local government and nonprofit agencies (HUD, 1999, 2000; Popkin, Katz, et al., 2004; Schwartz, 2015).

The HOPE VI program has five important objectives: 1) change the physical shape of public housing; 2) reduce the concentration of poverty through scattered-site development; 3) provide comprehensive support services to promote self-sufficiency and empower residents; 4) establish and maintain high standards of community and personal responsibility; and 5) develop partnerships between public and private agencies and organizations (HUD, 1992, 1999, 2000; Popkin et al., 2000; Popkin, 2002; GAO, 2002; Popkin, Katz, et al., 2004; Gilderbloom & Hanka, 2006; Brazley & Gilderbloom, 2007; Gilderbloom, 2008; Hanka, 2009; Schwartz, 2015).

Since its inception, 260 HOPE VI grants have been awarded, totaling over $6 billion to 134 local public housing authorities, with 10 cities receiving more than five grants (Hanlon, 2010; Gress, Cho, & Joseph, 2016). HOPE VI projects occurred in larger metropolitan areas like New York, Chicago, and Los Angeles, but also in medium and smaller cities like Louisville, Newport, and Covington, Kentucky, which we will discuss later in this chapter. HOPE VI is more than the physical demolition and redevelopment of distressed properties; it also provides social services to residents through Community and Supportive Services (CSS), the case management program of HOPE VI (HUD, 1992, 1999, 2000; Popkin, et al., 2000; Varady & Preiser, 1998; Popkin, 2002; Popkin, Katz, et al., 2004; Turner et al., 2007).

CSS supports the development of local strategies and programs to help public housing residents obtain employment, and provide training assistance through education, employment counseling, job training, household skills training, childcare services, transportation, substance abuse treatment and counseling, along with homeownership counseling that will lead to self-sufficiency and economic independence (HUD, 1999; HUD, 2000; Popkin, Katz, et al., 2004; Gilderbloom & Hanka, 2006; Brazley & Gilderbloom, 2007; Gilderbloom, 2008; Hanka, 2009).

Besides changing the physical shape of housing and providing support services, HOPE VI emphasizes personal and community responsibility through "community sweat equity," by instilling in residents that economic independence and self-sufficiency come with an obligation and responsibility to give back to one's community (Popkin, Katz, et al., 2004; HUD, 2000; Thompson, 2006). The HOPE VI program provides underserved communities with access to the social and economic capital necessary to create and revitalize neighborhood and community institutions, such as strong schools, businesses, and community organizations, which are the necessary building blocks for sustainable, stable, attractive, and livable communities (Gilderbloom, 2008).

HOPE VI IMPACTS

Laying the groundwork for HOPE VI began with the 1976 Supreme Court decision (*Gautreaux v. CHA*) that found the Chicago Housing Authority (CHA) guilty of racial discrimination. This forced the CHA to create new public housing in scattered sites through deconcentrating poverty and dispersing the poor into the private rental market known as the Gautreaux project, named after Chicago housing activist Dorothy Gautreaux. This program created 7,100 Section 8 certificates for current and former CHA residents in neighborhoods that were less than 30 percent Black (Brazley, 2002; Popkin, Buron, Levy, & Cunningham, 2000).

Over the next 20 years, Chicago received four HOPE VI grants for developments in Robert Taylor Homes, Rockwell Gardens, Stateway Gardens, and Henry Horner Homes. These HOPE VI projects resulted in the demolition of 51 high-rise public housing and several hundred middle and low-rise units, eliminating 14,000 units and relocating 6,000 families, and replacing them with 6,100 mixed income units and 9,500 senior citizen rehabilitated units at a cost of $1.5 billion (Popkin et al., 2000; Thompson, 2006).

In 2000, HUD published its first evaluation report of HOPE VI, which examines the accomplishments of HOPE VI development in eight U.S. cities: Atlanta, Baltimore, Columbus, El Paso, Milwaukee, Oakland, San Francisco, and Seattle (HUD, 2000). According to this report, HOPE VI fulfilled its main goals and objectives of community building, helping residents achieve self-sufficiency through improving education, job training, and homeownership through CSS. HOPE VI increased employment opportunities and income, dramatically reduced crime and violence, improved the physical shape of the housing, community policing, and improving crime prevention programs.

Also, HOPE VI eliminated the isolation of public housing through scattered site development and leveraged public investments in community development and neighborhood revitalization (HUD, 2000; GAO, 2002; Popkin, Katz, et al., 2004). Wyly and Hamel (1999), Byrne (2003), and Lees, et al. (2008) showed that the redevelopment of public housing in HOPE VI programs opened areas for investment and integrated residential neighborhoods by income. This is a "startling contrast to the patterns that have typified metropolitan development for 100 years" (Byrne, 2003, p. 429).

As noted by Gress et al. (2016), the HOPE VI program demolished 98,592 public housing units and replaced them with 97,389 units. Of the 97,389 units produced at HOPE VI sites during the 20 years of the program, 49,949 were public housing rentals and 5,369 units were public housing homeownership units totaling 55,318 units. The old public housing stock was replaced with 28,979 rental and homeownership affordable housing units, and 13,092 rental and homeowner market rate units, with only 35 percent of those for-sale units (see Table 8.1 below). Of the total number of public housing units, only 10 percent were homeownership. The older HOPE VI sites (12 years or older) have more public housing than affordable housing rental units, and most of the HOPE VI revitalization projects (161 out of 260) did not provide either affordable units or market rate units.

Table 8.1.   Total Number of HOPE VI Units Constructed

	Rental	Homeowner	Total
Public Housing	49,949	5,369	55,318
Affordable Housing	23,899	5,080	28,979
Market Rate	8,530	4,562	13,092
Total	82,378	15,011	97,389

Source: Gress, Cho, & Joseph, 2016.

The literature also focuses on the costs associated with HOPE VI developments. The average median cost per unit is $160,400, which encompasses the total cost of the home, including construction and labor costs, of which 37 percent of the cost is covered by HUD funds and 25 percent of the costs comes from private sources (Turner et al., 2007). The average cost of a mixed construction and rehabilitation unit is $165,800, and the median rehabilitation unit cost is $131,800, while the median unit cost for medium size metropolitan areas is $172,800 (Turner et al., 2007). The total cost of each unit also includes the costs associated with CSS.

Also, HOPE VI funding has an economic multiplier and leveraging effect. For every $1 of federal funds spent on HOPE VI, between $1.8 and $1.85 is leveraged from other sources, such as other public housing funding, federal, and non-federal funds (GAO, 2002; Popkin, Katz, et al., 2004; Gress et al., 2016). With approximately $6 billion spent on HOPE VI since 1993, approximately $11 billion in funds ($9 billion of that non-HUD funds) has been leveraged primarily through other federal, state, and other private sources (GAO, 2002; Popkin, Katz, et al., 2004; Gress et al., 2016).

The Government Accountability Office (GAO) estimated in 1999 that 61 percent of the original public housing residents would return to the new HOPE VI developments (Schwartz, 2015). However, Gress et al. (2016) show that only 21 percent of the former public housing residents will return to live in a HOPE VI development. Out of the 1,273 households who lived in the Cotter and Lang public housing projects in Park DuValle in Louisville, only 150 households (less than 12 percent) were selected to live in the new HOPE VI development (Brazley, 2002; Brazley & Gilderbloom, 2007; Gilderbloom, 2008).

Critics of Moving to Opportunity (MTO) housing programs, such as Section 8 and HOPE VI, argue that crime would increase in areas where residents moved (i.e., displaced persons would bring the crime with them) (Rosin, 2007). Due to lack of funding, HOPE VI reduced its ability and capacity to serve the "hard to house" residents—the elderly and the disabled, one-strike families with ex-offenders and convicted criminals, grandparents who are the primary caregivers for their grandchildren, and large families with a high number of occupants in the housing dwelling (Cunningham, Popkin, & Burt, 2005; Popkin, Theodos, Roman, Guernsey, & Getsinger, 2008).

Studies by Popkin (2000) and Popkin and Cunningham (1999, 2000) revealed that public housing residents were not prepared to face extraordinary challenges in transitioning to the private housing market. This difficulty was due to violent conditions in public housing, residents with criminal records, residents lacking the skills and knowledge to make the transition, as well as personal problems (Popkin et al., 2000). Cunningham (2001) showed the presence of HOPE VI gentrified neighborhoods reduced affordable housing in distressed neighborhoods, especially in neighborhoods with rents and home prices spiraling upward (Lees et al. 2008).

Robert Taylor Homes and Cabrini Green in Chicago, and the Pruitt Igoe Housing Development in St. Louis, are examples of the failure of public high-rise housing projects. Pruitt-Igoe housed 10,000 people in 33 eleven-story buildings covering 57 acres. It closed in 1976 because of high levels of despair, vandalism, and crime (Von Hoffman, 2012). Robert Taylor Homes housed 20,000 residents in 28 sixteen-story buildings covering 92 acres. Out of a population of three million people, Robert Taylor Homes represented 11 percent of Chicago's murders, 9 percent of rapes, and 10 percent of the aggravated assaults in 1980 (Wilson, 1987). The highly dense, high-rise physical shape of the public housing and its location related to basic services, schools, and employment opportunities produced an isolating and segregating effect from other communities, including residents who wanted to keep poor public housing residents out of their neighborhoods and communities.

The Cabrini Green HOPE VI project was one of the most acrimonious HOPE VI projects, due to significant residential opposition to one of the most dangerous public housing projects in the nation (Goetz, 2000). Nevertheless, the HOPE VI program eliminated the barracks style and high-rise public housing and replaced it with new urbanist designs, using traditional housing types and vernacular styles that deconcentrated poverty and provided new subsidized and market rate housing, making it indistinguishable from market rate housing in other neighborhoods (Bohl, 2000).

Place and geography have enormous impacts on where people live and whether people become homeowners (Dreier, Mollenkopf, & Swanstrom, 2014; Galster & Killen, 1995; Galster & Mikelsons, 1995; Reid, 2007). According to Dreier et al. (2014), place matters, because where you live has a powerful effect on the choices and opportunities and the quality of life of the area. In order to deconcentrate poverty, people must move from areas of high concentrations of poverty into more affluent areas. Moving the poor to more affluent areas would reduce the gap between rich and poor and increase the likelihood of economic integration (Dreier et al., 2014). Through government intervention, HOPE VI created new localities to deconcentrate poverty, promote economic integration, empower the underclass, and improve the lives of the poor and marginalized.

Scattered site housing, as seen in HOPE VI, and other public housing initiatives, is derived from the geography of opportunity hypothesis, which argues that where an individual lives influences his or her opportunities and life outcomes (Rosenbaum, 1995). Briggs (2005) describes an "uneven geography of opportunity," where the location of housing restricts access to economic and social opportunities and increases a resident's exposure to air pollution and highway congestion. Even though the uneven geography of opportunity hurts suburban residents as much as inner-city residents, especially through the increase of urban sprawl, suburban residents still have greater economic advantages (Briggs, 2005). The Gautreaux study in Chicago looked at how escaping concentrated poverty, the uneven geography of opportunity, and integrating low-income individuals into middle class areas will lead to improvements in employment, education, and social integration (Rosenbaum, 1995; Galster & Killen, 1995; Wilson, 1987; Brazley, 2002; Briggs, 2005; Gilderbloom, 2008).

Imbroscio (2008) challenged advocates of the Moving to Opportunity (MTO) and assisted mobility programs like Gautreaux, otherwise known as the "dispersal consensus." He argued the low-income residents' decisions to move to middle- and upper-class areas do not consider the contexts of their decisions and their choices to move. Their decisions become nothing more than "a desperate response to a desperate set of conditions with little to do with any real notion of freedom of choice" (Imbroscio, 2004; Imbroscio, 2008, p. 115).

Galster and Mikelson (1995), Galster (1996), and Reid (2007) extrapolate the geography of opportunity hypothesis and the linkages between geography and opportunity into the metropolitan opportunity structure, which is the interaction of a set of institutions, markets, social and administrative systems and networks, and the individual's perception of the structures available to them, influenced by geography, impact an individual's socioeconomic mobility. Where a person buys a home will affect their opportunities, because it may provide greater home equity through increased property values, as well as increased opportunities in education and employment, reduced exposure to crime, and an increase in self-esteem, satisfaction, and well-being (Rohe & Watson, 2007).

Place and geography have enormous impacts on where people live and whether people become homeowners (Dreier et al., 2014; Galster & Killen, 1995; Galster & Mikelsons, 1995; Reid, 2007). Removing public housing residents from their place and location through scattered-site housing not only deconcentrates poverty, but it removes the sense of identity the residents have about living in public housing. The demolition of the public housing through HOPE VI was viewed as an attack on residents' identity, and potential displacement from public housing dwellings ultimately disrupts friendship ties and social networks (Gotham, 2003).

The scattered-site housing approach has produced high levels of neighborhood satisfaction among former public housing residents, has reduced fears of crime, provided better employment opportunities for adults, increased educational opportunities for children, increased neighborhood social interaction, and reduced the cost burden of housing (Burby & Rohe, 1989; Rosenbaum & Popkin, 1990; Rosenbaum, 1995; Galster & Killen, 1995; Goetz, 2000; Varady & Preiser, 1998; Brazley, 2002; Popkin et al., 2000; Gilderbloom, 2008).

Varady and Walker (2003) argue that the use of housing vouchers (tenant-based subsidies) has deconcentrated poverty in some areas by improving the quality of life of former public housing residents, by moving them into neighborhoods that have higher mobility, better schools, and safer neighborhoods. In large urban areas like Chicago, recipients who used vouchers lived in neighborhoods with less drugs and crime and lower poverty rates than their old public housing (Varady & Walker, 2003).

HOPE VI RESIDENTIAL SATISFACTION

Studies on whether public housing residents benefit from scattered-site housing like HOPE VI showed greater residential satisfaction and improved quality of life (Burby & Rohe, 1989; Rosenbaum & Popkin, 1990; Rohe & Stegman, 1994; Popkin et al., 2000; Rosenbaum & Harris, 2001; Varady & Preiser, 1998; Varady, Walker, & Wang, 2001; Popkin, 2002; Popkin, Katz, et al., 2004).

Popkin et al.'s (2000) study of impact of the Gautreaux housing project in Chicago and Brazley's (2002) study of the HOPE VI project in Park DuValle, in Louisville's West End, measured the neighborhood and residential satisfaction of residents, showing that the majority of the lives of the residents in the new Villages of Park DuValle and the Oaks of Park DuValle were improved as a result of HOPE VI (see also Brazley & Gilderbloom, 2007; Gilderbloom, 2008). In Chicago, 63 percent of the residents reported their new housing was in good or excellent condition, and most said their new neighborhoods had less poverty than their previous neighborhoods (Popkin, 2002).

Varady and Preiser (1998) found that three-fourths of the Cincinnati Metropolitan Housing Authority (CMHA) residents surveyed, living in single-family, scattered-site units, and three-fifths in clustered scattered-site units, were satisfied, while only a third of the residents in traditional developments were satisfied. These high levels of satisfaction, according to Varady and Preiser (1998) were analyzed according to the following: 1) demographic characteristics, such as age, income, education employment status; 2) locational characteristics, such as traditional, clustered scatted-site or single-family scattered site, and whether one lives in the city or suburbs; 3) housing characteristics, such as the quality of the home and the maintenance of the home or unit; and 4) housing attitudes, such as the presence of crime, whether the resident felt safe or not, civic and neighborhood involvement by residents in their neighborhoods, and their involvement in the decision-making process in their neighborhood or community. Varady, Walker, and Wang (2001) also examined the relationship between relocation and housing satisfaction and found that residents who moved to a nearby housing development were just as likely to be satisfied as those who moved much farther away. In addition, receiving moderate relocation counseling helped improve housing choice and housing satisfaction.

Homeownership initiatives like HOPE VI are more likely to provide enormous stability in a neighborhood, higher levels of self-esteem and personal freedom, and improved quality of life for children. Homeowners are more likely to participate in civic activities and experience greater physical and psychological health and satisfaction from owning a home (Rohe, Van Zandt, & McCarthy, 2001). According to Varady, Walker, and Wang (2001), and Rohe and Stegman (1994), homeowners expressed greater residential satisfaction than those renting and living in apartments. These attitudes of satisfaction among residents come from the personal attitudes of the residents themselves, the characteristics of their own dwelling units, and the physical, geographic, and socioeconomic status of the area.

HOPE VI SELF-SUFFICIENCY PROGRAM

To elaborate further, Community and Supportive Services (CSS) was formed in response to the Personal Responsibility and Work Opportunity Reconciliation Act of 1996, which helped residents find jobs and transition to better jobs as a means to self-sufficiency, such as literacy training, job training, preparation, and retention, counseling, personal management skills, daycare, youth activities, health services, drug treatment, and information about relocation opportunities, which is a mandatory component of the HOPE VI CSS program (Kingsley & Corvington, 2000; Gilderbloom & Hanka, 2006; Gilderbloom, Hanka, & Lasley, 2008; Gress et al., 2016). Much of the literature on HOPE VI's self-sufficiency programs are case studies in places such as Denver, the state of North Carolina, Louisville, and New York City (Rohe & Kleit, 1997; Van Ryzin, Ronda, & Muzzio, 2001; Brazley, 2002; Santiago & Galster, 2004; Kleit & Rohe, 2005; Brazley & Gilderbloom, 2007).

Self-sufficiency services like CSS are an important holistic and comprehensive approach that helps residents find and maintain employment and relocate to another housing development, while addressing the needs of residents with physical and mental disabilities, older adults and senior citizens, and individuals who experience domestic violence, substance abuse addiction, criminal records, and poor credit records (Popkin, 2002; Popkin, Katz, et al., 2004). Residents who qualified for CSS and HOPE VI often need to meet stricter requirements (e.g., background checks, credit checks, drug testing), which may explain why many former public housing residents didn't return to the new HOPE VI developments (Popkin, Katz, et al., 2004; Gress et al., 2016).

$714 million was budgeted for CSS in the first decade of the HOPE VI program (GAO, 2002; GAO, 2003; Popkin, Katz, et al., 2004), providing direct services to over 73,000 residents of the approximately 95,000 residents from the original caseload (as of 2014). Approximately 22,000 residents either refused CSS services, did not need, or were not authorized for services. Of those 73,000 residents, 75 percent were original residents and 25 percent were new residents. This did not necessarily mean the 75 percent of original residents lived in the HOPE VI development (Popkin, Katz, et al., 2004; Turner et al., 2007; Gress et al., 2016).

CRITIQUES OF HOPE VI

HOPE VI established positive incentives for resident self-sufficiency by providing comprehensive supportive services that empowered residents. While HOPE VI program forged partnerships with other agencies and local government, nonprofit organizations, and private businesses to gain leverage, support, and resources, these projects were not always well received by the communities themselves. Oftentimes, residents never got involved with the process, in part because of the lack of interest from the residents and the public housing authorities (PHAs), who failed to involve the original residents from the beginning (Pitcoff, 1999).

Residents relocating to deconcentrated minority areas have experienced difficulty in making the transition to their new housing, adjusting to a new housing environment, overcoming fears of discrimination in predominantly White areas, the lack of affordable housing, the lack of public transportation in the suburban areas, and landlords unwilling to accept vouchers (Varady & Walker, 2003; Popkin, 1999, 2000). Also, the most vulnerable public housing residents that experience the greatest social problems, such as substance abuse and domestic violence, may not qualify for assistance from HOPE VI and Section 8 vouchers, or receive any assistance on the private market (Popkin et al., 2000).

Although studies have shown that HOPE VI has significantly eliminated concentration of poverty through mixed income housing, little was done to reduce the large racial concentrations in many of these new developments (Brazley, 2002; Kingsley, Johnson, & Petit, 2003; Gilderbloom, 2008). Many of the HOPE VI projects were built on the old public housing sites, which reinforces the residential segregation in these public housing developments by failing to integrate into the larger community or falling through the cracks, as is the case with the HOPE VI program in Park DuValle in Louisville (Brazley, 2002; Gilderbloom, 2008). The Popkin, Katz, et al. (2004) study, done a decade after the first HOPE VI developments, shows much of the same challenges facing former HOPE VI residents, noting, "Some of the original residents of these developments may live in equally or even more precarious circumstances today" (p. 4; as cited in Mallach, 2009, p. 185).

Not following the one-for-one replacement requirement for HOPE VI, a requirement repealed by Congress in 1998, only worsened residents' situations because they couldn't return to the new housing development where they once lived, ultimately failing to assist those specific families most in need. As noted earlier, only 21 percent of those who lived in the former public housing moved into the new HOPE VI housing (Gress et al., 2016). Public housing authorities (PHAs) were required to develop relocation plans for every displaced resident, but it was often difficult and time-consuming to develop these plans. Much of HOPE VI and affordable housing policy of the 1990s, according to Mallach (2009), reflects an "upward bias in the direction of many affordable housing efforts away from the neediest and most impoverished households towards those who, although in need, have higher incomes, are more likely to have stable employment, and are close in their demographic and social features to mainstream middle America" (p. 185).

Critics have complained that HOPE VI has removed and demolished more affordable housing units than replaced, resulting in hundreds and thousands of displaced public housing residents. The HOPE VI program repealed the "one-for-one" public housing replacement requirement for public housing demolitions as a part of the 1987 Housing and Community Development Act, because this replacement was viewed as an obstacle towards demolishing these communities (Goetz, 2003). Section 24 of the Quality Housing and Work Responsibility Act of 1998 (QHWRA) also excused HOPE VI from the one-to-one replacement requirement, which has resulted in the replacement of only about one affordable unit for every five destroyed (Williams, 2003). The repeal of this requirement also eliminated many scattered site developments outside of minority areas, resulting in the rebuilding of highly concentrated segregated low-income neighborhoods that lacked adequate replacement housing to accommodate tenants who were displaced voluntarily by the HOPE VI redevelopment (Briggs, 2005; Popkin, Katz, et al., 2004).

NEW URBANISM

Fulton (1996, p. 2) defines new urbanism as "a movement in architecture, planning, and urban design that emphasizes a particular set of design principles, including pedestrian- and transit-oriented neighborhood design, and a mix of land uses, as a means of creating more cohesive communities." New urbanism uses the traditional urban form by creating new housing designs and new uses in land and physical spaces on a human scale that encourages social interaction with the neighborhood that develops meaningful and purposeful community, while reducing our impact on the environment and improving the overall health and quality of life of residents in these communities (Katz, 1994; Duany, Plater-Zyberk, & Speck, 2010; Kleit, 2005; Nguyen, Rohe, Frescol, Webb, Donegan, & Han, 2016).

The neighborhood is the organizing element for new urbanism (Katz, 1994; Duany et al., 2010). A new urbanist neighborhood includes a traditional neighborhood development (TND) with an identifiable center and a Main Street with a mix of commercial (shops and stores), residential, civic (meeting halls, government buildings, schools), and religious (worship spaces), incorporating quality architecture and urban design methods that are energy efficient and environmentally friendly while reinforcing connection, diversity, socialization, and community.

A new urbanist neighborhood gives priority to public spaces where civic buildings are located and utilized. New urbanist communities are compact, dense, and walkable (1/4-mile radius from edge to edge that can be walked in 5–10 minutes), with short blocks and narrow, modest-sized, interconnected streets and networks. These neighborhoods have mixed-use zoning, offer robust public transit, and emphasize walkability and less dependence on the automobile (Katz, 1994, Dunay et al., 2010). New urbanism embraces development that includes downtown apartment building styles, and shops on the ground floor close to the street, which enhance the public realm that connects people to place (Duany et al., 2010; Ross, 2015).

New urbanism is grounded in the City Beautiful and Garden City movements of the late 19th/early 20th century, and a reaction to the increase in sprawl and suburbanization after World War II, based on single use commercial and residential development connected by multi-lane roads that only exacerbate the growth of a metropolitan area (Upton, 2003; Sander, 2010). New urbanism is seen as a viable solution to many issues addressed in this book. New urbanism reshapes the physical and spatial configuration of the neighborhood and community through purposeful design in order to create and foster community and enhance civic engagement. (Duany et al., 2010).

In 1993, the Congress of New Urbanism (CNU) was created by a group of architects, planners, and policymakers, chief among them Miami-based planners Andres Duany and Elizabeth Plater-Zyberk, as well as noted urbanist and planner Peter Calthorpe (Conn, 2014). The Congress's charter states, "Through grids of streets, transportation choices and the saying of buildings along sidewalks, New urbanism brings destination within reach and allows for frequent encounters between citizens, in sharp contrast to sprawl" (CNU, 1993). The charter also fights for the "reconfiguration of sprawling suburbs into communities of real neighborhoods and diverse districts," and advocates that "communities should be designed for the pedestrian and transit as well as the car; cities and towns should be shaped by physically defined and universally accessible public spaces and community institutions; urban places should be framed by architecture and landscape design that celebrate local history, climate, ecology, and building practice" (CNU, 1993, Preamble).

While new urbanism is associated with public health and environmentalism, new urbanism is also an antithesis to sprawl and a rejection of suburbia (Ross, 2015). As a term, *sprawl* was first used in the 1930s to describe the growth and proliferation of new housing stock in the suburbs after World War II (11 million new homes) through low-cost mortgages from the FHA and VA loans, and facilitated by a new interstate highway system to transport people safely and quickly to the suburbs (Duany et al., 2010).

Squires (2001) defines *sprawl* as "a pattern of urban and metropolitan growth that reflects low density, automobile dependent, exclusionary, new development on the fringe of settled areas often surrounding a deteriorating city" (p. xx). Downs (1998) sees sprawl as the unlimited outward extension of new development, low density developments in new-growth areas, leapfrog development, and strip commercial development. Sprawl is often caused and influenced by the availability of land, where land consumption is not proportional to the changes in population growth in the suburbs, moving out of the central city and into the suburbs, falling household sizes, technological advances, the structure of local government, and federal and local policies (e.g., roads and highways, homeownership subsidies, zoning).

Sprawl has five key components: 1) housing subdivisions that consist only of residences and nothing else; 2) the presence of shopping centers (aka shopping malls, strip malls, or big box retail used exclusively for shopping); 3) office and business parks designed only for work; 4) the presence of civic institutions that replaced those in civic institutions that are large, cumbersome, and inaccessible by pedestrians; 5) and the presence of roadways that connect the other uses (Duany et al., 2010).

The implications of sprawl include economic discrimination between the rich, the middle- and upper-middle-class and poor neighborhoods; the increase of environmental pollution due to runoff; the increase in greenhouse gases; and the loss of greenspace. Sprawl also has exacerbated the separation between the private and public realm (Duany et al., 2010). The private realm consists of the house and the inside of one's house (Americans have the largest homes per square foot in the world), while the public realm 100 years ago consisted of narrow streets, schools, parks, grocery stores, and other amenities within walking distance. Today, the public realm has been replaced with subdivisions, multi-lane roads, and parking lots that provide no sense of belonging.

For new urbanist residents, "new suburban development does not provide them with any more of the satisfying private realm that they love; it only gives them more of the degraded public realm toward which they feel indifferent at best" (Duany et al., 2010, p. 42). Sprawl creates the opposite of community, according to Richard Sexton, where "residents of suburbia try to own individually what the community once provided for all. They don't share, but hoard, as each homesite seeks to be a self-sufficient entity" (as cited in Conn, 2014, p. 284).

New urbanism focuses on policy solutions, such as mixed-income affordable housing and transit-oriented developments (TND), for both the city and the suburbs, and covers a wide range of incomes (Calthorpe, 2009). New urbanism pushes for the adoption of form-based codes, which regulates the size, shape, and placement of buildings on the outside. Ross (2015) notes that form based codes alter the power dynamics between citizens, the government and developers, because the citizens and the government have more control outside the building and can determine if it's a single or mixed-use building (Duany et al., 2010).These contributions to the new urbanist movement have challenged and ultimately discredited the role of physical determinism that has determined what can and cannot be designed to solve the problems of the city (Bohl, 2000).

SEASIDE, FLORIDA

One of the earliest developments that embraced new urbanism principles is Seaside, Florida, in Walton County, on the Florida panhandle near Destin and Panama City, Florida. This site was designed in 1981–1982 by Duany and Plater-Zyberk, and developed by Robert Davis, and these architects wanted to show a sense of community through their design and planning. Seaside had a central square town center surrounded by a Greek revival post office, an outdoor market and boutique shops, with streets, boulevards, and walkways. Private buildings filled in the surrounding public spaces near the town center. Seaside was also the setting for the 1998 film *The Truman Show* starring Jim Carrey (Katz, 1994; Hayden, 2003). The 80-acre site of Seaside can only be reached by car and sits across from the beach on Florida state highway 30A. It was designed to be pedestrian-oriented, to "recreate the ambiance of a southern beach resort of eighty to a hundred years ago, in the era of the horse and buggy" by using "neo-traditional vernacular houses set in indigenous landscaping" (Hayden, 2003, pp. 203, 205).

Seaside has 750 units, including 350 homes and 300 other apartments and hotel rooms, with a population of 2,000 at its peak. Seaside's lots are small, and the density is high. Lots were priced as high as $12,000. A 700 square foot home sold for $475,000, and a 2,100 square foot home sold for $1.1 million, while waterfront properties cost $1.7–$2 million (Hayden, 2003). The architectural styles of Seaside are diverse, ranging from traditional Victorian Southern and modern and postmodern styles, such as wood framed cottages and bungalows that use form-based codes to determine how the building and the physical space should look (i.e., lot size, setbacks, and landscape regulations) (Katz, 1994; Fulton, 1996).

CELEBRATION, FLORIDA

The next major new urbanism development in the 1990s was Celebration, Florida, a community that sits on 5,000 acres in unincorporated land in Osceola County in Central Florida, adjacent to the Walt Disney World Parks and Resort located in the Reedy Creek Improvement District (the planning district that includes the Disney parks and hotels) in Lake Buena Vista (Stern, 2019; Hayden, 2003; Conn, 2014). Designed in 1994, Celebration aimed "to recapture the idea of the traditional town, traditional in spirit, but modern in terms of what we know about how people live," according to Celebration designer and planner Robert Stern (Celebration Foundation, 2020, Program Overview).

The Walt Disney Company spent $2.5 billion on the Celebration development, which opened in 1996 and at its peak had as many as 2,000 residents. Celebration was created to resemble a "19th century town for the late 20th century" (Shibley, 1998, p. 81). Like the other new urbanist developments, "the Disney vision of village life, community, safety, a modest miniaturization of scale, and convenience . . . relies on down-scaled neighborhood centers" (Shibley, 1998, p. 81).

Celebration evolved into a vast network of buildings, roads, parks, a post office, and shops with a town center, but also has a golf course, a hotel, public schools, and an office park just outside town (Hayden, 2003). Celebration has a range of different architectural styles using new urbanist principles (i.e., classical, Victorian, Colonial revival, and Mediterranean) in the cottage homes, townhomes, and estate homes. The prices range from $250,000 for townhomes to $600,000 and above for the estate homes (Hayden, 2003). Celebration was built in several phases, including Celebration West that includes an additional 6.7 million square feet of retail, commercial, and industrial development.

Disney's new urbanist experiment, and its desire to control the built environment, is similar to its control of the amusement parks, through the strict regulation of the physical appearance of the homes (Conn, 2014). Unlike Seaside, which has a town council and governance structure, Celebration is a real estate development where staff, or "cast members" as they are called in the Disney World realm, provide street maintenance and contract out services to private companies (mowing, garbage pickup, other maintenance). Disney received favorable attention in the development of Celebration to create and invest in "substantial, attractive public realm intended to shame get-rich-quick developers of edge nodes, malls, and fringe subdivisions" (Hayden, 2003, p. 215).

Figure 8.1.   Aerial photo of Seaside, Florida. *Source:* Alex MacLean, Landslides

CRITIQUES OF NEW URBANISM

New urbanism is not a "magic wand" (Bohl, 2000, p. 791) designed to change and solve all the city's and the world's social, political, and economic problems. Bohl (2000) argues that new urbanism is a not a housing, economic development, or social service program, and architects and planners have often relied too heavily on design-based solutions to solve entrenched urban problems.

Some critics say new urbanism applies only to suburbs, is a scheme designed to make a profit by developers by appealing to nostalgia, is bourgeois and artificial, and features very little low-income housing, Such neighborhoods are "feel-good faux-towns, cozy and nostalgic developments which feign urbanity without making the effort to actually be urban" (DeWolf, 2002, para. 2). Conn (2014) says new urbanism is not new and did not solve all the problems it intended to solve. Gordon and Richardson (1998) argue that new urbanism is "pie-in-the-sky social engineering based on a false diagnosis of society's urban problems, an excessive faith in the ability to change the world, and the prescription of policies that are implementable only under very special circumstances" (para. 4).

New urbanism cannot replicate or recreate the physical structure and recreate the social and civic behavior of a traditional neighborhood (Gordon &

Richardson, 1998). You cannot build a sense of community using "spatial determinism" where engagement and interaction with residents and neighbors are created and developed by "the organizing power of space" (Talen, 1997, p. 1364). New urbanism promotes an ideology of community that suggests that reframing or reshaping the image of community, through the spatial ordering of place and design, will solve all of society's ills and problems (Harvey, 1997). Instead, new urbanism fails to understand how the spatial ordering of place serves as a "vehicle for controlling history and process," and fail to resolve issues of urban poverty and decay (Harvey, 1997, p. 68).

The organic growth and multiple uses seen in a normal urban landscape are not easily replicated in a new urbanism development, because of the continued use of standard planning practices through segregated uses that resembles a suburb more than a small town or neighborhood they aim to be (DeWolf, 2002). While the town center of a new urbanist community may be walkable and compact, the spatial segregation of commercial and residential areas are not easily accessible by foot, ultimately failing to live up to the promise of creating more walkable and less automobile dependent neighborhoods (DeWolf, 2002). Many of the critics contend that it is difficult to know exactly what a new urbanist community would look like (Upton, 2003).

While Durack (2001) does not reject new urbanism outright, she argues the new strategies towards building a village or city are incompatible and contradictory with sustainability:

> We must adopt a way of thinking about the world that accepts unpredictability, coincidence and the accidental; that delights in diversity, multiplicity, and contrast; that embraces change and the exercise of individual choice. Perhaps the best way of putting it is that we must find a way of thinking that concedes to the future, not in an acquiescent or submissive way, but as an act of affirmation and supreme optimism, proffered with sufficient humility to acknowledge that the next generation just may come up with better ideas than ours. (para. 12)

Another major skeptic and critic of new urbanism was Jane Jacobs, who believed that new urbanism artificially recreates the urban environment at the neighborhood and street level and "seeks to shortcut the temporal process that transforms the fringe into the center" (Grant, 2011, p. 98). Time and history will ultimately influence the development of the city and neighborhood, according to Jacobs (1961). For Jacobs (1961), it is also a question of inappropriate scales. The social networks and social capital generated on the street level are what give the neighborhood its diversity and vitality, compared to artificially creating a suburb or a small town. Creating a monolithic monoculture suburb all at once, instead of over time, by using traditional design elements does not create vitality. Also, a new urbanist neighborhood does not have the ability to transform as conditions change, making it difficult to readapt the physical character and design of the buildings and neighborhood (Jacobs, 1961; Grant, 2011).

HOPE VI AND NEW URBANISM

Despite those criticisms, some of the best outcomes of new urbanism have occurred through the HOPE VI program. HOPE VI has contributed to the urban renaissance of the 1990s and the early 21st century (Conn, 2014). The redevelopment projects of major American cities, such as Philadelphia, Boston, Chicago, and Atlanta, were inspired by new urbanism to resolve important issues affecting earlier public housing developments. Almost 300,000 HOPE VI housing units have been developed using new urbanist principles (Duany, 2019).

Calthorpe (2009) discussed four new urbanist principles in HOPE VI: 1) diversity through mixed-use and mixed income design and development; 2) human scale that featured walkable safe neighborhoods that are pedestrian-oriented, transit-oriented, and accessible to services and amenities; 3) the restoration of the social and physical infrastructure of the neighborhoods; and 4) continuity of the new projects with the surrounding neighborhoods and the city. HOPE VI enhances new urbanist principles by focusing on the social and economic planning aspects that enable residents to be self-sufficient through the introduction of CSS programs administered by the public housing authorities (PHAs), as discussed earlier.

HOPE VI would completely tear down all the modernist high-rise buildings with vertical designs and replace them with lower-rise horizontal buildings, using traditional architecture design built for single-family uses with porches near the streets and sidewalks. Smith (1999) argues that HOPE VI places too much emphasis on aesthetic principles and physical design, creating mixed-income, mixed-use neighborhoods with small scale commercial business (retail, restaurants, grocery stores) and homes that are both subsidized and market rate, to encourage homeownership (Conn, 2014). Unlike the isolation of residents in suburbia, HOPE VI ended the isolation of residents in the old public housing projects by recreating the traditional neighborhood form using new urbanist design principles to create viable and sustainable communities.

HOPE VI PROGRAMS IN LOUISVILLE, KENTUCKY

In the first three years of the HOPE VI program, HUD awarded HOPE VI grants to public housing authorities in the 40 largest U.S. cities (Goetz, 2003). Louisville received its first grant in 1996 and received two more over the next 15 years. Louisville is the largest city in Kentucky and is situated close to most of the eastern half of the United States. It is a midsized city on the border of the South and Midwest and sometimes referred to as the "Gateway to the South" (Ambrosius et al., 2010). Like the other cities we have discussed, Louisville is a river city with a deep and long history. Louisville was founded in 1778 by Revolutionary War General George Rogers Clark, on Corn Island at the Falls of the Ohio, and named after King Louis XVI of France. In its earliest days, when the city charter was approved, Louisville belonged to Virginia before Kentucky became the 15th state in 1792.

Louisville grew into an important steamboat port because of its location at the Falls. It became an important economic center along the Ohio River and played a pivotal role in the slave trade and the growing economy of the 19th century (Kleber, 2001). The development of the Louisville and Nashville (L&N) Railroad, the hosting of the Southern Exposition of 1893, and the establishment of a parks system designed by architect Frederick Law Olmsted enabled Louisville to grow further and become a regional and national economic engine (Kleber, 2001). Louisville was on the front lines of manufacturing and industry at the beginning of the 20th century, and Camp Taylor became a major World War I post. Louisville and much of the Ohio River Valley was devastated by the largest flooding disaster of the 20th century in January 1937, but it also became an important war production center during World War II.

Like many post-industrial cities in their region, Louisville experienced a decline in population and flight to the suburbs, due to the depletion of manufacturing and industrial jobs. As the suburbs grew, much of its divisions were demarcated along racial and socioeconomic lines, with the poorer African-American neighborhoods in the west, the working-class neighborhoods in the south, and the wealthier, middle class white neighborhoods to the east (Ambrosius et al., 2010). Louisville has a relative monocentric homogeneous downtown central business district and is more representative of a typical city in the United States (Ambrosius et al., 2010).

Park DuValle

Park DuValle is a neighborhood in west Louisville that dates to the 1880s, once a section of the Parkland neighborhood known as Little Africa (Gilderbloom, 2008). After urban renewal leveled the neighborhood, two public housing developments were constructed in the 1950s: Cotter Homes in 1952, named after educator and poet Joseph Cotter, and Lang Homes in 1958 (Brazley, 2002; The Planning Report [TPR], 2005). Cotter and Lang Homes, along with nearby Algonquin Square, represented some of the youngest, poorest, and highest crime neighborhoods in Louisville (LHMA, 2020). Cotter and Lang Homes were deemed "the meanest street corner in Louisville," by a newspaper reporter in 1986 (Engdahl, 2009, p. 121). In 1994 alone, the crime rate in Park DuValle was 137 percent above the city average; 78 percent of the residents were living in poverty, and the unemployment rate was 34 percent (Engdahl, 2009).

Cotter Homes contained 620 apartment units in 55 buildings that were low-density barracked style housing, and Lang Homes consisted of 496 apartments in 63 buildings (LMHA, 2020a). After trying and failing to secure an Empowerment Zone (EZ) designation, the Louisville city government, led by Mayor Jerry Abramson, and the Louisville Housing Authority (LHA)[1] received a $20 million HOPE VI grants in October 1996. This grant was combined with $31.4 million in special development public housing funds from LHA (Besel & Andreescu, 2013), and $14 million in Community Development Block Grants (CDBG) for infrastructure improvements to demolish the Cotter and Lang Homes and develop and revitalize the Park DuValle neighborhood (Hanlon, 2010; Raffel, Denson, Varady, & Sweeney, 2003; LHMA, 2020a).

Widely considered one of the most successful HOPE VI revitalization projects in the nation (Hanlon, 2010), the Park DuValle project totaled approximately $237 million, including $51 million in federal grants, leveraged with approximately $186 million in funding through public-private partnerships and other local and federal sources (Brazley, 2002; Brazley & Gilderbloom, 2007; Engdahl, 2009; Hanlon, 2010). The Park DuValle project demolished 1,116 units in Cotter and Lang Homes and relocated 1,273 households. Of these households, 611 households relocated to other public housing units, 232 moved to Section 8 housing, 198 were evicted, and 232 household moved to other housing situations (bought a new home, lived with relatives, became homeowners, etc. (Gilderbloom, 2008). Only 150 households planned to live in the new HOPE VI development, consistent with other similar HOPE VI developments' percentages of returning residents (Brazley, 2002; Brazley & Gilderbloom, 2007; Gilderbloom, 2008).

The Park DuValle HOPE VI program consisted of four phases, which included the construction of 1,213 new units: 450 for homeowners, 150 off site units, and 613 rental units (363 were set aside for public housing tenants). The project was designed as a mixed income development, with 1/3 of all the units developed for public housing, 1/3 for affordable housing (30 percent–60 percent area median income—AMI) and 1/3 for market-rate housing, bucking the trend of the majority of HOPE VI developments and revitalization projects that did not include a such a mixture of housing types (Raffel et al., 2003).

Phase I of the project included the construction of the Oaks at Park DuValle, which consists of 100 rental units with a mixture of single-family residences, townhouses, and apartments in various income levels (30 percent–80 percent AMI). The Oaks was approved in early 1997 and completed in spring 1998. By 1999, there was a waiting list (Raffel et al., 2003). Phase II included the construction of the Villages of Park DuValle, which consists of 213 rentals and 147 homeownership units (Raffel et al., 2003). Rents ranged from $430 to $808 a month, and homes for sale ranged from $70,000 to $217,000 (Engdahl, 2009). These units used Victorian colonial revival and craftsman architectural styles and include suburban style custom-built homes with driveways, front and back yards, narrow streets, and sidewalks (Gilderbloom, 2008; Engdahl, 2009; Hanlon, 2010). According to Brazley (2002), 51 percent of the units at the Villages of Park DuValle sold to households at 80 percent area median income (AMI) and 49 percent were sold to any family regardless of income.

A major goal of the Park DuValle HOPE VI program was to attract families of higher income into the area. The median family income in Park DuValle rose from $5,269 to $29,849 (Besel & Cherubin, 2013), and the prices for the higher end Estate Homes went for $278,000–$325,000 (Engdahl, 2009). Many of the apartments and homes built in the first two phases were in high demand, and a waiting list also emerged in Phase II for these units shortly after they were built in 2002–2003 (Raffel et al., 2003). Phase III of the Park DuValle revitalization began in 2001 and consisted of 25,000 square feet of retail space, 100 apartments for seniors, and 150 other off-site developments. While Phase III was going on, the old DuValle Education Center was renovated in the neighborhood to become Carter Traditional Elementary School.

The Park DuValle HOPE VI project had an enormous impact on a variety of quality-of-life indicators. In terms of economic development, the leveraging effect was 10.867 for every $1 in federal funds, much higher than the 1.85 average seen among other HOPE VI developments (GAO, 2002; Popkin, Katz, et al., 2004; Hanlon, 2010). The annual income of residents rose from $5,000 in 1994 to $26,134 in 2001, while unemployment decreased from 71 percent to around 35 percent and the poverty rate fell 50 percent to around 28 percent (Brazley, 2002; Hanlon, 2010; Clark, 2013). The total number of crimes dropped from 530 in 1994 to 2 in 1998 and 13 in 2002 (Raffel et al., 2003).

In terms of property values, Hanka (2009) expanded on previous studies (Ambrosius et al., 2010; Gilderbloom, Ambrosius, & Hanka, 2008) by documenting the trend of property value appreciations in Louisville over a seven-year period, 2000–2006, analyzing whether mid-sized cities are moving toward successful megacities like New York, Los Angeles, and Chicago, or becoming more like declining post-industrial cities like Buffalo, Cleveland, Detroit, and Cincinnati.

Many of the studies analyzing historic trends in real estate only looked at median housing values and raw changes in property values. This can paint an inaccurate and incomplete picture of the dynamics of contemporary housing markets. Using percent change as a measure of contemporary housing dynamics, the raw dollar change over housing value at the beginning of the period in the year 2000 better captures contemporary housing dynamics (Gilderbloom et al., 2008). Park DuValle ranked as having the highest percentage increase in neighborhood property values from 2000 to 2006, at 240 percent, compared to 169 other Louisville neighborhoods without HOPE VI developments, which had an average increase of approximately 32 percent.

Hanka (2009) shows that HOPE VI is a consistently positive and significant predictor in measuring changes in neighborhood housing dynamics and shows the traditional predictor of median household income is diminished when predicting percentage change. The HOPE VI neighborhood in Park DuValle significantly increased property values, showing the highest increase in neighborhood property values among all 170 neighborhoods in Louisville from 2000 to 2006. Measuring the impact of HOPE VI as a policy intervention using percentage change captures the impact greater than median housing value or raw dollar change.

The Park DuValle HOPE VI program attracted middle class households who could afford market rate housing, decreased the concentration of poverty, increased property values, and added more amenities such as a health clinic and a new community center (Raffel et al., 2003). However, Park Du-Valle HOPE VI failed to reduce the racial concentration of African American residents with only two White households resided in Park DuValle among the 1,213 new units built. The program didn't allow many former public housing residents to return to the new HOPE VI development, and it lacked the wherewithal to create new neighborhoods that eliminated the isolation of the old neighborhood by failing to connect the new HOPE VI residents to the wider Louisville community (Brazley, 2002; Brazley & Gilderbloom, 2007; Gilderbloom, 2008; Engdahl, 2009; Axtell & Tooley, 2015). New business and investment, including shopping and other services, did not come to Park DuValle (Axtell & Tooley, 2015).

While many city officials and planners applauded the Park DuValle HOPE VI program, America's first new Black urbanist development, as something shiny, beautiful, and pleasant, they made the major mistake in placement and geography. They made a major error in Park DuValle by placing the new development near the deadly chemical factories of nearby Rubbertown which spew out toxic poisons that have been found by Gilderbloom, Squires, and Meares (2020) and Gilderbloom, Meares, and Squires (2020) to cause a reduction of lifespan by an average of ten years, record low test scores in elementary school children, and a steep decline in housing values. Also, the development was located in a food desert with little access to stores that sell daily needs. Walkability scores were low because there was nowhere to walk to nor many tree-lined streets to protect residents from the sun and the elements (Gilderbloom and Meares, 2020). Moreover, Park DuValle created a major heat island where temperatures are often five degrees higher than the rest of the city that already suffers enough from the heat island effect.

Liberty Green

The HOPE VI Liberty Green project was Louisville's second HOPE VI grant located in downtown Louisville next to the Louisville medical campus and within walking distance of Main Street and the Central Business District (CBD). The predecessor to Liberty Green was the Clarksdale Public Housing projects. According to Clark (2013), HUD chose Clarksdale for a HOPE VI grant because of its proximity to downtown and its timing with downtown revitalization in the late 1990s and early 2000s. This included the development of Waterfront Park, the construction of Louisville Slugger Field baseball stadium on Main Street, the revitalization and redevelopment of the East Market Street corridor that would become the NuLu district, and other amenities meant to boost the housing stock and increase residential opportunities downtown (Clark, 2013).

The Louisville Metro Housing Authority (LMHA) used the experiences and lessons learned from the Park DuValle project to assist with the Liberty Green project (LHMA, 2020b). The Liberty Green HOPE VI program significantly transformed the Clarksdale neighborhood. The number of households decreased in the Clarksdale/Liberty Green Census tract area, from 2,499 in 2000 to 1,987 in 2010 (5,071 total population in 2000 to 3,805 in 2010), an unintended consequence of HOPE VI due to the relocation of residents. Of those residents who moved from Clarksdale, 41 percent moved to other public housing developments in the city, 12 percent moved to scattered sites, and 27 percent used housing vouchers. Less than 2 percent of the original residents moved back into the Liberty Green development (Stone, Dailey, Barbee, & Patrick, 2011; Stone, Vanderpool, Barbee, & Patrick. 2011; Clark, 2013; Clark & Negrey, 2017).

This HOPE VI project in Clarksdale, that would become Liberty Green, was developed in two phases with a $20 million federal grant in each phase: in the demolition of 713 units that were 65 years old at time of demolition, and the relocation of 700 residents (Clark, 2013). The total cost of the revitalization of Clarksdale was $250 million (Axtell & Tooley, 2015).

Clarksdale was one of the most impoverished areas in Louisville. According to (Stone, Dailey, et al., 2011; Stone, Vanderpool, et al., 2011), most of the Clarksdale residents (73 percent of those surveyed) were unemployed and most of those surveyed lived below the poverty level. Like Park DuValle, Clarksdale was overwhelmingly African American, and just over half of the population was 18 years of age and younger (Stone, Dailey, et al., 2011). Also, most of the households in Clarksdale were headed by a female, which is roughly the same population of female heads of household (217 out of 234) eligible for Community and Supportive Services (CSS), which was introduced after the Louisville Housing Authority failed to provide supportive services during the Park DuValle HOPE VI project.

Construction of Liberty Green units began in 2005 and was completed in 2009, but occupancy began as soon as 2006 (Clark & Negrey, 2017). A community center at Liberty Green was completed in spring 2010. Phase I of the Clarksdale revitalization area is a four-block area bounded by Jefferson Street to the north, Muhammad Ali Blvd. to the south, Jackson Street to the west, and Clay Street to the east. Phase I included 500 new units that were a mixture of apartments, town homes, and homes for sale (LHMA, 2020b). The Phase II area is a two-block area bound by Jefferson Street to the north, Muhammad Ali Blvd. to the south, Clay Street to the west, and Shelby Street to the east. The HOPE VI revitalization also included the development of 176 public housing rental units off-site for Phase I and 218 rental units for Phase II. Rents for the apartments for the apartments and town homes ranged from $475 to $699 per month, and the town homes, known as THE EDGE at Liberty Green, ranged from $105,000 to $300,000 (LMHA, 2020).

In census tract 59 where Clarksdale/Liberty Green is located, median home values rose from $63,800 in 2000 to $142,000 in 2010, and around 13 percent of the owner-occupied homes priced $200,000–$300,000, compared to zero before the revitalization (Clark & Negrey, 2017). The number of renters decreased, the poverty level decreased 16 percentage points from 57 percent to 41 percent, while educational attainment increased for those with a high school diploma by 16 percent. Bachelor's degrees rose by more than 2 percent,

Figure 8.2.   Liberty Green HOPE VI. *Source:* **Sherman Carter Barnhart Architects**

while median household income increased from $9,367 in 2000 to $15,439 in 2010 (U.S. Census, 2000; Stone, Dailey, et al., 2011; Clark, 2013; Clark & Negrey, 2017). Some of the notable accomplishments of the HOPE VI Liberty Green project included market rate housing within walking distance to the medical campus and other amenities, including student housing for medical school students and other professionals working in Downtown Louisville.

In the follow-up survey of former Clarksdale residents, 76 percent were satisfied with their current housing, 54 percent responded that they considered moving to Liberty Green, and around 44 percent said the housing was better compared to Clarksdale. However, 42 percent of respondents were unhappy about moving out of Clarksdale (Stone, Dailey, et al., 2011).

To avoid repeating the problems with the CSS in the Park DuValle HOPE VI project, Louisville Metro Housing Authority (LMHA) assumed a greater leadership role in the administration of CSS, combining it with Family Supportive Services (FSS) to provide better case management services to Clarksdale residents. Two hundred thirty-four families were eligible for the CSS program. In terms of the results from the CSS in Clarksdale and Liberty Green, Stone, Dailey, et al. (2011) found that more residents participated in these CSS program and demonstrated improvement in school attendance and achievement through the tutoring and mentoring youth programs, improvement in one grade level for adult education, and improvements in job readiness, life skills, and homeownership readiness.

For the most part, the Liberty Green HOPE VI program produced positive results and outcomes for the residents. While only two percent of the total number of former Clarksdale residents moved back to Liberty Green, it was "an indication that the program succeeded to integrate the families in their new neighborhoods—that was a good thing!" (Stone, 2020). Those who moved back, especially seniors and single families, were happy with having a place to call home, having their own backyard, and living in a safe neighborhood with better schools (Stone, 2020). Stone (2020) said, "Based on my experience with the program, the conversations I had with the residents and the survey data, I think the program made a difference in many people's lives. It definitely made a difference for the city; a walk in the neighborhood should be sufficient to tell the difference. . . . I focused on the people. The reality is that there is no perfect program; people can choose to look at a program as 'half glass empty' or 'half glass full.' That's their choice."

Marxist critics have been relentless in attacking HOPE VI developments and have focused heavily on Liberty Green by romanticizing old toxic public housing that became unlivable with poor plumbing, electric, heat, air conditioning, poor sunlight, and dangerous carcinogens that have hurt the residents' overall health. A study done by Johns Hopkins University found that Kentucky public housing barracks were so toxic for residents, it was the equivalent of smoking three packs of cigarettes a day. Critics argue that African Americans didn't want a HOPE VI development with modern appliances with heat and air conditioning that is safe and healthy for each resident, and instead were satisfied with the barrack like public housing units. Yet, surveys show that two-thirds to three-fourths of residents are happier with new housing choices like HOPE VI, and some even used Section 8 vouchers to find a home. HOPE VI developments are simply more humane, walkable, safer, and more welcoming place for residents. Critics are barking up the wrong tree by insisting that HOPE VI is a racist conspiracy to displace Blacks and leave them homeless. HOPE VI learned from the lessons and scandals of urban renewal programs and did not repeat those mistakes.

Sheppard Square

One of the last HOPE VI grants awarded, the Louisville Metro Housing Authority (LMHA) received a $22 million HUD HOPE VI Revitalization grant, awarded on May 20, 2011, as a part of a $167 million public-private investment to create a mixed-income neighborhood (Marshall, 2011). Sheppard Square is named after William Henry Sheppard, who moved to Louisville in 1912 as pastor of Grace Hope Presbyterian Church and became a prominent community leader in the Smoketown neighborhood and a prominent figure in the Black Presbyterian church (Kleber, 2001; Marshall, 2011; LMHA,

2020c). Sheppard Square housing development was constructed in 1942 and sits on 16.5 acres bordered by Finzer, Clay, Lampton, and Preston Streets in the historic Smoketown neighborhood (LMHA, 2020c). Construction of the original Sheppard Square buildings was completed in 1942 at a cost of $1.5 million and consisted of 326 apartments (Marshall, 2011; LMHA, 2020c).

Unlike the other HOPE VI projects in Louisville, more new units replaced the number of units that were demolished. Two hundred sixty-seven households were relocated from Sheppard Square, and 454 units were to be constructed or rehabilitated, 310 of them located on the old Sheppard Square public housing site (287 are mixed-income rental units and 23 are homeownership), while 32 units for the elderly and disabled would be in the old Presbyterian Community Center (PCC) building. Like Liberty Green, 144 of the new units were off-site and scattered in different sites, including nine single family units in Smoketown, 91 public housing rental units, and 54 units associated with the downtown Family Scholar House on 2nd Street (LMHA, 2020c).

Demolition on Sheppard Square began in 2012 and was completed the following year. Construction on the first phase of 60 units was completed in summer 2014, and three units were completed in 2017. The renovation of the old Presbyterian Community Center began in 2015 and was completed in 2018. Like the Liberty Green project a few blocks north, the Sheppard Square community aimed to be pedestrian friendly and transit-oriented with close accessibility to public transit. According to the Louisville Metro Housing Authority, the HOPE VI grant for Sheppard Square would be leveraged with more than $74.5 million public and private funds for physical infrastructure and $4.2 million in CSS (LMHA, 2020c).

Like the other CSS programs, Sheppard Square's CSS program includes legal aid services, accessible and affordable health care referral services, job placement, financial skills training, a scholarship program for residents who are high school/GED graduates who wish to pursue higher education, recruitment for Early Childhood Education programs, transportation assistance, homeownership counseling and a Section 8 Homeownership program which offers subsidy towards a mortgage payment for eligible candidates, as well as a computer lab for residents who do not have computer access at home (LMHA, 2020c). A major success of the Sheppard Square HOPE VI program is $2.5 million dedicated to education and job training for Sheppard Square residents (Marshall, 2011).

While some Sheppard Square residents complained about restricted access because of the electronic security system in each building, and not receiving mail packages directly to their apartments, the residents enjoyed a safe, peaceful, and more pleasant neighborhood, and even those who didn't move back were happy to see the neighborhood around Sheppard Square transform

(Stone, 2020). Individual lives were also saved and transformed, including a resident of Sheppard Square, according to Stone (2020), who expressed appreciation for HOPE VI when she needed it the most, including finishing high school, taking courses at Jefferson Community College, while working part-time to save for a down payment through her participation in the FSS program.

Figure 8.3.   Sheppard Square HOPE VI. *Source:* **Sherman Carter Barnhart Architects**

NEWPORT, KENTUCKY HOPE VI PROGRAM

Newport, Kentucky, located in Northern Kentucky at the confluence of the Ohio and Licking Rivers south of Cincinnati, is an important part of the greater Cincinnati metropolitan area, with a population of approximately two million residents in the Cincinnati metropolitan statistical area (MSA). The population of Newport is 14,932, down from 15,273 in the 2010 Census, which is about 9 percent less than the 2000 population of 17,048 (U.S. Census, 2020). Newport was founded in 1795 by Colonel James Taylor and son Hubbard Taylor, who named the new city after Captain Christopher Newport, the commander of the first English ship to settle Jamestown, Virginia (Hanka, 2009).

The unique and colorful history of Newport contributes to its character. While Cincinnati outpaced Newport and Covington in terms of growth, Newport established a unique identity that complemented the area, because of its

German and Italian immigrants, many of whom settled in the city's west side, known as Spaghetti Knob. That influx of immigrants, along with migrants from Eastern Kentucky moving to the region, helped intensify urban/rural tensions and class warfare between the migrants and Newport residents (Clift, Daniels, Fennell, & Whitehead, 1995; Hanka, 2009). The sagging economy and erosion of the industrial and manufacturing employment sector in the early 20th century gravitated people towards gambling and vice.

For much of the early to mid-20th century, Newport was a center of prostitution, gambling, and vice, and the city was controlled by corrupt elected officials and organized crime. Newport was the "vice capital of the south." The presence of organized crime syndicates manipulated the political machine of Newport to elect officeholders friendly to the mob, in part because local elected officials could only serve one term under Kentucky law.This system proved incapable of ridding Newport of vice and corruption (Hanka, 2009).

During the 1960s and 1970s, little business and economic activity occurred in Newport. The deteriorating economy of the city caused a shrinking of the middle and professional class, resulting in the third highest White underclass among cities in the United States (Clift et al., 1995). Newport city government was overwhelmed and ill equipped to handle the city's mounting problems, such as curbing unemployment and poverty that persisted until the 1980s. Despite attempts at reform, big changes did not occur until the election of Thomas Guidugli, Sr. as Mayor of Newport in 1992, who served four terms until 2008, thanks to the reversing of a Kentucky law allowing mayors and commissioners to be elected to more than one term (Hanka, 2009).

One of Guidugli's attempts to revitalize Newport resulted in a $28 million HOPE VI grant from HUD in 2002. Administered by the Housing Authority of Newport (HAN), the HOPE VI project in Newport replaced 202 severely distressed public housing units with 325 mixed-income units (192 rental units and 133 homeownership units) that were a mixture of new construction single-family dwellings, townhouses, in the Liberty Row neighborhoods, and multi-unit apartments, as well as rehabbed single-family and multi-family units (Hanka, 2009; Hanka, Gilderbloom, Meares, Khan, & Wresinski, 2015). Unlike other HOPE VI developments that tore down the old public housing and built the new housing units on the same site, Newport used a scattered site approach, through infill development and rehabilitation projects in other areas of the city, away from the original public housing site. Newport was only one of the few HOPE VI projects that replaced more units than it tore down.

One infill site for Newport HOPE VI was Liberty Row Housing, which included 13 newly constructed homes and one rehabilitated home with an average price ranging between $123,000 and $130,000 (see Figures 8.4 and 8.5)

(Hanka, 2009; Hanka, Gilderbloom, et al., 2015). The major rehabilitation HOPE VI project converted Corpus Christi Church into Corpus Christi Apartments, a 20-unit project that used Low Income Housing Tax Credit (LIHTC). HAN qualified for the LIHTC for ten years, as long as a specific proportion of units would be set aside for lower income households and these rents would be at least 30 percent of the adjusted median income (AMI) (HUD, 2003). All 20 units in Corpus Christi were tax credit units (50 percent of AMI) designed for senior living. The units range from 628–767 square feet and remained at 100 percent occupancy.

Figure 8.4.   Liberty Row in the HOPE VI Newport project. *Source:* John Gilderbloom

Unlike other HOPE VI programs, where the local public housing authority (PHA) provides the community and supportive services, HAN contracted with local nonprofit organization Brighton Center, Inc. to provide these one-stop shop services available to CSS families, such as credit counseling, employment training, youth activities, GED classes, budgeting classes, family health services, childcare services, classes for employment and homeownership training, and educational opportunities. Brighton Center is within walking distance to most of the new HOPE VI sites, including affordably priced residential neighborhoods and the existing Housing Authority in Newport public housing neighborhood, located south of the old public housing.

Figure 8.5. Corpus Christi Apartments converted from old church. *Source:* John Gilderbloom

Of the original 179 households eligible for the Newport HOPE VI CSS at the beginning of the program in the early 2000s, ten households purchased homes, 26 moved to the south site of the Housing Authority, nine used their Section 8 vouchers in Newport, and 14 households used their vouchers elsewhere in Northern Kentucky and Greater Cincinnati area. Two households were in senior buildings in Newport, 20 had an unknown address, five signed out of the program, 51 were evicted, three residents died, and 37 relocated on their own. Also, 28 individuals completed "Yes You Can" classes, a first step toward homeownership, while 41 individuals enrolled in the Money Matters classes offered through credit counseling services. Nine residents completed Brighton Center's Center for Employment Training (CET). Nine were working full-time jobs, and seven were working full-time with benefits.

The goals of the CSS program were revised and clarified in June 2004 (Gilderbloom, 2004), labeled as processes rather than outcomes as defined by HUD (Popkin et al., 2000; Popkin, Katz, et al., 2004; Popkin, Levy, et al., 2004; HUD, 1999; HUD, 2000). All 34 scheduled supportive services programs were utilized. HAN provided home maintenance classes given by their maintenance supervisors upon purchase of a home. All 10 homeowners who participated in Brighton Center's CSS program completed this class. Twenty-seven of 34 (79 percent) support service participation processes were met or exceeded at the end of the program. Thirty-two of the 34 (94 percent) support service program processes exceeded 50 percent of the original participation processes, while nine of the 35 (29 percent) participation processes were exceeded by over 100 percent.

Table 8.2. CSS WORKPLAN PROCESSES up to June 30, 2007—Newport HOPE VI

Program /Activity	Participation Process	Participation to Date
Jobs Center / One Stop	25 Persons	58 Persons
Job Training Development		(Process exceeded)
Assist families with entering post-secondary	7	25
degree program /training		Process exceeded
Enroll residents in a certificate or degree	7	10
program @ NK Vocational-Tech or NKU		Process exceeded
Residents will enroll in the Bureau of	7	8
Vocational Rehabilitation Program		Process exceeded
Career training through CET	35	29
Residents completing CET will obtain full-	16	9
time employment		
Residents completing CET will obtain full-	12	9
time employment for 9 months		
Residents completing CET will be offered	12	9
health insurance		
Residents will complete CET	20	9
Individuals will attend Newport Adult or	25	44
Community Learning Center		Process exceeded
Residents will obtain GED or increase TABE	12	Increase TABE: 27
by four grade levels		Received GED: 13
		Process exceeded
Youth will participate in the YLD/Summer	10	18
Youth program		Process exceeded
Youth participation in YMCA activities	30	55
		Process exceeded
Form a girl scout troop	10 Girls	21
		Process exceeded
Youth participation in boys & girls club	15	42
activities		Process exceeded
Participation in W/A youth programs	8	8
		Process met
Participants awareness of childcare	45	56
availability and funding		Process exceeded

Table 8.2. *(continued)*

Program /Activity	Participation Process	Participation to Date
Health Point will provide services to families on a sliding scale fee	60	97 Process exceeded
Families will purchase a new residence	10	10 Process met
First-time moms will receive home visits from "Every child succeeds"	10	16 Process exceeded
Families will receive health insurance for kids through K-chip	10	24 Process exceeded
Moms and babies will visit the healthy moms and babies van	15	19 Process exceeded
Newport school-based health center will provide families with monthly care	10	28 Process exceeded
North key will provide mental health and substance abuse serious to families	15	48 Process exceeded
NHA maintenance department will provide basic home maintenance *Housing Authority Directed.*	20	3
Participants will go through the NKU Entrepreneurship Center for Small Business program	10	6
Participants will receive HUD mortgage counseling through BC	30	33 Process exceeded
Participants will complete HUD mortgage counseling through BC	16	21 Process exceeded
Families will receive budget counseling through the CSS worker.	40	90 Process exceeded
Families had credit reports pulled	40	62 Process exceeded
Families will resolve credit issues	20	38 Process exceeded
Families will receive transportation assistance	31	50 Process exceeded
Families will be given information about TANK routes, and increase usage of public transportation	20	49 Process exceeded

Abbreviations Used in Table:

BC: Brighton Center	NHA: Newport Housing Authority
YLD: Youth Leadership Program	NK: Northern Kentucky
CET: Center for Employment Training	TABE: Test of Adult Basic Education
CSS: Community Social Services	TANK: Transit Authority of Northern Kentucky
GED: Graduate Equivalency Degree	HUD: Housing and Urban Development

Source: Gilderbloom, Hanka, & Lasley, 2008; Gilderbloom, 2008.

Processes that did not meet expectations were enrollment in the Center for Employment Training (CET) career training program, completion of the CET program, obtaining full-time employment for nine months, and offers of health insurance for CET participants. CSS also observed low participation in HAN's basic home maintenance program for residents and low participation in classes at the Northern Kentucky University (NKU) Entrepreneurship Center for Small Business. The success in meeting participation processes is surprising considering the decreases in HOPE VI-eligible families because of evictions or residents moving out of the area.

Analysis of Newport HOPE VI

By 2007, 100 families remained who participated in CSS. Hanka (2009) conducted a survey of these residents with a 54 percent response rate. Eighty-nine percent of the respondents were female, and only 17 percent of the households were married. The mean age was 44 years old and most respondents lived in households of one or two persons. Sixty-eight percent of the respondents were White, and over one-fourth were African American, which is comparable to the racial composition of residents living in HOPE VI developments and the total public housing stock in Newport (Hanka, 2009). The median household income was $643 per month, roughly $7,716 per year; 62 percent of the respondents have a high school diploma or less, while 79 percent were unemployed (either out of the labor force, on disability, or receiving Social Security income). Also, 55 percent of the residents surveyed did not own a car and 72 percent did not own a bicycle.

The survey also asked questions regarding overall neighborhood and residential satisfaction of the HOPE VI residents, with respect to CSS, and whether these programs and services improved the quality of life of the individuals and families who participated, whether residents were satisfied with their neighborhood, and the overall health of the neighborhood from the inception of the HOPE VI program in 2000 to the end of the study period in 2007. The survey also asked about recreation, transportation, education, and employment opportunities in the new neighborhood as a result of participating in CSS, along with community residents' perceptions of safety, cleanliness, involvement in community activities, the presence of crime and drugs in the neighborhood, and whether the residents felt there were enough opportunities for safe and affordable housing alternatives, such as subsidized, Section 8, and market-rate housing.

The HOPE VI program in Newport improved residential satisfaction and quality of life among the residents who participated in the CSS program. An overwhelming majority of residents were satisfied with where they lived and felt pride in their communities. An overwhelming majority of these residents knew their neighbors, were satisfied with relocating to a safer neighborhood, and were satisfied with the recreational and entertainment opportunities for both children and adults within walking distance of where they live. They were satisfied with the programs and services offered by Brighton Center and HAN, including childcare services, classes for employment and home-ownership training, and educational opportunities. Participants surveyed also agreed with the greater presence of safe and affordable housing, such as more Section 8 housing, less of a Section 8 waiting list, and more market rate housing available.

The residents surveyed believed that their neighborhood was safe and clean, and the housing was well maintained, and the neighborhood is diverse. Residents felt safe to walk or bike to school or work. They felt safe because of the adequate presence of street lighting. They believed that the police presence in their neighborhood reduced crime and gun violence. Many parents surveyed agreed they felt comfortable allowing their children to play outside with other children in the community. Residents felt the facilities were accessible for the disabled and elderly and were afforded many options for transportation. An overwhelming majority of residents surveyed noted that the programs offered by Brighton Center's CSS improved their quality of life.

The CSS program offered by Brighton Center and HAN also provided greater self-sufficiency to participants in the program. The residents overwhelmingly agreed that they gained more educational and employment opportunities and received the necessary job skills and training to be employable, such as resume and interview skills. They were provided opportunities to take classes to earn a GED and participated in credit and debt counseling classes and homeownership training classes. The skills taught by Brighton Center and HAN enabled residents to be more self-sufficient, eventually owning their own home, and become productive, contributing members of their community.

Overall, residents felt pride in their community, and most residents attended festivals and/or meetings in their community. However, a large majority of residents at the time did not belong to a community organization or group. The lack of participation and involvement in a civic or community organization may be attributed to the decline in social capital, which is important for a community because of its benefits to individuals and groups—i.e., the attributes and qualities citizens gain by participation in local and neighborhood organization, such as civic-mindedness, cooperation, and public-spiritedness (Putnam, 1995, 2000). Also, many families in CSS had jobs, and many of them were on disability, which may have impacted whether they were involved in the community.

Property values in neighborhoods with HOPE VI intervention (Saratoga Street and Liberty Row) increased between 94 and 520 percent. One neighborhood without the HOPE VI intervention, East Row Historic District, increased by 136 percent, 42 percent higher than the Liberty Row HOPE VI neighborhood. This anomaly could be explained by the higher quality of life and architectural integrity of the historic designated districts, versus non-designated neighborhoods, which could have affected higher property values in these areas along with the increased desire to live in older housing (Gilderbloom, House, & Hanka, 2008). The non-HOPE VI neighborhood, Southwest Downtown, experienced a 75 percent increase in property values, less than the increases experienced in both HOPE VI neighborhoods.

A major economic benefit of large-scale public housing development is in the multiplier effect, which is the change in total local employment divided by a change in export employment; thus, for every dollar spent, how many times is that same dollar re-spent in the neighborhood, creating other jobs, a phenomenon known as indirect effects (Bogart, 1998; O'Sullivan, 1993; Richardson, 1985; Weiss & Gooding, 1968; cited in Hanka, Gilderbloom, et al., 2015). An increase in spending produces an increased in costs and consumption. The job multiplier used in Newport showed between 17 to 19 jobs per $1 million spent. Also, the city of Newport has partnered with developed Corporex in a $1 billion investment on the vacant site of Newport Housing Authority's former public housing development called Ovation. The proposed Ovation development would offer first class and mixed-use development, such as retail, offices, 900 residential units, a hotel and additional entertainment, lodging, and recreational amenities near Downtown Newport, including a 2,700 seat indoor music venue (Owen, 2020).

Does the presence of scattered-site developments in Newport's HOPE VI program indicate success, when compared to the Louisville Park DuValle HOPE VI program? Park DuValle faces many challenges as a neighborhood, such as its lack of walkability, isolation from the rest of the city and adjacent neighborhoods, racial concentration of African Americans, limited number of new businesses, and limited access to public transportation and other amenities.

Newport, on the other hand, placed new residents in new scattered-site HOPE VI developments in Liberty Row and Saratoga Street, both within walking distance of downtown businesses, shops, stores, restaurants, Newport on the Levee, and Downtown Cincinnati. HOPE VI integrated into the Liberty Row neighborhood, representing approximately 22 percent of the total number of properties; the Saratoga Street HOPE VI neighborhood represented nine percent of the total properties in the neighborhood. These HOPE VI developments contributed to the increase in property values in these HOPE VI neighborhoods, the non-HOPE VI neighborhoods in our comparison (East Row Historic District and Southwest Downtown), the rest of Newport, and the Cincinnati metropolitan area.

Former Mayor Guidugli was aggressive in seeking federal grants like HOPE VI, as well as other economic development opportunities like the Ovation project on the old public housing site. Guidugli's consistent and steady leadership enabled him and his staff to stay focused on the goal to implement a common-sense strategy for revitalizing Newport. Newport's 180-degree turn, from its sordid organized crime past, has transformed this small river city into a premier destination for tourists, residents, businesses, and homeowners in the region.

The HOPE VI program in Newport has contributed to promoting sustainability by encouraging living downtown and encouraging the reuse and rehabilitation of older historic buildings and homes. The HOPE VI program in Newport fulfilled a main objective of HOPE VI by integrating neighborhoods into mixed-income communities. HOPE VI homes also promoted energy efficiency, through the rehabilitation of older homes and the construction of energy efficient homes that provide residents with low monthly utility bills, a departure from the $400 per month energy bills paid by residents in the old public housing site.

Unlike previous HOPE VI studies in other cities, the Newport HOPE VI project did not reinforce patterns of segregation and concentrated poverty, instead using the scattered site development approach, which increased property values in the HOPE VI and non-HOPE VI neighborhoods in Newport and the surrounding cities in the region. The HOPE VI program in Newport fulfilled its main objectives of reducing the concentration of poverty, revitalizing distressed communities, removing the old physical structure of the housing, providing support services to residents through Brighton Center, promoting personal and community responsibility, and developing public and private partnerships.

COVINGTON, KENTUCKY HOPE VI PROGRAM

Covington, Kentucky, located on the east side of the Licking River from Newport, at the Ohio River and south of Cincinnati, is another important city in the Greater Cincinnati metropolitan area. Covington's 2019 population is 40,341, slightly down from the 2010 Census population of 40,640 (U.S. Census, 2020). The city was named in honor of General Leonard Covington, an American officer who was killed in the War of 1812. After becoming an incorporated city in 1815, Covington grew as German immigrants moved into the city from New York, and like Newport, many rural migrants from eastern Kentucky also settled in Covington (Gilderbloom et al., 2014).

While Covington avoided the vice and corruption that was common in Newport, the city suffered the loss of many manufacturing and industrial jobs from the 1930s to 1960s caused a movement in population to the suburbs, which was not uncommon among other American cities. Despite annexation of the city, Covington's population did not rebound, and the city's prospects never recovered. By the 1970s, HUD named Covington one of American's most blighted cities (Gilderbloom et al., 2014).

In the 1980s, Covington saw a rebirth because of new investment, especially with the formation of the Mainstrasse entertainment and business district in the downtown area, along with the development of the Covington riverfront, including the Northern Kentucky Convention Center, an Embassy Suites hotel and office tower, and the popular condominium project, called *The Ascent*, near the famous Roebling bridge on the Ohio River. New sports stadia were built in Cincinnati in the 2000s: the Paul Brown Stadium for the Cincinnati Bengals in 2000 and the Great American Ball Park in 2003 for the Cincinnati Reds. Cincinnati, Hamilton County, and Ohio taxpayers subsidized the sports stadia, producing enormous benefits for residents and businesses in both Newport and Covington.

Figure 8.6.   Covington HOPE VI. *Source:* John Gilderbloom

The Covington Housing Authority received a $19 million HOPE VI grant in 2005 to revitalize the city by dismantling the old Jacob Price public housing development, built in 1939 and named after Jacob Price, a former slave, businessman, and minister. Jacob Price housed 163 apartments and had as many as 500 residents living there (Hanka, Gilderbloom, et al., 2015). Much of the area around Jacob Price was flood prone because of its proximity to the Licking River and could not be salvaged. Redeveloping the site as a HOPE VI development resulted in 149 single family and multifamily housing units with mixed use development, subsidized and market rate, at River's Edge at Eastside Pointe, along with the City Heights development (Hanka, Gilderbloom, et al., 2015; Gilderbloom et al., 2014). River's Edge at Eastside Pointe was positioned closer to downtown Covington, which offered frequent bus service and was closer to jobs, medical care, and educational opportunities.

Jacob Price rents ranged from $360 to $674 per month, and market rate housing ranged from $725 for a one-bedroom unit, to $1,200 for two or more bedrooms (Gilderbloom et al., 2014). Much of the new housing incorporated sustainable green principles into the design, resulting in the new development receiving LEED certification. In the HOPE VI program, based on 140 residents who qualified and were a part of CSS as of mid-October 2015, 35 were left in the HOPE VI Jacob Price development and River's Edge. An overwhelming majority of the survey respondents were female, two-thirds of the residents were African American, around 82 percent were single, and almost 70 percent of the residents were children under 17 years of age. The mean age of the respondent was 37 years old with an average monthly income of $703. Almost all the residents had subsidized rent, and many did not own a car or a bicycle (Gilderbloom et al., 2014).

Covington HOPE VI Survey Analysis

Gilderbloom et al. (2014) conducted a 106-item survey to each of the 35 asking questions about neighborhood satisfaction, community and safety, community activity and involvement, available affordable housing, technology, education, health and fitness, green features of the new HOPE VI housing, and demographics. Of the 35 HOPE VI residents returning a completed survey, most residents had a favorable opinion of the Housing Authority of Covington (HAC) and most took pride in their community. An overwhelming majority liked the appearance of the housing units and felt that the public transportation was easy to use. Also, most of the residents reported having a grocery store within walking distance and most felt there was adequate health care near the neighborhood.

The overwhelming majority felt safe in their neighborhood, and more than half believed there had been a decrease in crime compared to their old neighborhood, while the majority believed there was an adequate police presence. Also, nine out of ten HOPE VI residents believed that the HOPE VI/Jacob Price revitalization project was good for Covington.

From a social capital standpoint, while a majority of respondents participated in community events in their neighborhood or in Covington, almost 69 percent reported that they were not a member of a community group or organization (Gilderbloom et al., 2014), similar to the Habitat for Humanity study discussed in chapter 3. Eighty percent of the HOPE VI residents believed that the houses were affordable, almost 89 percent felt they were well maintained in their neighborhood, and three-quarters felt there were opportunities to purchase housing.

Most residents reported having access to a computer and more than half had internet access whenever they needed it. Nearly all residents reported owning a cellular phone, and over three-quarters had an email address. Of the residents with children in school, most reported they volunteered and were involved in after-school activities. All but one resident reported that they were satisfied with the early childhood education and most of them were able to get their child into such a program. Over three-quarters were satisfied with their child's school.

Regarding health indicators, almost all the respondents felt their insurance was high quality. In the past thirty days, almost 62 percent of the residents reported a physical illness or injury; around half reported issues related to stress and being unable to do usual activities due to physical or mental health issues. In the last year, 63 percent were worried about not having enough money to pay their rent or mortgage, but less than half were worried about having enough money to buy nutritious food for their family.

Gilderbloom et al. (2014) also conducted independent t-tests to examine differences between HOPE VI residents and non-HOPE VI residents. There were several areas where HOPE VI residents reported better outcomes than their non-HOPE VI neighbors. HOPE VI residents took significantly more pride in their community than others. Further, they liked their community more than non-HOPE VI residents and felt their community was cleaner. There was less fear about riding a bike and less perceived crime from HOPE VI residents. More HOPE VI residents owned a cell phone, were registered to vote, and had a grocery store in walking distance than their non-HOPE VI neighbors. More program participants had a primary health care provider and residents reported less stress about having money to purchase food.

Gilderbloom et al. (2014) examined both HOPE VI and River's Edge residents to look for differences between neighbors in other communities.

These residents had thirty-two outcomes in which they were significantly different from their neighbors in other communities. The combined residents had significantly more pride and liked living in their neighborhood, felt their neighborhoods were cleaner, and liked the appearance of the housing much more. Those in either HOPE VI or River's Edge also felt safer walking or riding their bike and had easier access to public transportation. More of the combined group wanted to stay in their current neighborhood and appreciated the easier access to the grocery store. Those living in River's Edge or in HOPE VI also had a significantly more positive perception of the revitalization of Covington.

Covington Economic Multiplier Analysis

Hanka, Gilderbloom, et al. (2015) shows the significant role HOPE VI has had in creating jobs, using the three economic multiplier models—the Preservation Economic Impact (PEI), the Economic Impact Forecasting System (EIFS), and the IMPACT analysis for planning. The HOPE VI programs in Newport and Covington helped create jobs at a crucial time when unemployment was at its highest in two decades (see Shierholz & Mishel, 2009).

While the EIFS model generated a job multiplier of 43–49 jobs per $1 million spent (Hanka, Gilderbloom, et al., 2015), we use a conservative multiplier of 17 jobs per $1 million for Newport (see also Hanka et al., 2007), resulting in 480–680 jobs. For our Covington analysis, we used the IMPLAN model, because the EIFS did not include indirect and induced job creation. The job estimator was based on limited citywide census data and did not use zip codes, which would have generated more accurate numbers.

For urban areas, however, IMPLAN is widely used to evaluate fiscal and economic impacts of various projects and programs on municipalities and metropolitan regions. Hanka, Gilderbloom, et al. (2015) tested the IMPLAN system to determine its accuracy, using the IMPLAN's direct job estimates and comparing them with the actual number of persons hired in a development. This helped confirm the accuracy and precision of the system. IMPLAN offers two types of data: countywide and zip code data. Although countywide data are known to be accurate, the zip code dataset provides finer granularity and seemed better suited for our analysis.

According to City of Covington officials, an estimated $42 million would be invested directly in new construction and building renovations. Using this estimate, we were able to create an analysis to predict the number of jobs that would be created from the construction in the area of interest. It was estimated that, by direct effect, the project would produce 242 jobs (a labor income of roughly $20 million) in addition to the approximately $22 million in value to the city's industries, resulting in a total output of almost $42 million. The indirect effect from the project would lead to the production of 43 jobs and generate $1.86 million in labor income. Also, Covington's industries would gain about $2.7 million in value and an output of roughly $4.5 million. The induced effect will increase jobs by 95, spawn an additional $3.5 million in labor income, and add $7 million in value with an output of approximately $10.5 million. Overall, the project will add 380 jobs to the city, generate approximately $25.1 million in labor income, and add approximately $31.9 million of value to Covington and its industries, with an overall output of approximately $57 million.

Of the 242 new jobs into the Covington economy as a result of the direct effect of the HOPE VI program, 125 jobs were in construction of new residential structures and 116 in maintenance and repair of existing residential structures. The indirect and induced effect of the HOPE VI program included the creation of 16 jobs in food service and drinking establishments, 11 in the food and beverage retail sector, and 10 jobs in real estate establishments. Retail for motor vehicles and parts and retail stores for electronics would add six jobs, while nursing and residential care facilities, architectural, engineering, and related services, and private hospitals would each experience an increase of five jobs (Hanka, Gilderbloom, et al., 2015).

Our analysis showed that HOPE VI helped revitalize two small Kentucky cities: Newport and Covington. Not only did the HOPE VI programs in Newport and Covington create attractive, affordable housing, but they helped create jobs in a number of sectors at a crucial time when unemployment was at its highest in two decades (Shierholz & Mishel, 2009). These findings suggest that policymakers should focus on job creation when planning programs like HOPE VI.

HOPE VI AND SOCIAL CAPITAL

How does HOPE VI enhance social capital? Social capital is all about "who you know" and the type of social networks and access to information and resources an individual possesses. When a person spends hours talking to neighbors, coworkers, and friends, they are building a social network and the social capital that develops will provide support during difficult economic and financial times, and ultimately, improve quality of life and personal success. When the community improves its social capital, change can happen. People can leverage networks to help influence better quality of life outcomes through community and economic development.

The connections between social capital, new urbanism, and HOPE VI are important. During the past 40 years of new urbanism, and the past 25–30 years of HOPE VI, scholars have wondered whether the physical design and configuration of a new HOPE VI neighborhood using new urbanist principles create social capital for residents, improve and enhance their connections and networks, and create a sense of community. Studies from Clampet-Lundquist (2004, Barrett, Geisel, & Johnson (2006) and Goetz (2003) show that very few households developed social ties and supportive relationships in their new neighborhood after being displaced by HOPE VI, exhibited fewer "neighboring behaviors" (talk with a neighbor or watch a neighbor's child) (Goetz, 2010, p. 11), and had limited interactions with their new neighbors. Only households who were moved voluntarily experienced greater interaction or became friends with their new neighbors or became involved in volunteer activities in their communities than households who were displaced involuntarily (Goetz, 2003, p. 217; Goetz, 2010, p. 11).

Pollner (2002) studied two Boston HOPE VI developments, Mission Main and Orchard Gardens, and showed that despite the new elements of a HOPE VI development, there was an "unimpressive level of bridging social capital" (as cited in Sander, 2002, p. 222) even though there had been no baseline measurement to determine whether social capital levels would be higher or lower without the development. Pollner (2002) argues that poor bridging social capital "reflects a lack of 'investment' in and identification with their HOPE VI development as a community" (as cited in Sander, 2002, p. 222). Pollner (2002) found more bonding social capital, in terms of checking in on neighbors or doing favors for each other, even though residents at both sites still found it difficult to get to know their neighbors more and meet new people, but found that no one learned about a job from their neighbor.

HOPE VI neighborhoods were designed to be places of shared interaction with new mixes of people that would provide opportunities for residents to be involved in their neighborhood, through social activities, volunteering, or serving on a resident council or a housing association (Sander, 2002). Pollner`s (2002) study showed that residents in Mission Main and Orchard Gardens, whether they were old residents who had lived on the site before HOPE VI or newer residents who came from somewhere else; or whether they lived in market rate, public, or affordable subsidized units in the HOPE VI development, acknowledged the difficulties of meeting new people and being more engaged and involved in their community (p. 11; as cited in Sander, 2002, p. 233).

The evolution of the HOPE VI self-sufficiency programs (Nguyen et al., 2016) has contributed to positive effects of social capital, as evidenced from the results of Louisville's Park DuValle HOPE VI program. Studies from

Buron, Popkin, Levy, Harris, and Khaduri (2002) and Schwartz and Tajbakhsh (1997) (as cited in Nguyen et al., 2016) have noted that mixing lower and middle incomes in the HOPE VI development does not alone lead to greater economic mobility, but requiring intentional interventions like CSS, might improve economic mobility (see also Kleit, 2001, 2002).

Nguyen et al. (2016) evaluated the Boulevard Homes HOPE VI project in Charlotte, North Carolina, and studied the residents over a two-year period, who participated in the CSS case management program. They found that former public housing residents who had high levels of satisfaction and positive relationships with their case manager (the bridging social capital that is formed through formal social supports) had better employment outcomes; however, individuals who had high levels of bonding social capital through informal social support, such as knowing one's neighbors, had negative employment outcomes. These positive and supportive relationships with case managers represented a long-term commitment toward clients' progress, through mentorship, guidance, and connection to information and resources, instead of simple job referral. While the new physical housing did not impact economic mobility, Nguyen et al. (2016) argue that CSS interventions may have led to greater economic mobility if the programs had been targeted to those ready for employment or with employment.

What role and responsibility does the public housing authority (PHA) that developed the HOPE VI site, or the CSS program, have in empowering the residents and helping them on a path towards self-sufficiency and good citizenship? Axtell and Tooley (2015) provide a good warning from their study of HOPE VI in Park DuValle:

> The processes did not take seriously the social nature of humans and therefore did not create the conditions that foster participation in the economic system, the community, and political engagement. . . . Priority must be given to the shape and composition of social capital and the recognition of the ways that it enhances community development and well-being. Further, processes must ensure autonomous freedom for representative resident bodies, and points of disagreement should be resolved through negotiation or mediation. At a minimum, the city must abide by all agreements with residents. In fact, in future projects, no demolition should take place until these envisioning, clarifying, and negotiating processes are nearly complete. It has taken a long time to get to the present moment; sufficient time will be required to build new patterns. (p. 296)

Social capital is also lost when families and residents are dislocated from their original neighborhoods and moved to new locations. Axtell and Tooley (2015) reported that former residents of Clarksdale felt more unsafe and unwelcome in new neighborhoods (i.e., did not accept our Clarksdale residents into Sheppard Square) and were disappointed at the loss of their social safety networks. Stone, Dailey, et al. (2011) conducted a survey of former Clarksdale residents, using a social capital measurement to determine involvement in the community. Respondents were spilt on participating in volunteer activities. There were as many respondents who never participated in volunteer activities as those who participated a few times a year, a few times a month, or once or more per week; this is consistent with other HOPE VI and community development projects. The overwhelming majority of respondents (76 percent) attended a religious service at least a few times a year, with almost one-fourth attended one or more religious service per week. Communities with members engaged in social activities also were more likely to develop their own social networks and their own sources of support (Stone, Dailey, et al., 2011).

CONCLUSION

During its 20 years of successes and failures, $6 billion in total investment, and another $11 billion leveraged from the private and nonprofit sector, HOPE VI has shown that homeownership is the best way to ensure livable and sustainable communities and revitalize distressed communities throughout the United States. HOPE VI is the solution to bad government public housing policy.

While it's difficult to generalize the effect of HOPE VI, because the variation is great in terms of scale, features, design, and demographics, further studies and research should be undertaken to analyze HOPE VI's impact in more medium and small size cities (Mallach, 2009). Whether Chicago or Covington, New York or Newport, Los Angeles or Lincoln, small, medium, and large cities need to grow and pursue developmental policies to establish their bargaining positions in the marketplace (Logan & Molotch, 1987).

If resources are available, studies should conduct a comparison across metropolitan areas, analyzing the impact and effectiveness of HOPE VI, including controlling HOPE VI with other intervening factors. The foresight and wherewithal for cities like Newport, Louisville, and Covington to seek federal grants like HOPE VI provided the catalyst to turn around these cities, their neighborhoods, and communities. Despite its flaws and criticisms, HOPE VI has enabled improvement and change in people's lives, making homeownership a possibility, so they too can live the American Dream, involve themselves in communities, and become responsible and productive citizens.

NOTES

Portions of this chapter were previously published in the article Hanka, Matthew J et al. "Measuring Job Creation for HOPE VI: a Success Story for Community Development Efforts." *Community development (Columbus, Ohio)* 46.2 (2015): 133–148, and is reprinted here with the permission of the published, Taylor & Francis, ltd. and from Hanka, M. J. (2009). From vice to nice: A case study of the HOPE VI program in Newport. Doctoral dissertation. Louisville, KY: University of Louisville.

1. The Park DuValle Project occurred prior to the approval of the Louisville and Jefferson County government merger in 2000 and that went into effect in 2003. Prior to merger, the city's housing authority was called the Louisville Housing Authority (LHA) and was called Louisville Metro Housing Authority (LMHA) after merger.

Chapter Nine

Placemaking and Social Capital

Much of this book has showcased the important role federal housing policy played in destroying urban neighborhoods and communities, including the 1949 Housing Act, which brought urban renewal and slum clearance programs, and the Federal Highway Act of 1956, which created the interstate highway system bisecting our major cities and led to massive suburbanization and sprawl. According to Kunstler (2004; as cited in Kayegama, 2011, pp. 13, 18), sprawl in America has created 38,000 places in the United States that "are not worth caring about." The creation of single tract suburban homes and "McMansions" have detached people from the notion of a public place worth caring about (Kunstler, 2004; Duany et al., 2010; Kayegama, 2011). The growth and development of suburbia has led to the neglect, disrepair, and disinvestment of cities, which also has led "to a psychic disconnection for people between the suburbs and their city" and "a bitterly divided national consciousness" (Kayegama, 2011, p. 17).

Another consequence of White flight to the suburbs through the interstate highway system was perpetuated by the creation of multi-lane one-way streets, which create hazards and unsafe conditions for pedestrians and bicyclists. One-way streets have negatively affected business and lowered housing values and have made it more difficult to notice crime and illegal activities, especially when motorists move through the neighborhood at high speeds (Hanka & Gilderbloom, 2008; Riggs & Gilderbloom, 2015).

In the past 30 years of the back-to-the-city movement, many scholars and urbanists have tried to understand how physical spaces and places influence social interactions and relationships. A space, either public or private, focuses on how the physical elements and design create a need for place, as well as how spaces help define social relations determining the use, meaning, and purpose of place for those individuals using it (Brown, 2006; Neethi, Kamath, & Paul, 2019).

Place defined by Friedmann (2010, p. 154) is "a small three-dimensional urban space that is cherished by the people who inhabit it," where it encompasses both the physical environment at the neighborhood level but also the subjective feelings the place's inhabitants have towards it. Place defined by Massey (1997) is a "socially constructed process through which imagination, memories, and experiences form content-specific identities and functions that remain fluid across social and physical boundaries" (cited in Neethi et al., 2019, p. 3). The context of place examined in this chapter is not the home or a workplace, but a public place, sometimes referred to as a third place, a place where the community comes together in an informal way, to see familiar and unfamiliar faces, where civic discourse and community connections can happen" (Oldenburg, 2002, p. 2; as cited in Silberberg, 2013, p. 6). For Oldenburg (2002), these places include gyms, coffee houses, taverns, and even a street in Chicago called Maxwell Street, where the Juketown Community bandstand performs every day.

Placemaking, on the other hand, "is the process of creating quality places that people want to live, work, play and learn in" (MSU Land Policy Institute, 2019) that also "concerns the deliberate shaping of an environment to facilitate social interaction and improve a community's quality of life" (Silberberg, 2013, pp. 1–2). Placemaking's major proponents include urbanist William Whyte, Kevin Lynch, and Jane Jacobs (Silberberg, 2013). Jacobs in her famous book, *The Death and Life of Great American Cities*, challenged the traditional planning establishment by envisioning public spaces based on what people want and need in their daily lives.

Placemaking touches many of the human sciences, such as social anthropology, environmental psychology, landscape architecture, planning, and philosophy. Placemaking also touches on a range of concerns and issues facing cities large and small, from healthy living, community capacity-building, social justice, economic revitalization, and childhood development, and involves many stakeholders, including local officials, visitors, workers, and residents (Silberberg, 2013).

Placemaking is one of the trendiest terms going around, but why is it important? Placemaking always starts with the basics. People want to live in communities that provide amenities. People want places where they can make connections with other people and their surroundings. In Indiana, for example, placemaking initiatives are a retention strategy to keep people in the state, since 50 percent of Indiana native college students leave the state within five years of graduation. According to Drew Klacik of the Indiana University Public Policy Institute, most Hoosiers value family, tradition, and loyalty to place, and most want to invest in a future that honors the unique history of the past (Klacik, 2017).

Wyckoff (2014) argues that placemaking is a process, a means to an end, where the end is the creation of quality places that evoke a strong sense of place in a physical building, location, or space that serves as a magnet for people, creativity, and new development. Placemaking inspires a community to collectively reimagine how citizens can be involved in shaping the built environment to be more community-friendly and promote belonging (Block, 2008). Placemaking enables citizens to help reinvent public spaces that become the heart of a community and to reinvent the spaces of major public institutions such as schools, public transportation systems, museums, playgrounds, social services, colleges, and universities (Katz & Nowak, 2017).

While place is also important, empowering the community through the placemaking process is critical. The making of place is continuous and cyclical, so once a placemaking project ends, another one begins. This process democratizes the space for placemakers because the layperson, citizen, resident, and professional are equal partners in the community of makers (Silberberg, 2013). The hands-on citizen-driven design approach of placemaking transforms a place to be "an authentic expression of the voices of the citizens who will occupy that space" (Block, 2008, p. 159). Places do not happen overnight but are created over time. People desire places where they can live and thrive.

Dreier, Mollenkopf, and Swanstrom (2014) identify the reasons place matters. Where we live tells a story. The values, characteristics, and identity of a place, including its history, geography, industry, institutions, culture, and landmarks, enhance a resident's emotional attachment and love for community. The Knight Foundation's Soul of the Community study (2010; as cited by Loflin, 2013) asked what makes people love where they live and why place matters. The Knight Foundation discovered that places and communities with significant levels of attachment experience an increase in local economic growth and development, have more productive workers, and have more people who want to stay in place (Loflin, 2013).

People's attachment to a community is driven by the social offerings (places where people meet and the care and concern people have for each other), openness (how welcoming the community is to different kinds of people, and the aesthetics (the physical beauty and amenities) (Knight Foundation, 2010). Loflin says, "You need civic engagement *plus* the belief that you can make a difference in order for it to create greater attachment. We can't just provide civic engagement opportunities, we also have to create a culture of success around engagement if we want it to translate to feelings of greater attachment to a place" (PPS, 2013, para 10).

People move to a city or community because of what a place has to offer. Florida (2014) says, "Place has become the central organizing unit of our economy and society" (p. 288). How we make that place depends on what the residents do, but also what cities and neighborhoods do to attract businesses, jobs, and residents. Placemaking means cities use place-based revitalization strategies, to transform "Anytown, USA" to a unique location where people want to live, work, and play (Klacik, 2017).

Transformative initiatives like placemaking have largely been ignored by local politicians and policymakers, according to Project for Public Spaces (PPS), one of the nation's foremost organizations on placemaking. Right now, no city or municipal department or community organization anywhere in the country oversees creating good places (Kent, 2013b). Whether government views placemaking as too large for any government to do without the private sector, or the local political culture won't allow it, crosscutting initiatives such as placemaking need less of a transactional and passive model (i.e., a citizen pays for services to a distant government or a citizen receives rights and protections and the government leaves them alone), and more of a model that involves more people directly in the civic decision-making process (such as residents themselves who know the neighborhood inside and out), instead of only the professionals (e.g., engineers and architects). This model is referred to as place governance (Kent, 2013a, 2013b).

Whereas government represents the formal institutions, processes, and administrative structures of a jurisdiction, and is top-down, hierarchical, and formal in its structures, governance is horizontal, decentralized, and informal, focusing on the laws, rules, actions, activities, methods, procedures, arrangements, and practices that reflect the pattern of government activity in a jurisdiction. The power in place governance lies in the networks between public, private, and civic actors, locally and around the world, along transnational lines of capital, trade, and innovation (Katz & Nowak, 2017). Place governance "meets people where they are and makes it easier for them to engage in shaping their communities" (Kent, 2013a, para. 6). PPS believes city and municipal governments and their departments have a collective role in creating place under a place governance model that results in the creation of place capital, defined as "the shared wealth (built and natural) of the public realm" (Kent, 2011, para. 2). It is this place capital that is important in generating sustainable economic growth and development for communities (Kent, 2011, 2013b).

There are four kinds of placemaking. The first is standard placemaking, focused on incremental change based on how a place can be improved over a specific period of time (Wyckoff, 2014). Standard placemaking is often project-based, involving many separate small projects and/or activities, but also creates larger scale transformative projects and activities that can convert a place in a relatively short period of time. A lot of normal standard place-making involves the renewal and adaptive reuse of old abandoned industrial buildings that are transformed into residential and commercial sites, artist studios, and performance centers (Katz & Nowak, 2017).

Strategic placemaking is a comprehensive targeted approach to community revitalization focused on goals and strategies. Over a specific period (3–5, 5–10, or 5–15 years), a community will develop places that fulfill these specific goals and strategies. It might be strategic to create places that attract certain businesses or firms, or offer certain amenities. Strategic placemaking "aims to create quality places that are uniquely attractive to talented workers," which results in the creation of jobs and income for individuals who want to live and work there (Wyckoff, 2014, p. 5).

Creative placemaking moves away from strategies, and focuses on the intentional integration of the arts, culture, creativity, and design in comprehensive community development. Creative placemaking involves partners from all sectors (public, private, nonprofit, community, and social) to "strategically shape the physical and social character of a neighborhood, town, city, or region around arts and cultural activities," for the good of the community (Markusen & Gadwa, 2010, p. 3; as cited in Lee et al., 2016, p. 34). Creative placemaking attracts the creative class, discussed in chapter 2, by emphasizing people first, and how a diverse group can address the many problems in communities to build better places to live, work, play, and visit (Vazquez, 2016).

Creative placemaking can "do more than 'develop' a location; it holds the promise of elevating the identity of a place by enhancing its essence through a collection of visual, cultural, social, and environmental qualities that inspire the community to be engaged" (Kelkar & Spinelli, 2016, p. 55; see also McMahon, 2010). Creative placemaking plays an important role in resolving community issues, through arts and culture, heritage, and history in important places like museums, art galleries, orchestra halls, and performing arts centers. Creative placemaking can also enhance a community's physical and social fabric (Vazquez, 2016). Vazquez (2016) further says:

> A new performance arts center in a poor part of town may be successful in bringing wealthy people to its theaters and halls. However, if those people just go to the performance arts centers (PAC) and leave without spending money anywhere nearby, that PAC is not achieving the kind of economic impact that community leaders imagined. (And because the community probably spent a lot of time and money to build the PAC, it might be costly to the people it is designed to help.) (cited in Phillips, 2016, p. 305)

These institutions need to be planned appropriately in scale so that they do not create more problems rather than addressing and resolving the problems and issues already facing the community.

Creative placemaking also enhances the various kinds of social capital, through engagement with the community (Kelkar & Spinelli, 2016). Linking bridging social capital and creativity "pushes us to see the joy, excitement, fear, and discomfort inherent in valued change and community building. And the arts may be uniquely positioned to build inclusive communities as they make room for all of these human experiences simultaneously" (Thomas, Pate, & Ranson, 2015, p. 75). Działek (2014) and Lorenzen (2007) share the effect place has on social capital and economics by being "more conducive to the development and strengthening of social relations" (Działek, 2014, p. 179).

Kelkar and Spinelli (2016) developed a model illustrating the interconnectivity between community design, identity and productivity, and their influence on building social capital through creative placemaking. This begins with a community-led design process that puts people at the center of the creative placemaking process, from which community identity emerges. What follows is the community's realization that the formation of bridging and linking social capital, through involvement in external organizations, allows a community to better understand its identity. This process enables the creation of capital that helps people identify their local assets, which builds capacity and trust, and enhances relationships with the community. This enables the community to act as a catalyst for community change because of these relationships to develop placemaking initiatives.

A study by the Mortimer and Mimi Levitt Foundation (Lee, Linnt, Baltazaer, & Woronkowicz, 2016) assessed audience and community engagement in two cities—Memphis, Tennessee, and Pasadena, California—where the foundation had built permanent arts venues. The study shows that attending a concert at a music venue enhances bonding social capital, through the interactions one has with family and friends who attend the concert and know one another, but also enhances bridging social capital by enabling participants to interact and connect with groups and communities outside their social network (Lee et al., 2016). These experiences are not "a random coming together of people from different walks of life in a public park, but rather a shared, communal experience that diverse individuals have together as a community" (Lee et al., 2016, p. 35). The Crosstown Arts initiative in Memphis creates an "ethic of belonging" in one of the most ethnically diverse areas in the city, despite the dilemmas, issues, and challenges in promoting community-based and community-driven arts organizations (Thomas et al., 2015, p. 86).

The fourth type of placemaking, tactical placemaking, uses a deliberate, often phased approach to change, which begins with a low-cost, short-term project or a mix of projects that can demonstrate what could happen when there are changes in the environment, in public spaces, and in the neighborhood. Sometimes referred to as tactical urbanism (or guerrilla urbanism, pop-up urbanism, or DIY urbanism) (Wyckoff, 2014), this approach is "grassroots, ad-hoc, often temporary, and sometimes unsanctioned efforts" to remake a neighborhood (Speck, 2018, p. 232). Tactical urbanists are working to "reimagine underused or dilapidated city spaces as spots for community congregation" (Bartram, 2014, p. 14).

Tactical urbanism enables a community to "wrest control of its streets from the firm grip of the automobile and create more valuable public space experiences" (Klayko, 2016, p. 2). The first tactical urbanists date back to the 1500s in France, called the Les Boquinistes, who set up stalls to sell books on the Seine River, but were banned in the next century, then reinstated after a public outcry. Even though it took 500 years, Les Boquinistes accomplished their goal to "encourage lasting, alternative uses for urban spaces" (Bartram, 2014, p. 14).

Tactical urbanism ranges from demonstrations, pop-ups, and pilot projects to permanent installations that can transform an area quickly. A common tactical urbanist strategy is Park(ing) day, where residents convert a parking space or spaces into a functioning garden, a playground, or a mini park (Meeks, 2018). Tactical urbanism is low risk with the possibility of high reward, but it is also important in developing social capital between citizens, and building organizational capacity between the public, private, and nonprofit sectors (Bartram, 2014).

A unique example of tactical placemaking and tactical urbanism is the creation of a parklet, which consists of a parking-space-sized space on an elevated platform that includes a large table for several small groups or one large group with benches of the edges of the parklet with bike parking on one side, and trees and shrubbery on the other side (see Figure 9.1). The parklet is also handicap accessible for wheelchairs (Klayko, 2016). For instance, Louisville's first parklet, known as the Community Table, was designed by architectural firms Gresham Smith & Partners in Louisville and Nomi Design in Lexington in 2016 and sat on Louisville historic West Main Street District (Klayko, 2016).

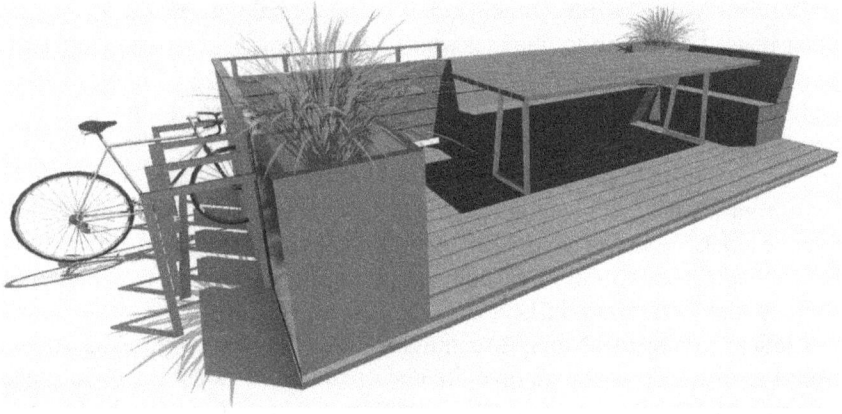

Figure 9.1. Rendering of Community Table in Louisville, KY. *Source:* **Gresham, Smith, and Brothers**

Covington, KY, created several tactical placemaking parklets on its downtown streets. A local program called Curb'd created a process in which local businesses and organizations pitched ideas for potential parklet projects. This process produced five projects funded at $15,000 each, such as the Wish Igloo that includes people hanging handwritten notes, Hopscotch Gardens where children can meander through a maze of nooks and crannies and play hopscotch while adults sit enjoying a beer, and a boxing-ring theme parklet with Rock 'Em Sock 'Em Robots located outside the retro storefront of the local barbershop that sponsors this project (Anzilotti, 2016).

Figure 9.2. Wish Igloo. *Source:* **Curb'd in Covington**

Placemaking can happen anywhere. Silberberg (2013) emphasizes placemaking that includes smaller cities as well as urban areas, because it enhances both social and economic capital, when people visit and spend money. Placemaking is a retention and attraction strategy for cities, especially creative placemaking, that attracts businesses and skilled workers. Through placemaking amenities, businesses can become competitive nationally and globally. Placemaking also creates a growing tax base and tax revenues to support needed urban services, while improving return on investment (ROI) for developers. Placemaking creates a higher quality of life through urban redevelopment that builds on existing and historic structures and infrastructure with better urban form, improved design, and use of the public realm (MSU Center for Land Policy Institute, 2015).

FOUNDING MOTHER OF PLACEMAKING: JANE JACOBS

Jane Jacobs, a writer without any formal training in urban planning, challenged the orthodox urbanism of Ebenezer Howard, Le Corbusier, and Lewis Mumford, preaching about the important role a neighborhood plays in building and making place and social capital. Jacobs discussed the classical urban form with mixed use and small blocks, and she emphasized the importance of sidewalks as more than a way to move pedestrians to and from a destination. Sidewalks are the veins in which the blood of urban life flows, and sidewalks are public spaces where people should feel safe (Jacobs, 1961).

Sidewalks, for Jacobs, must have three qualities; the public and private spaces are clearly marked; there are "eyes upon the street" that ensure the safety of residents and strangers; and the sidewalks must be used by pedestrians continuously, where residents can watch the activity of the street and the sidewalks from where they live (1961, p. 35). The continuous eyes on the street are "an almost unconscious assumption of general street support" (Jacobs, 1961, p. 56) or "trust," formed over time from contact between pedestrians and residents that can help build social networks and bridging social capital.

Sidewalks are one of the spaces in the city that does effective placemaking. For Jacobs, sidewalks maintain the order of the city and represent

> an intricate ballet in which the individual dancers and ensembles all have distinctive parts which miraculously reinforce each other and compose an orderly whole. The ballet of the good city sidewalk never repeats itself from place to place, and in any one place is always replete with new improvisations. (Jacobs, 1961, p. 50)

This ballet brings forth an urban dance that exposes people to unexpected things to see, hear, and feel in a neighborhood (Thomas et al., 2015).

The conversion of one-way streets to two-way streets has contributed to improvements in neighborhoods' quality of life. The streets themselves act as a part of the nervous system of the neighborhood, according to Jane Jacobs (1961, as cited in Riggs & Gilderbloom, 2015, p. 105). A street that is one-way does not train the pedestrian's eye to observe what is around them. The only focal point is the cars and the oncoming traffic. If a street is converted to two ways, the traffic will slow down, balancing traffic flow, and increasing pedestrian activity on and around the street. Two-way streets enable pedestrians and motorists to safely interact with the streetscape and activity around them (Hanka & Gilderbloom, 2008).

A study by Riggs and Gilderbloom (2015) on converting one-way streets (Brook and 1st streets) to two-way streets in downtown Louisville, KY, found that traffic accidents decreased 36–60 percent, crime dropped 23 percent, auto theft declined by 33 percent, and property values increased 2.8 percent each year on converted 1st Street, compared to one-way 2nd and 3rd streets. Property values increased more than 27 percent after Brook Street converted to two-way (Riggs & Gilderbloom, 2015). Converting one-way streets to two-way streets helps revitalize and reinvent our downtowns and neighborhoods (Hanka & Gilderbloom, 2008).

Parks are another venue for placemaking. While Jacobs calls them "volatile spaces," you need eyes on them just like the street. Parks create and enhance social capital by enabling "social friction," the interaction between people who would otherwise not meet (Sennett, 1992; Silberberg, 2013, p. 6; Thomas et al., 2015, p. 79). Playgrounds and parks are a perfect example of "volatile spaces," allowing children and families to connect and build social networks centered around the park.

Effective placemaking, for the most part, creates authentic, inclusive public spaces that enable many different people to live in places that reveal common ownership, belonging, and shared identity (Katz & Nowak, 2017). Social capital is closely related to placemaking that helps build associations and network structures that link individuals and develop trust and reciprocity. The social relationships and attachments one has to a place, space, locality, or territory over time is important in our understanding of placemaking, for it

> becomes the geographical expression of social power where space, time, and society are interrelated and co-exist and co-construct one another on a common crucible. Localism and territoriality then dovetail neatly to the process of placemaking, where place is elevated beyond just a physical location to a crucible of physical elements, activities, and meaning interlaced by a plethora of actors bounded by intergenerational social networks. (Neethi et al., 2019, p. 12)

The idea behind placemaking is changing the way cities work. The hands-on approach of placemaking improves the city or region and strengthens the connections between the people where they live. Placemaking generates jobs and incomes, creates new products and services, and attracts new businesses and creative industries, such as social media, design services, advertising, publishing, broadcasting, musical recordings, and video productions.

EXAMPLES OF PLACEMAKING

The Project for Public Spaces (PPS) uses a tool for placemakers called the Power of 10+, which explains that a place should have 10 or more reasons for people to be there, or 10 or more things to do in that place. It might be a place to sit, a playground, an art installation, food, music, people, or any unique activity that reflects the culture and history of the community (PPS, 2020). A neighborhood with 10 or more things to do, near to other neighborhoods that have 10 things to do, creates a district of interest. PPS (2020) says when a city contains 10 or more districts of interest, "their public perception begins to shift amongst both locals and tourists, and urban centers can become better equipped for generating resilience and innovation."

Creating place is an important aspect that determines how people feel about their city, community, or the neighborhood in which they live, work, and play. Kayegama (2011, 2014) cites some amazing projects that create a sense of place and community, including a love notes project, based on writing handwritten love notes that describe how a person feels about their community.

An important event promoting placemaking was a one night only event called Fall in Love on Main. This was a pop-up event for Valentine's Day, in Downtown Evansville, that offered two catered tasting sessions, a full bar, a chocolate vendor, and live music and dancing throughout the night (VOICE, 2020). Hundreds enjoyed an interesting and unique evening in Downtown Evansville because of the work of community leaders, business owners, and volunteers (VOICE, 2020). In February 2020, the Downtown Alliance, the division of the Southwest Indiana Chamber focused on downtown development and revitalization, created an opportunity to promote Downtown Evansville, and offer a unique experience by placing a lighted red heart on Main Street, and invited residents and pedestrians to take a photo inside the heart.

A special placemaking initiative that employs creative placemaking, emerging over the past decade, is located at Haynie's Corner in Evansville. Named after George Haynie, who owned a drug store in this area, Haynie's Corner is surrounded by four neighborhoods (Riverside, Culver, Goosetown, Blackford's Grove) that encompass the Haynie's Corner Arts District, where the corner meets at a fountain constructed in 1979 (Haynie's Corner, 2020).

Every first Friday of the month, Haynie's Corner hosts a mixture of live music, street performers, and vendors located around the fountain and outside the Alhambra theater, the historic Spanish style theater across from the fountain. The neighborhood's art galleries, boutiques, and retail spaces, as well as the neighborhood's restaurants and businesses, are open throughout the evening where everything comes alive (Haynie's Corner, 2020).

Another placemaking activity, using tactical urbanism, is an event in Louisville, known as CycLOUvia, where major streets in Louisville are shut down on a Sunday afternoon so that bikers, walkers, skaters, and joggers can use them in a safe, car-free environment (Kiger, 2016). The event began in 2016 by bike enthusiast, advocate, and former University of Louisville archivist, Louisville alderman, and Metro Council member Tom Owen. The festive community atmosphere of CycLOUvia is unparalleled, creating a festive community atmosphere that integrates "hard infrastructure" into new ways that connect residents to their urban environment (Kiger, 2016).

Figure 9.3.   CycLOUvia in the Highlands neighborhood, Louisville, KY. *Source:* Louisville Metro Government

Placemaking creates healthy communities with walkable neighborhoods that are compact and mixed-use. Placemaking helps the environment by creating public spaces that reduce our carbon footprint and our dependence on automobiles. Placemaking creates spaces that meet everyone's basic needs, while preserving historical, social, and cultural assets. Placemaking is about being authentic and the best version of what a community can be. Placemaking is about a city's unique identity and story. Placemaking is not solitary. It is a collaborative process, involving everyone, embracing a unique place, and envisioning what it could become.

How do we know placemaking is working? When we see greater investment and buy-in from all stakeholders and constituencies. When more housing is being built, more jobs are created, and more adaptive reuse projects are happening. When important quality-of-life indicators improve, such as low crime, good schools, infrastructure, and other amenities. Placemaking does not happen overnight but is created over time. People want places where they can live and thrive. Place matters. Placemaking matters. Everybody can contribute to making place. How will you make your place?

Conclusion

Lessons Learned in Community Development and Collective Impact

Community development is not conducted in a vacuum. Effective community development strategies, as we have explored in this book, do not assume community wants or needs; rather, the community itself serves as its own voice and writes its own story. The community is viewed as the expert in what its members need. Through self-reflection, collecting data, developing a community profile, doing a needs assessment, and engaging in a facilitated comprehensive community development initiative, goals, objectives, and strategies emerge from the community, to solve the problems of the community.

Over the years, positivist and postpositivist approaches have been used to analyze data or information. The positivist approach uses a scientific model focusing on facts or data only; whereas the current postpositivist approach recognizes the complexity of human observation, guided not solely by data (Hutchison, 2019). Although controversial, these approaches apply when working with communities. Past models emphasize a positivist or scientific approach in assuming that the outside so-called experts that only use data or technical expertise know what's best for a community. The current approach utilizes a contemporary postpositivist or postmodern approach, with emphasis on the community as the expert. The community developer acts as the guide to help hear individual and collective voices and narratives of community members (Hutchison, 2019).

Many challenges, failures, and lessons learned over time occur because a developer or a community organizer believes they alone know what the community wants or needs. Any community development project needs to have a goodness of fit for that community, rather than forcing a model that does not reflect the needs or desires of the community. On the other hand, there are comprehensive community development and collective impact initiatives where the residents and indigenous community leaders look to someone to assist them in their process. They believe nothing will happen without the help and assistance of the experts. A partnership, with the collaboration of experts and community input, needs to be built together (Hutchison, 2019).

It is a fine line to walk, and there is rarely a magic solution. Sometimes, the solution you think is going to work does not, while a solution for which you have doubts or suspicions may be the best choice. Even if collective impact and comprehensive community development efforts fail or do not get off the ground, the attempts bring a sense of hope and optimism to communities who believe that their lives and their futures can improve (Hanleybrown et al., 2012).

In this book, we shared the results of studies showing the effects of social capital at the program and neighborhood level, and several case studies that examined how social capital and social networks are enhanced by community development efforts. We examined the effects of strong and weak ties on community development, and whether communities with little to no social capital can build networks to enhance their chances for development. What are the levels and types of social networks and support in the community? What community development efforts help build and sustain social interaction that will generate trust and reciprocity? How does an increase in social capital impact civic participation and involvement in local voluntary organizations and how many? (Green & Haines, 2016) Some communities may include the recipients of the services themselves to serve on the board of the local neighborhood associations, or on the board of the CDC, or on the steering committee or planning development committee for the community development initiative.

Collaboration, with commitment and shared values, is key. In February 2018, I was appointed by Mayor Lloyd Winnecke of Evansville, Indiana, to serve as the Director of the Commission on Homelessness for Evansville and Vanderburgh County, whose goal is to advise the city and county on issues related to homelessness. As a joint commission, it has up to 25 members, which is a large commission, but many different stakeholders are at the table, including the chair of our Homeless Services Council of Southwest Indiana, the United Way of Southwestern Indiana (the largest collective impact organization in the region), and the executive directors of the four main homeless service providers in the area.

Evansville is effective in dealing with homelessness because of the intentional collaboration the Commission on Homelessness has with all the homeless service agencies throughout our community. It is impossible to deal with a crosscutting issue like homelessness through only one agency. It involves multiple agencies and stakeholders. One agency works on housing and feeds the most vulnerable and chronically homeless for one night or an extended period. Another agency works towards providing solutions to ending chronic homelessness through the Housing First approach, which advocates permanent supportive housing (PSH), while another agency only serves women and families. None of these agencies or organizations can accomplish their goals without the collaboration and commitment they have with other agencies in the community. This has been on full display while solving the chronic homelessness issues during the COVID-19 epidemic, where all the agencies and providers have come together and have worked with the City of Evansville and the Catholic diocese of Evansville to house homeless individuals who test positive for COVID-19 and are recovering from the virus in the Diocese of Evansville's retreat center.

Collaboration is not strong without trust. We've discussed the research from Putnam and others about the role of trust in building social capital, but the success of community development and collective impact initiatives cannot be accomplished without trusting the experts or facilitators you bring in, trusting one's neighbors and fellow community members, and trusting the collaborative process. Without trust, there is no ability to build the social capital necessary to change communities. Without trust, communication breaks down, which can result in lack of commitment to the process.

The strategic planning process for the University of Southern Indiana (USI) we discussed in chapter 6 is a perfect example of collaboration from all stakeholders and constituencies. When I co-convened USI's strategic plan in 2015, a former alumnus and chair of the pharmacology department at one of America's most prestigious medical schools emphasized the power of collaboration and interdisciplinarity in trying to solve or create solutions to cross cutting and cross-disciplinary issues facing the community. He said, "If the issue can only be solved by one discipline, then it's not big enough of a problem."

USI's strategic plan required total collaboration from many disciplines and viewpoints to achieve the goals. We convened a diverse steering committee of faculty, staff, alumni, students, parents, and community members. We organized workshops, meetings, and other planning exercises with multiple stakeholders and constituencies throughout the university, from executive-level administrators to low-level staff members. We sought input from all units and departments on our three strategic goals: excellence in learning for the entire USI community, access and opportunity by design, and purposeful and sustainable growth. Each unit and department on campus provided strategies and metrics on how we might achieve these three goals.

To move away from the model of working *for* the community as the hired experts (technical assistance), to a model working *with* the community (self-help), there must be an understanding of shared vision and power. In a community development context, who is in charge or who is in control often has a thankless, stressful, and cumbersome task. Sometimes, these community groups organize efforts and initiatives with too many leaders and not enough followers. What is important is who will own this process (the community) when the community developers leave or step away, and who will share the power among multiple stakeholders and constituencies. People with power often want prestige and credit for the work accomplished, which matters only to the individuals who want it or for whom it matters, and not always by the residents and the community itself. Lynn Miller Pease of Leadership Everyone in Evansville, Indiana, who we featured in chapter 7 as a collective impact case study, said, "It's amazing what we can accomplish when it doesn't matter who gets the credit."

A major component of these efforts involves passion, which is best shared by all stakeholders and constituencies. It involves a passion for the community members who have lived in the community for one or multiple generations, with strong roots but a passion and willingness to convene and work with a community to make a difference. This passion is real and shared among all residents, but the passion must exist in the leaders themselves, for without their passion and commitment, the rest of the community will not follow. Lori Reed in Glenwood may have been the "buzzing bee"; her passion for community development infected and impacted everyone in the neighborhood, but if that same passion for the community was not felt by Lucy Williams, the Glenwood Neighborhood Association president, then it would have been difficult for her neighbors to be passionate about the community development initiative and be motivated to change their neighborhood. At it's completion, will the neighbors feel satisfied and attached to their neighborhood, and will social capital grow as a result? At the end of the day, how we establish the process from beginning to end is critical towards the sustainability of a community development process and the overall future health of the community.

In our efforts, we learned about the power of facilitation and having the right training and the right facilitator necessary to best capture the thoughts, needs, and desires of the community. A good facilitator can balance these issues. While the Simplex method has been viewed by some as more adaptable to the corporate environment than a community development model, its effectiveness lies in the strength and skill of the facilitator, evident in the comprehensive community development initiatives in Glenwood, Jacobsville, and the East End of Henderson. The facilitator needs to work with the community, through a holistic process that includes residents and stakeholders. A good facilitator can take a proverbial horse to water but cannot make the horse drink.

With respect to social capital and community development, further research should focus on linking social capital to enhance communities that in some ways balance the growth of bonding social capital and the decline of bridging social capital (Halsted & Deller, 2015). Social capital is a necessary but not sufficient condition for economic development (Halsted & Deller, 2015), but chapter 4 adds to our understanding of social capital and economic development by examining its effects at the neighborhood and individual level.

No two communities are the same. While we have scratched the surface of our understanding of these topics, especially collective impact, we need to be mindful of paradigm-shifting seismic events that disrupt and transform our society and our communities. Due to the COVID-19 pandemic that began during the spring of 2020, our concept of community, and how we choose to initiate or create change in that community, has been disrupted. How we now approach and define community may be different going forward. However, good community development is open-minded, flexible, adaptable, and willing to make compromises in order to achieve the goal of improving and enhancing the quality of life of one's community. Community is what you make of it. Community matters. Community development matters. Building social capital matters. Making place matters.

References

Abiona, A., & Bello, W. N. (2013). Grassroots participation in decision-making process and development programmes as correlate of sustainability of community development programmes in Nigeria. *Journal of Sustainable Development 6*(3), 47–57.

Alinsky, S. (1971). *Rules for radicals: A practical primer for realistic radicals.* New York: Vintage Books.

Allen, J. A. (2011, March 10). "Memo to a divided church: Meet the Focolare." *National Catholic Reporter.* https://www.ncronline.org/blogs/all-things-catholic /memo-divided-church-meet-focolare.

Allison, M., & Kaye, J. (2015). *Strategic planning for nonprofit organizations: A practical guide for dynamic times* (3rd ed.). Hoboken, NJ: Wiley and Sons.

Almond, G. A., & Verba, S. (1963). *The civic culture: Political attitudes and democracy in five nations.* Princeton, NJ: Princeton University Press.

Alvarez, B. (2012). *Indiana school becomes the heart of the community.* Washington, DC: National Education Association Priority Schools Campaign. http:// priorityschools.org/engaged-families-and-communities/indiana-school-becomes -the-heart-of-a-community.

Ambrosius, J. D., Gilderbloom, J. I., & Hanka, M. J. (2010). Back to black . . . and green? Location and policy interventions in contemporary neighborhood housing markets. *Housing Policy Debate, 20*(3), 457–484.

AmeriCorps VISTA Campus (2021). *Thirteen lessons about poverty.* Washington, D.C.: Corporation for National and Community Service. https://www.vistacampus .gov/thirteen-lessons-about-poverty/.

Anzilotti, E. (2016, July 4). These whimsical parklets promote walkability. *City Lab.* https://www.citylab.com/solutions/2016/07/whimsical-parklets-spring-up-in covington-kentucky/489794/.

Aristotle. (2010). *Politics.* (C. Lord, Trans.) Chicago: University of Chicago Press.

Armstrong, K. (2008). Ethnography and audience. In P. Alasuutari, L. Bickman, & J. Brannen (Eds.). *The SAGE handbook of social research methods* (pp. 54–63). Thousand Oaks, CA: SAGE Publications.

Arrow, K. (1972). Gifts and exchanges. *Philosophy and Public Affairs, 1*(4), 343–362.

Audubon Kids Zone. (2020). *Five goals of AKZ*. https://www.audubonkidszone.com /our-values.

Axtell, R., & Tooley, M. (2015). The other side of hope: Squandering social capital in Louisville's HOPE VI. *Journal of Poverty, 19*(3), 278–304.

Bachrach, P., & Baratz, M. (1970). *Power and poverty*. New York: Oxford University Press.

Baker, B., & Johannes, E. M. (2013). Measuring social capital change using ripple mapping. *New Directions for Youth Development, 138*, 31–47.

Banerjee, D. (2008, July 31). *Justice-as-rights: Environmental justice and the human rights question*. Paper presented at the annual meeting of the American Sociological Association Annual Meeting, Sheraton Boston and the Boston Marriott Copley Place, Boston, MA. http://citation.allacademic.com/meta/p242680_index.html.

Banfield, E. C. (1958). *The moral basis of a backward society*. Glencoe, IL: The Free Press.

Baradaran, M. (2017). *The color of money: Black banks and the racial wealth gap*. Cambridge, MA: Harvard University Press.

Barakat, S., & Chard, M. (2002). Theories, rhetoric, and practice: Recovering the capacities of war-torn societies. *Third World Quarterly, 23*(5), 817–835.

Baron, R. A., & Markman, G. D. (2003). Beyond social capital: The role of entrepreneurs' social competence in their financial success. *Journal of Business Venturing, 18*(1), 41–60.

Barrett, E. J., Geisel, P., & Johnston, J. (2006). *The Ramona Utti Report: Impacts of the Ripley Arnold Relocation Program: Year 3 (2004–5)*. Paper prepared for the City of Fort Worth, Texas.

Bartram, S. (2014). Grassroots Placemaking. *Parks & Recreation, 49*(9), 14–15. Retrieved from https://www.nrpa.org/parks-recreation-magazine/2014/september /grassroots-placemaking/.

Basadur, M. S. (1999). *Simplex: A flight to creativity*. Buffalo, NY: The Creative Education Foundation.

Basadur, M. S. (2003). *Simplex process. An 8-step process that askes "How might we . . . ?" from problem finding to action taking*. Burlington, ON, Canada: Basadur Applied creativity, Inc.

Beaudoin, C. E. (2009). Social capital and health status: Assessing whether the relationship varies between blacks and whites. *Psychology & Health, 24*(1), 109–118.

Beaudoin, C. E. (2011). News effects on bonding and bridging social capital: An empirical study relevant to ethnicity in the United States. *Communication Research, 38*(2), 155–178.

Benhabib, J., & Spiegel, M. M. (1994). The role of human capital in economic development evidence from aggregate cross-country data. *Journal of Monetary Economics, 34*(2), 143–173.

Bergstrom, J. C., Cordell, H. K., Ashley, G. A., & Watson, A. E. (1990). Economic impacts of recreational spending on rural areas: A case study. *Economic Development Quarterly, 4*, 29–39.

Berry, B. J. L. (1992). *America's utopian experiments: Communal havens from long-wave crises.* Hanover, NH: Dartmouth College Press.

Berry, W. E. (1969). *The long-legged house.* Berkeley, CA: Counterpoint Press.

Besel, K., & Andreescu, V. (2013). *Back to the future: New urbanism and the rise of neotraditionalism in urban planning.* Lanham, MD: University Press of America, Inc.

Besser, L. M., Marcus, M., & Frumkin, H. (2008). Commute time and social capital in the U.S. *American Journal of Preventative Medicine, 34*(3), 207–211.

Bhattacharyya, J. (1995). Solidarity and agency: Rethinking community development. *Human Organization, 54*(1), 60–69.

Bhattacharyya, J. (2004). Theorizing community development. *Community Development: Journal of the Community Development Society, 34*(2), 5–34.

Block, P. (2008). *Community: the structure of belonging.* San Francisco, CA: Berrett-Koehler Publishers, Inc.

Blouin, D. D., & Perry. E. M. (2009). Whom does service learning really serve? Community-based organizations' perspectives on service learning. *Teaching Sociology, 37*(2), 120–135.

Bogart, W. T. (1998). *The economics of cities and suburbs.* Upper Saddle River, NJ: Prentice Hall.

Bohl, C. (2000). New urbanism and the city: Potential applications and implications for distressed inner-city neighborhoods. *Housing Policy Debate, 11*(4), 761–801.

Bolland, J. M., & McCallum, D. M. (2002). Neighboring and community mobilization in high-poverty inner-city neighborhoods. *Urban Affairs Review, 38*(1), 42–69.

Borzaga, C., & Defourny, J. (2001). *The emergence of social enterprise.* Florence, KY: Routledge.

Bourdieu, P. (1986). The forms of capital. In J. G. Richardson (Ed.), *Handbook of theory and research for the sociology of education* (pp. 241–258). Westport, CT: Greenwood Press.

Bozalek, V., & Biersteker, L. (2010). Exploring power and privilege using participatory learningand action techniques. *Social Work Education, 29*(5), 551–572.

Bradshaw, J. (1972). The concept of social needs. *New Society, 19*, 640–643.

Brazley, M. E. (2002). *An evaluation of residential satisfaction of HOPE VI: A study of the Park DuValle revitalization project.* Louisville, KY: University of Louisville.

Brazley, M. E., & Gilderbloom, J. I. (2007). HOPE VI housing program: Was it effective? *American Journal of Economics and Sociology, 66*, 433–442.

Brewer, P. (1986). *Shaker communities, Shaker lives.* Hanover, NH: University Press of New England.

Brewer, P. (1997). *Shaker communities.* In D. E. Pitzer, (Ed.) (1997). *American communal utopias.* Chapel Hill, NC: The University of North Carolina Press.

Brisson, D., & Usher, C. L. (2007). The effects of informal neighborhood bonding, social capital, and neighborhood context on homeownership for families living in poverty. *Journal of Urban Affairs, 29*(1), 65–75.

Brown, A. (Ed.). (2006). *Contested space: Street trading, public space, and livelihoods in developing cities.* Warwickshire, UK: ITDG Publishing, Inc.

Brown, A. & Weiner, E. (1985). *Supermanging: How to harness change for personal and organizational success.* New York: Mentor.

Brown, S. L. (Ed.). (2002). *Intentional community: An anthropological perspective.* Albany, NY: State University of New York (SUNY) Press.

Bryson, J. M. (2011). *Strategic planning for public and nonprofit organizations: A guide to strengthening and sustaining organizational achievement* (4th ed.). San Francisco, CA: Jossey-Bass.

Burby, R. J., & Rohe, W. M. (1989). Deconcentration of public housing: Effects on residents' satisfaction with their living environments and their fear of crime. *Urban Affairs Quarterly, 25*(1), 117–141.

Buron, L., Popkin, S. J., Levy, D. K., Harris, L. E., & Khaduri, J. (2002). *The HOPE VI resident tracking study: A snapshot of the current living situation of original residents from eight sites.* Washington, DC: The Urban Institute.

Caiazza, A., & Putnam, R. D. (2005). Women's status and social capital in the United States. *Journal of Women Politics and Policy, 27*(1/2), 69–84.

Calhoun, C. J. (1994). *Social theory and the politics of identity.* Cambridge, MA: Blackwell Publishing, Inc.

Campbell, D. E. (2000). Social capital and service learning. *PS: Political Science and Politics,* 641–645.

Caparo, J. (2013). Can successful community development be anything but comprehensive? *Shelterforce Magazine.* https://shelterforce.org/2013/07/17/can_success ful_community_development_be_anything_but_comprehensive/.

Carroll, M. C., & Smith, B. W. (2006). Estimating the economic impact of universities: The case of Bowling Green University. *The Industrial Geographer, 3*(2), 1–12.

Carroll, R. (2020, May 15). Interview about Audubon Kids Zone. Evansville, IN.

Carpiano, R. M., & Kimbro. R. T. (2016). Neighborhood social capital, parenting strain, and personal mastery among female primary caregivers of children. *Journal of Health and Social Behavior. 53*(2), 232–247.

Center for Urban and Public Affairs (CUPA). (2013). *Raider Country Creative Industries Economic Impact Analysis.* http://corescholar.libraries.wright.edu/cgi /viewcontent.cgi?article=1004&context=cupa_econdev.

Center for Urban Transportation Research (CUTR). (2000). *Community impact assessment: A handbook for transportation professionals.* Tampa, FL: Center for Urban Transportation Research, University of South Florida. https://www.cutr.usf .edu/wp-content/uploads/2012/08/CIA_handbook.pdf.

ChangingAging (2018, October 27). *Minka MAGIC homes and communities.* https:// changingaging.org/blog/minka-magic-homes-and-communities/

Chaskin, R. J., & Joseph, M. L. (2011). Social interaction in mixed-income developments. relational expectations and emerging reality. *Journal of Urban Affairs, 33*(2), 209–237.

Checkoway, B. (2013). Social justice approach to community development. *Journal of Community Practice, 21*, 472–486.

Christensen, K., & Levinson, D. (Eds.) (2003). *Encyclopedia of community, From the village to the virtual world* (Volumes I–IV). Thousand Oaks, CA: SAGE Publications.

Christenson, J. A., & Robinson, J. W. (Eds.). (1989). *Community development in perspective*. Ames, IA: Iowa State University Press.

Christian, D. L. (2007). *Finding community: How to join an ecovillage or intentional community*. Gabriola, BC: New Society.

Cisneros, H. G., & Engdahl, L. (Eds.). (2009). *From despair to hope: HOPE VI and the new promise of public housing in America's cities*. Washington, DC: Brookings Institution Press.

Clampet-Lundquist, S. (2004). Moving over or moving up? Short-term gains and losses for relocated HOPE VI families. *Journal of Policy Development and Research, 7* (1), 57–80.

Claridge, T. (2018). *What is linking social capital?* https://www.socialcapital research.com/what-is-linking-social-capital/.

Clark, J. (2013). *Hope for people or help for cities? HOPE VI at Liberty Green*. Master Thesis. Louisville, KY: University of Louisville.

Clark, J., & Negrey, C. (2017). Hope for cities or hope for people: Neighborhood development and demographic change. *City and Community, 16*(2), 169–188.

Clark, T., Lloyd, R., Wong, K. K., & Jain, P. (2002). Amenities drive urban growth. *Journal of Urban Affairs, 24*(5), 493–515.

Clift, K. M., Daniels, B. M., Fennell, E. P., & Whitehead, M. (1995). *Newport, Kentucky: A Bicentennial history*. Newport, KY: Otto Zimmerman and Son, Inc

Cohen, C. J. (2001). Social capital, intervening institutions, and political power. In S. Saegert, J. P. Thompson & M. R. Warren (Eds.), *Social capital and poor communities* (pp. 267–289). New York: Russell Sage Foundation.

Coleman, J. C. (1988). Social capital in the creation of human capital. *American Journal of Sociology, 94*, S95–S120.

Coleman, J. C. (1990). *Foundations of social theory*. Cambridge, MA.: Harvard University Press.

Collins, C. R., Neal, J. W., & Neal, Z. P. (2014). Transforming individual civic engagement into community collective efficacy: The role of bonding social capital. *American Journal of Community Psychology, 54*(3–4), 328–336.

Congress for the New Urbanism (CNU) (1993). *The Charter of the New Urbanism*. https://www.cnu.org/who-we-are/charter-new-urbanism.

Conn, S. (2014). *America against the city: Anti-urbanism in the twentieth century*. New York: Oxford University Press.

Cooper Marcus, C. (2006). *House as a mirror of self: Exploring the deeper meaning of home*. Berwick, ME: Nicolas-Hays, Inc.

Costa, D. L., & Kahn, M. E. (2003). Understanding the American decline in social capital, 1952–1998. *Kyklos, 56*(1), 17–46.

Coyle, D. J. (1993). *Property rights and the Constitution: Shaping society through land use regulation.* Albany: NY: SUNY Press.

Cramer, E. P., Brady, S. R., & McLeod, D. A. (2013). Building capacity to address the abuse of persons with disabilities. *Journal of Community Practice, 21*, 124–144.

Creative Placemaking for Comprehensive Community development. Building community resilience through placemaking. Columbia, MD: Enterprise Community Partners. https://community-wealth.org/sites/clone.communitywealth.org/files/downloads/building%20community_1.pdf.

Croninger, R., & Lee, V. (2001). Social capital and dropping out of high school: Benefits to at-risk students of teachers' support and guidance. *The Teachers College Record, 103*(4), 548–581.

Cunningham, J. L. (2001). Service-learning in faith-based programs for children and youth from low-income urban families. *Journal of Teaching Marriage and Families, 1*, 28–44.

Cunningham, L. E. (2001). Islands of affordability in a sea of gentrification: Lessons learned from the DC Housing Authority's HOPE VI projects. *Journal of Affordable Housing and Community Development Law, 10*(4), 353–371.

Cunningham, M. K., Popkin, S. J., & Burt, M. R. (2005, June). *Public housing transformation and the "Hard to house."* (Brief No. 9). Washington, DC: The Urban Institute.

Curley, A. M. (2010). Relocating the poor: Social capital and neighborhood resources. *Journal of Urban Affairs, 32*(1), 79–103.

Dagger, R., (1981). Metropolis, memory, and citizenship. *American Journal of Political Science, 25*(4), 715–737.

Dakhli, M., & De Clercq, D. (2004). Human capital, social capital, and innovation: a multi-country study. *Entrepreneurship & regional development, 16*(2), 107–128.

Dalton, R.J. (2005), The social transformation of trust in government. *International Review of Sociology, 15*(1), 133–154.

Deaton, A. (2003). *Health, income, and inequality.* National Bureau of Economic Research Reporter: Research Summary. Retrieved August 15, 2009.

DeFilippis, J. (2001). The myth of social capital in community development. *Housing Policy Debate, 12*(4), 781–806.

DePaola, T. (2014). Collaborating for social justice through service learning. *New Directions for Community Colleges, 165*, 37–47.

DeWolf, C. (2002, February 18). Why new urbanism fails. *Planetizen.* https://www.planetizen.com/node/42.

Diehl, D. (2019a, November 19). *Evaluation framework and annual report review.* Presentation given to the Promise Zone Governance Committee. Evansville, IN.

Diehl, D. (2019b). *Promise Zone annual report.* Evansville, IN: Diehl Consulting, Inc.

Diehl, D. (2020). *Results of 2019 Evansville Promise Zone community survey.* Evansville, IN: Diehl Consulting.

Direct Action Research Center (2016): Mission, history, and values. https://thedart center.org/our-mission-and-history-2/.

Dobbie, W., & Fryer, R. G. Jr. (2009). *Are high quality schools enough to close the achievement gap? Evidence from a social experiment in Harlem.* Cambridge, MA: Harvard University National Bureau of Economic Research (NBER) Working Paper 15473.

Dodd, E. P., Bryant, F. C., Brennan, L. A., Gilliland, C., Dudensing, R., & McCorkle, D. (2013). An economic impact analysis of South Texas landowner hunting operation expenses. *Journal of Fish and Wildlife Management, 4*, 342–350.

Doeksen, G. A., Johnson, T., Biard-Holmes, D., & Schott, V. (1998). A healthy health sector is crucial for community economic development. *The Journal of Rural Health,* 14, 66–72.

Donner, W., & Rodríguez, H. (2008). Population composition, migration anti Inequality: The influence of demographic changes on disaster risk and vulnerability. *Social Forces, 87*(2), 1089–1114.

Donovan, T., & Hoover, K. (2014). *The elements of social scientific thinking* (11th ed.). Boston, MA: Wadsworth Cengage Learning.

Douglas, A. J., & Harpman, D. A. (1995). Estimating recreation employment effects with IMPLAN for the Glen Canyon Dam region. *Journal of Environmental Management, 44*, 233–247.

Draughon, K., Hanka, M. J., Khayum, M., Opartny, M., Phillips, I., & Priest, R. (2012). *Impact of homeownership and affiliate experiences.* Evansville, IN: University of Southern Indiana, Center for Applied Research.

Dreher, C. (2002, June 6). Be creative—or die. *Salon.* https://www.salon.com /2002/06/06/florida_22/.

Dreier, P., Mollenkopf, J., & Swanstrom, T. (2014). *Place matters: Metropolitics for the twenty-first century* (3rd ed. revised). Lawrence, KS: University Press of Kansas.

Duany, A., Plater-Zyberk, E., & Speck, J. (2010). *Suburban nation: The rise of sprawl and the decline of the American dream* (10th anniversary ed.). New York: North Point Press.

Duany, A. (2019, June 12). *Principles of new urbanism.* Lecture given at the Congress of New Urbanism (CNU) 27 Conference, Louisville, Kentucky.

Durack, R. (2001). Village vices: The contradiction of new urbanism and sustainability. *Places Journal, 14*(2), 64–69. https://placesjournal.org/article/village-vices -the-contradiction-of-new-urbanism-and-sustainability/?cn-reloaded=1.

Durham, W., Hanka, M. J., McKibban, A., Priest, R., & Raymond, P. (2012). *Jacobsville Initiative: Neighborhood assessment report.* Evansville, IN: University of Southern Indiana, Center for Applied Research.

Działek, J. (2014). Is social capital useful for explaining economic development in Polish regions? *Geografiska Annaler; Series B, Human Geography, 96*(2), 177–193.

Economic Development Authority (2014, May 28). *Economic Development: A definition and model for investment.* https://www.eda.gov/tools/files/research-reports /investment-definition-model.pdf.

Edwards, C., & Imrie, R. (2015). *The short guide to urban policy*. Bristol, UK: Policy Press.

Eisinger, P. (2000). The politics of bread and circuses: Building the city for the visitor class. *Urban Affairs Review, 35*(3), 316–333.

Ellspermann, S. (2008). *USI community facilitation institute concept paper*. Unpublished manuscript. University of Southern Indiana, Evansville, IN: Center for Applied Research.

Ellspermann, S., Recker, G., & Kleindorfer, K. (2010, December 13). *PowerPoint presentation on a future USI community facilitation institute*. Evansville, IN: USI Division of Outreach and Engagement.

Ellwood, D. T., & Jencks, C. (2004). The spread of single-parent families in the United States since 1960. In D. P. Moynihan, T. M. Smeeding, & L. Rainwater, *The future of the family* (pp. 25–65). New York: Russell Sage Foundation.

Emery, M. E. (2013). Social capital and youth development: Toward a typology of program practices. *New Directions for Youth Development, 138*, 49–59.

Emery, M. E., & Flora, C. (2006). Spiraling-up: Mapping community transformation with community capitals framework. *Community Development: The Journal of the Community Development Society, 37*(1), 19–35.

Enfield, R. (2008, Spring). *Social capital and implications for positive youth development. Monograph*. 4-H Center for Youth Development, University of California-Davis. https://robertoigarza.files.wordpress.com/2009/04/art-social-capital-and-implications-for-positive-youth-development-enfield-2008.pdf.

Engbers, T. A., & Rubin, B. (2016). Policy recommendations for fostering economic development through social capital. Paper presented at the Urban Affairs Association Conference, San Diego, CA.

Engbers, T. A., Rubin, B., & Aubuchon, C. P. (2017). Social Capital and Metropolitan Economic Development. *Economic Development Quarterly, 31*(1), 37–49.

Engbers, T. A., Thompson, M., & Slaper, T. (2017). Theory and measurement in social capital research: *Social Indicators Research, 132*(2–1), 537–558.

Ennis, G., & West, D. (2010). Exploring the potential of social network analysis in asset-based community development practice and research. *Australian Social Work, 63*(4), 404–417.

Enterprise Community Partners. (2017). *Creative placemaking through comprehensive community development. Building community resilience through placemaking*. Columbia, MD: Enterprise Community Partners. https://www.enterprisecommunity.org/resources/creative-placemaking-community-developers-5901.

Erickson, B. H. (2001). Good networks and good jobs: The value of social capital to employers and employees (pp. 127–158). In N. Lin, K. Cook, & R. Burt (Eds.), *Social capital: Theory and research*. Brunswick, NJ: Transaction Publishers.

Erickson, D., Galloway, I., Cytron, N. (2012). Routining the extraordinary. In N. Andrews and D. J. Erickson (Eds.), *Investing in what works for America's communities*. San Francisco, CA: Federal Reserve Bank of San Francisco.

Etzioni, A. (1993). *The spirit of community. The reinvention of American society*. New York: Simon and Schuster.

Etzioni, A. (1996). *The new golden rule: Community and morality in a democratic society*. New York: Basic Books.

Euchner, C. C. (1998). *Playing the field: Why sports teams move, and cities fight to keep them*. Baltimore, MD: The Johns Hopkins University Press.

Evans, J. (2019, November 26). *Interview on the Dream Center, Jacobsville community development, and the Peacemakers program*. Evansville, IN.

Evansville Promise Zone. (2016, February 10). *PowerPoint Presentation on establishing a Promise Zone in the City of Evansville*. Evansville, IN: CK Newsome Center.

Eversley, M. (2006, December 20). Cities changing one-way streets back. *USA Today*.

Ferguson, R. F., & Dickens, W. T. (Eds.). (1999). *Urban problems and community development*. Washington, DC: Brookings Institution Press.

Field, J. (2017). *Social capital* (3rd ed.). New York: Routledge.

Fine, A. (2011). *Integrating high quality academic programs and supportive health, social, and community services*. Washington, DC: Center for Study of Social Policy.

Florida, R., Cushing, R., & Gates, G. (2002, August). When social capital stifles innovation. *Harvard Business Review*. https://hbr.org/2002/08/when-social-capital -stifles-innovation.

Florida, R. (2002). *The rise of the creative class, and how it's transforming work, leisure, community, and everyday life*. New York: Basic Books, Inc.

Florida. R. (2005). *Cities and the creative class*. New York: Basic Books, Inc.

Florida, R. (2014). *The rise of the creative class and how it's transforming work, leisure, community, and everyday life, revisited*. New York: Basic Books, Inc.

Focolare Movement. (2021). *About us*. https://www.focolare.org/en/chi-siamo/

Fowler, R. B. (1991). *The dance with community—the contemporary debate in American political thought*. Lawrence, KS: University Press of Kansas.

Freeman, J. B. (2012). *American empire: 1945–2000. The rise of a global power: The democratic revolution at home*. New York: Penguin Books, Inc.

Freire, P. (1970). *Pedagogy of the oppressed*. New York: Continuum.

Freire, P. (1973). *Education for critical consciousness*. New York: Sheed & Ward Ltd.

Friedmann, J. (2010). Place and place making in cities: A global perspective. *Planning Theory and Practice, 11*(2), 149–165.

Fukuyama, F. (1996). *Trust: The social virtues and the creation of prosperity*. New York: The Free Press.

Fulton, W. (1996). *The new urbanism: Hope or hype for American communities?* Cambridge, MA: Lincoln Institute of Land Policy.

Galster, G. C. (1987). *Homeowners and neighborhood investment*. Durham, NC: Duke University Press.

Galster, G. C., & Killen, S. P. (1995). The geography of metropolitan opportunity: A reconnaissance and conceptual framework. *Housing Policy Debate, 6*(1), 7–43.

Galster, G. C., & Mikelsons, M. (1995). The geography of metropolitan opportunity: A case study of neighborhood conditions confronting youth in Washington, DC. *Housing Policy Debate, 6*(1), 73–104.

Gaventa, J. (1980). *Power and powerlessness: Quiescent and rebellion in an Appalachian Valley.* Urbana, IL: University of Illinois.

Gazley, B., Bennett, T. A., & Littlepage, L. (2013). Achieving the partnership principle in experiential learning: The nonprofit perspective. *Journal of Public Affairs Education, 19*(3), 559–579.

Gilchrist, A. (2004). *The well-connected community: A networking approach to community Development.* Bristol: Policy Press.

Gilderbloom, J. H., Meares, W. L., & Squires, G. D. (2020) "Mama, I can't breathe." Louisville's dirty air has steep medical and economic costs, *Local Environment, 25*(8), 619–626.

Gilderbloom, J. H., Meares, W. L., & Squires, G. D. (2020). Pollution, place, and premature death: Evidence from a mid-sized city. *Local Environment, 25*(6), 419–432.

Gilderbloom, J. H., & Meares, W. L. (2020). How inter-city rents are shaped by health considerations of pollution and walkability: A study of 146 mid-sized cities. *Journal of Urban Affairs, 42*(6), 1–17.

Gilderbloom, J. I. (2008). *Invisible city: Poverty, housing, and new urbanism.* Austin, TX: University of Texas Press.

Gilderbloom, J. I., Brazley, M., Alam, M. A., Ashan, M. & Ramsey, S. (2002). *Newport's HOPE VI project baseline evaluation: Volume 1.* Louisville, KY: University of Louisville, Center for Sustainable Urban Neighborhoods.

Gilderbloom, J. I., Hanka, M. J., & Ambrosius, J. D. (2012). Without bias? Government policy that creates fair and equitable property tax assessments. *American Review of Public Administration, 42*(5), 591–605.

Gilderbloom, J. I., & Mullins, R. L. (2005). *Promise and betrayal: Universities and the battle for sustainable urban neighborhoods.* Albany, NY: SUNY Press.

Gilderbloom, J. I., & Hanka, M. J. (2006). *Newport's HOPE VI project evaluation: Volume IX.* Louisville, KY: University of Louisville, Center for Sustainable Urban Neighborhoods.

Gilderbloom, J. I., Hanka, M. J., & Lasley, C. B. (2008). Amsterdam: planning and policy for the ideal city? *Local Environment, 14*(6), 473–493.

Gilderbloom, J. I., Hanka, M. J., & Lasley, C. B. (2008). *Newport's HOPE VI project evaluation: Final Volume.* Louisville, KY: University of Louisville, Center for Sustainable Urban Neighborhoods.

Gilderbloom, J. I., Hargrove, E., & Canfield, J. (2014). *From blighted to beautiful: Covington HOPE VI Final Report.* Covington, KY: Housing Authority of Covington.

Glaeser, E. (2004). Review of Richard Florida's *Rise of the creative class. Regional Science and Urban Economics, 35*(5), 593–596.

Glickman, N. J., & Wilson, R. H. (2008, July 10). *Urban policy in the 21st century: Legacies of the Johnson administration.* Presentation at the American College Schools of Planning (ACSP) and Association of European Schools of Planning (AESOP) 4th Joint Congress, Chicago, IL.

Goetz, E. G. (2000). The effects of subsidized housing on communities. *Just in time research: Resilient communities.* Minneapolis, MN: Hubert H. Humphrey Institute of Public Affairs/University of Minnesota Extension Service.

Goetz, E. (2003). *Clearing the way: Deconcentrating the poor in urban America.* Lanham, MD: Rowman & Littlefield Publishers, Inc.

Goetz, E. (2010). Better neighborhoods, better outcomes? Explaining relocation outcomes in HOPE VI. *Cityscape: A Journal of Policy Development and Research, 12*(1), 5–31.

Gold, L. (2003). The roots of the Focolare Movement's economic ethic. *Journal of Markets and Morality, 6*(1), 143–159.

Gorby, C. (2019). New Harmony as an evolving commemorative environment. In B. Nicholson & M. Sabatino (Eds.), *Avant-garde in the cornfields: Architecture, landscape, and preservation in New Harmony* (pp. 65–103). Minneapolis, MN: University of Minnesota Press.

Gordon, P., & Richardson, H. W. (1998). *A critique of new urbanism.* Presented at the Meeting of the American Collegiate Schools of Planning (ACSP), Pasadena, CA). http://www.petergordon.us/urbanism.html#intro.

Gotham, K. F. (2003). Toward an understanding of the spatiality of urban poverty: The urban poor as spatial actors. *International Journal of Urban and Regional Research, 24*(3), 723–737.

Granovetter, M. S. (1973). The strength of weak ties. *American Journal of Sociology, 78*(6), 1360–1380.

Grant, J. (2011). Time, scale, and control: How new urbanism (mis)uses Jane Jacobs. In M. Page & T. Mennel (Eds.), *Reconsidering Jane Jacobs.* Chicago and Washington, DC: American Planning Association Planner Press.

Greely, A. (1997). Coleman revisited: religious structures as a source of social capital. *American Behavioral Scientist, 40*(5), 587–594.

Green, G. P. (2001). Amenities and community economic development—Strategies for sustainability. *Journal of Regional Analysis and Policy, 31*(2), 61–75.

Green, G. P., & Haines, A. (2016). *Asset building and community development* (4th and 7th ed.). Thousand Oaks, CA: SAGE Publications, Inc.

Gregory, H. Jr., Van Orden, O., Jordan, L., Portnoy, G. A., Welsh, E., Betkowski, J., Charles, J. W., & Di Clemente, C. C. (2012). New directions in capacity building: Incorporating cultural competence into the interactive systems framework. *American Journal of Community Psychology, 50*, 321–333.

Gress, T., Cho, S., & Joseph, M. (2016). *HOPE VI data compliation anaylsis.* Washington, DC: Office of Policy Development and research (PD&R) U.S. Department of Housing and Urban Development (HUD) and National Initiative on Mixed Income Communities. Case Western Reserve University.

Grummon, P. T. H. (2013). A primer on environmental scanning in higher education. *Planning for Higher Education, 41*(2), 69–74.

Habitat for Humanity International (2007). *Habitat homeowners.* Atlanta, GA: HFHI, Inc. http://www.habitat.org/homeowners.

Habitat for Humanity International (2020a). *About Habitat for Humanity.* Atlanta, GA: HFHI, Inc. http://www.habitat.org/about.

Habitat for Humanity International (2020b). *History of Habitat for Humanity.* Atlanta, GA: HFHI, Inc. http://www.habitat.org/about/history.

Habitat for Humanity International (2020c). *What is sweat equity?* Atlanta, GA: HFHI, Inc. https://www.habitat.org/stories/what-is-sweat-equity.

Habitat for Humanity International (2020d). *40 Facts about Habitat and housing.* Atlanta, GA: HFHI, Inc. https://www.habitat.org/stories/40-facts-about-habitat-humanity-and-housing.

Habitat for Humanity of Evansville. (2011). *Three-year evaluation report (2008–2010) of the Glenwood Community Development Initiative.* Evansville, IN: HFH Evansville.

Halpern, D. (2005). *Social capital.* Cambridge, UK: Polity Press.

Halsted, J. M., & Deller, S. C. (Eds.). (2015). *Social capital at the community level: An applied interdisciplinary perspective.* New York: Taylor and Francis.

Haman, L. (2010). Civic culture. In H. K. Anhiere & S. Toepler (Eds.), *International Encyclopedia of Civil Society.* New York: Springer. https://doi.org/10.1007/978-0-387-93996-4.

Hanka, M. J., Kumaran, M., & Gilderbloom, J. I. (2007, October). *Estimating the economic effects, consequences, and impacts of President Clinton's community economic empowerment programs: An analysis of Empowerment Zones in Enterprise Communities.* Paper presented at the 28th Annual Southern Industrial Relations and Human Resources Conference, Louisville, KY.

Hanka, M., & Gilderbloom, J. I. (2008, February 1). "Time to End One-Way Thinking." Louisville, KY: *The Courier-Journal.* http://sun.louisville.edu/ preservation /one-waystreetver12-012908-5B1-5D%20.pdf.

Hanka, M. J. (2009). *From vice to nice: A case study of the HOPE VI program in Newport.* Doctoral dissertation. Louisville, KY: University of Louisville.

Hanka, M. J., Gilderbloom, J. I., Meares, W. L., Khan, M., & Wresinski, K. (2015). Measuring job creation for HOPE VI: A success story for community development efforts. *Community Development: The Journal of the Community Development Society, 46*(2), 133–148.

Hanka, M. J., Valadares, K. J., & Bennett, L. L. M. (2015). Changing the landscape at the University of Southern Indiana through a locally developed, customized environmental scanning process. *Planning for Higher Education, 43*(2), 4–14.

Hanka, M. J., & Engbers, T. A. (2017). Social capital and economic development: A neighborhood perspective. *Journal of Public and Nonprofit Affairs, 3*(3), 272–291.

Hanleybrown, F., Kania, J., & Kramer, M. (2012). Channeling change: Making collective impact work. *Stanford Social Innovation Review*, 1–8.

Hanlon, J. (2010). Success by design: HOPE VI, New urbanism and the neoliberal-transformation of public housing in the United States. *Environment and Planning, 42*, 80–98.

Hanson, D. (2013, March 6). *Assessing the Harlem Children's Zone.* Washington, DC: The Heritage Foundation. Center for Policy Innovation. Discussion Paper No. 8.

Harlem Children's Zone (2020). *Our programs.* New York: HCZ. www.hcz.org.

Harper, C. R., Kupermine, G. P., Weaver, W. R., Enshoff, J., & Erickson, S. (2014). Leveraged resources and systems change in community collaboration. *American Journal of Community Psychology, 54*, 348–357.

Harrison, L. E., & Huntington, S. P. (2000). *Culture matters: How values shape human progress*. New York: Basic Books.

Harvey, D. (1997). The new urbanism and the communitarian trap. *Harvard Design Magazine*, *1*, 68–69. http://www.harvarddesignmagazine.org/issues/1/the-new -urbanism-and-the-communitarian-trap.

Harwood, R. C. (2015). *Putting community in collective impact*. Bethesda, MD: Harwood Institute for Public Innovation.

Hawkins, R. L., & Maurer, K. (2010). Bonding, bridging and linking: How social capital operated in New Orleans following Hurricane Katrina. *British Journal of Social Work*, *40*, 1777–1793.

Hayaloğlu, P. (2015). The impact of developments in the logistics sector on economic growth: The case of OECD countries. *International Journal of Economics and Financial Issues*, *5*(2), 523–530.

Hayden, D. (2002). *Redesigning the American dream: The future of housing, work, and family life* (Revised and expanded ed.). New York: W. W. Norton and Co.

Hayden, D. (2003). *Building suburbia. Green field and urban growth*, 1820–2000. New York: Pantheon Books.

Haynie's Corner Arts District. (2020). Evansville, IN: http://hayniescorner.com

Hays, R. A. (2002). Habitat for Humanity: Building social capital through faith-based service. *Journal of Urban Affairs. 24*(3), 247–269.

Hays, R., & Kogl, A. M. (2007). Neighborhood attachment, social capital building, and political participation: A case study of low- and moderate-income residents of Waterloo, Iowa. *Journal of Urban Affairs, 29*(2), 181–205.

Hebert, S., Vidal, A., Mills, G., James, F., & Gruenstein, D. (2001). *Interim assessment of the Empowerment Zones and Enterprise Communities (EZ/EC) Program: A progress report*. Washington, DC: U.S. Department of Housing and Urban Development, Office of Policy Development and Research (PD&R).

Heckman, J. J., Stixrud, J., & Urzua, S. (2006). *The effects of cognitive and non-cognitive abilities on labor market outcomes and social behavior* (No. w12006). Washington, DC: National Bureau of Economic Research.

Heenan, D. (2004). Learning lessons from the past or re-visiting old mistakes: Social work and community development in Northern Ireland. *British Journal of Social Work, 34*(6), 793–809.

Heiman, R. (2011). *A story of leadership: Southern Indiana Higher Education. How Evansville got a state university (almost in spite of itself)*. Evansville, IN: M.T. Publishing, Inc.

Hein, K., Hanka, M. J., & Gogel, T. (2013). *Engage Henderson evaluation*. Evansville, IN: University of Southern Indiana, Center for Applied Research.

Helliwell, J. F. & Putnam, R. D. (1995). Economic growth and social capital in Italy. *Eastern Economic Journal, 21*(3), 295–307.

Helms, M. M., & Nixon, J. (2010). Exploring SWOT analysis—where are we now? A review of academic research from the last decade. *Journal of Strategy and Management, 3*(3), 215–251.

Hendricks, P. (1998). Developing youth curriculum using the targeting life skills model. Ames, IA. Iowa State University Extension. (1998). http://www.extension . iastate.edu/4h/explore/lifeskills.

Hess, D. R. (1999). *Community organizing, building, and developing: Their relationship to comprehensive community initiatives.* COMM-ORG: The On-Line Conference on Community Organizing and Development. https://comm-org.wisc.edu /papers99/hesscontents.htm.

Hill, M. (2002). Network assessment and diagrams: A flexible friend for social work practice and education. *Journal of Social Work, 2*, 233–254.

Himmelman, A. (2002). *Communities working collaboratively for a change.* Minneapolis, MN: Himmelman Consulting Group.

Hinds, W. A. (1961). *American communities.* New York: Corinth.

Historic Evansville. (2020). http://www.historicevansville.com/jacobsville.php.

Holloway, M. (1966). *Utopian communities in America, 1680–1880.* Mineola, NY: Dover Publications, Inc.

Holmes, G. M., Slifkin, R. T., Randolph, R. K., & Poley, S. (2006). The effect of rural hospital closures on community economic health. *Health Services Research, 41*, 467–485.

Honadle, B. W. (2008). Federal grant programs for community development: Deja vu and policy paradoxes in an ill-fated initiative. *Journal of Public Budgeting, Accounting & Financial Management, 20*(1), 72–86.

Hondagneu-Sotelo, P., & Raskoff, S. (1994). Community service-learning: promises and problems. *Teaching Sociology, 22*, 248–254.

HOPE VI Study by University of Louisville. (2005, February). The Planning Report. https://www.planningreport.com/2005/03/03/hope-vi-study-university-louisville.

Hopkins, D., & Williamson, T. (2012). Inactive by design? Neighborhood design and political participation. *Political Behavior, 34*(1), 79–101.

Hoyman, M., and Faricy, C. (2009). It takes a village: A test of the creative class, social capital, and human capital theories. *Urban Affairs Review, 44*(3), 311–333.

Hustedde, R. J. (2016). Seven theories for seven community developments. In R. Phillips & R. H. Pittman (Eds.), *An introduction to community development* (2nd ed.). New York: Routledge.

Hutchison, E. D. (2019). *Dimensions of human behavior (person and environment)* (6th ed.). Thousand Oaks, CA: SAGE Publications.

Imbroscio, D. (2004). Fighting poverty with mobility: A normative policy analysis. *Review of Policy Research, 21*(3), 447–461.

Imbroscio, D. (2008). "[U]nited and actuated by some common impulse of passion": Challenging the dispersal consensus in American housing policy research. *Journal of Urban Affairs, 30*(2), 111–130.

Ivery, J. (2010). Partnerships in transition: Managing organizational and collaborative change. *Journal of Human Behavior in the Social Environment, 20*(1), 20–37.

Jackman, S. (2000). Models for ordered outcomes. http://web.stanford.edu/class /polisci203/ordered.pdf.

Jackson, A. P., & J. Sedehi. (1998). Homevisiting. *Journal of Social Work Education, 34*(2), 283–290.

Jacobs, J. (1961). *The death and life of great American cities.* New York: Random House, Inc.

Jacobsville five-year strategic plan. (2008). Evansville, IN: Jacobsville Area Community Corporation (JACC).

Jacobsville Neighborhood Revitalization Strategy Area (NRSA) plan. (2018). Evansville, IN: City of Evansville Department of Metropolitan Development.

Jacobsville redevelopment area plan. (2013). Evansville, IN: Jacobsville Area Community Corporation (JACC).

Jameson, J. K., Clayton, P. H., & Ash, S. L. (2013). Conceptualizing, assessing, and investigating academic learning in service learning. In P. H. Clayton, R. G. Bringle, & J. A. Hatcher (Eds.), *Research on service learning: Conceptual frameworks and assessment* (Vol. 2A, pp. 85–110). Sterling, VA: Stylus.

Janson, N. (2016). *It takes a village—but the village needs a vision: The role of the "quarterback" organization in comprehensive community development.* Cambridge, MA: Harvard's Joint Center for Housing Studies and NeighborWorks America.

Jennings, C. (2016). *Paradise now: The story of American utopianism.* New York: Random House, Inc.

Jobson, D. (2017, May 4). Is the *Harlem Children's Zone accomplishing its goal? Should HUD's Promise Zone initiative be the future of American public education.* New Haven, CT: Yale University Education Studies. http://debsedstudies.org/harlem-childrens-zone.

Johnson, D. E., Meiller, L. R., Miller, L. C., & Summers, G. F. (1987). *Needs assessment. Theory and methods.* Ames, IA: Iowa State University Press.

Johnson, J. A., Honnold, J. A., & Threlfall, P. (2011). Impact of social capital on employment and marriage among low-income single mothers. *Journal of Sociology & Social Welfare, 38*(4), 9–31.

Johnson, R. L., & Moore, E. (1993). Tourism impact estimation. *Annals of Tourism Research, 20,* 279–288.

Johnson, S. (1999). Applying social capital theory to needs assessment, social program development, and evaluation: A practitioner's perspective. *Administrative Theory and Praxis, 21*(1), 12–21.

Jones, B. L., Pomeroy, E. C., & McClain, S. (2009). University-community partnerships and community-based participatory research: One community's approach to enhance capacity in end-of-life and bereavement practice, research, and education. *Journal of Social Work in End-of-Life & Palliative Care, 5,* 94–104.

Jones, D. D., & Pitzer, D. E. (2012). *New Harmony, Then and Now.* Bloomington, IN: Quarry Press, an imprint of Indiana University Press.

Kania, J., & Kramer, M. (2011). Collective impact. *Stanford Social Innovation Review, 36*–41.

Kapucu, N., & Petrescu, C. (2006). Capacity building through service learning. *Academic Exchange, 132*–138.

Katz, P. (1994). *The new urbanism: Toward an architecture of community.* New York: McGraw Hill, Inc.

Katz, B., & Nowak, J. (2017). *The new localism: How cities can thrive in the age of populism*. Washington, DC: Brookings Institution Press.

Kaufman, J. E., & Rosenbaum, J. (1992). The education and employment of low-income black youth in white suburbs. *Educational Evaluation & Policy Analysis, 14*(3), 229–240.

Kawachi, I., Kennedy, B. P., Lochner, K., & Prothrow-Stith, D. (1997). Social capital, income inequality, and mortality. *American Journal of Public Health, 87*(9), 1491–1498.

Kayegama, P. (2011). *For the love of cities: The love affair between people and their places*. St. Petersburg, FL: Creative Cities Productions.

Kayegama, P. (2014). *Love where you live. Creating emotionally engaging places*. St. Petersburg, FL: Creative Cities Productions.

Kearns, K. P. (2000). *Private sector strategies for social sector success: The guide for strategy and planning for public and nonprofit organizations*. San Francisco, CA: Jossey Bass.

Keeter, S., Kennedy, C., Dimock, M., Best, J., & Craighill, P. (2006). Gauging the impact of growing nonresponse on estimates from a national RDD telephone survey. *The Public Opinion Quarterly, 70*(5), 759–779.

Keeter, S., Miller, C., Kohut, A., Groves, R. M., & Presser, S. (2000). Consequences of reducing nonresponse in a national telephone survey. *Public Opinion Quarterly, 64*(2), 125–148.

Kelkar, N. P., & Spinelli, G. (2016). Building social capital through creative placemaking. *Strategic Design Research Journal, 9*(20), 54–66.

Kent, E. (2011, April 20). *Place capital: The shared wealth that drives thriving communities*. https://www.pps.org/article/place-capital-the-shared-wealth-that-drives-thriving-communities.

Kent, E. (2013a, March 16). *Stronger citizens, stronger cities: Changing governance through a focus on place*. https://www.pps.org/article/stronger-citizens-stronger-cities-changing-governance-through-a-focus-on-place.

Kent, E. (2013b, September 4). *Toward place governance: what if we reinvested civic infrastructure around placemaking?* New York: Project for Public Spaces. https://www.pps.org/article/toward-place-governance-civic-infrastructure-placemaking.

Kent, E. (2014, March 13). *Social capital and placemaking. An interview with Ethan Kent*. New York: Project for Public Spaces, Inc. https://naturesacred.org/social-capital-and-placemaking-an-interview-with-ethan-kent/.

Kiger, P. J. (2016, October 31). *Placemaking for mid-sized cities: Rebuilding waterfront parks and "Bourbonism."* Chicago, IL: Urban Land Institute. https://urbanland.uli.org/planning-design/rose-center-fellows-share-lessons-placemaking/.

Kim, P. H., & Aldrich, H. E. (2005). Social capital and entrepreneurship. *Foundations and Trends in Entrepreneurship, 1*(2), 55–104.

Kingsley, G. T., & Corvington, P. A. (2000). *Case management and self-sufficiency: The challenge for HOPE VI*. Washington, DC: The Urban Institute.

Kingsley, G. T., & Fortuny, K. (2010). *Urban policy in the Carter administration*. Washington, DC: The Urban Institute. https://www.urban.org/sites/default/files/publication/28631/412091-Urban-Policy-in-the-Carter-Administration.PDF.

Kingsley, G. T., Johnson, J., & Petit, K. L. S. (2003). Patterns of Section 8 relocation in the HOPE VI program. *Journal of Urban Affairs, 25*(4), 427–447.

Kingsley, G. T., McNeely, J. B., & Gibson, J. O. (1997). *Community building: Coming of age*. Washington, DC: The Urban Institute and the Development Training Institute.

Kinsey, S. (2013). Using multiple youth programming delivery modes to drive the development of social capital in 4-H participants. *New Directions for Youth Development, 138*, 61–73.

Klacik, D. (2017, October 10). *Comprehensive community development and place-making for all Hoosier communities*. Presentation given at the Accelerate Indiana Municipalities (AIM) Ideas Summit 2017, Evansville, IN.

Klayko, B. (2016, September 27). Louisville's first parklet debuts at IdeaFestival, headed for Portland restaurant. *Broken Sidewalk*. https://brokensidewalk.com /2016/the-community-table-parklet/.

Kleber, J. (Ed.). (2001). *The encyclopedia of Louisville*. Lexington, KY: The University Press of Kentucky.

Kleinberg, B. (1995). *Urban America in transformation: Perspectives on urban policy and development*. Thousand Oaks, CA: SAGE Publications.

Kleit, R. G. (2001). The role of neighborhood social networks in scattered-site public housing residents' search for jobs. *Housing Policy Debate, 12*(3), 541–573.

Kleit, R. G. (2002). Job search networks and strategies in scattered site public housing. *Housing Studies, 17*(1), 83–100.

Kleit, R. G., & Rohe, W. M. (2005). Using public housing to achieve self-sufficiency: Can we predict success? *Housing Studies, 20*(1), 81–105.

Knack, S., & Keefer, P. (1997). Does social capital have an economic payoff? A cross-country investigation. *Quarterly Journal of Economics, 112*(4), 1251–1288.

Knight Soul of the Communities. Why people love where they live and why it matters: A national perspective. (2010). Miami, FL: The Knight Foundation, Inc.

Knoke, D., & Kuklinski, J. (1982). *Network analysis*. Thousand Oaks, CA: SAGE Publications.

Kolzow, D. (2009). Developing community leadership skills. In R. Phillips & R. Pittman. *Introduction to community development* (pp. 119–132). New York: Routledge.

Krätke, S. (2010). 'Creative Cities' and the rise of the dealer class: A critique of Richard Florida's approach to urban theory. *International Journal of Urban and Regional Research, 34*(4), 835–853.

Krosnick, J. A., Presser, S., Fealings, K. H., & Ruggels, S. (2012). *The future of survey research: Challenges and opportunities*. The National Science Foundation Advisory Committee for the Social, Behavioral and Economic Sciences Subcommittee on Advancing SBE Survey Research. National Science Foundation, Washington, DC.

Kunstler, J. H. (2004). The ghastly tragedy of the suburbs. TED presentation. Monterey, CA. https://www.ted.com/talks/james_howard_kunstler_the_ghastly_tragedy _of_the_suburbs/transcript?language=en.

Landes, D. S. (1998). *The wealth and poverty of nations: Why some are so rich and some so poor.* New York: W. W. Norton.

Lapin, J. D. (2004). Using external environmental scanning and forecasting to improve strategic planning. *Journal of Applied Research in the Community College, 11*(2), 105–113.

Lapin, J. D. (2014, July). Using external environmental scanning and forecasting to improve strategic planning. Workshop given at the Society for College and University Planning (SCUP) annual conference, Pittsburgh, PA.

Leadership Everyone (2021). *About Leadership Everyone.* https://leadershipevery one.org/about/

Ledwith, M. (2011). *Community development: A critical approach* (2nd ed.). Bristol, England: The Policy Press.

Lee, S., Linett, P., Baltazar, N., &.Woronkowicz, J. (2016, Novembeer). Setting the stage for community change: Reflecting on creative placemaking outcomes. Los Angeles, CA: Mortimer & Mimi Levitt Foundation https://levitt.org/ckeditor/user files/images/1478133733_Levitt_white-paper_setting-the-stage-for-community -change_creative-placemaking-outcomes-study_2016.pdf

Lees, L., Slater, T., & Wyly, E. (2008). *Gentrification.* New York: Routledge.

Leistritz, F. L. (1994). Economic and fiscal impact assessment. *Impact Assessment, 12,* 305–317.

Lelieveldt, H. (2004). Helping citizens help themselves: Neighborhood Improvement programs and the impact of social networks, trust and norms on neighborhood-oriented forms of participation. *Urban Affairs Review, 39*(5), 531–551.

Lepofsky, J., & Fraser, J. C. (2003). *Building community citizens: Claiming the right to placemaking in the city.* Urban Studies, 40(1), 127–142.

Levi, M. (1996). Social and unsocial capital: A review essay of Robert Putnam's *Making Democracy Work. Politics and Society, 24*(1), 45–55.

Levy, D. K., & Woolley, M. (2007). *Relocation is not enough: Employment barriers among HOPE VI families.* Washington, DC: The Urban Institute.

Lewis, T. (2004). Service learning for social change? Lessons from a liberal arts college. *Teaching Sociology, 32,* 94–108.

Light, I., Kwoun, I. & Zhong, D. (1990). Korean rotating credit associations in Los Angeles. *Amerasia, 16*(1), 35–54.

Linfield, K., & Posavac, E. (2018). *Program evaluation: Methods and case studies* (9th ed.). New York: Routledge.

Local Initiatives Support Corporation (2020). *About us.* www.lisc.org/section/about -us/.

Lockhart, W. H. (2005). Building bridges and bonds: Generating social capital in secular and faith-based Poverty-to-Work programs. *Sociology of Religion, 66*(1), 45–60.

Lofland, L. H. (2000). Urbanity, tolerance and public Space: The creation of cosmopolitans. In L. Deben, W. Heinemeijer, & D. van der Vaart (Eds.), *Understanding Amsterdam: Essays on economic vitality, city life and urban form* (pp. 143–160). Amsterdam, the Netherlands: Het Spinhuis.

Loflin, K. (2013, June 13). *Knight Foundation's Soul of the Community report*. Presentation given at the Southwest Indiana Speaker Series, Huntingburg, IN.

Logan, J., & Molotch, H. (1987). *Urban fortunes: The political economy of place*. Berkeley, CA: University of California Press.

London, S. (2002). *Organic democracy. On the political philosophy of John Dewey*. Unpublished manuscript.

Lorenzen, M. (2007). Social capital and localised learning: Proximity and place in technological and institutional dynamics. *Urban Studies, 44*(4), 799–817.

Louisville Metro Housing Authority (LMHA) (2020a). Park DuValle Revitalization. Louisville, KY: LMHA, Inc. http://www.lmha1.org/hope_vi/fact_sheet.php.

Louisville Metro Housing Authority (LMHA) (2020b). *Clarksdale HOPE VI Revitalization*. Louisville, KY: LMHA, Inc. http://www.lmha1.org/hope_vi/clarksdale_hope_vi_revitalization.php.

Louisville Metro Housing Authority (LMHA) (2020c). *Sheppard Square HOPE VI revitalization*. Louisville, KY: LMHA, Inc. http://www.lmha1.org/hope_vi/sheppard_square_hope_vi_revitalization.php.

Loury, G. (1977). A dynamic theory of radical income differences. In P. Wallace & A. LeMund (Eds.), *Women, minorities, and employment discrimination*. Lexington, Mass.: Lexington Books.

Lozier, G. G., & Chittipeddi, K. (1986). Issues management in Strategic Planning. *Research in Higher Education, 24*(1), 3–14.

Ludy, M. (2005). *The flower man*. Longmont, CO: Scribble and Sons Publishing.

Lukes, S. (1974). *Power: A radical view*. London: Macmillan Publishing.

Machlup, F. (2014). *Knowledge: Its creation, distribution and economic significance, Volume III: The Economics of Information and Human Capital*. Princeton University Press.

Majee, W., & Hoyt, A. 2013. Are worker-owned cooperatives the brewing pots for social capital? In V. Gonzales & R. G. Phillips (Eds.), *Cooperatives and community development* (pp. 111–124). New York: Routledge.

Mallach, A. (2009). *A decent home: Planning, building, and preserving affordable housing*. Chicago and Washington, DC: American Planning Association Planner Press.

Mannheim, K. (1952). The problem of generations. In K. Manheim (Ed.), *Essays on the sociology of knowledge* (pp. 276–320). London, Routledge.

Marcuse, P. (2001). The liberal/conservative divide in the history of housing policy in the United States. *Housing Studies, 16*(6), 717–736.

Maridal, J. H. (2013). Cultural impact on national economic growth. *The Journal of Socioeconomics, 47(c)*, 136–146.

Marini, M. (2004). Cultural evolution and economic growth: A theoretical hypothesis with some empirical evidence. *The Journal of Socioeconomics, 33*, 765–784.

Markusen, A. (2006). Urban development and the politics of the creative class: Evidence from the study of artists. *Environment and Planning A, 38*(1), 1921–1940.

Markusen, A., & Gadwa, A. (2010). *Creative placemaking*. White paper for Mayor's Institute on City Design. Washington, DC: National Endowment for the Arts. https://www.leoweekly.com/2011/09/rise-and-fall/.

Marshall, A. (2011, September 28). *Rise and fall: With demolition ahead, a look back at Sheppard Square's 70 years.* Louisville, KY: Louisville Eccentric Observer (LEO). Retrieved from https://www.leoweekly.com/2011/09/rise-and-fall/.

Martinson, M., Minkler, M., & Garcia, A. (2013). Honoring, training, and building a statewide network of elder activities: The California senior Leaders program (2002–2012). *Journal of Community Practice. 21L*, 327–355.

Maslow, A. H. (1943). A theory of human motivation. *Psychological Review, 50*(4), 370–396.

Massey, D. S., & Denton, N. A. (1993). *American apartheid: Segregation and the making of the underclass.* Cambridge, MA: Harvard University Press.

Masters, T., & Uelman, A. (2011). *Focolare: Living in a spirituality of unity in the United States.* Hyde Park, NY: New City Press.

Mathie, A., & Cunningham, G. (2003). From clients to citizens: Asset-based community development as a strategy for community-driven development. *Development in Practice, 13*, 474-486.

Mattessich, P. W. (2016). Social capital and community building. In R. Phillips & R. H. Pittman (Eds.), *An introduction to community development* (2nd ed.). New York: Routledge.

Mattessich, P. W., & Monsey, B. (1997). *Community building: What makes it work: A review of factors influencing successful community building.* St Paul, MN: The Wilder Foundation.

Maurer, R. (2000). *Building capacity for change sourcebook.* Maurer & Associates.

McAtee, C. (2019). The rib cage of the human heart: Philip Johnson's Roofless Church. In B. Nicholson & M. Sabatino (Eds.), *Avant-garde in the cornfields: Architecture, landscape, and preservation in New Harmony* (pp. 105–169). Minneapolis, MN: University of Minnesota Press.

McClelland, D. C. (1961). *The achieving society.* Princeton, NJ: Van Nonstrand.

McMahon, E. (2010). The place making dividend. *Planning Commissioners Journal, 80*, 16–17.

Meeks, S. (2016). *The past and future city: How historic preservation is reviving American's communities.* Washington, DC: Island Press.

Miller-Pease, L. (2015, August 4). Interview on Leadership Evansville and the VOICE visioning process. Evansville, IN.

Miraftab, F. (2004), Making neo-liberal governance: the disempowering work of empowerment. *International Planning Studies, 9*(4), 239–259.

Mobley, C. (2007). Breaking ground: Engaging undergraduates in social change through service learning. *Teaching Sociology, 35*(2), 125–137.

Montgomery, J. (2005). Beware 'the creative class:' Creativity and wealth creation revisited. *Local Economy, 20*(4), 337–343.

Moreland, J. J., Raup-Krieger, J. L., Hecht, M. L., & Miller-Day, M. M. (2013) The conceptualization and communication of risk among rural Appalachian adolescents, *Journal of Health Communication, 18*(6), 668–685.

Morris, M., & Frisman, L. K. (1987). The competent community revisited: A case study of networking in policy implementation. *Journal of Community Psychology, 15*, 29–34.

Morrison, J. L., & Held, W. G. (1989). Developing environmental scanning/forecasting systems to augment community college planning. *Virginia Community Colleges Association Journal, 4*(1), 12–20.

Narayan, D., & Nyamwaya. D. (1996). *Learning from the poor: A participatory poverty assessment in Kenya.* Environment Department Papers, Participation Series 34. Washington, DC: World Bank, Social Policy and Resettlement Division.

National Youth Leadership Council. (2008). *K–12 service-learning standards for quality practice.* http://www.nylc.org/sites/nylc.org/files/files/Standards_Oct2009-web.pdf.

Neal, J. (1977). *The Kentucky Shakers.* Lexington, KY: University Press of Kentucky.

Neckerman, K. M., & Torche, F. (2007). Inequality causes and consequences. *Annual Review of Sociology, 33,* 335–357.

Neethi, P., Kamath, A., & Paul A. M. (2019). Everyday place making through social capital among street vendors at Manek Chowk, Gujaratya, India. *Space and Culture,* 1–15.

Newcomer, K. E., Hatry, H. P., & Wholey, J. S. (Eds.). (2015). *Handbook of practical program evaluation* (4th ed.). Hoboken, NJ: John Wiley and Sons, Inc.

Newman, O. (1973). *Defensible space.* New York: Collier Books.

Nguyen, M. T., Rohe, W., Frescol, K., Webb, M., Donegan, M., & Han, H. (2016). Mobilizing social capital: Which informal and formal supports affect employment outcomes for HOPE VI residents? *Housing Studies, 31*(7), 785–808.

Nichols, L., & Winston. N. (2014). *Undergraduate students an applied sociologist: Community-based research addresses homelessness, Footnotes.* American Sociological Association.

Nicholson, B. (2019). The New Harmony Atheneum; White collage. In B. Nicholson & M. Sabatino (Eds.), *Avant-garde in the cornfields: Architecture, landscape, and preservation in New Harmony* (pp. 261–304). Minneapolis, MN: University of Minnesota Press.

Nicholson., B., & Crout, W. R., (2019). Frederick Kiesler's Grotto: A Promethean spirit in New Harmony. In B. Nicholson & M. Sabatino (Eds.), *Avant-garde in the cornfields: Architecture, landscape, and preservation in New Harmony* (pp. 171–225). Minneapolis, MN: University of Minnesota Press.

Nicholson, B., & Sabatino, M. (Eds.) (2019). *Avant-garde in the cornfields: Architecture, landscape, and preservation in New Harmony.* Minneapolis, MN: University of Minnesota Press.

Nisbet, R. (1953). *The quest for community.* Oxford, England: Oxford University Press.

O'Connor A. (1999). Swimming against the tide: A brief history of federal policy in urban communities. In R. F. Ferguson & W. T. Dickens (Eds.), *Urban problems and community development* (pp. 77–137). Washington, DC: Brooking Institution Press.

O'Sullivan, A. M. (1993). *Urban economics* (2nd ed.). Homewood, IL: Irwin.

Oh, Y., Lee, I. W., & Bush, C. B. (2014). The role of dynamic social capital on economic development partnerships within and across communities. *Economic Development Quarterly, 28,* 230–243.

Ohmer, M. L. (2008). Assessing and developing the evidence base of macro practice interventions with a community and neighborhood focus. *Journal of Evidence-Based Social Work, 5*(3–4), 519–547.

Ohmer, M. L. O., & Koff, W. S. (2006). The effectiveness of community practice interventions: A review of the literature. *Research on Social Work Practice, 16*(2), 132–145.

Oldenburg, R. (2002). *Celebrating the third place: Inspiring stories about the "Great Good Places" at the heart of our communities.* New York: Marlowe & Company.

Olsen, E. (2021). *An overview of mission statements.* Reno, NV: On Strategy. Retrieved from https://onstrategyhq.com/resources/mission-statements/.

Onyenemezu, C. E. (2014). The imperative of citizen's participation in community development. *Academic Research International, 5*(1), 209–215.

Onyx, J., & Leonard, R. J. (2010). Complex systems leadership in emergent community projects. *Community Development: The Journal of the Community Development Society, 46*(4), 593–510.

Osterling, K. L. (2007). Social capital and neighborhood poverty: Toward an ecologically grounded model of neighborhood effects. *Journal of Human Behavior in the Social Environment, 16*(1/2), 123–147.

Ostrom, E. (1990). *Governing the commons.* Cambridge: Cambridge University Press.

Ostrom, E., Gardner, R., & Walker, J. (1994). *Rules, games, and common-pool resources.* Ann Arbor, MI: The University of Michigan Press.

Owen, D. (2020, April 24). "Construction at Ovation site in Newport ongoing; goal is completion of music venue by end of 2020." *Northern Kentucky Tribune.* https://www.nkytribune.com/2020/04/construction-at-ovation-site-in-newport-ongoing-goal-is-completion-of-music-venue-by-end-of-2020/.

Painter, M. A., & Paxton, P. (2014). Checkbooks in the heartland: change over time in voluntary association membership. *Eastern Sociological Society, 29*(2), 408–428.

Patterson, J. T. (1994). *America's struggle against poverty, 1900–1994.* Cambridge, MA: Harvard University Press.

Paxton, P. (1999). Is social capital declining in the United States? A multiple indicator assessment. *American Journal of Sociology, 105*(1), 88.

Pearson, D. E. (1995). Community and sociology. *Society, 32*(5), 44–50.

Peck, J. (2005). Struggling with the creative class. *International Journal of Urban and Regional Research, 29*(4), 740–770.

Pendall, R., & Hendey, L. (2013). *A brief look at the early implementation of Choice Neighborhoods.* Washington, DC: The Urban Institute.

Phillips, I., Bennett, S., Opartny, M., Priest, R., & Khayum, M. (2008). *Habitat for Humanity of Evansville impact study.* Evansville, IN: University of Southern Indiana, Center for Applied Research.

Phillips, R., & Pittman, R. H. (Eds.). (2015). *An introduction to community development* (2nd ed.). New York: Routledge.

Phipps, D. J., & Shapson, S. (2009). Knowledge mobilization builds local research collaboration for social innovation. *Evidence & Policy, 5*(3), 211–227.

Pillisuk, M., McAllister, J., & Rothman, J. (1996). Coming together for action: The challenge of contemporary grassroots community organizing. *Journal of Social Issues, 52*(1), 15–37.

Pitcoff, W. (1999). New hope for public housing? *Shelterforce Magazine, 21*(2), 18–22.

Pitzer, D. E. (Ed.). (1997). *America's communal utopias.* Chapel Hill, NC: The University of North Carolina Press.

Placemaking assessment tool. (2015). East Lansing, MI: Michigan State University Land Policy Institute. https://www.canr.msu.edu/landpolicy/uploads/files /Resources/Tools/MIplace_Partnership_Initiative/PlacemakingAssessmentTool _LPI_WCAG2.0_updated_041515.pdf.

Plotkin, W. (2001, Spring). "Hemmed in:" The struggle against racial restrictive covenants and deed restrictions in post-WWII Chicago. *Journal of the Illinois State Historical Society,* 1–18.

Polgar, M. (2008). *Teaching sociology of homelessness and poverty in the United States.* Paper presented at the annual meeting of the American Sociological Association Annual Meeting, Sheraton Boston and the Boston Marriott Copley Place, Boston, MA.

Pollner, L. (2002). The HOPE VI program: Developing social capital and community in public housing. Unpublished paper.

Popkin, S. J., Buron, L. F., Levy, D. K., & Cunningham, M. K. (2000). The Gautreaux legacy: What might mixed income and dispersal strategies mean for the poorest public housing tenants. *Housing Policy Debate, 11*(4), 911–942.

Popkin, S. J., & Cunningham, M. K. (1999). *CHAC, Inc. Section 8 program: Barriers to successful leasing up.* Washington, DC: Urban Institute.

Popkin, S. J., & Cunningham, M. K. (2000). *Searching for rental housing with Section 8 in Chicago.* Washington, DC: Urban Institute.

Popkin, S. J. (2002). *The HOPE VI Program—What about the residents?* Washington, DC: The Urban Institute. http://www.urbaninstitute.org/UploadedPDF/310593 _HopeVI. pdf

Popkin, S. J., & Cunningham, M. K. (2005). Beyond the projects: Lessons from public housing transformation. In X. de Souza Briggs (Ed.), *Chicago in the geography of opportunity, race and housing choice in metropolitan America* (pp. 176–196). Washington, DC: Brookings Institution Press.

Popkin, S. J., Theodos, B., Roman, C., Guernsey, E., & Getsigner, L. (2008). *The Chicago family case management demonstration: Developing a new model for serving "hard to house" public housing families.* Washington, DC: The Urban Institute.

Popkin, S. J., Katz, B., Cunningham, M. K., Brown, K. D., Gustafson, J., & Turner, M. (2004). *A decade of HOPE VI: Research findings and policy challenges.* Washington, DC: The Urban Institute and The Brookings Institution.

Popkin, S. J., Levy, D., Harris, L., Comey, J., Cunningham, M., & Buron, L. (2004). The HOPE VI program: What about the residents? *Housing Policy Debate, 15*(2), 385–414.

Portes, A. (1998). Social capital: Its origins and applications in modern sociology. *Annual Review of Sociology, 24*, 1–24.

Portney, K. E., & Berry, J. M. (1997). Mobilizing minority communities: Social capital and participation in urban neighborhoods. *American Behavioral Scientist, 40*(5), 632–645.

Project for Public Spaces (PPS) (2020). *The power of 10+*. New York: PPS, Inc. https://www.pps.org/article/the-power-of-10.

Putnam, R. D. (1993). The prosperous community: Social capital and public life. *The American Prospect, 4*(13), 35–42.

Putnam, R. D. (1995). Bowling alone: America's declining social capital. *Journal of Democracy, 6*(1), 65–78.

Putnam, R. D. (2000). *Bowling alone: The collapse and revival of American community*. New York: Simon and Schuster.

Putnam, R. D (2001). Social capital: Measurement and consequences. *Canadian Journal of Policy Research,* 2(1), 41–51.

Putnam, R. D., & Feldstein, L. M. (2003). *Better together: Resolving the American community*. New York: Simon and Schuster.

Putnam, R. D., Leonardi, R., & Nanetti, R. Y. (1993). *Making democracy work: Civic traditions in modern Italy*. Princeton University Press.

Raffel, J. A., Denson, L., Varady, D., & Sweeney, L. (2003). *Linking housing and public schools in the HOPE VI public housing revitalization program: A case study analysis of four developments in four cities*. Newark, DE: University of Delaware School of Urban Affairs and Public Policy.

Raiser, M., Haerpfer, C., Nowotny, T., & Wallace, C. (2002). Social capital in transition: A first look at the evidence. *Sociologický časopis/Czech Sociological Review, 38*(6), 693–720.

Rankin, B. H., & Quane, J. M. (2000). Neighborhood poverty and the social isolation of inner-city African American families. *Social Forces, 79(*1), 139–164.

Recker, G., & Reed, L. (2013). *Shaping the future through learning and innovation: A case for the Center for Collective Impact*. Unpublished paper. University of Southern Indiana Division of Outreach and Engagement, Evansville, IN.

Reed, L. (2015, July 28). Interview on comprehensive community development. Evansville, IN.

Reed, S., Rosenberg, H., Statham, A., & Rosing, H. (2015). The effect of community service learning on undergraduate persistence in three institutional contexts. *Michigan Journal of Community Service Learning,* Spring, 22–36.

Reid, C. K. (2007). Locating the American dream—Assessing the neighborhood benefits of homeownership. In W. M. Rohe & H. L. Watson (Eds.), *Chasing the American dream: New perspectives on affordable homeownership* (pp. 233–277). Ithaca, NY: Cornell University Press.

Renault, V. (2010) *Community tool box: SWOT analysis: strengths, weaknesses, opportunities, and threats*. Lawrence, KS: University of Kansas Center for Community Health and Development. https://ctb.ku.edu/en/table-of-contents/assessment /assessing-community-needs-and-resources/swot-analysis/main.

Richardson, H. W. (1985). Input-output and economic base multipliers: Looking backward and forward. *Journal of Regional Science, 25*, 607–661.

Riggs, W., & Gilderbloom. J. I. (2016). Two-way street conversion: Evidence of increased livability in Louisville. *Journal of Planning Education and Research. 36*(1), 105–118.

Robinson, J. W., Jr. (1989). The conflict approach. In J. A. Christenson and J. W. Robinson, Jr. (Eds.). *Community development in perspective*. Ames, IA: Iowa State University Press.

Robinson, J., & Godbey, G. (1997). *Time for Life: The surprising ways Americans use their time* (2nd ed.). University Park, PA: Pennsylvania State University Press.

Robinson, J. P., & Martin, S. (2010). IT use and declining social capital? More cold water from the General Social Survey (GSS) and the American Time-Use Survey (ATUS). *Social Science Computer Review, 28*(1), 45–63.

Robison, L. J., Seles, M. E., & Jin, S. (2011). Social capital and the distribution of household income in the United States: 1980, 1990, 2000. *Journal of Socioeconomics, 40*, 538–547.

Rockfellow, J. D. (1994). Wild cards: Preparing for the big one. *The Futurist, 28*(1), 1–14.

Rode, S. A. (2018). *George Rapp: Thoughts on the destiny of man, particularly with reference to the present times by the Harmony Society in Indiana, A.D. 1824.* Indianapolis, IN: IUPUI Max Kade German American Center.

Rode, S. A. (2019, October 11). *Harmonist society in theory and practice, or socialism and capitalism under God.* Presentation at the Atheneum 40th Anniversary Celebration Speaker Series, New Harmony, IN.

Rodrik, D., Subramanian, A., & Trebbi, F. (2004). Institutions rule: the primacy of institutions over geography and integration in economic development. *Journal of Economic Growth, 9*(2), 131–165.

Rogers, S. H., & Jarema, P. M. (2015). A brief history of social capital research. In J. M. Halsted & S. C. Deller (Eds.), *Social capital at the community level. An applied interdisciplinary perspective* (pp. 14–30). New York and London: Routledge Taylor & Francis Group.

Rohe, W. M., & Kleit, R. (1997). From dependency to self-sufficiency: An appraisal of the gateway transitional families program. *Housing Policy Debate, 7*, 75–108.

Rohe, W. M., & Stegman, M. (1994). The effects of homeownership on the self-esteem, perceived control, and life satisfaction of low-income people. *Journal of the American Planning Association, 60*(1), 173–184.

Rohe, W. M., & Watson, H. L. (Eds.). (2007). *Chasing the American dream: New perspectives on affordable homeownership.* Ithaca, NY: Cornell University Press.

Rohe, W. M., Van Zandt, S., McCarthy, G. (2001). *The social benefits and costs of homeownership: A critical assessment of the research* (Working Paper LIHO-01.12). Cambridge, MA: Joint Center for Housing Studies, Harvard University.

Rose, A. (1995). Input-output economics and computable general equilibrium models. *Structural Change and Economic Dynamics, 6*, 295–304.

Rosenbloom, J. E., & Popkin, S. J. (1990). *Economic and social impacts of housing integration.* Evanston, IL: Northwestern University, Center for Urban Affairs and Policy Research.

Rosenbaum, J. E. (1991). Black pioneers: Do their moves to the suburbs increase economic opportunity for mothers and children? *Housing Policy Debate 2*(4), 1179–1214.

Rosenbaum, J. E. (1995). Changing the geography of opportunity by expanding residential choice: Lessons from the Gautreaux program. *Housing Policy Debate, 6*(1), 231–269.

Rosenbaum, E., & Harris, L. E. (2001). Low-income families in their new neighborhoods: The short-term effects of moving from Chicago's public housing. *Journal of Family Issues, 22*(2), 183–210.

Ross, B. (2015). *Dead end: Suburban sprawl and the rebirth of American urbanism.* New York: Oxford University Press.

Ross, C. E. (2000). Neighborhood disadvantage and adult depression. *Journal of Health and Social Behavior, 41,* 177–187.

Rossi, P. H., Lipsey, M., & Freeman, H. E. (2004). *Evaluation, a systematic approach* (7th ed.). Thousand Oaks, CA; Sage Publications

Rothstein, R. (2017a). *The color of law: A forgotten history of how our government segregated America.* New York: W. W. Norton.

Rothstein, R. (2017b, May 17). *'The Color of Law'* details how *U.S. housing policies created segregation.* Interview by Ari Shapiro on All Things Considered. Washington, DC: National Public Radio (NPR).

Rotuman, J., & Gant, L. M. (1987). Approaches and models of community intervention. In D. E. Johnson, L. R. Meiller, L. C. Miller & G. F. Summers (Eds.), *Needs assessment: Theory and methods.* Ames, IA: Iowa State University Press.

Royle, E. (2003). *Robert Owen.* In K. Christensen & D. Levinson (Eds.), *Encyclopedia of community, From the village to the virtual world* (Volume III, pp. 1051–1052). Thousand Oaks, CA: SAGE Publications.

Rubin, H. J. (2000). *Renewing hope; within neighborhoods of despair: The community-based development model.* Albany, NY: State University of New York Press.

Rubio, M. (1997). Perverse social capital: Some evidence from Colombia. *Journal of Economic Issues, 31*(3), 805–816.

Rupasingha, A., Goetz, S. J., & Freshwater, D. (2002). Social and institutional factors as determinants of economic growth: Evidence from the United States counties. *Papers in Regional Science, 81*(2), 139–155.

Ruskay, S. (2012). How to turn a year of service into a lifetime of commitment: A case study of AVODAH: The Jewish Service Corps, *Journal of Jewish Communal Service. 87,* 113–121.

Ryan, L. A. (2003). Exploring poverty: Classroom activities combined with service learning, *Journal of Teaching in Marriage and Family, 3,* 85–101.

Sabatini, F. (2005). *Social capital as social networks: A new framework for measurement,* Working Paper no. 83, Department of Public Economics, Universitia di Roma la Sapienza, Rome, Italy.

Saegert, S., Thompson, J. P., & Warren, M. R. (Eds). (2001). *Social capital and poor communities.* New York: Russell Sage Foundation.

Safford, S. (2009). *Why the garden club couldn't save Youngstown: The transformation of the rust belt.* Cambridge, MA: Harvard University Press.

Salama, J. J. (1999). The redevelopment of distressed public housing: Early results from HOPE VI projects in Atlanta, Chicago, and San Antonio. *Housing Policy Debate, 10*(1), 95–142.

Sales, W. W. Jr., & Bush, R. (2000). The political awakening of Blacks and Latinos in New York City: Competition or cooperation? *Social Justice, 27*(1), 19–42.

Sander, T. H., & Putnam, R. D. (2010). Still Bowling Alone? The Post-9/11 Split. *Journal of Democracy, 21*(1), 9–16.

Sander, T. H. (2002). Social capital and new urbanism: Leading a civic horse to water? *National Civic Review, 91*(3), 213–234.

Sanders, I. T. (1958). Theories of community development. *Rural Sociology, 23*(1), 1–12.

Santiago, A. M., & Galster, G. C. (2004). Moving from public housing to home-ownership: Perceived barriers to program participation and success. *Journal of Urban Affairs, 26*(3), 297–324.

Saunders, J. A., & Marchik, B. M. A. (2007). Building community capacity to help persons with mental illness: A program evaluation. *Journal of Community Practice, 15*(4), 73–96.

Schnurbein, G. V. (2014). Managing organizational social capital through value configurations. *Nonprofit Management and Leadership, 24*(3), 357–376.

Schutt, R. K., (2015). *Investigating the social world: The process and practice of research* (8th ed.). Thousand Oaks, CA: SAGE Publications.

Schwadel, P., & Stout, M. (2012). Age, period, and cohort effects on social capital. Social Forces, *91*(1), 233–252.

Schwartz, A., & Tajbakhsh, K. (1997). Mixed-income housing; unanswered questions. Cityscape, *3*(2), 71–92.

Schwartz, A. F. (2015). *Housing policy in the United States: An introduction* (3rd ed.). New York: Routledge Press.

Seider, S. C., Rabinowicz, S. A., & Gillmor, S. C. (2010). Changing American college students' conceptions of poverty through community service learning. *Analyses of Social Issues and Public Policy, 10*(1), 215–236.

Sennett, R. (1992). *The fall of public man.* New York: W. W. Norton & Company.

Seymore, B. (2015, July 16). *Interview on Engage Henderson.* Evansville, IN.

Seymore, B. (2020, May 22). *Phone conversation on Engage Henderson and Audubon Kids Zone,* Evansville, IN.

Sharp, E. B. (2005). Cities and subcultures: Exploring validity and predicting connections. *Urban Affairs Review, 41*(2), 132–156.

Shibley, R. G. (1998). The complete New urbanism and the partial practices of place-making. *Utopian Studies, 9*(1), 80–102.

Siegel, D. I. (2011). The role of the neighborhood in making welfare reform possible. *Journal of Sociology & Social Welfare, 38*(3), 123–150.

Siegel, P. B., & Leuthold, F. O. (1993). Economic and fiscal impacts of a retirement/recreation community: A study of Tellico Village, Tennessee. *Journal of Agriculture and Applied Economics, 25,* 134–147.

Silberberg, S. (2013). *Places in the making: How placemaking builds places and communities.* Department of Urban Studies and Planning. Massachusetts Institute of Technology, Cambridge, MA.

Society for Human Resource Management. (2012). *Strategic planning: What are the basics of environmental scanning?* http://www.shrm.org/ templates/tools/hrqa /pages/cms_021670.aspx.

Sousa, F., Pellissier, R., & Monteiro, I. (n.d.). *Creativity and problem solving in the development of organizational innovation.* Unpublished manuscript.

Speck, J. (2018). *Walkable city rules: 101 steps to making better places.* Washington, DC: Island Press.

Squires, G. D. (Ed.). (2002). *Urban sprawl: Causes, consequences, and policy responses.* Washington, DC: The Urban Institute Press.

Stadtler, L., & Probst, G. (2012). How broker organizations can facilitate public-private partnerships for development. *European Management Journal, 30*(1), 32–46.

Steffensmeier, D., & Ulmer, J. T. (2006). Black and white control of numbers gambling: A cultural asset—social capital view. *American Sociological Review, 71*(1), 123–156.

Stone, R. (2020. November 6). Personal e-mail communication.

Stone, R., Dailey, A., Barbee, A. P., & Patrick, D. (2011). *Clarksdale HOPE VI Community Supportive Services Program evaluation. How do former Clarksdale residents fare after relocation?* Unpublished evaluation. Louisville, KY:

Stone, R., Vanderpool, R. C., Barbee, A. P., & Patrick, D. (2011). Quality of life in Clarksdale public housing before HOPE VI. *Revista de Asistenta Sociala, anul x, 1,* 89–105.

Stoutland, S. E. (1999). Community development corporations: Mission, strategy, and accomplishments. In R. F. Ferguson & W. T. Dickens (Eds.), *Urban problems and community development* (pp. 193–240). Washington, DC: Brookings Institution Press.

Sullivan, H., Barnes, M., & Matka, E. (2002). Building collaborative capacity through 'theories of change.' *Evaluation, 8*(2), 205–226.

Summers, G. F. (1987). Democratic governance. In D. E. Johnson, L. R. Meiller, L. C. Miller, & G. F. Summers (Eds.), *Needs assessment. Theory and methods.* Ames, IA: Iowa State University Press.

Szreter, S., & Woolcock, M. (2004). Health by association? Social capital, social theory, and the political economy of public health. *International Journal of Epidemiology, 33,* 650–667.

Talen, E. (1999). Sense of community and neighborhood form: An assessment of the social doctrine of New Urbanism. *Urban Studies, 36(*8), 1361–1379.

Tedeschi, B. (2018, January 4). A physician homebuilder tries to upend the nursing home industry—and give seniors back their independence. Stat News. https:// www.statnews.com/2018/01/04/minka-homes-seniors-bill-thomas/.

Temkin, K., & Rohe, W. (1998). Social capital and neighborhood stability: An empirical investigation. *Housing Policy Debate, 9*(1), 61–88.

Tesdahl, E. A. (2015). More than the sum of its parts: cooperation and mutual commitment inmulti-issue congregation-based community organizing. *Sociological Inquiry, 85*(1), 148–171.

The Planning Report. (2005, February). *HOPE VI study by University of Louisville.* https://www.planningreport.com/2005/03/03/hope-vi-study-university-louisville.

Thissen, M. (2020, May 22). E-mail correspondence on the Simplex method.

Thomas, E., Pate, S., & Ranson, A. (2015). The Crosstown Initiative: Art, community, and placemaking in Memphis. *American Journal of Community Psychology, 55*(1–2), 74–88.

Thomas, J. B., & McDaniel, R. R. (1990). Interpreting strategic issues: Effects of strategy and the information-processing structure of top management teams. *Academy of Management Journal, 33*(2), 286–306.

Thomas, W. H. (2006). *In the arms of elders: A parable of wise leadership and community building.* St. Louis, MO; VanderWyk & Burnham.

Thompson, M. (2006). Relocating from the distressed public housing on the difficulties of the private market: How the move threatens to push families away from opportunity. *Journal of Law and Social Policy, 1*(1), 1–32.

Tighe, J. R. (2012). How race and class stereotyping shapes attitudes toward affordable housing. *Housing Studies, 27*(7), 962–983.

Tocqueville, A. de. (1966). *Democracy in America.* J. P. Meyer & Max Lerner (Eds.). New York: Harper & Row Publishing.

Trigilia, C. (2001). Social capital and local development. *European Journal of Social Theory, 4*(4), 427–442.

Turner, M. A., Woolley, M., Kingsley, G. T., Popkin, S. J., Levy, D., & Cove, E. (2007). *Estimating the public costs and benefits of HOPE VI investments: A methodological report*: Washington, DC: The Urban Institute.

University of Louisville (2019). *International Service Learning Program (ISLP).* Retrieved from https://louisville.edu/islp.

University of Southern Indiana (2021a). *Enrollment trends.* https://www.usi.edu/about/enrollment-trends/

University of Southern Indiana (2021b). *Academics.* https://www.usi.edu/about/academics/.

Upton, D. (2003). New urbanism. In K. Christensen & D. Levinson (Eds.), *Encyclopedia of community, From the village to the virtual world* (Volume III, pp. 1089).

U.S. Census Bureau. (2000). *Census of population and housing.* Kentucky State Data Center, University of Louisville, Louisville, KY.

U.S. Census Bureau. (2016). *Community Facts: Evansville city, Indiana.* https://factfinder.census.gov/faces/nav/jsf/pages/community_facts.xhtml.

U.S. Census Bureau. (2020a). *Community Facts: Covington city, Kentucky.* https://factfinder.census.gov/faces/nav/jsf/pages/community_facts.xhtml.

U.S. Census Bureau. (2020b). *Community Facts: Newport city, Kentucky.* https://factfinder.census.gov/faces/nav/jsf/pages/community_facts.xhtml.

U.S. Department of Housing and Urban Development. (1992). *Final report of the National Commission on Severely Distressed Public Housing: A report to Congress and the Secretary of Housing and Urban Development.* Washington, DC: HUD.

U.S. Department of Housing and Urban Development. (1999). *HOPE VI: Building communities, transforming lives.* Washington, DC: HUD. https://www.huduser.gov/publications/pdf/hope.pdf.

U.S. Department of Housing and Urban Development. (2000). *Community building makes a difference*. Washington, DC: HUD.

U.S. Department of Housing and Urban Development. (2003). *Updating the Low-Income Housing Tax Credit (LIHTC) database projects placed in service through 2003*. Washington, DC: HUD. Office of Economic Affairs. Office of Policy Research and Development. https://www.huduser.gov/datasets/lihtc/report9503.pdf.

U.S. Department of Housing and Urban Development. (2014). The Community Development Block Grant (CDBG) program- Frequently asked questions. Washington, DC: HUD. https://www.hudexchange.info/sites/onecpd/assets/File/The-Community-Development-Block-Grant-FAQ.pdf.

U.S. Department of Housing and Urban Development. (2016). HOME and CDBG Guidebook. https://files.hudexchange.info/resources/documents/HOME-CDBG Guidebook.pdf.

U.S. Department of Housing and Urban Development. (2020a). Ginnie Mae Program. Washington, DC: HUD.

U.S. Department of Housing and Urban Development. (2020b). Choice Neighborhoods Program. Washington, DC: HUD.

U.S. Department of Housing and Urban Development. (2020c). Promise Zone.Washington, DC: HUD.

U.S. Government Accountability Office (2002). *Public housing: HOPE VI leveraging has increased, but HUD has not met annual reporting requirement* (GAO Publication No. GAO-03-91). Washington, DC: U.S. Government Printing Office.

U.S. Government Accountability Office (2003). *Public housing: HOPE VI resident issues and changes in neighborhoods surrounding grant sites.* GAO Publication No. GAO-04-109). Washington, DC: U.S. Government Printing Office.

U.S. Government Accountability Office (2006). *Faith-based and community initiative: Improvements in monitoring grantees and measuring performance could enhance accountability.* (GAO Publication No. GAO-06-616). Washington, DC: U.S. Government Printing Office.

University of Southern Indiana (2018, October 24). *USI unveils robotic manufactured "MAGIC" house designed by renowned aging expert Dr. Bill Thomas* [Press release]. https://www.usi.edu/news/releases/2018/10/usi-unveils-robotic-manufactured-magic-house-designed-by-renowned-aging-expert-dr-bill-thomas/.

Van Ryzin, G., Ronda, M., & Muzzio, D. (2001). Factors related to self-sufficiency in a distressed public housing community. *Journal of Urban Affairs, 23*(1), 57–69.

Varady, D. P., & Preiser. W. F. (1998). Scattered-site public housing and housing satisfaction. *Journal of the American Planning Association, 64*(2), 189–207.

Varady, D. P., & Walker, C. C. (2003). Housing vouchers and residential mobility. *Journal of Planning Literature, 18*(1), 17–30.

Varady, D. P., Walker, C. C., & Wang, X. (2001). Voucher recipient achievement of improved housing conditions in the US: Do moving distance and relocation services matter? *Urban Studies, 38*(8), 1273–1304.

Vazquez, L. (2015). Creative placemaking, In R. Phillips & R. H, Pittman, (Eds.), *An introduction to community development* (2nd ed.) (pp. 305-306). New York: Routledge.

Vidal, A. C. (2001). *Faith-Based Organizations in Community Development*. Washington, DC: U. S. Department of Housing and Urban Development, Office of Policy Development and Research.

VOICE Visioning: Fact Sheet (2013). Evansville, IN: Leadership Evansville, Inc.

VOICE Visioning: Impact on Community. (2015). Evansville, IN: Leadership Evansville, Inc.

Von Hoffman, A. (2012). The past, present, and future of community development in the United States. In *Investing in What Works for America's Communities*. San Francisco, CA: Federal Reserve Bank of San Francisco.

Wade, J. L. (1989). Felt needs and anticipatory needs: Reformulation of a basic community development principle. *Community Development: Journal of the Community Development Society, 20*(1), 116–123.

Walker, C., Simonson, J., Kingsley, G. T., Ferguson, B., & Boxall, P. (1994). *Status and prospects of the nonprofit housing sector*. Report prepared for the U.S. Department of Housing and Urban Development. Washington, DC: The Urban Institute.

Walker, G. W., Kulash, W. M., & McHugh, B. T. (2000). Downtown streets: Are we strangling ourselves in one-way networks? http://onlinepubs.trb.org/onlinepubs/circulars/ec019/Ec019_f2.pdf.

Walsh, J. (1997). Community building in theory and practice: Three case studies. *National Civic Review, 86*(4), 291–314.

Wang, L., & Graddy, E. (2008). Social capital, volunteering, and charitable giving. *Voluntas: International Journal of Voluntary & Nonprofit Organizations, 19*(1), 23–42.

Warren, M. R., Thompson, P. J., & Saegert, S. (2001). The role of social capital in combating poverty. In S. Saegert, P. J. Thompson, & M. R. Warren (Eds.), *Social capital and poor communities*. New York: Russell Sage Foundation Press.

Waters, E. C., Holland, D. W., & Weber, B. A. (1997). Economic impacts of a property tax limitation: A computable general equilibrium analysis of Oregon's Measure 5. *Land Economics, 73*, 72–89.

Weaver, R. R., & Rivello, R. (2006). The distribution of mortality in the United States: The effects of income (inequality), social capital, and race. *Omega: Journal of Death & Dying, 54*(1), 19–39.

Weber, M. (1905). *The Protestant ethic and the spirit of capitalism*. London and Boston: Unwin Hyman.

Webman, J. A. (1981). UDAG: Targeting urban economic development. *Political Science Quarterly, 96*(2), 189–207.

Weinzapfel, C. A., Bigham, D. E., & Branigin, S. R. (2000). *Images of America: Historic New Harmony*. Charleston, SC: Arcadia Publishing, Inc.

Weiss, S. J., & Gooding, E. C. (1968). Estimation of differential employment multipliers in a small regional economy. *Land Economics, 44*, 235–244.

West, M., & Kraeger P., & Dahlstrom, T. R. (2016). Establishing community-based organizations. In R. Phillips & R. H. Pittman (Eds.), *An introduction to community development* (2nd ed.) (pp. 154–177). New York: Routledge.

Westbrook. R. (1991). *John Dewey and American democracy*. Ithaca, NY: Cornell University Press.

Westlund, H., & Adam, F. (2010). Social capital and economic performance: A meta-analysis of 65 studies. *European Planning Studies, 18*(6), 893–919.

Whitehurst, G. J., & Croft, M. (2010). *The Harlem Children's Zone, Promise Neighborhoods, and the broader, bolder approach to education.* Washington, DC: Brookings Institution Brown Center on Education Policy.

Whiteley, P. F. (2000). Economic growth and social capital. *Political Studies, 48*(3), 443–466.

Whitley, S. (2013). Changing times in rural America: Food assistance and food insecurity in food deserts. *Journal of Family Social Work, 16*(1), 36–52.

Wiggins, N., Kaan, S., Rios-Campos, T., Gaonkar, R. Morgan, E. R., & Robinson, J. (2013). Preparing community health workers for their role as agents of social change: Experience of the community capacitation center. *Journal of Community Practice, 21,* 186–202.

Wilkins, J. (2014). Stewardship of public service renewal and reform. *International Journal of Leadership in Public Services, 10*(4), 188–199.

Williamson, T., Imbroscio, D., & Alperovitz, G. (2003). *Making a place for community: Local democracy in a global era.* New York: Routledge.

Wilson, M. (2020, March 6). EPA is continuing its cleanup of toxic soil in Evansville's center city. Evansville, IN: *Evansville Courier & Press.* https://www.courierpress.com/story/news/local/2020/03/06/epa-cleanup-evansville-toxic-soil-superfund-lead-arsenic-jacobsville/4965996002/.

Wilson, W. J. (1987). *The truly disadvantaged: The inner city, the underclass and public policy.* Chicago: The University of Chicago Press.

Wolff, T. (2016). Ten places where collective impact gets it wrong. *Global Journal of Community Psychology Practice, 7*(1). https://www.gjcpp.org/en/resource.php?issue=21&resource=200.

Woodhouse, A. (2006). Social capital and economic development in regional Australia: A case study. *Journal of Rural Studies, 22*(1), 83–94.

Woolcock, M. (1998). Social capital and economic development: Toward a theoretical synthesis and policy framework. *Theory and Society, 27*(2), 151–208.

Woolcock, M., & Narayan, D. (2000). Social capital: Implications for development theory, research, and policy. *The World Bank Research Observer, 15*(2), 225–249.

Woolcock, M. (2000). Social capital: Implications for development theory, research, and policy. *The World Bank Research Observer, 15*(2), 225–49.

Woolcock, M. (2001). The place of social capital in understanding social and economic outcomes. *Canadian Journal of Policy Research, 2*(1), 1–17.

Wright, T. C. (2018). *Dorothy Day: An introduction to her life and thought.* San Francisco, CA: Ignatius Press.

Wyckoff, M. (2014). *Definition of placemaking: Four different types.* East Lansing, MI: Michigan State University Land Policy Institute. https://www.canr.msu.edu/uploads/375/65814/4typesplacemaking_pzn_wyckoff_january2014.pdf.

Zander, K. (2006). The impact of service learning on basic sociological knowledge, *Sociological Imagination, 42,* 25–32.

Index

About the Author and Contributors

Matthew J. Hanka is associate professor of political science at the University of Southern Indiana (USI) in Evansville, Indiana. Hanka earned a B.A. in History and Politics from The Catholic University of America in Washington, DC, and an M.A. in Political Science and a Ph.D. in Urban and Public Affairs, both from the University of Louisville. Dr. Hanka served as Director of the Master of Public Administration (MPA) program at USI from 2010 to 2018. Hanka has taught over 20 different courses at both the undergraduate and graduate level. His research interests include housing policy, community development, urban policy and governance, strategic planning, and social capital. His academic work has been published in 11 different peer-reviewed journals. He has also given over 40 conference presentations and has co-authored nine technical reports and six newspaper articles. Hanka served as co-convener of USI's strategic plan for 2016–2020 and has also consulted other nonprofit organizations on their strategic planning processes. He served as director of the Commission on Homelessness for Evansville and Vanderburgh County in 2018 and 2019 and is president of the Evansville Morning Rotary Club for 2021–2022. He also provides political commentary during election seasons on local media around the Evansville area. Hanka lives in Evansville, Indiana with his wife Ann and their two sons, MJ and David.

Trent A. Engbers is a former Peace Corps volunteer, an experienced college educator, and nonprofit consultant living in Evansville, Indiana. His primary appointment is as associate professor of Political Science and Public Administration and Director of the Master of Public Administration program at the University of Southern Indiana. He has taught in a number of public administration programs, including the Truman School of Public Affairs at the University of Missouri, the DePaul School of Public Service, the Mendoza

College of Business at the University of Notre Dame, and the O'Neill School of Public and Environmental Affairs (SPEA) at Indiana University. Engbers is an award-winning teacher and was appointed to serve as the faculty representative on the Indiana Commission for Higher Education for 2019–2021 by Governor Eric Holcomb. Engbers holds degrees from Xavier University, the University of Maryland, University of Missouri, and Indiana University. His research on leadership, economic development, and civic engagement has been published widely in *Social Science Quarterly*, *Public Administration Review*, and the *Journal of Leadership Education*, among other publications. He lives in Evansville with his wife Kimberly and their four children.

John I. "Hans" Gilderbloom is professor in the Graduate Planning, Public Administration, Sustainability, and Urban Affairs program at the University of Louisville, where he also directed the Center for Sustainable Urban Neighborhoods (SUN) for 30 years before moving to Washington DC in 2020 to become a fellow at the Neighborhood Associates Corporation. In an international poll of thousands of urbanists, planners, and architects, Professor Gilderbloom was ranked one of the "top 100 urban thinkers in the world." Gilderbloom's research in urban sustainability has appeared in eight edited books, 60 scholarly peer-reviewed journals, 30 chapters in edited books, 11 monographs, and 35 opinion pieces in newspapers and magazines including the *Wall Street Journal, Washington Post, Los Angeles Times, Chicago Sun-Times, San Francisco Chronicle, The Courier-Journal, USA Today Magazine*, and with City Lab/Bloomberg, and *The New York Times*. His most recent book, *Chromatic Homes*, focuses on stabilizing and regenerating neighborhoods. He has consulted for Presidents Bush, Clinton, and Obama, over 50 U.S. mayors, U.S. Senators Chuck Schumer and Mitch McConnell, former governor of California Jerry Brown, and former Secretaries of the U.S. Department of Housing and Urban Development Andrew Cuomo and Henry Cisneros, along with the mayors of Moscow, Havana, and San Jose, Costa Rica. He has brought in over $3.5 million in federal, state, and local grants and has won numerous awards, including the University of Louisville medal for outstanding research.

Ramona Harvey is a disability advocate and consultant. She is a certified ADA Coordinator. She received her bachelor's degree in Psychology from DePauw University and a Master of Public Administration (MPA) from the University of Southern Indiana. She is actively involved in empowering marginalized individuals to live independently in the community. She is a proponent of universally-designed, affordable, and accessible housing. In her spare time, she writes poetry and is the author of the book *Unclipped Wings*.

Mohammed Khayum is provost at the University of Southern Indiana. His current research interests include the impact of communication and information technologies on entrepreneurship in the 21st century and he has published peer-reviewed articles in the areas of service sector growth, consumption behavior, and exchange rate determination. He has authored two books on economic issues in developing countries. He regularly shares his perspectives about regional economic developments in Evansville, Indiana.

Helen Rosenberg received her Ph.D. from Northwestern University in 1989 and became a faculty member in the Sociology Department at the University of Wisconsin-Parkside in 1991. She teaches in the general area of deviant behavior, with specialties in mental illness, gerontology, and substance use and abuse. She received a grant from the National Institutes of Justice in 1995 to study community policing and consulted on the CAPS program in Chicago. She emphasizes community engagement in her classes and has published on best practices and methods of assessing service learning, service-learning work with people with mental illness, service learning with older, non-traditional students, and study abroad as experiential learning.

Anne Statham is Professor Emerita of Sociology at both the University of Southern Indiana and the University of Wisconsin-Parkside and was founding director of service-learning programs on both campuses. She has published many scholarly articles and books on various topics, including the process and efficacy of service learning, taught many service-learning courses, and led major community engagement projects.

www.ingramcontent.com/pod-product-compliance
Lightning Source LLC
Chambersburg PA
CBHW022301280326
41932CB00010B/934